Authors:

Michael A. Putlack
Michael A. Putlack graduated from Tufts University in Medford, Massachusetts, USA, where he got his B.A. in History and English and his M.A. in History. He has written a number of books for children, teenagers, and adults.

e-Creative Contents
A creative group that develops English contents and products for ESL and EFL students.

영어 슈퍼 리딩 훈련

2019 발행   2019년 5월 20일

저자   Michael A. Putlack | e-Creative Contents
펴낸이   김기중(Keyjoong Kim)
펴낸곳   (주)키출판사(Key Publications)

Tel 02)1644-8808 Fax 02)733-1595
등록 1980. 3. 19 (제 16-32호)

정가 19,800원 (본책+훈련북+MP3 파일 무료 다운로드)
ISBN 978-89-7457-994-4 13740

이 책의 무단 복제, 복사, 전재는 저작권법에 저촉됩니다.
잘못 만들어진 책은 구입처에서 바꾸어 드립니다.

Copyright ⓒ 2019 by Key Publications
Photo Credits ⓒ Photos.com,
                Key Publications

http://www.englishbus.kr
email: company@keymedia.co.kr

All rights reserved. No part of this publication may be reproduced,
stored in a retrieval system, or transmitted, in any form or by any means,
without the prior written permission of the copyright owner.

세계 명작, 유명 단편소설에서 선별한
15편의 스토리로 연습하는 **슈퍼 리딩 스토리 6단계 훈련**

영어 슈퍼 리딩 스토리 훈련

SUPER READING TRAINING BOOK

MAIN BOOK

Michael A. Putlack | e-Creative Contents 지음

교육 R&D에 앞서가는
Key 키출판사

Introduction

원서 읽는
슈퍼 리딩 스토리 훈련

이번엔 영어 소설 읽기다!!

　영어가 경쟁력이 되면서 좀 더 쉽고 효과적인 비법을 가르쳐 주겠다는 각종 학습서가 넘쳐나고 있습니다. 하지만 남의 나라 언어를 하루아침에 마스터할 수 있는 비법 같은 것은 있을 리 없습니다. 영어가 모국어가 아닌 나라에서 태어나 '제법 영어 좀 한다'하는 소리를 듣는 영어의 달인들은 대개 수년 동안 혹은 수십 년 동안 각고의 노력을 기울인 분들이지요.
　《영어 슈퍼 리딩 스토리 훈련》은 미국 교과 과정의 과목별 핵심내용을 다양한 학습방식으로 프로그램화하여 많은 학습자들의 사랑을 받고 있는 베스트셀러《영어 슈퍼 리딩 훈련》의 두 번째 훈련북입니다.
　《영어 슈퍼 리딩 훈련》이 논리적이고 딱딱한 문체의 논픽션 읽기에 초점을 맞추었다면, 《영어 슈퍼 리딩 스토리 훈련》은 비교적 부드럽고 긴 만연체의 픽션 읽기를 통해, 보다 다양한 어휘와 문장에 익숙해지고 영어를 영어 그대로 이해하는 즐거움을 배가시킬 수 있도록 구성하였습니다.

사전 없이 영어 소설을 읽는 감동의 영어 체험

　독해력을 키우는 왕도로 늘 권장되는 학습법은 역시 많이 읽고 많이 듣는 것입니다. 이미 알고 있는 이야기를 통해 좀 더 친근하게 영어에 접근하는 '명작 읽기'는 그 중 가장 효과적인 학습법 중의 하나입니다.

《영어 슈퍼 리딩 스토리 훈련》은 세계적으로 널리 읽히고 있는 명작동화와 단편소설 15개를 선별하여 6단계로 난이도를 조절하고, 다양한 학습장치를 마련하여 초보학습자들도 쉽고 재미있게 원서를 읽어나갈 수 있도록 하였습니다. 특히 영어를 영어 그대로 이해할 수 있도록 배려한 본책과, Close Up · Grammar Point · 직독직해 연습 등을 통해 영어 문장구조에 훤해지도록 구성된 훈련북은 이 책의 자랑입니다.

이런 분들께 강추!

- 희미하게 잔해만 남아 있는 내 영어, 기초부터 차근차근 다시 세우고 싶다.
- 뉴욕타임즈 베스트셀러 소설을 원서 그대로 읽고 싶다.
- 토익, 토플 등 각종 영어시험에서 고득점을 얻고 싶다.
- 영어로만 수업하는 이중언어교육 또는 몰입교육에 대비하고 싶다.
- 해외유학을 준비 중이다.

이미 수많은 학습자들이 〈영어 슈퍼 리딩〉 시리즈를 통해 비약적인 영어 실력 향상의 기쁨을 맛보고 있습니다.

사전 없이 원서 소설을 읽는 영어 실력,
이제 당신의 경쟁력으로 만드십시오.

How to Use This Book

《영어 슈퍼 리딩 스토리 훈련》은 영어로만 구성한 본책 1권과 직독직해 능력 및 영어문장구조에 대한 이해를 근본적으로 향상시킬 수 있는 훈련북 1권으로 구성되어 있습니다

 본책   본책은 **Step 1**부터 **Step 6**까지 6단계로 나누어 총 15개의 스토리로 구성되어 있습니다.

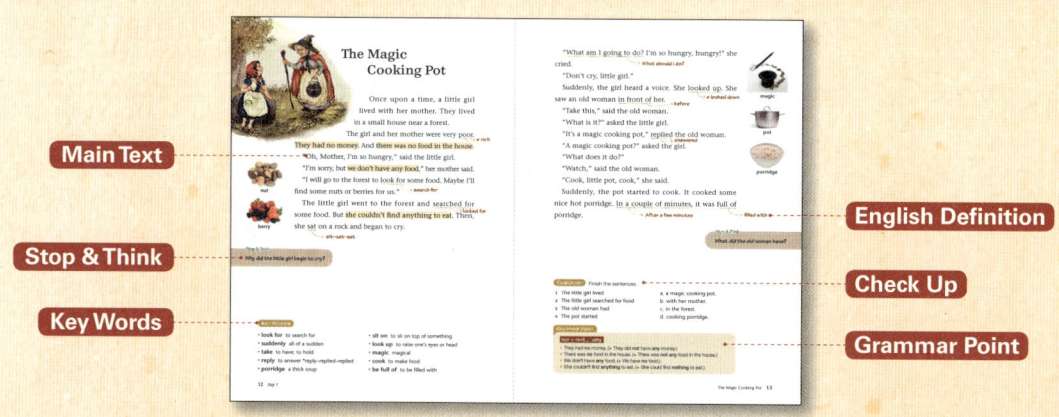

1 Main Text 본문 읽기

먼저 영어로만 구성된 본문을 읽습니다. 모르는 단어나 표현은 유의어, 반의어, 뜻풀이 등 다양한 방식으로 설명되어 있는 영영풀이 사전과 그림사전, 그리고 Key Words, Grammar Point 등의 도움을 받아 앞뒤 문맥을 파악하도록 노력합니다. 이 단계에서는 함께 제시되어 있는 사진이나 각종 학습장치의 도움을 받으며 영어를 영어로 이해하는 것이 중요합니다. 모르는 어휘나 표현은 체크하여 두었다가 그 스토리를 다 읽은 후 훈련북에서 확인하도록 합니다.

2 Stop & Think / Check Up 문제 풀어보기

본문을 읽은 후, Stop & Think, Check Up의 문제들을 풀어 보며 내용을 제대로 이해했는지 확인합니다. 문제는 main idea(주제)와 details(세부사항)를 묻는 Reading Comprehension(이해력) 문제와 Vocabulary(어휘) 문제로 구성되어 있습니다. 각종 영어시험에 빈번히 출제되는 형식이므로 독해력과 함께 각종 시험에 대한 적응능력을 키울 수 있습니다.

 **MP3 무료 다운로드**   이 책의 본문은 모두 원어민의 정확한 발음으로 녹음되어 있습니다. www.englishbus.co.kr에서 MP3 파일을 무료로 다운로드 받으세요.

 훈련북

훈련북에서는 정답 및 해설뿐만 아니라 직독직해에 필수인 의미단위별 끊어읽기(/)와 구문별 영어 표현을 제공합니다. 또한 Close Up과 Grammar Point에 대한 설명을 추가하여 학습자들이 영문 구조를 제대로 이해할 수 있도록 도와줍니다. 훈련북을 잘 활용하면 영문에 대한 이해력은 물론 어휘와 문장구조 파악 능력까지 근본적으로 향상시킬 수 있으므로 반복학습하도록 합시다.

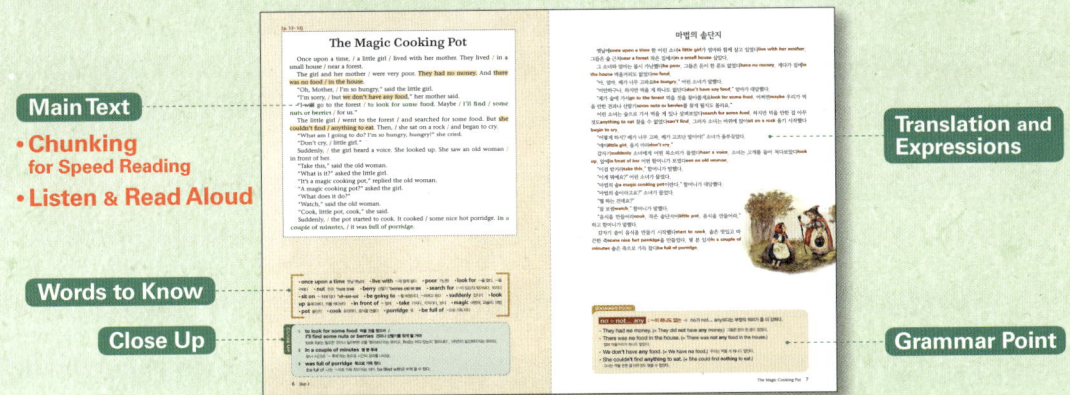

3 우리말 뜻과 영어표현 확인하기

자, 이제 훈련북을 보면서 본책에서 미처 이해하지 못한 어휘와 표현을 확인하고 영문을 완벽하게 소화하도록 합시다. 먼저 〈Words to Know〉에 있는 단어들을 한번 훑어 봅니다. 그런 다음 위의 영어 본문을 읽으며 한글 번역과 대조해 나갑니다. Close Up과 Grammar Point를 통해 영문구조도 완벽하게 이해하도록 합시다. 또한 번역과 함께 제시된 영어표현은 영문을 의미단위로 이해하는 키워드이므로 반복해서 읽으며 완벽하게 이해하도록 합시다.

4 도전! 직독직해 & 의미 덩어리별 끊어읽기(Chunking)

이제 번역을 보지 말고 위의 영어 본문을 혼자 해석해 봅니다. 이때 의미 덩어리별 끊어읽기(/) 표시를 활용하면 순차적으로 영문을 읽어 나가는 데 많은 도움이 됩니다. 모르는 부분이 있으면 우리말 뜻과 영어표현을 다시 한번 확인하며 완전히 이해될 때까지 반복하도록 합시다.

5 오디오 들으며 따라 읽기

영어는 눈으로만 읽는 것보다 소리와 함께 익히는 것이 기억에 더 오래 남습니다. 이 책의 본문은 모두 원어민의 정확한 발음으로 녹음되어 있습니다. www.englishbus.co.kr에서 MP3파일을 무료로 다운로드 받으세요. 그런 다음 본문을 2회 반복해서 들으며 정확한 발음과 억양을 익힙니다. 스크립트에는 슬래시(/)로 끊어읽기가 표시되어 있습니다. 본문을 들을 때는 끊어읽기를 참고하여 원어민의 발음, 억양, 연음 등에 주의를 기울여 듣습니다. 스크립트 위에 억양, 연음 등을 표시해도 좋습니다. 그런 다음 2회 더 반복해서 들으며 큰 소리로 따라 읽습니다. 이때 원어민을 똑같이 흉내 내어 읽는 것이 중요합니다.

6 오디오 없이 혼자서 소리 내어 읽기

다음은 오디오 없이 본문을 소리 내어 읽으며 원어민처럼 흉내 내어 봅니다. 발음이나 억양이 어색한 부분이 있으면 다시 한번 오디오를 들으며 확인합시다.

7 영어 본문에 다시 한번 도전

이제 다시 본책으로 돌아가 영어 본문을 읽고 문제를 풀어 봅시다. 영어로만 읽어도 아주 쉽게 읽히고 문제를 이해할 수 있게 될 것입니다.

★ 정답은 Training Book의 〈Answers & Translations〉에서 확인하실 수 있습니다.

Table of Contents

Step 1

- **The Magic Cooking Pot** | 12
  마법의 솥단지

- **The Shoemaker and the Elves** | 18
  구두장이와 꼬마 요정들

- **Jack and the Beanstalk** | 24
  잭과 콩나무

- **The Ugly Duckling** | 30
  미운 오리 새끼

- **Aesop's Fables** 이솝 우화
  - **The Ants and the Grasshopper** | 38
    개미와 베짱이
  - **The Hare and the Tortoise** | 40
    토끼와 거북이
  - **The Sick Lion** | 42
    병든 사자
  - **The Boy Who Cried Wolf** | 44
    늑대가 나타났다고 외친 소년 (양치기 소년과 늑대)

Step 2

- **The Little Mermaid** | 48
  인어공주 – Hans Christian Andersen

Step 3

- **Beauty and the Beast** | 68
  미녀와 야수 – Beaumont, Madame de
- **The Stars** | 88
  별 – Alphonse Daudet

Step 4

- **What Men Live By** | 102
  사람은 무엇으로 사는가 – Leo Tolstoy
- **How Much Land Does a Man Need?** | 122
  사람에게 필요한 땅은 얼마만큼인가 – Leo Tolstoy

Step 5

- **A Christmas Carol** | 144
  크리스마스 캐럴 – Charles Dickens

Step 6

- **The Last Leaf** | 172
  마지막 잎새 – O. Henry

Super Reading Story Training Book

Step 1

The Magic Cooking Pot

•

The Shoemaker and the Elves

•

Jack and the Beanstalk

•

The Ugly Duckling

•

Aesop's Fables

The Magic Cooking Pot

Once upon a time, a little girl lived with her mother. They lived in a small house near a forest. The girl and her mother were very poor. They had no money. And there was no food in the house.

≠ rich

"Oh, Mother, I'm so hungry," said the little girl.

"I'm sorry, but we don't have any food," her mother said.

"I will go to the forest to look for some food. Maybe I'll find some nuts or berries for us."

→ search for

The little girl went to the forest and searched for some food. But she couldn't find anything to eat. Then, she sat on a rock and began to cry.

→ looked for

→ sit-sat-sat

nut

berry

Stop & Think
Why did the little girl begin to cry?

Key Words

- **look for** to search for
- **suddenly** all of a sudden
- **take** to have; to hold
- **reply** to answer *reply–replied–replied
- **porridge** a thick soup
- **sit on** to sit on top of something
- **look up** to raise one's eyes or head
- **magic** magical
- **cook** to make food
- **be full of** to be filled with

12 Step 1

"What am I going to do? I'm so hungry, hungry!" she cried.
→ *What should I do?*

"Don't cry, little girl."

Suddenly, the girl heard a voice. She looked up. She saw an old woman in front of her.
→ ≠ *looked down*
→ *before*

magic

"Take this," said the old woman.

"What is it?" asked the little girl.

"It's a magic cooking pot," replied the old woman.
→ *answered*

pot

"A magic cooking pot?" asked the girl.

"What does it do?"

"Watch," said the old woman.

"Cook, little pot, cook," she said.

porridge

Suddenly, the pot started to cook. It cooked some nice hot porridge. In a couple of minutes, it was full of porridge.
→ *After a few minutes*
→ *filled with*

Stop & Think
What did the old woman have?

CHECK UP Finish the sentences.

1 The little girl lived
2 The little girl searched for food
3 The old woman had
4 The pot started

a. a magic cooking pot.
b. with her mother.
c. in the forest.
d. cooking porridge.

GRAMMAR POINT

no = not... any
- They had **no** money. (= They did **not** have **any** money.)
- There was **no** food in the house. (= There was **not any** food in the house.)
- We do**n't** have **any** food. (= We have **no** food.)
- She could**n't** find **anything** to eat. (= She could find **nothing** to eat.)

The Magic Cooking Pot

amazing

delicious

magic words

"Wow!" said the girl.

"That's amazing. Let's eat the porridge."
→ very surprising

"Wait," said the old woman.

"First, the pot must stop."

Then, she said to the pot, "Stop, little pot, stop."

The pot immediately stopped cooking.
→ instantly

"You must always say those words, or the pot will keep cooking porridge. Now, you can eat."
→ or else, otherwise

"It's delicious!" said the little girl.

"You can have this pot," said the old woman.
→ take

"Oh, I am so happy. Thank you so much."

"Just don't forget the magic words," said the old woman.
→ remember

The little girl took the pot and ran back to her home.
→ take–took–taken   → run–ran–run

"Mother," shouted the little girl.

"Look at what I have. It's a magic cooking pot."

> **Stop & Think**
> What should the little girl do to stop the pot from cooking?

KEY WORDS

- **amazing** very surprising
- **keep -ing** to continue doing something
- **magic words** words that can do magic
- **run back** to return
- **go out** to leave *go–went–gone

- **immediately** instantly; at once
- **forget** to not remember
- **take** to hold; to carry *take–took–taken
- **shout** to yell loudly
- **be out** to be away

The girl's mother looked at the pot.

"Magic? Are you sure?"

"Of course. Watch this," answered the little girl.

"Cook, little pot, cook."

Immediately, the pot cooked some nice hot porridge. In a couple of minutes, it was full of porridge.

"Wait a minute, Mother," said the little girl.
→ Wait a second, Hold on

"We have to say the magic words to stop the pot. Stop, little pot, stop," she said.

The pot immediately stopped cooking.

The little girl and her mother ate porridge every day. They were not hungry anymore.

One day, the little girl went out to play with her friends. She was out for a long time. Her mother became very hungry. So she decided to eat without her daughter.
→ go-went-gone

play

daughter

Stop & Think
Why did the mother decide to eat without her daughter?

CHECK UP Put the right words.

| full   immediately   porridge   ran back |

1. The little girl took the pot and _____ to her home.
2. Soon, the pot was _____ of porridge.
3. The pot _____ stopped cooking.
4. The little girl and her mother ate _____ every day.

GRAMMAR POINT

stop -ing / keep -ing / decide to
- The pot immediately **stopped** cook**ing**.
- The pot will **keep** cook**ing** porridge.
- She **decided to** eat without her daughter.

overflow

spill

surprised

"Cook, little pot, cook," she said.

The pot started cooking some porridge. After a few minutes, the pot was full of porridge. The mother wanted the pot to stop cooking.

"No more, little pot, no more," said the mother.

But the pot did not stop cooking. Those were not the magic words.

"Stop cooking, little pot, stop cooking," she cried. → shouted

But those were not the magic words either.

Soon, the porridge began to overflow from the pot. It spilled onto the floor. The mother did not know what to do. She kept trying to stop the pot. But she did not remember how to make it stop.
→ run over
→ overflowed
→ continued *keep–kept–kept
→ forgot

The kitchen filled with porridge. Then, the porridge spilled into the street and went into the next house. The villagers were surprised.

"What's happening?" they asked.
What's going on?

"The magic pot will not stop cooking," answered the mother.

Stop & Think
Why did the pot keep making porridge?

KEY WORDS

- **cry** to shout *cry–cried–cried
- **spill** to flow over; to fall *spill–spilled–spilled
- **villagers** the people who live in a village
- **scoop up** to draw up
- **continue -ing** to keep doing something
- **overflow** to run over; to flow over
- **fill with** to be full of; to be filled with
- **be surprised** to be shocked
- **take away** to remove
- **come back** to return

16 Step 1

The villagers scooped up the porridge with buckets and took it away. But the magic pot continued cooking. Soon, there was porridge in every house in the village.
→ removed it   → kept

Just then, the little girl came back to her home.
→ returned

"Stop, little pot, stop," she shouted.

The magic cooking pot immediately stopped cooking.

"It's a good little pot. But you must say the right words!" said the little girl.
→ ≠ wrong

scoop up

bucket

CHECK UP Choose the right words.

1. The mother did not remember _____ make it stop. (how to | what to)
2. The porridge _____ onto the floor. (filled | spilled)
3. Every house in the village had _____ in it. (porridge | pot)

GRAMMAR POINT

what to ~ / how to ~
- The mother did not know **what to** do.
- She did not remember **how to** make it stop.

The Shoemaker and the Elves

shoemaker

a pair of shoes

gold coin

There was once an old shoemaker. He owned an old shoe shop. He worked on the first floor, and he and his wife lived on the second floor. The shoemaker and his wife were very poor. Few people visited his shop, so he did not make much money.

One day, the shoemaker told his wife.

"One last pair of shoes. That's all I can make. We don't have any money. What are we going to do?"

"It is late. So we should go to bed. Make the shoes in the morning," answered the shoemaker's wife. The shoemaker and his wife went upstairs and went to bed.

The next morning, the shoemaker and his wife went downstairs. There was something on the table. It was a pair of shoes.

Stop & Think
Were there many customers in the shop?

Key Words

- **shoemaker** a person who makes shoes
- **make money** to earn money
- **pair** a duo; a couple; a set
- **go upstairs** ≠ go downstairs
- **magic** super powers
- **own** to have *own–owned–owned
- **wife** ≠ husband
- **go to bed** to go to sleep
- **a pair of** a couple of
- **gold coin** a coin that is made of gold

"Look at these," the shoemaker said. "What beautiful shoes! It's magic."

Just then, a lady came into the store. The lady looked at the shoes and said, "What beautiful shoes! I'll take them." She gave the shoemaker three gold coins for the shoes.

came into = walked into
I'll take them = I'll buy them.

"Three gold coins! Now I can make two more pairs of shoes," the shoemaker said. So he went out and bought some more leather. He came back and cut the leather.

buy–bought–bought
cut–cut–cut

"It is late. Make them in the morning," said his wife. The shoemaker and his wife went upstairs and went to bed.

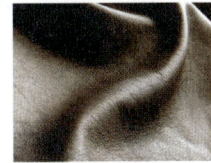
leather

Stop & Think
Who made the beautiful shoes?

Check Up True or false?

1. The shoemaker was very poor. _____
2. The shoemaker finished his last pair of shoes. _____
3. The lady gave the shoemaker three gold coins for the shoes. _____
4. The next morning, the shoemaker made two more pairs of shoes. _____

Grammar Point

What ~! / How ~! (exclamation)
- **What** beautiful **shoes**!
- **How beautiful** they are!

The next morning, the shoemaker and his wife came down. They saw two beautiful pairs of shoes on the table.

came downstairs ← came down

"Look at these," he said. "More magic."

The shoemaker put the shoes in the window. A man saw them. He walked into the shop. "How beautiful they are! I must buy them. Here are six gold coins."

placed, displayed → put
see–saw–seen → saw
came into → walked into
What beautiful shoes they are! ← How beautiful they are!

"Now I can buy enough leather to make four pairs of shoes," the shoemaker said. So he went out and bought some more leather. He came back and cut the leather.

"It is late," said his wife. "So we should go to bed." The shoemaker and his wife went upstairs and went to bed.

Key Words

- **come down** to go down
- **a while later** after a while; later on
- **pay** to give money *pay–paid–paid
- **wonder** to be curious about
- **put** to place; to display
- **customer** someone who buys goods; a shopper
- **twelve** 12; a dozen
- **hide** to keep from being seen *hide–hid–hidden

The next morning, the shoemaker and his wife came down. They saw four beautiful pairs of shoes on the table.

"Look at these," he said. "They're beautiful. Even more magic."

A while later, two customers entered the store. They looked at the shoes and said, "Those shoes are beautiful. We'll take them." They paid the shoemaker twelve gold coins for the shoes.

→ After a while
→ came into
→ pay-paid-paid

The shoemaker and his wife were very happy. But they wondered, "Who is making these shoes? We must know."

→ were curious

That night, the shoemaker cut the leather for the shoes. But he and his wife did not go upstairs. Instead, they hid downstairs. They waited and waited.

→ hide-hid-hidden

customer

twelve

wonder

hide

Stop & Think
Why did the shoemaker and his wife hide downstairs?

Check Up Put the right words.

| twelve   hid   came down   pairs of |

1. The next morning, the shoemaker and his wife _____.
2. They saw two beautiful _____ shoes on the table.
3. The two customers paid _____ gold coins for the four pairs of shoes.
4. The shoemaker and his wife _____ downstairs.

Grammar Point

enough ~ to...
- Now I can buy **enough** leather **to** make four pairs of shoes.

The Shoemaker and the Elves 21

elf

sew

At midnight, two elves came into the shoemaker's shop. They jumped onto the table. *sg. elf

"Look at this leather," one said.

"Let's make some beautiful shoes with it," said the other.

The elves worked hard all night long. They made several beautiful pairs of shoes. When the sun rose, they left. → a few   rise–rose–risen
leave–left–left

"Those elves are very kind," said the shoemaker.

"You're right," answered his wife. "We should do something for them."

"What can we do?" asked the shoemaker.

"I know," said his wife. "Their clothes looked poor. Let's make some clothes for them."

So the shoemaker and his wife made some tiny clothes for the elves. They sewed → very small
sew–sewed–sewed

Stop & Think
Who made the beautiful shoes?

Key Words

- **midnight** twelve at night (≠ noon)
- **jump onto** to leap onto
- **rise** move upward *rise–rose–risen
- **look poor** to appear to have no money
- **sew** to make clothes *sew–sewed–sewed
- **stay** to be in one place (≠ leave)
- **elf** fairy *pl. elves
- **several** a few; more than two but not many
- **leave** ≠ arrive; stay
- **tiny** very small
- **put on** to put clothes on (≠ take off)

tiny pants, shirts, hats, and boots for the elves. Then, they put the new clothes on the table.

pants

That night, the shoemaker and his wife hid again. At midnight, the elves came into the shoemaker's shop. When they jumped onto the table, they saw the clothes.

"What are these?" one said. "Are these clothes for us?"

"Yes," said the other. "They are for us."

shirt

The elves put their new clothes on. Then, they danced with each other.
→ ≠ take off

→ no longer
"We cannot stay here any longer," said the first elf.

hat

"You're right. They know about us. Now it's time for us to go," said the second elf.

"Goodbye, shoemaker," they said.

The elves left and never came back. But now the shoemaker could make good shoes. He worked hard, too. So he and his wife became very rich. And they lived happily ever after.
→ become-became-become
→ forever

boots

Stop & Think
Why did the elves leave?

Check Up Choose the right words.
1. Two _____ made the shoes at night. (elves | customers)
2. The shoemaker and his wife made tiny _____. (clothes | shoes)
3. The _____ left and never came back. (elves | customers)
4. The shoemaker and his wife became _____. (rich | poor)

Grammar Point

it's time for ~ to…
- Now **it's time for** us **to** go.

Jack and the Beanstalk

cottage

cow

bean

Long ago, there lived a mother and her son. The son's name was Jack. They lived in a small cottage. They were very poor. Their only valuable possession was an old cow. (→ property)

One day, the mother said to Jack.

"We've got no money, Jack. Go and sell the cow." (→ We have no money)

So Jack took the cow and walked toward the town. On his way to the town, he met a strange old man. He (→ While going to) (→ odd) asked Jack, "Where are you going with that cow?"

"I'm going to town to sell the cow so that we can buy some food," said Jack.

"Ah... but the town is so very far away... I will gladly buy the cow from you," the old man said. (→ happily)

"Take a look at these." The old man (Look at ←) showed Jack some beautiful beans. "These are magic beans. I will give you five magic beans for your cow," he offered. (→ proposed)

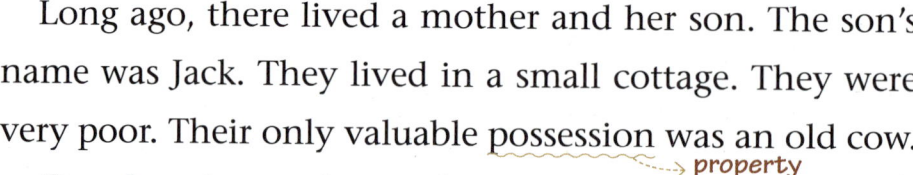

Stop & Think
What did the strange old man offer Jack?

KEY WORDS

- **valuable** worth a lot of money
- **on one's way to** on the way to; while going to
- **be far away** to be a long distance from
- **be impressed by** to be amazed by
- **amazing** very surprising; incredible
- **possession** something a person owns
- **so that** in order that
- **offer** to suggest; to propose
- **throw out** to throw away *throw–threw–thrown
- **climb up** to go up (≠ climb down)

Jack was impressed by the magic beans. So he sold the cow to the old man for five beans. Jack was very proud of himself.

But when he got home, his mother was angry.

"What? Beans!" she cried. "You sold our cow for five beans? You fool! Only a fool would exchange a cow for five beans. No supper for you. Go to bed right now," she told him. Then, Jack's mother threw the beans out the window.

The next morning, Jack looked out the window and saw an amazing sight. There was an enormous beanstalk growing next to the window. It rose so high that he could not see where it ended.

"The old man was right," said Jack. "They were magic beans." Jack started climbing up the beanstalk. He climbed for hours and hours. Finally, he got to the top of the beanstalk.

beanstalk

CHECK UP — Answer the questions.

1. What did Jack sell the strange old man?
   a. magic beans   b. some food   c. a cow
2. What did Jack's mother do with the beans?
   a. She ate them.   b. She threw them out the window.   c. She planted them.

GRAMMAR POINT

so that… / so ~ that…

- I'm going to town to sell the cow **so that** we can buy some food.
- It rose **so** high **that** he could not see where it ended.

Jack and the Beanstalk

There, high in the clouds, was a huge castle.

"I wonder who lives there," thought Jack as he walked toward the castle. When Jack got to the castle, he tripped over an enormous foot. It belonged to the biggest woman he had ever seen.

→ while
→ fell over

"You, boy," said the woman. "What are you doing here? My husband is a giant. He loves to eat little boys like you."

→ likes to

"Please don't let him eat me," answered Jack. "I just came here because I smelled breakfast, and I am so hungry."

castle

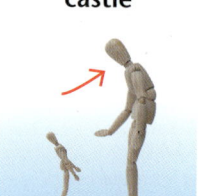
giant

The giant's wife was kindhearted, so she gave Jack some food. All of a sudden, the ground began to shake. "Hide, boy," said the woman. "My husband is coming."

→ kind, nice ≠ mean
→ Suddenly

"Fee, fi, fo, fum, I can smell a little boy," said the giant when he walked into the kitchen. "Are you cooking a boy for me for breakfast?"

→ came into

smell

"No, dear," she answered. "You probably smell the boy you ate last week."

→ eat-ate-eaten

Stop & Think
Who lived in the castle?

KEY WORDS

- **castle** a palace
- **enormous** huge; very large
- **kindhearted** nice; kind (≠ mean)
- **ground** land; earth
- **take out** to put out; to pull
- **run out** to use all of something

- **trip over** to fall over
- **giant** a very tall person
- **all of a sudden** suddenly
- **shake** to move back and forth
- **fall asleep** to get to sleep (≠ wake up)
- **go away** to leave

The giant sat down and ate his breakfast. Then, he took out a huge bag. It was filled with gold. After a while, he fell asleep at the table. Then, Jack came out quietly. He took the bag of gold and ran out of the castle. He climbed down the beanstalk and showed his mother the gold. She was very pleased with him.

Annotations: fell asleep → put out; fell asleep ≠ woke up; took → grabbed, stole; ran → run-ran-run; climbed down ≠ climbed up; very pleased → very happy

Jack and his mother lived happily. But they soon ran out of gold. Jack decided to climb the beanstalk again. He got to the top of the beanstalk and walked to the castle.

Annotation: ran out of → used up

"Oh, it's you again?" said the giant's wife. "Go away! You're a bad boy. Didn't you take my husband's gold?"

Annotation: Go away! → Get out! / Leave!

"That wasn't me. That was another boy," answered Jack.

The giant's wife believed Jack. She gave him some food. Then, the ground began to shake. "He's coming," said the woman. "**Hide, or he will find you.**"

bag

fall asleep

hide

find

> **Stop & Think**
> Why did Jack climb the beanstalk again?

CHECK UP Finish the sentences.

1. The giant's wife
2. The giant's huge bag
3. Jack stole

a. the giant's gold.
b. was kindhearted.
c. was filled with gold.

GRAMMAR POINT

Hide, or... (imperative + or...)
- **Hide, or** he will find you. (= **If you don't hide,** he will find you.)

Jack and the Beanstalk 27

hen

lay an egg

thief

harp

"Fee, fi, fo, fum, you have a boy for me today, don't you?" said the giant.

"Sorry, dear. I don't. But here are some bacon and eggs for you," she said.

After breakfast, the giant said, "Wife, bring me my hen. I want some golden eggs." So she brought the hen to the table. "Lay," said the giant. The hen laid a golden egg.
→ bring-brought-brought
→ lay-laid-laid

After a while, the giant fell asleep at the table. Then, Jack came out of his hiding place. He grabbed the hen and ran out of the castle. He climbed down the beanstalk and showed his mother the hen. They became very rich.
→ took
→ became bored

But Jack got bored one day, so he climbed up the beanstalk again. He went to the castle, but he hid from the giant's wife this time.

"Fee, fi, fo, fum, I can smell a little boy," roared the giant.
→ yelled loudly

"Can you? Maybe it's that thief again," said the giant's wife. "Let's find that boy."

They looked in the kitchen, but they could not find Jack. Soon, they gave up and ate breakfast. Then, the giant got his harp. "Play," he said. The harp began to play some beautiful music.
→ stopped
→ grabbed, took

Key Words

- **lay an egg** to produce an egg
- **get bored** to become bored (≠ get excited)
- **give up** to stop doing; to abandon
- **steal** to take without permission
- **cut down** to chop down
- **grab** to take *grab–grabbed–grabbed
- **thief** a person who steals things
- **master** an owner
- **chase** to run after
- **fall down** to fall to the ground

After a while, the giant fell asleep at the table. Then, Jack came out of his hiding place. He grabbed the harp and ran out of the castle. But the harp called out, "Master, save me! The boy is stealing me!"
called out → shouted
Master, save me → help me

The giant woke up and chased Jack. Jack ran to the beanstalk and began climbing down it. The giant started climbing down, too.
woke up ≠ fell asleep
chased → ran after
climbing down → going down

"Mother, get the axe. Quick! The big giant is coming," shouted Jack. When he reached the bottom, he grabbed the axe. He cut down the beanstalk.
reached → got to

The beanstalk fell, and the giant fell down with it. His head hit the ground. Thump! He was dead. Jack never went back to the giant's castle.
fell — fall–fell–fallen
hit the ground → fell to the ground

axe

Stop & Think
Why did Jack cut down the beanstalk?

CHECK UP   Put the right words.

| laid | stole | harp | cut down |

1. The hen _____ golden eggs.
2. The _____ played beautiful music.
3. Jack _____ the harp and ran out of the castle.
4. Jack _____ the beanstalk with an axe.

GRAMMAR POINT

~, don't you? (tag question)

- You have a boy for me today, **don't you?**

Jack and the Beanstalk

The Ugly Duckling

duck

crack

duckling

One summer in a country farmyard, Mother Duck was sitting on her new eggs. She sat on them for a long time. Finally, the eggs began to crack. Six little ducklings popped out and started to cry out, "Quack, quack!" ⇢ came out
Mother Duck was very pleased. "My little ducklings!" she said. ⇢ happy

She looked inside her nest. One egg had not opened.

"That's strange," she thought. "This egg is bigger than the other ones." ⇢ odd

⇢ remember
Mother Duck couldn't recall laying that seventh egg. How did it get there? "Did I count the eggs wrongly?" Mother Duck wondered. ⇢ stopped by   incorrectly ≠ rightly

An old duck came by to see the ducklings.

"Hello, Mother Duck. I see your eggs have hatched. How are the ducklings?" the old duck asked.

Stop & Think
How did the seventh egg look?

Key Words

- **farmyard** the area around a farm
- **duckling** a baby duck
- **recall** to remember
- **hatch** to come out of an egg
- **crack** to break open
- **pop out** to come out
- **wonder** to think about
- **look like** to resemble; to look the same as

"Almost all of them have hatched. There is only one egg left," Mother Duck answered.

"That egg looks strange. It looks like a turkey egg. Leave it alone," said the old duck.
→ Do not take care of it.

"No, I can't do that. It's my egg, so I must wait for it," said Mother Duck. She got back into her nest and sat on the big egg. After a while, the egg finally hatched.
→ went back
→ with shock

They looked at the last baby duckling with great surprise. He looked nothing like the other ducks. In fact, he did not look like much of a duck at all. He was big, gray, ugly, and strange looking.
→ did not look like
→ Actually
→ ≠ beautiful, handsome

"Well, he certainly is an unusual-looking duckling," said the old duck.
→ surely
→ strange-looking

"Hmm," said Mother Duck, "he was in the egg for so long, so he must be so big. I am sure he will become a proper-looking duck."
→ normal-looking

nest

hatch

turkey

Stop & Think
How did the ugly duckling look?

CHECK UP True or false?

1. Mother Duck did not remember the seventh egg. _____
2. The last baby duckling looked strange. _____
3. The ugly duckling looked like the old duck. _____

GRAMMAR POINT

look + adjective / look like + noun

- That egg **looks** strange.
- It **looks like** a turkey egg.
- He **looked** nothing **like** the other ducks.
- He did not **look like** much of a duck at all.

pond

peck at

laugh at

goose

Mother Duck took her children to the pond. They all jumped into the pond one by one. The ugly duckling swam very well. *[swim–swam–swum]* Actually, he swam even better than the others. *[In fact]* Mother Duck was pleased.

All of the animals gathered around *[came around]* Mother Duck and her ducklings. "What a beautiful family!" they all said. Then, they noticed *[saw, found]* the ugly duckling. "What is wrong with that big duckling? He's very ugly," they said. One of the ducks even pecked at *[What happened to]* the ugly duckling. This made the ugly duckling very sad.

Mother Duck and her ducklings went swimming in the pond every day. And, every day, the ducks and other animals laughed at *[made fun of]* the ugly duckling. Even the farm girl disliked *[≠ liked]* the ugly duckling. "Go away," she said. "You are an ugly duckling."

The ugly duckling felt very sad. "Nobody loves me. They all tease me! *[make fun of]* Why am I different from my brothers?"

Stop & Think
Why was the ugly duckling sad?

Key Words

- **gather around** to come around
- **laugh at** to make fun of
- **tease** to make fun of
- **run away** to flee
- **noise** a sound
- **scared** afraid

- **notice** to be aware of; to pay attention to
- **dislike** to hate; to not like
- **be different from** to not be the same
- **loud** noisy (≠ quiet)
- **rifle** a long gun
- **hunter** a person who hunts animals

One night, he ran away from the farm. He traveled a long, long way until he finally found a huge field. He soon fell asleep. When he woke up, he was by a lake. He looked up in the sky and saw two geese.

ran away → fled
woke up → wake-woke-woken
geese → sg. goose

rifle

hunter

"You look very strange," they said. "But we like you. Do you want to fly with us?" they asked the ugly duckling.

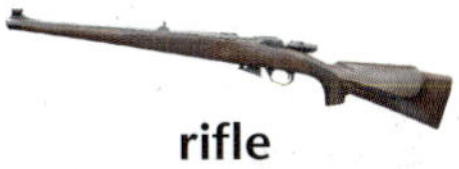

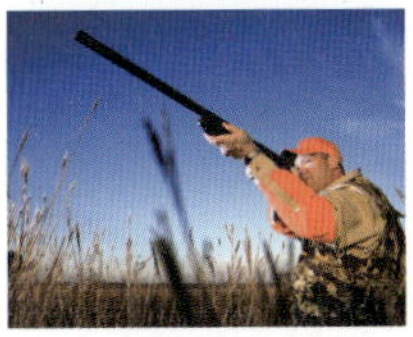

The ugly duckling agreed, but he suddenly heard a loud noise. "Bang! Bang!"

loud noise → very big sound

The two geese fell to the ground. They were dead. In the distance, the ugly duckling saw some men with hunting rifles. He got very scared. He ran away from the hunters. He ran and ran until he was very far away.

fell → fall-fell-fallen
In the distance → From a distance
got very scared → was very afraid

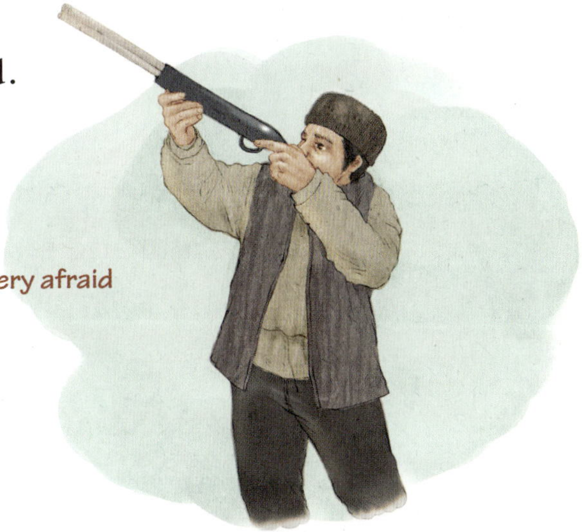

Stop & Think

Who killed the two geese?

CHECK UP Choose the right words.

1 The ugly duckling was a ____________ swimmer. (good | bad)
2 The farm girl ____________ the ugly duckling. (liked | disliked)
3 The ugly duckling ____________ the farm. (ran to | ran away from)
4 Hunters with ____________ killed the two geese. (rifles | knives)

GRAMMAR POINT

-er + than... (comparative)

- He swam even **better than** the others.

hut

at sunrise

flight

swan

Finally, he found an old hut in the forest. He entered the hut. There were a woman, a cat, and a hen. The woman was very old. "What are you? A duck?" she asked. "How wonderful! You can stay here and lay eggs for me."

The next day, the cat asked the ugly duckling, "Where are your eggs?"

"I don't have any eggs," he answered.

"Then you are useless. You must leave," the hen said.
↳ worthless ≠ valuable

The ugly duckling left the hut. The weather was getting colder. ≠ getting hotter

One day at sunrise, he saw something beautiful and strange overhead. ↳ over his head It was a flight of beautiful birds—three swans! ↳ a group of They had long necks and soft white wings. They were migrating south.
↳ moving south

Stop & Think
What did the ugly duckling see in the sky?

Key Words

- **hut** a small house
- **useless** worthless
- **flight** a group of flying birds
- **freeze** to become ice
- **pick up** to lift
- **survive** to live; to not die
- **lay eggs** to produce eggs
- **overhead** over one's head; up in the air
- **migrate** to move somewhere else to live
- **lie** to be on the ground
- **be able to** can; to have an ability to
- **set free** to let go; to release

"Oh, what beautiful birds!" he thought. He called to them. "Who are you? Take me with you." But they did not hear him.

Winter came, and the water in the lake froze. **The poor ugly duckling could not even swim in the water.** He was cold and had no food to eat.

A farmer walked by the lake. He saw the ugly duckling lying on the ice. "You poor bird," he said. "I will take you home and help you." He picked up the ugly duckling and took him home. The man had a wife, a son, and a daughter. They took good care of the ugly duckling. Slowly, he started to get better. **Thanks to them, the ugly duckling was able to survive the cold winter.**

However, by springtime, he had grown so big. The farmer decided to set the ugly duckling free by the pond.

lie

pick up

set free

Stop & Think
How did the ugly duckling survive the winter?

Check Up
Answer the questions.

1. Why couldn't the ugly duckling swim in the lake?
   a. There was no water.   b. He was a bad swimmer.   c. The water froze.
2. When did the farmer set the ugly duckling free?
   a. in the winter   b. in the spring   c. in the summer

Grammar Point

can / be able to

- The poor ugly duckling **could** not even swim in the water.
- Thanks to them, the ugly duckling **was able to** survive the cold winter.

flap

garden

shy

reflection

The ugly duckling was alone again. [→ by himself] He was swimming alone in the pond. Then, suddenly, he started to flap his wings and flew into the sky. [→ move quickly] "I can fly. I can fly!" shouted the ugly duckling. [→ fly–flew–flown] "This is amazing."

The ugly duckling flew all around the land. Then, he looked down and saw a garden. It was a garden with a pond. "That's a beautiful garden," he thought. "I will go there."

He landed in the pond in the garden. [→ went down onto] He looked over [→ looked around] and saw three swans. They were the three swans he had seen in winter. "Oh, they are so beautiful," he thought. "I have to speak to them."

But the ugly duckling did not know what to say. He suddenly felt shy. He looked down into the water. [≠ looked up] Then, he saw his reflection in the water. [→ image] He looked just like the swans. He was not an ugly duckling. He was a swan. "I'm a swan!" he cried.

Stop & Think
What was the ugly duckling?

Key Words

- **alone** by oneself
- **fly into** to fly up into
- **shy** ≠ brave
- **throw** to toss *throw–threw–thrown
- **flap one's wings** to move one's wings quickly
- **land** to go down to the ground from flying
- **reflection** an image reflected by a mirror or water
- **pleased** happy; glad

"Mother, look," some children shouted. "There's a new swan. Isn't he beautiful? He's the most beautiful of all the swans."

The children threw some bread into the pond for him to eat. He was so pleased. All his life, people had thought he was ugly. Now, they told him how beautiful he was. It was the happiest moment of his life.

→ throw–threw–thrown

→ happy, glad

→ ≠ the saddest

throw

Check Up Put the right words.

| the most | flew | reflection | ugly |

1. The ugly duckling _____ into the sky.
2. The ugly duckling saw his _____ in the water.
3. He was not an _____ duckling anymore.
4. The ugly duckling was _____ beautiful of all the swans.

Grammar Point

the + -est (superlative)
- He's **the most beautiful** of all the swans.
- It was **the happiest** moment of his life.

The Ugly Duckling 37

The Ant and the Grasshopper

One summer day, a grasshopper hops into a field. He sings happily because it is a beautiful summer day. He sees an ant pass by. The ant is working hard. It is carrying some corn to its home.
→ jumps into
→ go by

"Why don't you stay and chat with me?" asks the grasshopper. "That corn looks heavy. Why are you carrying it?"
→ talk with
→ ≠ light

"I'm saving food for the winter," answers the ant. "I recommend that you do the same thing. Then, you will have plenty of food for the winter."
→ keeping
→ advise, suggest
→ a lot of, lots of

"Winter?" says the grasshopper. "Why worry about that? We have lots of food right now. And winter is a long time away."
→ far in the future

grasshopper

ant

Stop & Think
Why does the ant work hard every day?

KEY WORDS

- **hop** to jump
- **recommend** to advise
- **gather** to collect
- **disappear** to vanish
- **look over** to look around
- **pass by** to go by
- **a long time away** far in the future
- **completely** entirely; totally
- **discover** to see; to realize
- **prepare for** to be ready for; to get ready for

The ant leaves the grasshopper. The ant works hard every day, so it gathers lots of food. After a while, the ant completely fills its house with food.
→ collects
→ entirely, totally

Meanwhile, the grasshopper stays in the field. But he does not work at all. Instead, he plays and sings every day.
→ In the meantime

Soon, summer turns to fall, and fall turns to winter. When the weather gets colder, the food starts to disappear. The grasshopper discovers that he has no food to eat. He looks over at the ant's house. The ant has plenty of food and a nice, warm house. The grasshopper realizes how foolish he was.
→ changes to
→ vanish ≠ appear
→ realizes
→ silly

That winter, there is lots of snow. Later, when spring arrives, the ant comes out of its house. The ant had enough food during winter. Now, it is ready to start gathering food for the next winter. When the ant looks around the field, there is no sign of the grasshopper.
→ comes

- Moral: Work hard today to *prepare* for tomorrow.
  be ready for ←

carry

plenty of

weather

Stop & Think
What does the grasshopper do every day?

Check Up Choose the right words.
1. The ant _____ a lot of food for the winter. (gathers | eats)
2. In winter, the _____ has no food to eat. (grasshopper | ant)
3. The grasshopper realizes how _____ he was. (fun | foolish)
4. Is the grasshopper in the field in the next spring? (Yes | No)

Grammar Point

see + O(object) + V(verb)
- He **sees** an ant **pass** by.

The Hare and the Tortoise

hare

tortoise

race

One day, a hare was bragging [→ boasting] about how fast he could run. "I am the fastest animal in the entire forest," he said. All the animals were tired of hearing the hare brag. They had heard his bragging many times before. [→ sick of]

The hare started to make fun of the tortoise. "You are so slow," laughed the hare. "A snail could run faster than you." [→ laugh at]

The tortoise smiled at the hare and replied, "Yes, I am slow. But I bet I can reach the end of this field before you. Let's run a race." [→ I'm sure]

"Oh, really? It's a bet," said the hare. "All right, everyone. Let's find out who the faster animal is." [→ betting] [→ learn, discover]

The tortoise and the hare went to the starting line. All the animals in the forest gathered to watch. "Ready. Go," shouted the fox. [≠ finish line]

Stop & Think
Why did the tortoise and the hare race?

Key Words

- **brag** to boast
- **be tired of** to be sick of
- **find out** to learn; to discover
- **leave ~ behind** to get ahead of
- **far behind** far away from ≠ far ahead of
- **cross** to go across; to pass

- **entire** all; total
- **bet** to be sure; to challenge; betting
- **race off** to run quickly
- **look back** to look behind oneself
- **get rest** to rest; to relax
- **steady** constant; regular

The hare raced off and left the tortoise behind. The tortoise simply kept moving as fast as he could.

When the hare was halfway across the field, he looked back. The tortoise was far behind him. "Ha," thought the hare. "It will take the tortoise all day to finish. I'm going to get some rest here." The hare rested, but he soon fell asleep in the warm sunshine.

The tortoise, in the meantime, walked and walked. He never stopped until he got to the finish line.

A few hours later, the hare woke up. "Oh, no!" the hare thought. He looked ahead toward the finish line. The tortoise was about to cross it. The hare ran as fast as he could, but it was too late. The tortoise crossed the finish line first. The tortoise had won.

get rest

cross

- Moral: *Slow and steady wins the race.*

> **CHECK UP** Finish the sentences.

1. The hare bragged
2. The tortoise bet
3. The tortoise
4. The hare woke up

a. kept walking to the finish line.
b. about how fast he could run.
c. too late.
d. he could beat the hare.

> **GRAMMAR POINT**

as ~ as one can/could

- The tortoise simply kept moving **as** fast **as he could**. (= **as fast as possible**)
- The hare ran **as** fast **as he could**. (= **as fast as possible**)

The Sick Lion

hunt

forest

cave

Once, there was a very old lion. As he got older, he became weak and slow. He could no longer hunt animals. So he was not able to eat any food.

The lion was sure he would soon die. He was very sad. As he slowly walked home, the lion told a bird about his sad situation. Soon, all of the animals in the forest heard about the lion.

The other animals felt sorry for the lion. "That's terrible," they said. "We should visit the lion and see how he is doing." So, one by one, they went to visit the lion in his cave.

The lion was old and weak, but he was also very wise. As each animal came into his cave, they were easy to catch and eat. Soon, the old lion became fat.

Still, he kept pretending to be sick. And the animals kept going into the lion's cave. After a while, many of the animals of the forest had disappeared.

Stop & Think
What did the lion do?

Key Words

- **situation** a condition
- **wise** very clever; smart
- **disappear** to vanish
- **die** to become dead
- **footprint** an impression of one's foot
- **terrible** awful; very bad
- **pretend** to act
- **call out** to yell; to shout
- **closely** carefully
- **misfortune** bad luck

One day, early in the morning, the fox went to the lion's cave. The fox was very wise, too. He slowly walked close to the cave. Standing outside the cave, the fox called out, "Hello. How are you feeling now?"

footprint

The lion answered, "I am not doing very well. Why don't you come in? I can't see you very well. Come closer and tell me some kind words. I am old and will die soon."

→ yelled, shouted (above "answered")

While the lion was talking, the fox was looking closely at the ground. The fox suddenly realized what the lion was doing.

→ carefully (above "closely")

Finally, the fox looked up and answered, "No thank you. I can see many footprints entering your cave. But I cannot see any footprints leaving your cave."

→ footsteps
→ going out of (below "leaving")

- Moral: A wise person learns from the misfortunes of others.

→ bad luck

Stop & Think
Why did the fox refuse to enter the cave?

Check Up   Put the right words.

| hunt   footprints   sorry   pretended |

1. The lion could not _____ animals anymore.
2. The animals felt _____ for the lion.
3. The lion _____ to be sick.
4. The fox looked at the _____ outside the cave.

Grammar Point

as (conjunction)
- **As** he got older, he became weak and slow.
- **As** he slowly walked home, the lion told a bird about his sad situation.
- **As** each animal came into his cave, they were easy to catch and eat.

The Boy Who Cried Wolf

shepherd

a flock of sheep

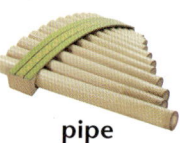
pipe

There once was a shepherd boy. He watched a flock of sheep at the bottom of a mountain. The shepherd boy was bored watching the sheep all day by himself. So he sometimes talked to his dog or played his pipe.

One day, he became very bored. So he thought of a plan to have some fun. He decided to play a trick on the villagers. He ran down toward the village and cried out, "Wolf! Wolf!"

The villagers heard the shepherd boy. The kind villagers ran up the mountain to help him. But when they arrived, they found no wolf.

"Where is the wolf?"

The boy laughed at the sight of their angry faces.

"Ha, ha, ha! I fooled all of you," he said.

"Don't cry 'wolf,' shepherd boy," said the villagers, "when there's no wolf!" They went back down the mountain.

Stop & Think
Why did the shepherd boy yell, "Wolf!" the first time?

Key Words

- **shepherd boy** a boy who watches sheep
- **bored** ≠ excited
- **play a trick on** to trick; to fool
- **fool** to trick
- **louder** ≠ quieter
- **scatter** to spread out
- **flock** a group of animals
- **by oneself** alone
- **run up** to go up quickly
- **frightened** scared
- **trick** to fool
- **liar** a person who tells lies

A few days later, the shepherd boy was bored again. So the boy cried out again, "Wolf! Wolf!" When the villagers arrived, the shepherd boy was laughing at them again.

frightened

One day while the boy was watching the sheep, a wolf really did come. It started attacking his sheep. The frightened boy ran toward the village and shouted even louder than before.

"Wolf! Wolf! A wolf is killing my sheep!"

But the villagers thought he was fooling them again. So they didn't come. "He will not trick us again," they said. Because none of them went to help the boy, the wolf killed many of the sheep. And the flock scattered.

- *Moral: No one believes liars even when they tell the truth.*

Stop & Think
Why did the villagers not go to help the shepherd boy?

Check Up — True or false?
1. The shepherd boy tricked the villagers by crying out, "Wolf!" _____
2. A wolf attacked the shepherd boy's sheep. _____
3. The shepherd boy killed the wolf. _____

Grammar Point

to + V (purpose)
- He thought of a plan **to have** some fun.
- The kind villagers ran up the mountain **to help** him.
- None of them went **to help** the boy.

Super Reading Story Training Book

Step 2

The Little Mermaid
– Hans Christian Andersen

The Little Mermaid

mermaid

tail

Deep beneath the sea, the Sea King lived. He lived with his six daughters, very beautiful mermaids, in a palace. His wife died many years ago. Their grandmother took care of the mermaid princesses.

Each princess was beautiful, but the youngest was the loveliest of all. Her skin was like a rose. Her eyes were deep sea-blue. Her long hair flew smoothly in the sea. And she had the most beautiful singing voice in the world. When she sang, the fish flocked from all over the sea to listen to her. She seemed like other girls on land. But, like all mermaids, she had no legs. She had a tail like a fish.

Key Words

- **take care of** to look after; to care for
- **loveliest** most beautiful
- **seem like** to resemble; to be similar to
- **for oneself** by oneself
- **stand by** to stand next to
- **princess** ≠ prince
- **flock** to gather around
- **keep ~ company** to be with another
- **hardly** barely
- **look up** to look toward the sky

The Little Mermaid had a wonderful life. She played and sang with her sisters all day long. She also liked to spend her time in her wonderful sea garden. The seahorses kept her company, and sometimes a dolphin would come and play.
→ played with her

seahorse

But the Little Mermaid was happiest when her grandmother told her stories. Her grandmother told her all about the world above the sea. She told her about beautiful ships, villages, and the people above.

dolphin

The Little Mermaid never went out of the sea.

"Oh, how I'd love to go up there and see the sky at last!"
→ I really want to

"You're still too young," said her grandmother.

"When you are fifteen, you can swim to the top of the ocean and see the wonderful things for yourself," said her grandmother.
→ by yourself
→ could not wait

The Little Mermaid could hardly wait. Every night, she stood by the window and looked up through the water. She often dreamed of the land above the water.
→ stand-stood-stood

ship

Check Up   Choose the right words.

1. The Little Mermaid had a _____ singing voice. (terrible | beautiful)
2. All mermaids have a _____ instead of legs. (tail | head)
3. The Little Mermaid dreamed of the _____ above the water. (land | sea)

Grammar Point

the loveliest of all (superlative + a group or place)
- The youngest was **the loveliest of all**.
- She had **the most beautiful** singing voice **in the world**.

The Little Mermaid   49

comb

wave

lightning

break apart

At last, the Little Mermaid turned fifteen. → became fifteen years old

"There, now you can go to the surface," said her father.

The Little Mermaid was so excited. She combed her long golden hair. She polished the scales on her tail. She kissed her grandmother goodbye.
→ thrilled ≠ bored
→ shined

In a second, the Little Mermaid swam up toward the surface of the sea. She swam so fast that even the fish could not keep up with her.
→ Quickly
→ swim–swam–swum
→ follow, run after

Suddenly, she popped out of the water. How wonderful! For the first time, she saw the great sky. It was full of red and orange clouds. The sun was setting. "It's so lovely!" she exclaimed happily.
→ came out of
→ going down
→ shouted

In front of her was a big ship. She swam close to the ship and looked inside. There was a big party. There were many handsome gentlemen, but the finest of all was a prince. He was laughing and shaking hands with everyone. She had never seen anyone like him before. She could not take her eyes off him.
← fine–finer–finest
→ stop looking at him

All of a sudden, the weather changed. The sky became dark, and heavy rain started to fall. The waves became very rough. Lightning flashed, and thunder boomed
← Suddenly
→ ≠ smooth
← made a loud sound

Stop & Think
Who did the Little Mermaid see inside the ship?

Key Words

- **polish** to shine; to clean
- **keep up with** to follow
- **flash** to make a bright light
- **roll up and down** to move up and down
- **in a second** quickly; swiftly
- **pop out of** to come out of
- **thunder** the loud sound caused by lightning
- **break apart** to come apart; to go to pieces

throughout the sky. The ship rolled up and down on the waves. Then, the ship broke apart and started to sink.
→ moved up and down

The Little Mermaid saw the prince fall into the sea. "People cannot breathe underwater," she thought. "I must save him." The Little Mermaid went diving down to look for him. He was sinking deep into the ocean. She seized his shoulder and took him to the surface.
→ go beneath the water
→ grabbed

When she got to land, she pushed the prince's body onto the shore. The prince was still not awake. The Little Mermaid looked into his handsome face all night long.
→ reached
≠ asleep

By the morning, the storm was finished, and the warm sun appeared. In the sunlight, the prince looked more handsome. His eyes were still closed. "Wake up. Please don't die," she whispered.
≠ disappeared
spoke softly

breathe

storm

Check Up True or false?

1 The Little Mermaid thought the prince was handsome. _____
2 The prince could breathe underwater. _____
3 The Little Mermaid saved the prince's life. _____

Grammar Point

so ~ that...
- She swam **so** fast **that** even the fish could not keep up with her.

The Little Mermaid 51

beach

rock

sorrow

look out

Now, she could see dry land ahead. She took the prince onto a pretty beach with calm water. She laid the prince on the warm sand. At that moment, she saw some girls walking along the sand. Quickly, she swam away and hid behind some rocks. She watched the prince. "I must stay here until someone comes to save him," she thought.

After a while, a pretty girl came along the beach. She saw the prince and ran to him. At that moment, the prince opened his eyes and smiled at the girl. The girl called for help. Soon, some people came and took the prince away.

The Little Mermaid felt so sad because she could not see him anymore. She swam back home full of sorrow.

"What did you see?" her sisters asked. But she told them nothing. She was too sad to speak. She was quiet all day long.

Days and weeks went by. The Little Mermaid could only think about the prince. She missed him so much. At night, she often swam to the beach. She looked for the prince, but she did not see him.

Stop & Think
Who found the prince on the beach?

KEY WORDS

- **calm** peaceful
- **take away** to carry away; to remove
- **go by** to pass
- **foam** bubbles
- **lay** to put down *lay–laid–laid
- **sorrow** sadness
- **wish** a desire; a dream
- **soul** a spirit

One day, she finally told her sisters her story. One of the sisters took her to his palace. He lived in a great palace by the sea. She could see the prince looking out his window. She was so happy. Every night, she swam near the palace and watched the prince.

→ at last

The Little Mermaid loved the world above the sea more and more. Now she had only one wish—to become a human.

→ desire, dream

"Grandmother," she asked one day. "Can humans live forever?"

→ without end

"No, they can't," said her grandmother. "Humans die. They live shorter lives than we do. Mermaids live for 300 years, and then we become foam on the sea. But humans have souls. Their souls live forever."

→ *sg. life
→ bubbles
→ spirits

foam

Stop & Think
What did the Little Mermaid wish?

Check Up Put the right words.

mermaids   souls   prince   rocks

1. The Little Mermaid hid behind some _____.
2. The Little Mermaid only thought about the _____.
3. _____ live for 300 years.
4. Humans have _____, but mermaids do not.

Grammar Point

see + O(object) + V(verb) / V-ing

- The Little Mermaid **saw** the prince **fall** into the sea.
- She **saw** some girls **walking** along the sand.
- She could **see** the prince **looking** out his window.

marry

witch

scary

bone

"I want to be like a person. Can I get a human soul?" asked the Little Mermaid. →human →have

"Don't say that," said her grandmother.

"Is there any way that I can get a soul?" she asked over and over again. →repeatedly

At last, her grandmother replied. →Finally

"There is only one way. If a man loves you with all his heart and marries you, then his soul can enter your body. Then, you would have a soul and would live forever," she continued. "But that will never happen because we have tails. Humans think tails are ugly. They prefer legs. No man will want to marry a mermaid." →truly →occur

The Little Mermaid looked at her tail and thought.

"I want to have two legs. I must win the prince's love and marry him. I love him. I will do anything for him. Maybe the sea witch can help me." →≠ lose

She swam off to see the sea witch. The sea witch lived in a horrible, scary place. Her house was made from the bones of dead sailors. And there were sea snakes →swam away awful← →frightening

Stop & Think
How can a mermaid get a soul?

KEY WORDS

- **over and over again** repeatedly
- **prefer** to like one thing more than another
- **scary** frightening
- **grant one's wish** to make one's wish come true
- **hurt** to feel pain; to cause pain
- **marry** to get married to; to wed
- **horrible** awful
- **afraid** scared; frightened (≠ brave)
- **split in** to divide into
- **bear pain** to stand being hurt

everywhere. The Little Mermaid felt very afraid. She almost left. Then, she thought, "The prince! And my soul! I must not be afraid."

> scared
> nearly went away

The Little Mermaid swam up to the sea witch. When the witch saw the Little Mermaid, she said, "I know what you want. I can give you a pair of human legs. Then, you will be able to walk on land. Come in."

> can

sailor

magic drink

The Little Mermaid followed the witch into the bone house.

"You are a stupid girl. You will be sorry. But I will grant your wish," the witch said.

> foolish
> regret
> make your wish come true

"I will make a magic drink for you. Tomorrow morning, before sunrise, you must swim to land and drink it. Then your tail will split in two, and you will have two legs. But it will be very painful. It will hurt every time you walk. Can you bear the pain?"

> ≠ sunset
> divide into
> cause pain
> stand, deal with

Stop & Think
How can the Little Mermaid become a human?

CHECK UP Finish the sentences.

1 Humans think
2 The sea witch's house
3 The Little Mermaid
4 The Little Mermaid's tail

a. wanted a pair of human legs.
b. was made from bones.
c. will split in two.
d. tails are ugly.

GRAMMAR POINT

will be able to / must be able to

- You **will be able to** walk on land. (*NOT* will can)
- I **must be able to** talk to the prince. (*NOT* must can)

The Little Mermaid 55

painful

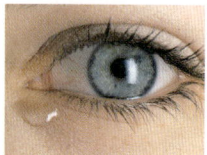
tears

"Yes," replied the Little Mermaid. "It doesn't matter!" whispered the Little Mermaid with tears in her eyes. "As long as I can go back to him!"

"But remember one more thing," the sea witch added. "Once you become a human, you can never become a mermaid again. You will never return to your father's palace. And if the prince marries another girl, you will turn into foam on the sea."
→ If
→ go back
→ change into

"I will do it," the Little Mermaid said.

"Ah, but there is one more thing," said the sea witch. "You must pay me. I want your voice. You have the prettiest voice in the world."
→ pretty–prettier–prettiest

KEY WORDS

- **pay** to give money for something
- **instantly** immediately; at once
- **pass out** to faint; to lose consciousness
- **fall in love with** to love; to be in love with
- **be gone** to disappear

"My voice? Then how can I speak?" the Little Mermaid asked. "How will I make the prince fall in love with me? I must be able to talk to him." *(fall in love → love me)*

"You are beautiful," said the sea witch. "You can dance. You can smile at him. Your deep blue eyes will speak for you. You do not need to talk."

"All right," the Little Mermaid agreed to the price. Instantly, her voice was gone. *(Instantly → Immediately; gone → disappeared)*

The sea witch made the magic drink for her. The Little Mermaid took the drink and swam to land. She reached the beach and then drank the magic drink. *(drink–drank–drunk)* Suddenly, she felt a horrible pain. It was like a knife in her body. She passed out in the sand. *(passed out → fainted)*

The next morning, the Little Mermaid woke up. She looked at her body. Her tail was gone. She had the prettiest legs on Earth. Then, she saw a shadow. She looked up. The prince was standing over her and looking down at her.

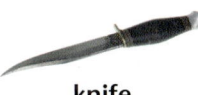
pay

knife

pass out

shadow

Stop & Think
What did the sea witch take from the Little Mermaid?

CHECK UP Answer the questions.

1 What will happen to the Little Mermaid if the prince marries someone else?
   a. She will lose her voice.   b. She will turn into foam.   c. She will get a soul.

2 What happened right after the Little Mermaid drank the magic drink?
   a. She became a human.   b. She found the prince.   c. She passed out.

GRAMMAR POINT

as long as / once
- **As long as** I can go back to him!
- **Once** you become a human, you can never become a mermaid again.

castle

jewelry

"Who are you? Where did you come from?" asked the prince.

But the Little Mermaid could not speak. She just looked deeply into his eyes with her sad blue eyes. At that moment, the prince had very strong feelings for her.

"I'll take you to the castle and look after you," he said. The prince took the Little Mermaid inside his castle. Every step felt like sharp knives. But she was with the prince, so she was happy.

→ take care of

≠ dull

In the days that followed, the Little Mermaid started a new life. The prince gave the Little Mermaid her own room. He gave her beautiful clothes and jewelry to wear, too. She was the most beautiful girl in the kingdom. But the Little Mermaid could not say anything to the prince. All she could do was smile at him.

In the days afterward

The prince held many parties. One night, some girls sang for the prince. They sang well, but the Little Mermaid was sad. "I used to sing much better than

→ had many parties

sing-sang-sung

Stop & Think
Where did the prince take the Little Mermaid?

Key Words

- **kingdom** a country that a king rules
- **suffer** to experience; to endure
- **have a picnic** to go on a picnic
- **ache** to hurt; to be sore
- **hold a party** to host a party; to have a party
- **be amazed by** to be very surprised by
- **go riding** to ride a horse
- **at those times** then

that," she thought. "I wish the prince could hear my singing voice."

Then, the girls started to dance. Now, the Little Mermaid could dance for the prince. She danced and danced. She suffered terrible pain throughout her body, but she danced so beautifully. Everyone was amazed by the Little Mermaid's dancing. The prince could not stop watching her.

have a picnic

go riding

After the party, the Little Mermaid and prince did everything together. They had picnics on the beach. They went riding together. They walked beside the calm ocean. The Little Mermaid's feet ached, but she did not care. She was happy to be with the prince.

Sometimes at night, she went to the ocean. She put her feet into the cool water. It always felt so good. At those times, she thought of her family. She missed them so much. "I hope they are well. I hope they understand me," she thought.

Stop & Think
What did the Little Mermaid do at the prince's party?

Check Up
Choose the right words.

1. _____ sang for the prince at the party. (Some girls | The Little Mermaid)
2. The Little Mermaid and the prince did _____ together. (everything | nothing)
3. The Little Mermaid _____ her family. (forgot about | missed)

Grammar Point

I wish ~ (subjunctive)
- **I wish** the prince **could hear** my singing voice.

drown

get married

sail

> As days went by

Day by day, the prince loved the Little Mermaid more and more. But he loved her like a sister. He did not think of marrying her.

One day, the prince told the Little Mermaid, "You are the sweetest girl I know. You remind me of a girl. This girl saved my life when my ship sank. I almost drowned. I only saw her once, but I cannot forget her. She is the only girl I can ever love."

> make me think of
> rescued

"I wish I could tell him it was me!" the Little Mermaid thought. "I saved you. But you don't know me." She felt so sad.

> I wish I were able to, I want to

One day, the king ordered the prince to visit the next kingdom. The king wanted the prince to marry the princess of the kingdom.

> commanded

"I must go there because my father ordered me," said the prince, "but no one can make me marry this princess. You remind me more of my lost love. If I must get married, I will marry you." He kissed the Little Mermaid. "Will you come with me? I want you to sail with me," he asked.

> not found, missing
> marry

Stop & Think

How did the prince feel about the Little Mermaid?

KEY WORDS

- **sweetest** the nicest; the kindest
- **save one's life** to rescue someone
- **come true** to become real; to happen
- **remind** to make one remember something
- **drown** to die in the water
- **be broken** to be shattered

The prince, the Little Mermaid, and many others got on a ship and sailed across the sea. At last, they arrived at a beautiful town. Many people came to the ship and welcomed the prince. And there was the princess. She had deep blue eyes, just like the Little Mermaid.

broken

"It is you," cried the prince. "My true love! You are the girl who saved my life. Let us get married tonight."

The prince turned to the Little Mermaid. He said, "My wish has come true. *(faced / become real)* I am so happy. I have found my true love. And I know you will be happy for me because you love me."

The Little Mermaid's heart was broken. She would never marry the prince now. *(break–broke–broken)* His wedding meant one thing. She must die. *(mean–meant–meant)*

Check Up   True or false?

1. The prince did not think of marrying the Little Mermaid. _____
2. The king ordered the prince to marry the Little Mermaid. _____
3. The prince met the girl he had been looking for. _____
4. The princess of the next kingdom saved the prince's life. _____

Grammar Point

who / whom (relative pronoun)

- You are *the girl* **who** saved my life.
- You are *the sweetest girl* **(whom)** I know.
- She is *the only girl* **(whom)** I can ever love.

The Little Mermaid

angel

bride

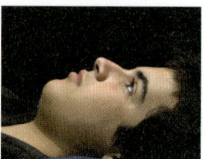
stay awake

That night, the prince and the princess got married on his ship. The wedding was beautiful. There was joyful music everywhere. But the Little Mermaid did not hear the music.
→ happy

"This is my last night on Earth," she said to herself. "Tomorrow, I will die and become foam on the sea."

At the wedding, the Little Mermaid danced for the last time. She moved like an angel. She danced more beautifully than ever. But her feet and heart were in pain. After that night, she would not see the prince again.
→ ≠ for the first time
→ hurt

At midnight, the music stopped, and the prince led his bride away. All was silent, yet the Little Mermaid stayed awake. She went out to look at the water by herself.
→ took away
→ quiet
→ ≠ went to sleep
→ alone

Just then, the Little Mermaid's sisters swam up to the ship. They looked different. Their beautiful hair was gone.
→ missing

Stop & Think
What did the Little Mermaid do at the wedding?

KEY WORDS

- **joyful** happy
- **lead away** to take away
- **silent** quiet (≠ loud)
- **rise** to come up
- **sneak** to move silently
- **be in pain** to hurt
- **bride** a wife (≠ groom)
- **stay awake** to remain alert (≠ go to sleep)
- **splash** to splatter; to spray
- **peacefully** quietly

"Little sister!" they cried. "We gave our hair to the sea witch. In return, she gave us a knife. Before the sun rises, you must kill the prince. When his blood splashes on you, your tail will return. You will become a mermaid again. Hurry up and do it. You must kill him before the sun rises, or it will be too late."

The Little Mermaid took the knife from her sisters. It was very sharp. She sneaked into the prince's room. The prince and the princess were sleeping peacefully. The Little Mermaid took the knife out. She looked at the knife. Then, she looked at the prince. No, she could not do it. She loved him. She threw the knife into the sea. Then, she jumped into the sea. The sun was rising.

splash

Check Up Finish the sentences.

1. The prince and the princess
2. The Little Mermaid's sisters
3. The Little Mermaid had to kill
4. The Little Mermaid

a. got married on the ship.
b. couldn't kill the prince.
c. gave their hair to the sea witch.
d. the prince before the sun rose.

Grammar Point

give A to B (= give B A)

- We **gave** our hair **to** the sea witch. (= We **gave** the sea witch our hair.)
- She **gave** us a knife. (= She **gave** a knife **to** us.)

floating

The Little Mermaid felt cold water. "I am dying," she thought.

But the Little Mermaid did not turn into foam. *(change into)* Suddenly, she felt her body rising into the air. *(going up)* She saw other lovely floating children. *(flying)* They were singing around her.

"Where am I? Who are you?" asked the Little Mermaid. She could speak again! She had a new voice. It was even more beautiful than before.

"You're with us in the sky. We are the fairies of the air," they responded. *(replied)* "You are now a fairy of the air. There are many ways to win a soul. *(get a soul)* We can get souls by doing good deeds," *(acts)* they continued.

"Mermaids only get souls if humans love them. But the fairies of the air can live for 300 years. If we do good deeds for 300 years, we can earn souls. You tried so hard to *(win souls, get souls)*

Stop & Think
What did the Little Mermaid become?

KEY WORDS

- **turn into** to change into; to become
- **lovely** beautiful
- **deed** an act
- **fly down** ≠ fly up
- **rise** to go up (≠ fall)
- **floating** flying
- **earn a soul** to win a soul; to get a soul
- **heaven** the place where souls go

earn a soul. You loved the prince so much that you gave your life for him. We will help you get a soul. Your soul will live forever."

fairy

"I can earn a soul? This is wonderful."

The Little Mermaid looked down at the ship. She saw the prince and the bride. The prince was looking sadly (≠ happily) into the ocean. He seemed to have guessed what had happened to her.

fly down

She flew down (≠ flew up *fly–flew–flown) to them. Of course, they could not see the Little Mermaid. She moved her body around them. **They felt the cool air move around them.** The Little Mermaid kissed the prince and his bride. Then, she smiled and flew up into the sky.

fly up

"In 300 years, I will have a soul," she said. "And I will see my prince in heaven."

Stop & Think
Why did the prince look sad?

CHECK UP Put the right words.

| guessed | fairy | soul | kissed |

1 The Little Mermaid became a _____ of the air.
2 The Little Mermaid can get a _____.
3 The prince _____ what had happened to the Little Mermaid.
4 The Little Mermaid _____ the prince and princess.

GRAMMAR POINT

feel + O(object) + V(verb) / V-ing

- They **felt** the cool air **move** around them.
- Suddenly, she **felt** her body **rising** into the air.

Super Reading Story Training Book

Step

3

Beauty and the Beast
– Beaumont, Madame de

•

The Stars
– Alphonse Daudet

Beauty and the Beast

merchant

greedy

Once, there was a rich merchant who had many ships. He bought and sold things from around the world. He lived in a big house by the sea. He had three daughters. The daughters were all very beautiful, but the youngest was the most beautiful of all. In fact, she was so beautiful that everyone called her "Beauty." Beauty was not only pretty but also kind and smart. She loved reading. Her two sisters were not very nice though. They were selfish and greedy. They liked to go to parties and to wear nice dresses. They were always mean to Beauty. They laughed at her when she read books. They only thought about marrying rich men.

Stop & Think

What kind of a person was Beauty?

Key Words

- **youngest** ≠ oldest; eldest
- **selfish** caring only for oneself
- **marry** to get married to; to wed
- **earn money** to make money
- **not only A but also B** B as well as A; both A and B
- **greedy** wanting more of everything
- **sink** to go beneath the water
- **be supposed to** to be expected to

One day, there was a terrible storm at sea. All the merchant's ships sank, so he lost everything. The man had to sell his big house and move into a small house in the countryside.

sink-sank-sunk *lose-lost-lost*

storm

"I'm sorry, my children. All my ships sank," said the man. "We have no money, so we have to work to earn money."

make money

"But, Father," said the eldest daughter, "we have never worked in our lives. We don't know how to work."

≠ youngest *sg. life*

sink

"We can't work. No rich man will want to marry us!" the middle daughter cried.

The family moved to the small country house.

"This house is so tiny," said the eldest daughter.

very small

"How are we supposed to live here?" the middle daughter cried.

How can we live here?

countryside

Stop & Think
What happened to the merchant's ships?

CHECK UP Put the right words.

tiny   countryside   selfish   enjoyed

1. Beauty's sisters were _____ and greedy.
2. Beauty was beautiful and _____ reading.
3. The merchant sold his house and moved to the _____.
4. Their new house was very _____.

GRAMMAR POINT

not only ~ but also...
- Beauty was **not only** pretty **but also** kind and smart.

Beauty and the Beast **69**

sit around

port

jump for joy

The two sisters did not stop complaining. But Beauty did not complain at all. Instead, she tried to be happy and to make everyone else happy.

→ grumbling

"I will clean the house, Father," she said. "This house is small, but we can be happy here."

Beauty worked hard every day. She woke up early in the morning and cleaned the house. She cooked breakfast, lunch, and dinner for her family. But her sisters never did any work. They sat around and complained all the time.

→ got up

sat and did nothing

One day, Beauty's father received a letter. He read the letter and instantly cheered up.

→ got

immediately, at once

"Children, I just heard some good news," he said. "One of my ships did not sink. It is bringing back lots of gold and silver for us. We are rich again. I must go to the port now."

hear-heard-heard

coming back with

Beauty's sisters jumped for joy. "We are rich! We are rich!" they cried.

were very happy

"Oh, Father, you must buy us some new dresses," said the two older sisters.

Stop & Think

How did Beauty's sisters like their new house?

Key Words

- **complain** to express dissatisfaction
- **cheer up** to become happy
- **jump for joy** to be very happy
- **steal** to rob; to take without permission
- **afford to** to have enough money to
- **sit around** to sit and do nothing
- **bring back** to come back with
- **pirate** a thief on the ocean
- **fix** to repair; to mend

"Yes, my dears, I will," said their father.

"And you, Beauty, what would you like me to get you?" asked her father.

rose

Beauty did not want anything. She was happy just because she could see her father happy. "Please bring me a rose, Father," said Beauty. "There are no roses in our garden."

pirate

Beauty's father hurried to the port. When he arrived there, he heard some bad news.

"The gold and silver are gone," his friend told him. "Pirates stole it. There is your ship. It has many holes in it, so you must fix the holes before the ship can sail again."

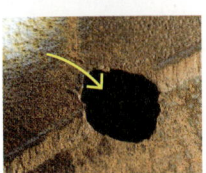
hole

Beauty's father fell to the ground.

"Without any gold or silver, I cannot afford to fix my ship," said Beauty's father sadly. "I will leave the ship there for now and return to the countryside."

Stop & Think

What happened to Beauty's father's ship?

Check Up — Finish the sentences.

1. Beauty worked hard and
2. One of Beauty's father's ships
3. Some pirates stole
4. Beauty's father could not

a. cleaned every day.
b. afford to fix the ship.
c. did not sink.
d. the gold and silver.

Grammar Point

would like ~ to...

- What **would** you **like** me **to** get you?

pocket

coin

howl

Then he remembered his daughters. He looked in his pockets and found only a few coins. "I don't have enough money to buy any dresses." Sadly, he started to walk back home.

→ recalled (remembered)

Suddenly, the weather became terribly cold. It began to snow, and the wind blew heavily. Soon, he was lost in a forest.

→ very, really (terribly)
blow–blew–blown
strongly (heavily)
got lost (was lost)

"This is very strange," he said to himself. "I have never seen this forest before. I must be lost."

He heard wolves howling loudly. He began to feel very afraid. "I must find some shelter. There is no way I will get home tonight," he said.

→ refuge (shelter)

He looked around and saw a light at some distance. "What is that? Is there a house there?"

→ in the distance

KEY WORDS

- **terribly** very; really
- **howl** to make a sound like a dog or wolf
- **look around** to look at everything in an area
- **burn** to be on fire
- **be full of** ≠ be empty
- **heavily** strongly; powerfully
- **shelter** a place that protects a person
- **wonder** to be curious about
- **fireplace** an indoor place to have a fire
- **starving** very hungry

72 Step 3

Beauty's father followed the light. After a few minutes, he found a castle.

"I wonder who lives here," he said. He went to the door of the castle.
→ am curious about

dining room

"Hello?" he called. But there was no answer. The door was open, so he walked inside. He saw no one. It was cold, and he was tired. He entered a large hall. It was a dining room. A huge fire was burning in the fireplace. And the dining table was full of food. There was a single plate on the table with a knife and fork beside it.
→ walked into
→ on fire
→ one

fireplace

plate

"This must be someone's dinner," he thought. He waited for the person to arrive, but no one came. Finally, after he had waited for a couple of hours, he sat down at the table and ate the food. Because he was starving, he ate all of the food. Then, he found a bedroom and fell asleep immediately.
→ two, a few
→ very hungry
→ instantly, at once

bedroom

Stop & Think
What did Beauty's father see in the dining room?

CHECK UP Choose the right words.

1. The weather suddenly became very _____. (cold | hot)
2. Beauty's father saw a _____ in the forest. (light | wolf)
3. There was _____ in the castle. (someone | no one)
4. Beauty's father sat down at the table and _____ the food. (ate | cooked)

GRAMMAR POINT

have/has + p.p. (present perfect: experience)
- I **have** never **seen** this forest before.

snowstorm

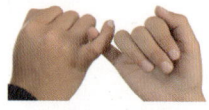
promise

rose bush

pick

In the morning, Beauty's father woke up. He looked around the room. He saw some breakfast on the table. But he did not see anybody. He sat down at the table and enjoyed breakfast. While he ate, he looked outside. *(enjoyed → ate, had)* He saw a beautiful garden full of flowers.

"That's strange," he thought. "Last night, there was a huge snowstorm, but the sun is shining now, and the flowers are blooming." *(huge → very big)*

Just then, he remembered the promise that he had made to Beauty. "A rose!" he said aloud. "**I promised Beauty I would bring her a rose.**" *(promised → made a promise)*

He went out to the garden and found a rose bush. It was full of beautiful red roses. He picked one. But as soon as he picked the rose, he heard a loud roar. And he saw a frightful, angry beast coming toward him. *(as soon as → the moment; roar → a loud sound; frightful → scary)*

"You dirty thief!" cried the Beast. *(thief → robber)*

"I saved your life and gave you food and a bed. But, in return, you are stealing my flowers. Now you're going to pay for it. I'm going to kill you." *(in return → as payment for it; pay for it → be punished for)*

Stop & Think
Why did Beauty's father go to the garden?

Key Words
- **snowstorm** heavy snow
- **frightful** scary
- **forgive** to pardon
- **bloom** to open, as in a flower
- **pay for** to be punished for; to suffer
- **angrily** with anger

Beauty's father fell to the ground and cried out, "Forgive me. I only wanted a single rose for my daughter. *Pardon* **I promised to bring a rose to my youngest daughter, Beauty.** Please do not kill me."

angrily

The Beast looked down at him angrily *(with anger)* and said, "All right. You may go home. But you have to send me your daughter. She must come here and live in this castle with me. If not, *(Otherwise)* then you must return here and die. Go back to your bedroom. There is a box of gold there. Take it and go."

box of gold

Stop & Think
What did the Beast want Beauty's father to do in return for sending him home?

Check Up True or false?

1. The garden had many yellow roses. _____
2. The Beast wanted to eat Beauty's father. _____
3. The Beast gave Beauty's father a box of gold. _____

Grammar Point

the usage of "promise"
- I **promised** Beauty **(that)** I would bring her a rose.
- I **promised to** bring a rose to my youngest daughter, Beauty.

say goodbye

ugly

Beauty's father hurried away from the castle as fast as he could. When he got home, he told his children what had happened.

as fast as possible

"I must return to the castle," he said. "I just wanted to say goodbye to all of you."

Beauty's sisters suddenly became angry at her. *upset with*

"Beauty, what have you done?" they shouted. "It's your fault. You wanted the rose, and now Father must die. You stupid girl!" *responsibility* *foolish*

"Father, I'll go to the Beast. I'm not afraid. I will go and live with the Beast," Beauty said quietly. *scared* *calmly*

"No, Beauty, no."

"There is no choice," she said. "The Beast will kill you and our family if I do not go."

Beauty's father was very sad. He went to his bedroom. Beauty followed him there.

"What is the Beast like, Father? Is he very ugly?" she asked. *bad-looking*

"Yes, the Beast is ugly, but he can also be kind. Look. He gave me this box of gold. But do not tell your

Stop & Think
What did Beauty ask her father about the Beast?

KEY WORDS

- **suddenly** instantly; at once
- **stupid** foolish; not smart
- **walk up to** to approach
- **weird** strange
- **angry at** upset with; mad at
- **arrive at** to get to
- **yell** to shout; to speak loudly
- **favorite food** the food that one likes the most

sisters about it. They will only want to spend it on new dresses."

"Father, please give the money to them," Beauty told her father. "While you *were away*, two men came here. My sisters are going to marry them, so they will have to buy many things. They need that money."

→ were out, were not here

marry

The next morning, Beauty said goodbye to her family and left for the castle. She was very sad, but she did not cry. Late in the evening, she finally *arrived at* the Beast's castle. The door was open, so she walked up to it. She saw nobody. "Hello?" she *yelled*, but no one answered.

→ ≠ left for
→ went near, approached

yell

"What a *weird* place!" thought Beauty. But she was very *brave*. She walked around the castle and found the dining room. There was a table with lots of food on it. All her *favorite* foods were on the table. There were two plates, two glasses, two forks, and two knives. Beauty *sat down* and ate the food.

→ strange
→ not afraid
→ most liked
→ ≠ stood up

favorite

Stop & Think
Who met Beauty at the castle?

CHECK UP Answer the questions.

1 What did Beauty's father show her?
   a. a box of gold   b. a picture of the Beast   c. a red rose

2 What was on the dining table?
   a. nothing   b. Beauty's favorite foods   c. some cakes and pies

GRAMMAR POINT

had + p.p. (past perfect: earlier past)

• When he <u>got</u> home, he <u>told</u> his children what **had happened**.

Beauty and the Beast 77

sign

pick up

note

After supper, Beauty started to look around the castle. *(supper → dinner)* It was a beautiful castle with many fine rooms. *(fine → very good, expensive)* When Beauty got to one room, she looked at the door. There was a sign on the door. It read "Beauty's Room."

"Is this my room? Well, if he gives me a special room, maybe he will not kill me," she thought.

Beauty opened the door and went inside. It was the most beautiful room she had ever seen. It was full of flowers, books, and beautiful clothes. She picked up one *(picked up → lifted)* book and opened it. Inside, there was a note. It read:

> Welcome, Beauty.
> Do not be afraid. *(afraid ≠ in danger)*
> You will be safe and happy here.
> I will do anything you want.
> You may have all of this.

"He must be very kind," Beauty thought. Beauty was very tired. She went to bed and fell asleep instantly.

Beauty spent the next day alone. *(alone → by herself)* In the evening, Beauty put on the most beautiful dress and went to the *(put on ≠ took off)*

Stop & Think
What did Beauty find in the book?

Key Words

- **look around** to explore
- **pick up** to lift
- **alone** by oneself
- **growl** a low sound an animal makes
- **kill** to make a living thing die
- **safe** secure
- **put on** to wear clothes or accessories
- **seem to** to appear; to look like

dining room. All of her favorite foods were on the table.

Beauty sat down. Suddenly, she heard a gentle growl, and the Beast came in. He was wearing fine clothes, but he had as much hair as a lion.

> gentle → soft
> as much hair as a lion → a lot of hair like

present

Beauty said, "Thank you for my present, sir."
> present → gift

"Call me Beast," said the Beast.

"Tell me, Beauty. Am I very ugly? Are you afraid of me?"
> afraid of → scared of

"Yes, Beast, you are ugly," said Beauty slowly. "But you seem to be very gentle. I'm not afraid of you because you're nice to me."
> seem → look
> nice → nice, kind

"Thank you for saying that," said the Beast.

That evening, Beauty and the Beast had dinner together. They talked about many topics. By the end of the dinner, Beauty thought that the Beast was not so frightening.
> had → ate
> frightening → scary

Check Up Put the right words.

| lion | frightening | ugly | sign |

1. The _____ on the door read "Beauty's Room."
2. The Beast had hair like a _____.
3. Beauty told the Beast that he was _____.
4. Beauty thought the Beast was not so _____.

Grammar Point

as much/many ~ as...

- He had **as much** hair **as** a lion.

Beauty and the Beast 79

mirror

heart

propose

The next day, Beauty went downstairs. There, she saw the Beast waiting for her. ≠ went upstairs

"There is a mirror in your bedroom," the Beast said. "It is a magic mirror. When you want to see your father, look into that mirror."

"That is very generous of you. Thank you," replied Beauty. → kind

"Beauty, I know that I am ugly," said the Beast. "I must be stupid as well because I cannot think of anything smart to say to you." ≠ smart   → also

Beauty felt bad. "I know many people who look → felt sorry
beautiful but have ugly hearts," she said. "I like you better than those people, Beast."

"Then will you marry me?" asked the Beast.

"Marry you? Oh, no. I'm sorry, but I cannot do that," she said.

Beauty lived in the castle with the Beast, and they were very happy. Every night at nine o'clock, Beauty and the Beast had dinner together and chatted. At the chat-chatted-chatted
end of every dinner, the Beast always proposed, "Will you marry me?" And Beauty always answered, "I like you, but I cannot marry you." asked to get married

Stop & Think
What did the Beast ask Beauty to do?

Key Words

- **generous** kind; sweet
- **feel bad** to feel sorry; to feel sad
- **propose** to ask someone to get married
- **be sick in bed** to be ill in bed
- **stupid** foolish; dumb
- **chat** to talk
- **sick** ill
- **all by oneself** all alone

For three months, Beauty lived at the castle. She was happy there. She read books and walked through the garden every day. But, one day, she looked into the magic mirror. She saw her father. He was sick in bed and was all by himself. *(all alone)*

"I must go and see my father. I must talk to the Beast at dinner," Beauty thought.

At nine o'clock, Beauty and the Beast had dinner together. The Beast said, "If you will not marry me, then will you be my friend? I want you to stay with me forever." *(always)*

"Of course I will," Beauty answered. "You are kind to me. I will stay here with you, but there is a problem. I looked into the magic mirror and saw my father. He is sick in bed and all by himself. Will you please let me go to visit him?"

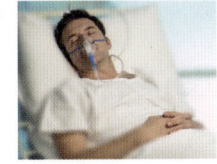

be sick in bed

> **Stop & Think**
> Why did Beauty want to go home?

CHECK UP — Finish the sentences.

1. The Beast gave Beauty
2. Beauty and the Beast
3. Beauty saw her father

a. had dinner together every night.
b. sick in bed.
c. a magic mirror.

GRAMMAR POINT

want + O(object) + to + V(verb) / let + O + V

- I **want** you **to stay** with me forever. (*NOT* want you stay)
- Will you please **let** me **go** to visit him? (*NOT* let me to go)

"If you leave, you will not come back," the Beast said. → go away   → won't

"I promise to come back," said Beauty. "But let me go there for one week."

The Beast thought for a moment and then said, "Okay. You may go." → for a while

He gave Beauty a ring and said, "Take this. Put on this ring and go to bed. Tomorrow, you will wake up in your father's home. After seven days, take the ring off and put the ring by your bed. You'll wake up in this castle." → wear ≠ take off   → ≠ put on   → place

"Goodbye, Beauty. Don't forget your promise. Come back in seven days."

Beauty thanked the Beast. She put the ring on and went to sleep. In the morning, when she woke up, she was in her father's home. She got up and ran to her father. → woke up

"Father, I'm home," she said.

"Oh, Beauty," he cried, "you have returned. I thought the Beast ate you. I'm so ill, and I am all alone. Your sisters are married, and they never visit me." → sick

ring

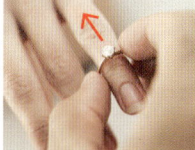
put on

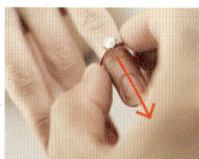
take off

Stop & Think

Why did the Beast give Beauty a ring?

KEY WORDS

- **put on** ≠ take off
- **take care of** to look after
- **respond** to answer
- **handsome** good-looking
- **promise** a vow
- **feel better** to get better
- **be good to** to be nice to
- **unkind** mean (≠ kind)

82 Step 3

"Father, I am only here for one week, but I will take good care of you. You will feel better soon," Beauty responded.
→ look after → get better
→ answered, replied

husband

Beauty's father looked at her. "You look beautiful," he said. "Your dress looks very nice. Is the Beast good to you?"
Is the Beast nice to you? ←

handsome

"Yes, he is very kind to me. I like him very much. Perhaps I almost love him," Beauty said.
→ Maybe
→ nearly

Her older sisters heard that Beauty was back. They came to visit her with their husbands. Both sisters were unhappy. One had a very handsome husband, but he was unkind. The other had a very smart husband, but he talked too much. When they saw Beauty in her beautiful dress, they both became angry.
→ ≠ kind
→ got angry

"Why is she always happy?" said one.

"I can't stand this. Let's keep Beauty here longer than a week. Then, the Beast will become angry with her. Maybe the Beast will eat her then." The other sister agreed.
→ can't bear
→ ≠ disagreed

Stop & Think
How did Beauty feel about the Beast?

CHECK UP Choose the right words.
1. Beauty _____ the ring and went to bed. (put on | took off)
2. In the morning, Beauty was in _____. (the Beast's castle | her father's house)
3. Beauty's sisters were very _____. (happy | unhappy)

GRAMMAR POINT

one / the other

- **One** had a very handsome husband. **The other** had a very smart husband.

have a dream

lie

grass

So they said to Beauty, "Oh, Beauty, we are so happy to see you. Please stay here for a few more days."

Beauty disliked seeing them sad. [≠ liked] So a week passed, [went by] but Beauty did not go back to the castle.

Then, one night, Beauty had a dream. [dreamed] In her dream, she saw the Beast. The Beast was lying on the grass. He was very sick and sad. He seemed to be dying. [looked like he was dying] Beauty heard the Beast saying, "Oh, Beauty! Beauty, why haven't you come back yet? I am dying."

Beauty woke up and jumped out of bed. It was the middle of the night. [midnight]

"I'm coming back, Beast!" she said. She removed [took off] the ring quickly and put it beside [next to] her bed. Then, she went back to sleep.

Beauty woke up in the castle. She jumped up and went looking for the Beast. [searching for] She tried every room in the castle, but she could not find the Beast anywhere.

Stop & Think
Where did Beauty see the Beast?

Key Words

- **dislike** to not like
- **have a dream** to dream
- **seem to** to look like
- **remove** to take off
- **pass** to go by
- **lie** to be on the ground
- **die** to stop living
- **lift** to raise

Step 3

Then, she remembered her dream. She ran into the garden and saw the Beast.

"Wake up, Beast. Wake up," she cried. "I'm back. I'm so sorry."

The beast slowly lifted his head. "I waited for you, Beauty. But you didn't come. Now it is too late. I'm going to die soon."

- lifted → raised
- late ≠ early

"No, Beast, you cannot die. I need you," said Beauty.

"I love you, Beast. Please don't die. I want to marry you." Beauty kissed his ugly face.

die

Stop & Think
What did Beauty tell the Beast?

Check Up
True or false?

1. The Beast was dying in Beauty's dream. _____
2. Beauty woke up from the dream and removed the ring. _____
3. Beauty found the Beast in the dining room. _____

Grammar Point

dislike -ing / go -ing

- Beauty **disliked** see**ing** them sad. (*NOT* disliked to see)
- She jumped up and **went** look**ing** for the Beast. (*NOT* went to look for)

prince

fairy

magic wand

At that moment, something magical happened. The sky was filled with bright light. In a moment, Beauty found herself inside the castle. The room was filled with flowers. But the Beast was not there. Next to Beauty was a very handsome young man. He was dressed like a prince.

- magical → magic
- bright → shining
- dressed → was wearing clothes

"What's going on here? Where is Beast?" Beauty asked.

- What's going on here? → What is happening here?

"I am here, Beauty," said the prince. "I am the Beast. Well, I was the Beast."

"A long time ago," said the prince, "I was selfish and unkind. A fairy touched me with her magic wand and put a spell on me. She turned me into a beast. She cursed me to be a beast forever until someone loved me. You broke the spell, Beauty. I became a man again because you love me."

- put a spell → cast a spell
- turned ~ into → changed ~ into
- broke the spell → stopped magic from happening

Then, the fairy suddenly appeared and said, "Yes, Beauty, you understand that kindness is more important

- appeared → came into sight

Stop & Think
What did the fairy do to the prince?

Key Words

- **magical** related to magic
- **be filled with** to be full of
- **fairy** an elf
- **curse** to use bad magic on someone
- **appear** to come into sight
- **invite** to ask someone to go somewhere; to ask for
- **happen** to take place; to occur
- **prince** ≠ princess
- **put a spell on** to cast a spell on
- **break a spell** to stop magic from happening
- **grant** to give

86   Step 3

than looks. Your sisters don't understand that. So now they are unhappy with their husbands. But you will be happy with your prince. You are the most beautiful couple in the world. I will marry you and give you happiness for the rest of your lives. And I will grant you many beautiful children, too."

appearance → (unhappy)
until you die → (rest of your lives)
give → (grant)

wedding

Beauty and the prince married soon. They had a wonderful wedding. Beauty invited her father to live in the castle with her. Beauty and the prince lived happily ever after.

Check Up Answer the questions.

1. How did Beauty break the spell?
   a. She kissed the Beast.   b. She married the Beast.   c. She loved the Beast.
2. What did the fairy promise Beauty and the prince?
   a. many children   b. long lives   c. lots of money

Grammar Point

-thing + adjective

- At that moment, **something magical** happened. (*NOT* magical something)

The Stars

shepherd

pasture

coal miner

I used to be a shepherd in the Luberon region of France. It was a very isolated place, so I was often all alone in the pasture. Sometimes, I did not see many people for weeks. During those weeks, I only had my dog and the flocks of sheep to accompany me.

From time to time, I saw a loner who lived on Mount Lure. He would come down to hear some news of the outside world. Also, I sometimes saw coal miners. They worked in the coal mines near my field, so I spoke with them as they went back and forth to the coal mines.

Once every two weeks, I got a visitor from the farm. This person was usually the farm boy or an old woman who worked at the farm. They were sent to bring me

Stop & Think
Who did the shepherd sometimes see?

Key Words

- **isolated** remote; separated from other things
- **accompany** to go with; to be with
- **supplies** food and other essential goods
- **delivery** the bringing of goods to someone's place
- **flock** a group of animals
- **loner** a person who spends much time alone
- **master** a boss; an employer
- **run out of** to be out of something

supplies on a mule. I was always happy to see them. *→ food and other essential goods*
They would tell me all of the news from the lowlands.

However, the news that interested me the most was about my master's daughter. Her name was Stephanette, and she was the most beautiful girl in the surrounding area. Without seeming to take too much interest, I would ask how Stephanette was doing. I asked if there were any young men who wanted to marry her.
an area of low
around the area
→ Pretending not to have much interest

Of course, I was just a lowly shepherd who worked for her father. I had to remind myself that there was no way that Stephanette would be interested in me. After all, there were many wealthy and handsome young men in the area.
→ unimportant, humble
→ make myself remember
→ Anyway
→ rich

One Sunday, I was waiting for the delivery boy to arrive. It had been two weeks since my last delivery, so I was running out of supplies. By ten o'clock, no one had arrived yet.
→ almost out of

mule

delivery

Stop & Think
What news interested the shepherd the most?

CHECK UP True or false?

1. The shepherd spent most of his time alone. _____
2. A person delivered supplies to the shepherd every week. _____
3. The shepherd often spoke with Stephanette. _____
4. One Sunday, the delivery boy arrived at ten o'clock. _____

GRAMMAR POINT

would
- He **would** come down to hear some news of the outside world.
- They **would** tell me all of the news from the lowlands.
- I **would** ask how Stephanette was doing.

The Stars

noon

dark clouds

ray

farmhand

"That's odd," I thought. "There must be a problem at my master's house."

→ strange

I continued to wait, but no one came by noon. "They must have forgotten to send my supplies," I said to myself.

Around noon, I noticed that a big storm was coming. In the distance, some dark clouds were gathering. Soon, heavy rain began to pour down. "Now I understand," I said to myself. "The bad weather has delayed the delivery person. The roads must be muddy by now. I should not expect him to arrive yet."

→ realized
→ fall heavily
→ made the delivery person late
→ full of mud

A few hours later, the storm was over. The sun shone high in the sky, and its warm rays spread bright light all over the fields.

shine–shone–shone ←

All of a sudden, I heard the familiar sound of the mule's bells. I eagerly looked to see if it was the farmhand or the old woman. However, it was neither the farmhand nor the old woman. It was the beautiful Stephanette! Oh, what a wonderful surprise that was!

well-known ←
→ excitedly
→ whether

She got off the mule, and then she said to me, "I got lost on my way up the hill."

↳ was lost

"Are you all right, mistress?" I asked.

≠ master

She smiled and nodded at me.

Key Words

- **odd** strange
- **delay** to make someone to be late
- **spread** to stretch out
- **eagerly** excitedly; enthusiastically
- **get off** ≠ get on
- **notice** to realize; to become aware of
- **muddy** full of mud; dirty
- **all of a sudden** suddenly
- **farmhand** a person who works on a farm
- **get lost** to lose one's way

"The farmhand is sick," said Stephanette, "and the old woman is visiting her children to spend the holiday with them. So my father sent me instead."

> holiday → vacation

I could not take my eyes off her. She looked so beautiful in that fresh afternoon air. In fact, I had never seen her so close before. And I had never spoken to her. I had only ever seen her from a distance.

> take my eyes off her → stop looking at her
> from a distance → from far away

When I returned to the lowlands in the winter, her father would invite me to dinner at his farm. At those times, she would walk silently across the room and not say a word to any of the servants. She had always looked very proud during those times. And now she was standing in front of me.

> servants → household workers

Stop & Think
Why did Stephanette come to the field?

CHECK UP Choose the right words.

1. The heavy _____ delayed the delivery person. (snow | rain)
2. The person on the mule was _____. (the old woman | Stephanette)
3. Stephanette _____ on her way to the field. (got lost | took a nap)
4. Had the shepherd ever spoken to Stephanette before? (Yes | No)

GRAMMAR POINT

neither ~ nor...
- It was **neither** the farmhand **nor** the old woman.

barn

straw

cape

stick

After she took my supplies off the mule, Stephanette looked around the area. She seemed curious about the pasture and the small barn. → interested in

"So this is where you live, shepherd?" she asked. She noticed my bed in the barn. It was a simple bed made of straw and sheepskin. There were a cape and a stick hanging on the wall above my bed.

"You must be lonely and bored because you are always alone," she continued. "What do you do all day long?"

I wanted to answer, "I only think about you, Stephanette," but I did not. As a matter of fact, I could not say a single word to her. How embarrassed I was.
→ In fact
→ a word
→ ashamed

Stephanette must have noticed my embarrassment. She started to tease me. → make fun of

"Do the fairies come to see you sometimes?" She was laughing with a twinkle in her eyes. I thought she was like a fairy, but I did not say those words. Instead, I said nothing.
→ pleasantly, happily

Stop & Think
What did the shepherd say to Stephanette?

Key Words

- **hang** to suspend
- **embarrassed** ashamed or nervous
- **tease** to make fun of
- **footstep** the sound or mark of walking
- **chore** a small duty or job
- **shiver** to shake
- **cross** to go across

- **lonely** lonesome
- **embarrassment** the state of being embarrassed
- **disappear** to vanish; to go away
- **remain** to stay
- **soaking wet** very wet
- **flood** to overflow
- **tremble** to shake

"Well, I must leave now," she said. Stephanette got back on the mule and said goodbye to me. Then, the mule led her back toward the farm. I watched her as she disappeared down the hill. The sound of the mule's footsteps continued for a while. The sound of those footsteps remained with me for a long time.

footstep

Later in the evening, I brought the flock of sheep back in from the fields. As I was completing my chores, I heard a voice calling my name. It was Stephanette. She had returned. But she was not smiling anymore. Now, she was soaking wet and shivering from the cold.

soaking wet

"At the bottom of the mountain, there is a river as you know. The rain from the storm caused the river to flood. The water has risen very high. I tried to cross the river, but I almost drowned in the water. I was so scared and didn't know what to do. So I just returned here," she said in a trembling voice.

flood

Stop & Think
Why did Stephanette return to the shepherd?

CHECK UP Finish the sentences.

1. The shepherd's bed was
2. The shepherd was
3. Stephanette left to go
4. The water in the river

a. embarrassed in front of Stephanette.
b. had risen too high.
c. made of straw and sheepskin.
d. back to the farm.

GRAMMAR POINT

"-ing" form (present participle)

- There were a cape and a stick **hanging** on the wall above my bed.
- She <u>was</u> **laughing** with a twinkle in her eyes.
- As I <u>was</u> **completing** my chores, I heard a voice **calling** my name.

make a fire

burst into tears

I was not sure what to do. It was not right for her to spend the night on the mountain. I also could not leave the flock of sheep to take her home. But then I thought, "The nights in July are short. It's only one night."

I immediately made a fire so that she could dry her feet and clothes. Then, I gave her some milk and cheese, but Stephanette was not interested in eating. She burst into tears. And I almost felt like crying, too. It was completely dark outside. I took her to the barn, and I prepared a bed for her. I laid out a new sheepskin on the fresh straw so that she could rest. I said goodnight and went outside.

I sat down in front of the door. I tried not to think of the young lady who was resting in my house. But all that I could think of was her. I was proud because I had assisted her. Tonight, it was my responsibility to keep her safe. In happiness, I looked up in the sky. The stars shone more beautifully than ever that night.

Stop & Think
How did the shepherd feel about taking care of Stephanette?

KEY WORDS

- **burst into tears** to start crying
- **completely** totally; entirely
- **lay out** to set out
- **keep ~ safe** to protect someone or something
- **frighten** to scare; to make someone afraid
- **almost** nearly
- **prepare** to get ready
- **be proud** to have a feeling of pride
- **normal** usual; regular
- **shooting star** a meteor

A while later, the barn door opened, and Stephanette came out.

"I cannot sleep," she said. "Do you mind if I sit next to the fire?"

frog

She sat down by the fire. I gave her a goatskin to wrap around herself. We sat by the fire in silence. That night, every creature seemed to come alive. The frogs in the pond croaked louder than normal. The insects sang loudly as well. The fire made a brilliant bright light as it burned through the night. Even the night air seemed to be fresher than normal.

shooting star

Some noises in the night frightened her. She moved closer to me. Just then, a shooting star passed in the sky above us. It was the most beautiful shooting star I had ever seen.

> Stop & Think
> What did Stephanette suddenly do?

Check Up Answer the questions.

1 Where did the shepherd make a bed for Stephanette?
   a. by the fire   b. in the barn   c. in the pasture

2 How did the noises make Stephanette feel?
   a. warm   b. frightened   c. angry

Grammar Point

it ~ to+V (preparatory "it")
- Tonight, **it** was my responsibility **to keep** her safe.
- **It** was not right **for her to spend** the night on the mountain.

plain

Milky Way

"What is that?" asked Stephanette.

"A soul that has entered Heaven," I responded.

Stephanette looked at me and said, "You are not like the other young men I know."

I answered, "I am probably like most other men, but my life in the field is very different from theirs. Here, I live close to the stars. I know what happens up there better than people from the plains."

(similar to — like)
(perhaps, maybe — probably)

Stephanette looked up into the sky and said, "Look! There is another shooting star." She pointed to a shooting star streaking across the sky.

(moving quickly — streaking)

point out

"It's so beautiful. I have never seen so many beautiful stars in my life. Do you know the names of the stars?"

Key Words

- **soul** a person's spirit
- **stretch** to extend
- **constellation** a group of stars
- **streak of light** a long band of light
- **point out** to show
- **form** to make; to create

"Of course, mistress, I do," I answered. "Look up there. Do you see the streak of light that travels across the sky? That is the Milky Way. The Milky Way stretches all across France and goes into Spain. Soldiers often use the Milky Way to find their way home."

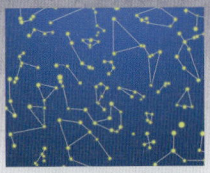
constellation

I continued to point out some of the stars to her. I explained constellations to her.

"Many stars combine to form constellations. They are like pictures in the sky. Can you see that group of stars? That is the Big Dipper. The three stars in front are the Three Animals. And there is Orion the Hunter up there."

Big Dipper

"Did you know that we shepherds are able to use the sky like a clock? I can tell the time by looking at the stars. For instance, right now, it is almost midnight." I kept talking.

- long band of light →
- extends →
- make →
- come together, unite ←
- can →
- know what time it is →
- continued →

Stop & Think
What did the shepherd show Stephanette in the sky?

CHECK UP Put the right words.

| tell | shooting star | Milky Way |

1. Stephanette pointed to a _____ in the sky.
2. The _____ stretches across all of France.
3. Shepherds can _____ time by looking at stars.

GRAMMAR POINT

to + V (purpose)
- Soldiers often use the Milky Way **to find** their way home.
- Many stars combine **to form** constellations.

The Stars

Evening Star

Saturn

"All of the stars are beautiful. But the most beautiful star of all is the Evening Star. It comes out first every night. It is the shepherd's friend. She lights our way at dawn when we take our flocks out to the fields → lead outside and also in the evening when we return. We call her Maguelonne. Maguelonne chases Saturn in the sky and → follows marries him every seven years."

"What? The stars can marry?" she exclaimed.

"Oh, sure. The stars can get married," I told her.

> **Key Words**
>
> - **dawn** daybreak
> - **enchanting** charming; attractive
> - **march** a movement
> - **brilliant** very bright and strong
> - **exclaim** to yell; to shout
> - **fade** to become weaker; to disappear gradually
> - **imagine** to think; to consider
> - **lose one's way** to get lost

I was just about to explain how the stars get married. Then, I felt as Stephanette laid her head on my shoulder and fell asleep. In the cool breeze, the ribbons in her hair danced, and I felt the touch of her curls against my neck. It was the most enchanting feeling.

curls

→ was going to
→ lay–laid–laid
→ a light wind
→ charming, attractive

We stayed like that until the stars began to fade and the first rays of dawn appeared. I wanted that night to last forever.

→ disappear gradually

All above us, the stars continued their march across the night sky. I imagined that one of the stars, the finest and the most brilliant, had lost her way and was resting her head on my shoulder.

→ movement
→ thought, considered
→ fine–finer–finest

Stop & Think
How did Stephanette fall asleep?

CHECK UP Choose the right words.

1. The _____ is the most beautiful star of all. (Evening Star | Saturn)
2. Stephanette _____ in front of the fire. (woke up | fell asleep)
3. Stephanette _____ her head on the shepherd's shoulder. (laid | stayed)

GRAMMAR POINT

the + -est (superlative)
- It was **the most enchanting** feeling.
- One of the stars, **the finest** and **the most brilliant**, had lost her way.

The Stars

Super
Reading
Story
Training
Book

Step 4

What Men Live By
– Leo Tolstoy

•

How Much Land Does a Man Need?
– Leo Tolstoy

What Men Live By

shoemaker

hut

fret

naked

There was once a poor shoemaker named Simon. He had no house or land. He lived in a hut with his wife and children. One morning, he went to the village to buy some sheepskins for a winter coat. He had only three rubles, but he planned to visit some of his customers on the way. They owed him five rubles for work he had already done.

Simon visited several customers' houses, but he could not collect any money. He went to the store and asked if he could buy the sheepskins on credit. But the shopkeeper refused to give them to Simon.

Simon felt downhearted and started walking homeward. "Though I have no sheepskin coat, I don't care. I can live without a coat. Yet my wife will surely fret," he thought.

While he was walking home, he passed by a church

> **Stop & Think**
> Why couldn't Simon pay for the sheepskins?

Key Words

- **on the way** while going somewhere
- **refuse** to turn down; to reject
- **homeward** toward home
- **robber** a thief
- **look back** to look behind oneself
- **owe** to have to pay money to
- **feel downhearted** to be sad; to be depressed
- **naked** having no clothes on
- **interfere** to get involved
- **frightened** scared

at the bend in the road. Simon saw something white behind the church. He did not know what it was. He came closer, and, to his surprise, it was a naked man. He was sitting against the church without any clothes on. → not wearing any clothes

Suddenly, Simon felt afraid. "Robbers must have killed him and stolen his clothes. If I interfere, I will have a big problem," Simon thought. → Thieves / steal-stole-stolen / get involved

Simon continued walking, but when he looked back, he saw the man was moving. Simon felt more frightened. → scared

"If I go there, he might kill me for my clothes. Even if he doesn't attack me, what can I do for him?" thought Simon. → Even though / ≠ defend

He ran down the road. But he suddenly stopped.

robber

> **Stop & Think**
> What did Simon see behind the church?

CHECK UP True or false?

1. Simon had five rubles. _____
2. Simon wanted to buy some sheepskins. _____
3. There was a robber next to the church. _____
4. Simon was afraid of the naked man. _____

GRAMMAR POINT

though / if / even if

- **Though** I have no sheepskin coat, I don't care.
- **If** I interfere, I will have a big problem.
- **Even if** he doesn't attack me, what can I do for him? (even if = even though)

What Men Live By

stick

surprised

felt boots

"What am I doing? The man could be dying!" He felt guilty, so he turned around and went back to the church. →felt bad   →turned back

When Simon went behind the church, he saw that the stranger was a young man. He was freezing and frightened. Simon immediately took off his coat and put it around the man. Then, he put boots on the man. Simon had an extra pair of boots. →very cold →removed ≠ put on →≠ took off →additional

"Can you walk?" asked Simon. "It's too cold to stay here. I will take you to my home. Here is a stick for you to lean on while you walk." →rest on

The man stood up and looked kindly at Simon. But he did not speak. As they walked to Simon's home, Simon asked him where he was from and how he got to the church. The man replied with a calm voice, "I'm not from around here. God has punished me." →got up *stand-stood-stood →quiet

Simon was surprised by the response. But he said, "Well, God rules all men. Come home with me and at →controls

Stop & Think
What did Simon give the man?

KEY WORDS

- **feel guilty** to feel bad
- **freezing** very cold
- **punish** to penalize a person for doing something wrong
- **disappointment** the state of being disappointed; displeasure
- **drunk** a person who is drunk
- **drunkard** a drunk
- **go back** to return
- **lean on** to lean against; to rest on
- **supper** a light dinner

least make yourself warm." As Simon walked with the stranger, he felt glad to help another person.

Simon's wife was preparing dinner when Simon and the man came into the house. Matryna noticed that the man had no hat and was wearing felt boots. And he was wearing her husband's coat. Simon had no sheepskins. Her heart was ready to break with disappointment. "He has been out drinking, and now he has brought another drunk home with him," she thought.

saw, became aware
was about to ≠ *satisfaction*
bring–brought–brought

drunk = drunkard

bench

vodka

Simon took off his hat and sat down on the bench as if things were all right. Then, he said, "Have a seat, my friend, and let us have some dinner."

Matryna became very angry and said, "I cooked dinner, but not for you. You went out to buy some sheepskins but bring a strange man home instead. He doesn't even have any clothes of his own. You must have spent all our money on vodka. I have no supper for drunkards like you."

drunks

Stop & Think
What did Simon's wife think about her husband?

CHECK UP Finish the sentences.

1. The man said that
2. Simon felt glad
3. Matryna was
4. Matryna thought that Simon

a. very disappointed with Simon.
b. to help another person.
c. was a drunkard.
d. God had punished him.

GRAMMAR POINT

what/where/how... + S + V (indirect question)

- Simon asked him **where he was** from and **how he got** to the church.

curious

anger

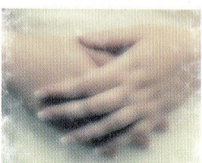
be folded

in pain

Simon tried to explain to his wife how he had met the man, but she did not listen. She angrily walked out the door, but then she stopped undecided; she wanted to work off her anger, but she also wanted to learn what sort of a man the stranger was. She was curious about the man.

> undecided → not decided, not determined
> work off → release

"If he were a good man, he would not be naked. Where is he from?" she asked.

"That's just what I'm trying to tell you," answered Simon. "When I passed the church, I saw him sitting there naked and frozen. God made me go to help him, or he would have died. What should I have done? So I helped him get up, gave him my coat, and brought him here. Don't be so angry with me. Anger is a sin."

> passed → went by
> frozen → ice cold
> anger → Being mad or angry

As Matryna listened to her husband, she looked closely at the man. He sat on the bench without moving. His hands were folded on his knees, and he looked down at the floor. His eyes were closed as if he were in pain.

> folded → fold–folded–folded
> in pain → hurting, pained

Stop & Think
What did Simon say to make Matryna calm down?

KEY WORDS

- **undecided** unable to make up one's mind
- **sin** something one does that is against the laws of God
- **be in pain** to hurt   • **soften** to become less hard (≠ harden)
- **feel pity for** to feel bad for someone (= take pity on)   • **feed** to give food to someone
- **reward** to give something to someone for doing a good deed

106   Step 4

"Matryna, don't you love God?" asked Simon.

Suddenly, her heart *softened* toward the stranger. She went back into the kitchen. She set the table and served dinner. While they were eating, Matryna *felt pity* for the stranger. She did not feel angry anymore. She even began to like him. At that moment, the man looked at Matryna and smiled at her. A light *seemed to* come from his face.

set the table

When they had finished supper, she asked the man where he was from. But the man said he did not know. All he said was, "God punished me. I was naked and freezing cold. Then, Simon saw me, *took pity on* me, and brought me here. You have *fed* me and *pitied* me, too. God will *reward* you."

- became soft
- felt sorry
- appeared to
- felt pity for, pitied
- feed-fed-fed
- pity-pitied-pitied
- repay ≠ punish

Check Up Answer the questions.

1. What did Matryna feel for the stranger?
   a. concern   b. love   c. pity

2. What happened after the man smiled?
   a. A light came from his face.   b. Simon felt pity for him.   c. Matryna's heart softened.

Grammar Point

if ~ (subjunctive)

- **If** he **were** a good man, he **would** not **be** naked.
- God made me go to help him, or he **would have died**.
  (= **If** God **had** not **made** me go to help him, he **would have died**.)

grieved

wake up

Matryna gave the man some clothes, and he went to get some sleep. Then, she and Simon went to bed, too, but Matryna could not sleep. She could not get the stranger out of her mind. Then, she suddenly remembered [forgot] that they had eaten their last piece of bread, so there was nothing left for tomorrow. She felt grieved. [felt sad, felt very bad]

"Simon, what will we do tomorrow?"

"As long as we are alive, we will find something to eat," Simon answered.

The next morning, Simon and Matryna woke up and saw that the stranger was already awake. He looked much better than the day before. [not sleeping ≠ asleep]

Simon said, "Well, friend, we have to work for a living. What work do you know?"

"I do not know anything," answered the man.

Surprised [Shocked], Simon said, "A man who wants to learn can learn anything."

"Then I will learn how to work."

"What is your name?" asked Simon.

Stop & Think
What work did Michael know?

Key Words

- **get ~ out of one's mind** to forget about something
- **feel grieved** to feel very bad
- **wake up** ≠ fall asleep
- **awake** ≠ asleep
- **carriage** a wagon drawn by horses
- **servant** a person who works for another
- **stride into** to walk into *stride–strode–stridden
- **master** a skilled person; a person in charge

"Michael."

"Well, Michael, if you work with me, I will give you food and shelter," offered Simon.

"May God reward you," answered Michael. "Show me what to do."

Simon showed Michael how to make boots. Michael learned quickly and was very skilled. He ate little food and almost never went anywhere.

He made boots so well that many people came to Simon's shop. Soon, Simon began to make a lot of money.

A year passed. Michael lived and worked with Simon. One day, Simon and Michael were working hard when a carriage drawn by three horses drove up to the hut. A servant opened the door, and a gentleman wearing a fur coat got out. He strode into the hut and asked, "Which of you is the master bootmaker?"

carriage

servant

fur coat

Stop & Think
Who was in the carriage?

Check Up — Put the right words.

> Michael   skilled   bread   shelter

1. Simon and Matryna had no more of _____.
2. The stranger's name was _____.
3. Simon offered Michael food and _____ in return for work.
4. Michael became a very _____ bootmaker.

Grammar Point

"-ing" form (present participle) / **"-ed" form** (past participle)

- A gentleman **wearing** a fur coat got out. (**active meaning**)
- A carriage **drawn** by three horses drove up to the hut. (**passive meaning**)

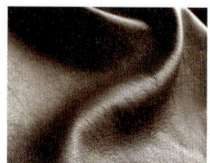
leather

lose one's shape

"I am, sir," Simon answered.

Then the gentleman said, "Do you see this leather here?"

"Yes, it is good leather, sir."

"You fool," laughed the gentleman. "It is the finest leather. It comes from Germany and is extremely expensive. I want you to make me a pair of boots that will last for years. If they lose their shape or fall apart, I will throw you into prison. After one year, if the boots are still good, I will pay you ten rubles for them," said the rich man.

Simon was terrified, but Michael advised him to make the boots. So Simon agreed, and then he measured the gentleman's feet. While he was doing that, Simon saw Michael was gazing behind the rich man as if someone were there.

Key Words

- **fool** an idiot; a stupid person
- **throw ~ into prison** to have someone arrested
- **terrified** very scared
- **gaze** to look at; to stare
- **cautious** ≠ careless
- **fall apart** to break
- **advise** to give advice
- **grin at** to smile at
- **make a mistake** to make an error

Suddenly, Michael smiled, and his face turned bright. [became]

"What are you grinning at [smiling at], you fool?" shouted the man. "You had better make these boots on time [not late]. I will come back in two days."

"They will be ready," answered Michael.

After he left, Simon looked at Michael and said, "Michael, we must be cautious [careful] with this expensive leather. We cannot make a single mistake."

Michael started cutting the leather, but he did not cut it for boots. Instead, he started to make soft slippers. Simon saw what Michael was doing, and he was shocked. [surprised]

"What are you doing, Michael? The gentleman ordered boots, not slippers. You've ruined [spoiled, destroyed] that leather. What's going to happen to me now?"

prison

measure

slippers

Stop & Think
What did Michael do when he looked behind the gentleman?

CHECK UP Choose the right words.
1. The gentleman showed Simon some _____ leather. (expensive | cheap)
2. The gentleman _____ Simon. (angered | terrified)
3. The gentleman wanted his boots in _____. (two weeks | two days)
4. Michael made _____ for the gentleman. (boots | slippers)

GRAMMAR POINT

as if ~ (subjunctive)
- Michael was gazing behind the rich man **as if** someone **were** there.

rush

corpse

crippled

At that very moment, the gentleman's servant rushed into the hut. *hurried into, ran into*

"My master does not need boots anymore," he announced. *stated, said* "He is dead. He did not even make it home alive as he died in the carriage. *because, since* My master's wife sent me here to cancel the order for boots. *stop* Instead, she wants you to quickly make a pair of soft slippers for his corpse." *dead body*

Simon was amazed. *shocked, stunned* Michael took the pair of soft slippers he made and handed them to the servant. *gave to*

More time passed, and Michael had now lived with Simon for six years. He never went anywhere, *didn't go anywhere* and he was always quiet. He had only smiled two times in six years: once when Matryna gave him food and a second *for* time when the rich man was in their hut. Simon adored *liked very much, loved* Michael and was afraid that Michael would leave him.

One day, one of Simon's sons came running to Michael. "Uncle Michael," he cried, "Look! A lady with two little girls is coming, and one of the girls is lame." *unable to walk properly*

Stop & Think
What happened to the gentleman?

Key Words

- **corpse** a dead body
- **hand ~ to** to give something to someone
- **lame** unable to walk properly
- **be a master at** to be very skilled at doing something
- **confused** puzzled; not understanding
- **give birth to** to bear; to produce a baby
- **amazed** shocked; stunned
- **adore** to like very much (≠ hate)
- **crippled** disabled
- **crush one's leg** to break one's leg

Michael immediately stopped work and looked out the window. Simon was surprised since Michael never looked outside. Simon also looked out and saw that a well-dressed woman with two little girls was coming to his hut. One of the girls was crippled in her left leg.
→ disabled

The woman came in and said, "I want leather shoes for these two girls for spring."

Simon answered, "I have never made such small shoes, but my assistant Michael is a master at making shoes, so he can do it."
→ helper   → is very skilled at

Michael was staring at the girls as if he had known them before. Simon was confused, but he began to measure the girls' feet. The woman mentioned that the girls were twins.
looking at, gazing at   → like
→ puzzled
→ said, told

Simon asked, "How did it happen to her? Was she born this way?"

"No," the woman answered. "Her mother crushed her leg. Their father died one week before they were born. And their mother died right after she gave birth to them."
broke, squashed ←
→ die–died–died
bore ←

twins

be born

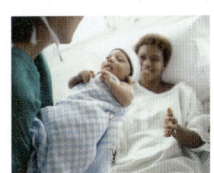
give birth to

> **CHECK UP** True or false?
>
> 1 Michael smiled two times in six years. _____
> 2 A woman with two girls came to Simon's hut. _____
> 3 The two girls were cousins. _____
> 4 The woman was the girls' mother. _____

> **GRAMMAR POINT**
>
> **tense agreement**
> • Simon **was** afraid that Michael **would** leave him.

nurse

sigh

wipe tears

She continued, "My husband and I were their neighbors. When I visited their hut, I found that the mother, when dying, had rolled on this child and crushed her leg. The babies were left alone. What could I do? I was the only woman in the village with a baby, so I took both girls and nursed them as well.

"I thought the crippled one would die, so I did not feed her at first. But I had so much milk that I could feed my son and both girls. Then, my own son died when he was two." She sighed.

"I thank God for giving me these two girls. I would be very lonely without them. They are precious to me."

She wiped some tears from her face as she told the story.

Then, Matryna said, "The old proverb is true. 'One may live without father or mother, but one cannot live without God.'"

Stop & Think
How did the girl's leg get injured?

Key Words

- **roll on** to roll over onto
- **nurse** to provide milk for a baby; to feed
- **lonely** feeling alone
- **proverb** a wise saying
- **forgive** to pardon *forgive–forgave–forgiven

- **crush** to break; to squash
- **sigh** to exhale loudly
- **precious** dear; valuable
- **bow** to bend over in a sign of respect
- **gloomy** sad; depressing

As they talked, suddenly a bright light filled the room. They looked at Michael, who was the source of this light. He was smiling and looking up at the heavens.

heavens

After the woman left with the girls, Michael bowed low to Simon and Matryna. "Farewell," he said. "God has forgiven me. I ask your forgiveness, too, for anything I have done wrong."

bow

They saw a light was shining from Michael. Simon bowed to Michael and said, "I see that you are not an ordinary man. But please tell me. When I first met you and brought you home, you were quite gloomy. But you smiled at my wife after she gave you some food. Then, when the rich man came and ordered boots, you smiled again. Finally, when the woman brought the girls, you smiled a third time. And now you have become as bright as day. Why is your face shining like that, and why did you smile those three times?"

shine

> **Stop & Think**
> What happened as everyone was talking?

Check Up Finish the sentences.

1. The woman said the girls
2. Michael asked Simon and Matryna
3. Simon realized that Michael

a. was not an ordinary man.
b. were precious to her.
c. to forgive him.

Grammar Point

may
- One **may** live without father or mother. (**possibility**)

angel

breast

pray

Michael answered, "Light is shining from me because I was punished, but now God has forgiven me. I smiled three times because God sent me here to learn three truths, and I have learned them. I learned the first ---> facts
when your wife pitied me, so I smiled then. I learned ---> at that time
the second when the rich man ordered the boots, so I smiled again. And I learned the third when I saw the little girls, so I smiled for the third time."

Simon asked, "Michael, why did God punish you? And what are the three truths? I would like to learn them for myself."

Michael answered, "God punished me because I disobeyed him. I was an angel in Heaven, but I ---> ≠ obey
disobeyed God. God sent me to take the soul of a ---> make the person die
woman. I came down to Earth and saw a sick woman lying alone. She had just given birth to twin girls. The woman saw me and said, 'Angel of God, my husband has just died, and there is no one to look after my girls.
---> nurse, take care of

Stop & Think
Why did God punish Michael?

KEY WORDS

- **disobey** to not follow a command or order
- **care for** to take care of
- **pray** to make a prayer
- **dwell** to live
- **lie alone** to be by oneself
- **breast** a woman's chest
- **stay alive** to not die
- **live by** to be supported by

116   Step 4

Do not take my soul. Let me live to care for my babies. Children cannot live without father or mother.'"

care for → take care of

Michael continued, "I put one child at her breast and put the other in her arms. Then, I returned to Heaven. I told God, 'I could not take the mother's soul. Her husband died, and the woman has twins and prays to stay alive.'

stay alive → live, not to die

"But God said, 'Go back and take the woman's soul, and learn three truths: Learn what dwells in man. **Learn what is not given to man.** And learn what men live by. When you learn all three things, you may return to Heaven.'"

dwells → lives
live by → be supported by

> **Stop & Think**
> What did God order Michael to learn about?

CHECK UP Answer the questions.

1. Why did Michael smile three times?
   a. He learned three truths.   b. He saw God.   c. He knew the little girls.

2. Whose soul was Michael supposed to take?
   a. Simon's soul   b. the mother's soul   c. the girls' souls

GRAMMAR POINT

> **be + p.p. (passive)**
> - I **was punished** (by God), but now God has forgiven me.
> - Learn what **is** not **given** to man.

What Men Live By

wings

crawl

frown

→ returned *fly–flew–flown

"So I flew back to Earth and took the mother's soul. The babies fell from her breast. Her body rolled over on the bed and crushed one of the baby's legs. I tried to fly up to Heaven with the mother's soul, but my wings suddenly dropped off. Then, I fell to Earth. That is how you found me, Simon."

→ fall–fell–fallen

→ fell off

Simon and Matryna now understood who had been living with them, so they began to cry for joy. → happiness

The angel Michael said, "I was alone in the field and naked. **I had never known cold or hunger until I became a man.** I crawled to a church. Then, I saw a man coming down the road.

"He frowned as he passed me, but he came back a few minutes later. He gave me some clothes and brought me to his house. When I entered the house, his wife seemed very angry. She wanted to send me back into the cold, but her husband mentioned God to her. The woman changed at once. When she brought me some

← looked

→ instantly

Stop & Think
What did Michael do when he returned to Earth?

KEY WORDS

- **drop off** to fall off
- **frown** ≠ smile
- **mention** to say about something
- **crawl** to walk on one's hands and feet
- **stand** ≠ sit
- **last** to continue in time; to remain in useful condition

food, I looked at her. I noticed she had changed. She had become alive, and God was in her.

"Then, I remembered the first lesson God had sent me. God told me, 'Learn what dwells in man.' I understood. It was love. Love lives in men. God had shown me the first truth, so I smiled.

"After a year, a rich gentleman came to order some boots. I looked at him and saw the Angel of Death standing behind him. Only I could see the Angel of Death, so I knew that he would die soon. The man was about to die, yet he wanted boots that would last for years.

"Then, I remembered God's second order: 'Learn what is not given to man.' I learned that men are not given the knowledge to know what they need. So I smiled for a second time.

> **Stop & Think**
> What was the second truth?

Check Up — Choose the right words.

1. Michael could return to _____ after he learned all three truths. (Heaven | Earth)
2. Michael learned the _____ truth from Matryna. (first | second)
3. Michael learned another truth from the _____. (rich man | poor man)

Grammar Point

not/never ~ until...
- I had **never** known cold or hunger **until** I became a man.

roof

ray of light

"I still did not know the third truth, so I have waited for God to reveal it.

→ show ≠ hide

"In my sixth year here, the woman and the two girls came. I recognized the girls and listened to how the woman had kept them alive. After she told the story, I realized that the woman had loved two children who were not her own. I saw the living God in her, and then I learned the last lesson: I learned what men live by. I knew God had revealed it to me and had forgiven me, so I smiled for a third time."

→ knew
→ living ≠ dead
→ was enclosed by

Just then, Michael's body was surrounded by a bright light. He said, "I have learned that all men live not by care for themselves but by love. I did not die because a man and his wife took pity on me and loved me. The

Stop & Think
What was the third truth?

Key Words

- **reveal** to show (≠ hide)
- **be surrounded by** to be enclosed by; to be encircled by
- **orphan** a child with no parents
- **spread** to extend
- **recognize** to know who a person is
- **ray of light** a sunbeam; sunlight
- **remain** to be left

→ children with no parents

orphans stayed alive because of the love of a woman who was not their mother. And all men live because love is in them. A person who has love is in God, and God is in that person because God is love."

Then, the roof opened, and a ray of light fell down from Heaven. Michael spread his wings and flew up in the light. Simon stood there, gazing after him. After a while, the roof was closed. No one but Simon and his family remained.

spread-spread-spread
→ went up
→ were left

Check Up Choose the right words.

1. Michael learned the _____ truth from the woman. (third | second)
2. A _____ light surrounded Michael's body. (dim | bright)
3. Did Michael fly away from Simon's house? (Yes | No)

Grammar Point

because + S + V / because of + noun

- I did not die **because** a man and his wife took pity on me and loved me.
- The orphans stayed alive **because of** the love of a woman.
- All men live **because** love is in them.

How Much Land Does a Man Need?

peasant

theater

entertainment

An elder sister went to visit her younger sister in the country. The elder sister was married to a tradesman in town and the younger sister to a peasant in the village. As the sisters sat over their tea talking, the elder began to boast about the advantages of town life. She talked about how comfortably they lived there, how well they dressed, what good things they ate and drank, and how she went to the theater and other types of entertainment.

The younger sister was annoyed and in turn mocked the life of a tradesman. She stood up for the life of a peasant.

"I would not change my way of life for yours," she said. "We may live roughly, but at least we are free from anxiety. You live in a better style than we do, but though you often earn more than you need, you are very likely to lose all you have."

Stop & Think

Why was the younger sister annoyed?

Key Words

- **peasant** a poor farmer
- **in turn** one after another; as a result of something
- **stand up for** to defend
- **chatter** talking; gossip
- **annoyed** bothered
- **mock** to make fun of; to laugh at
- **lie on** to recline on
- **the Devil** Satan; Lucifer

She continued, "We know the proverb 'Loss and gain are brothers twain.' It often happens that people who are wealthy one day are begging for their bread the next. Our way is safer. Though a peasant's life is not a fat one, it is long."

beg

Pahom, the master of the house, was lying on the top of the stove, and he listened to the women's chatter.

childhood

"It is perfectly true," he said. "Busy as we are from childhood farming Mother Earth, we peasants have no time to let any nonsense settle in our heads. Our only trouble is that we haven't got enough land. If I had plenty of land, I wouldn't fear the Devil himself!"

The women finished their tea, chatted a while about dresses, and then cleared away the tea things and lay down to sleep. But the Devil had been sitting behind the stove and had heard all that was said.

> **Stop & Think**
> How would Pahom feel if he had plenty of land?

Check Up
Answer the questions.

1. How did the younger sister feel about her way of life?
   a. She felt anxious.   b. She liked it.   c. She wanted to change it.
2. Where was the Devil sitting?
   a. on the stove   b. behind the stove   c. under the stove

Grammar Point

that + S + V (that-clause)

- It often happens **that** people who are wealthy one day are begging for their bread the next.
- Our only trouble is **that** we haven't got enough land.

seed

sow

harvest

plow

He was pleased to hear that the man had boasted that ==if he had plenty of land, he would not fear the Devil himself.==

"All right," thought the Devil. "We will have a contest. I'll give you enough land, and by means of that land, I will get you into my power."

→ compete, bet
→ through

One day, Pahom heard that a neighbor was going to buy fifty acres of land, so he felt envious. Pahom and his wife sold some of their property and borrowed some money. Then, they bought a farm of forty acres.

→ sell–sold–sold
→ was jealous
→ ≠ lent

So now Pahom had land of his own. He borrowed seed and sowed it on the land he had bought. The harvest was a good one, and within a year, he had managed to pay off his debts. So he became a landowner. When he went out to plow his fields or to look at his growing corn, his heart would fill with joy.

→ planted
→ pay back the money
→ be filled with

Key Words

- **property** land or buildings
- **trespass** to go onto land that is not one's own
- **district court** regional court
- **be taught a lesson** to be punished
- **sneak onto** to go somewhere without being seen
- **manage to** to be able to do; to deal with
- **lose patience** to become impatient
- **overlook** to ignore; to forget about
- **upset with** angry at
- **take someone to court** to sue a person

However, over time, some of the peasants in the neighborhood began to trespass across Pahom's land with their cows and horses. For a long time, Pahom forgave the owners. But at last he lost patience and complained to the district court. He thought, "I cannot go on overlooking it, or they will destroy all I have. They must be taught a lesson."

Pahom began to fine his neighbors for trespassing on his land. This made them very upset with him, so they started to trespass on his land on purpose. Sometimes, they even sneaked onto his land at night and chopped down his trees. Pahom was furious.

He tried to figure out who was doing it, and he decided that it was probably Simon. He took Simon to court, but Pahom had no evidence against Simon. The judges let Simon go, so Pahom got angry at them and quarreled with the judges and with his neighbors. Threats to burn his building began to be uttered.

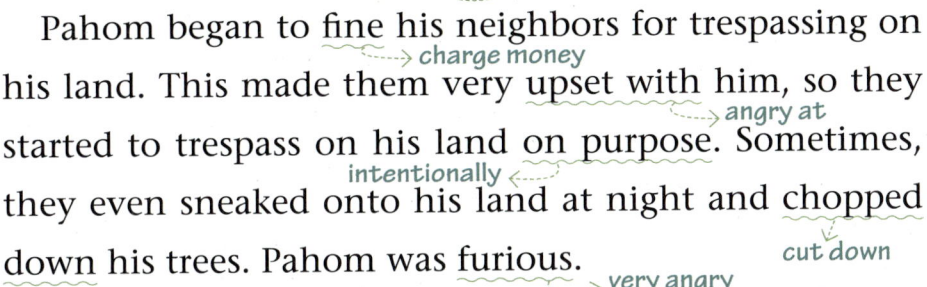

sneak

furious

judge

> Stop & Think
> Why did Pahom fine his neighbors?

Check Up Finish the sentences.

1. The Devil decided to
2. Pahom bought a farm
3. Pahom's neighbors began to
4. Pahom took Simon

a. and became a landowner.
b. trespass on his land on purpose.
c. have a contest with Pahom.
d. to court for trespassing.

Grammar Point

if ~ (subjunctive)

- If he **had** plenty of land, he **would** not **fear** the Devil himself.

rumor

estate

About this time, there was a rumor that many people were moving to a new place. "There's no need for me to leave my land," thought Pahom. "But some of the others might leave our village, and then there would be more room for us. I would take over their land myself and make my estate a bit bigger."

One day, Pahom was sitting at home when a peasant passing through the village happened to call on him. The peasant was allowed to stay the night, and supper was given to him. Pahom had a talk with this peasant and asked him where he had come from. The stranger answered that he had come from beyond the Volga River, where he had been working. He said that many people were moving there. Anyone who moved to the village was given twenty-five acres of land for free.

"The land there is very good," said the peasant. "One peasant moved to the village with nothing at all, but now he is very wealthy."

Pahom's heart was filled with desire. He thought, "Why should I suffer in this narrow hole if one can live

Stop & Think
What did the stranger tell Pahom about the village?

Key Words

- **rumor** gossip or information which may not be true
- **pass through** to go through
- **for free** without having to pay money for
- **find out** to learn about
- **grow tired of** to get tired of; to dislike
- **estate** a large amount of land
- **call on** to visit a person
- **suffer** to experience pain
- **better off** richer; wealthier
- **rush for** to hurry after; to run to

so well elsewhere? I will sell my land here, and with the money I get, I will start all over again with more land. But I must first go and find out all about it myself."

So Pahom went down to the land beyond the Volga. It was just as the stranger had said. The peasants owned plenty of land. The village gave each person twenty-five acres of land, and people could also buy as much land as they could afford. Pahom moved with his family to the new settlement.

Pahom had much more land than before. In fact, he was ten times better off than he had been. This made Pahom very happy. But after he got used to it, he began to think that even here he did not have enough land. He grew tired of having to rent other people's land every year. Wherever there was good land to be had, the peasants would rush for it and argue about the land.

ten times

argue

> **Stop & Think**
> Why was Pahom not happy in the village?

Check Up True or false?

1. The peasant came from a land beyond the Volga River. ____
2. The village beyond the Volga gave everyone 250 acres of land for free. ____
3. Pahom visited the village to find out about the land. ____
4. Pahom was ten times better off than before. ____

Grammar Point

where / wherever (relative adverb)

- He went to *a place* **where** they had pitched their tents.
- He had come from *beyond the Volga River*, **where** he had been working.
- **Wherever** there was good land to be had, the peasants would rush for it.

chief

prairie

gift

"If it were my own land," thought Pahom, "I would be independent, and there would not be all this unpleasantness."

So Pahom began looking out for land which he could buy. One day, a peddler went by his house. He said that he was just returning from the land of the Bashkirs, which was far away. There, he had bought thirteen thousand acres of land for 1,000 rubles.

"That area has so much land that you could walk for a year and still be in the land of the Bashkirs. They sell their land for very cheap prices. All one has to do is make friends with the chief. The land lies near a river, and the whole prairie is virgin soil."

Pahom was curious, so he made up his mind to visit the land of the Bashkirs. Before he went there, he bought some gifts. The peddler had told him that it was their custom to give gifts.

On the seventh day of his travels, he came to a place where the Bashkirs had pitched their tents. It was all just as the peddler had said. The people lived by a river on the steppes in felt-covered tents.

Stop & Think
How much land did the peddler buy?

Key Words

- **unpleasantness** ugliness; a bad situation
- **pitch** to put up a tent
- **felt-covered tent** a tent that has felt on it
- **uneducated** having no schooling
- **make up one's mind** to decide
- **steppe** a plain; a grassland
- **despite** in spite of

They were a simple people. They did not farm at all. The men merely sat around, drank tea, ate lamb, and played their pipes to make music. Still, despite being uneducated and knowing no Russian, they were good-natured enough.

lamb

cart

As soon as they saw Pahom, they came out of their tents and gathered around their visitor. An interpreter was found, and Pahom told them he had come about some land. They took Pahom and led him into one of the best tents. Pahom took some presents out of his cart and distributed them among the Bashkirs. The Bashkirs were delighted.

- merely → only, just
- despite → in spite of
- uneducated → not educated
- good-natured → warm-hearted, kind-hearted
- interpreter → translator
- distributed → gave, passed out
- delighted → very happy, pleased

Check Up Put the right words.

| tents | peddler | visit | interpreter |

1. The _____ said that the Bashkirs sold their land for cheap prices.
2. Pahom decided to _____ the land of the Bashkirs.
3. The Bashkirs pitched their _____ beside a river.
4. Pahom told the _____ that he had come about some land.

Grammar Point

which (relative pronoun)

- So Pahom began looking out for *land* **which** he could buy.
- He was just returning from *the land of the Bashkirs*, **which** was far away.

present

crowded

exhausted

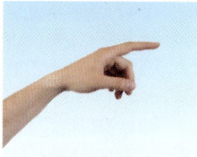
point out

The Bashkirs talked for a while and then told the interpreter to translate. "They wish to tell you," said the interpreter, "that they like you, and that it is our custom to do all we can to please a guest and to repay him for his gifts. You have given us presents. Now tell us which of the things we possess please you best so that we may present them to you."

"What pleases me best here," answered Pahom, "is your land. Our land is crowded, and the soil is exhausted; but you have plenty of land, and it is good land." The interpreter translated.

The Bashkirs talked among themselves for a while. Then, they were silent and looked at Pahom while the interpreter said, "They wish me to tell you that in return for your presents, they will gladly give you as much land as you want. You have only to point it out with your hand, and it is yours."

Stop & Think
What did Pahom say about the Bashkirs' land?

Key Words

- **translate** to interpret
- **possess** to have; to own
- **crowded** full of people (≠ empty)
- **in return for** as payment for something
- **have a dispute** to argue
- **rise to one's feet** to stand up
- **repay** to pay a person back for something
- **present** to give; to award
- **exhausted** used up; spent; old
- **point out** to show
- **in one's absence** while one is not around
- **address** to speak to

The Bashkirs talked again for a while and began to have a dispute. Pahom asked what they were arguing about. The interpreter told him that some of them thought they ought to ask their chief about the land and ought not to act in his absence.

> arguing → argue
> ought to → should
> in his absence → while he is not around

While the Bashkirs were arguing, a man in a large fox-fur cap appeared on the scene. They all became silent and rose to their feet. The interpreter said, "This is our chief himself."

> appeared on the scene → on the spot
> rose to their feet → stood up *rise-rose-risen

Pahom immediately took out the best dressing gown and five pounds of tea, and he offered these to the chief. The chief accepted them and seated himself in the place of honor. The Bashkirs at once began telling him something. The chief listened for a while and addressed himself to Pahom. Speaking in Russian, he said, "Well, let it be so. Choose whatever piece of land you like. We have plenty of it."

> offered → gave
> in the place of honor → at the top seat
> addressed himself to → spoke to

dispute

dressing gown

Stop & Think
What did Pahom give to the chief?

CHECK UP Choose the right words.

1. The Bashkirs wanted to _____ Pahom for his gifts. (repay | replay)
2. The Bashkirs told Pahom to _____ the land he wanted. (point out | purchase)
3. The _____ arrived while the Bashkirs were arguing. (interpreter | chief)
4. Did the chief speak to Pahom in Russian? (Yes | No)

GRAMMAR POINT

ought to / ought not to

- They **ought to** ask their chief about the land and **ought not to** act in his absence.

How Much Land Does a Man Need?

deed

"How can I take as much as I like?" thought Pahom. "I must get a deed to make it secure, or else they may say, 'It is yours,' and afterward they may take it away again."

To the chief, he said, "I must get a deed as a guarantee, or else you may take the land away from me in the future."

The chief said, "We will go to the town with you and make a deed for the land."

"And what will be the price?" asked Pahom.

The chief answered, "Our price is always the same: one thousand rubles a day."

Pahom did not understand. "A day? What measure is that? How many acres would that be?"

The chief said, "We don't know how to figure out the acres, so we sell land by the day. As much as you can go round on your feet in a day is yours, and the price is one thousand rubles a day."

Stop & Think
How much was the land Pahom wanted to buy?

Key Words

- **deed** a paper that gives a person ownership of property
- **take away** to take back; to steal
- **measure** a calculation
- **tract** an area of land
- **spot** a place
- **enormous** huge; very large
- **guarantee** a promise
- **figure out** to calculate
- **condition** a requirement
- **set** to go down
- **imagine** to think about; to picture

Pahom said, "But you can walk around a large tract of land in a single day." → one day
→ area

circle

The chief laughed and then answered, "It will all be yours. But there is one condition: If you don't return to the spot where you started on the same day, your money is lost. You must make a circle. You may make as large a circle as you wish, but you must return to your starting point before the sun sets. Then, all of the land that you walked around will be yours."
→ requirement
→ place
→ goes down

imagine

Pahom agreed to the chief's conditions, and they decided to start the next morning.

That night, Pahom lay in bed thinking about the land. He thought, "I can cover an enormous amount of land. I can easily walk thirty-five miles in one day. Imagine how much land that will be."
→ huge
→ Think, Suppose

Stop & Think
What was the condition the chief gave Pahom?

Check Up Answer the questions.

1 What did Pahom want the chief to give him with the land?
   a. a deed   b. some money   c. some servants
2 How far did Pahom think he could walk in one day?
   a. 20 miles   b. 35 miles   c. 50 miles

Grammar Point

`as ~ as...`
- How can I take **as much as** I like?
- **As much as** you can go round on your feet in a day is yours.
- You may make **as large** a circle **as** you wish.

How Much Land Does a Man Need?

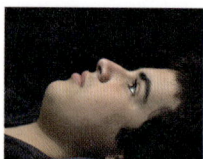
lie awake

doze off

hoof

horn

Pahom lay awake all night and dozed off only just before dawn. Hardly were his eyes closed when he had a dream. In his dream, the chief of the Bashkirs was sitting in front of a tent and laughing. "What are you laughing at?" he asked the chief. But the chief was no longer there. Instead, it was the peddler who had stopped at his house and told him about the Bashkirs. Then, the peddler disappeared, and the peasant who had told him about the land beyond the Volga River suddenly appeared. Then, he saw that it was not the peasant either, but the Devil himself with hoofs and horns, sitting there and chuckling. There was a man lying dead in front of the Devil, and it was Pahom himself. He awoke horror-struck.

- lay awake → did not sleep *lie-lay-lain
- dozed off → fell asleep for a short time
- Hardly → Scarcely
- disappeared → vanished
- appeared → came into sight
- chuckling → laughing
- horror-struck → very shocked and afraid

Looking round, he saw through the open door that the dawn was breaking. "It's time to wake them up," he thought. "We ought to be starting."

Pahom, the chief, and the other Bashkirs met on the land early in the morning. The chief stretched his arms out and said, "All of this land—as far as you can see—belongs to us. You may have any part of it you like."

- stretched → extended

Stop & Think
What happened to Pahom in his dream?

Key Words

- **lie awake** to lie in bed but not to sleep
- **appear** ≠ disappear
- **stretch out** to extend
- **dawn** the time when the sun rises
- **horror-struck** extremely shocked and afraid
- **spade** a shovel

The chief took off his fox-fur cap, placed it on the ground, and said, "This will be the mark. Start from here and return here again. All the land you go around shall be yours." Pahom took out his money and put it on the cap.

Pahom stood ready to start with a spade in his hand. He considered for some moments which way he had better go. Then, he concluded, "I will go toward the rising sun."

mark

spade

Stop & Think
What did the chief put down to mark the starting spot?

Check Up   Finish the sentences.

1. Pahom had a dream
2. The Devil was
3. Pahom put his money

a. on the fox-fur cap.
b. the night before the contest.
c. laughing in Pahom's dream.

Grammar Point

hardly ~ when...

- **Hardly** were his eyes closed **when** he had a dream.
 (= His eyes were **hardly** closed **when** he had a dream.)

How Much Land Does a Man Need?

girdle

ant

noon

lie down

Pahom started walking neither slowly nor quickly. After having gone a thousand yards, he stopped, dug a hole, and placed pieces of turf one on another to make it more visible. Then, he went on. Now that he had walked off his stiffness, he quickened his pace. After a while, he dug another hole.

→ can be seen ≠ invisible
→ walked enough to soften
→ moved faster

The weather was getting warmer. He looked at the sun. It was time to think of breakfast. "It is too soon yet to turn. I will just take off my boots," he said to himself. He sat down, took off his boots, stuck them into his girdle, and went on. It was easy to walk now.

put, pushed *stick-stuck-stuck
→ belt
→ kept walking

"I will go on for another three miles," he thought, "and then turn to the left. This land here is so nice that it would be a pity to lose it."

→ shame

He went straight on for a while, and then he looked back. The people on the hill where he had started were as small as ants. "Ah, I have gone far enough in this direction," he thought. "It's time to turn and go another direction. Besides, I'm getting tired and need something to drink."

→ went right ahead ≠ went backward

KEY WORDS

- **turf** grass; sod
- **quicken one's pace** to move faster (≠ slow down)
- **go straight** to go right ahead of oneself
- **lie down** to get down on the ground
- **damp** wet
- **stiffness** a feeling of inflexibility
- **a pity** a shame; a sad situation
- **look back** to look behind (≠ look ahead)
- **perceive** to notice
- **hollow** a valley

He looked at the sun and saw that it was noon. He sat down, ate some bread, and drank some water. But he did not lie down as he thought that if he did, he might fall asleep. After sitting for a little while, he went on again. It had become terribly hot, and he felt sleepy. Still, he went on, thinking, "An hour to suffer, a lifetime to live."

He went a long way in this direction also and was about to turn to the left again when he perceived a damp hollow. "It would be a pity to leave that out," he thought. So he went on past the hollow and dug a hole on the other side of it.

"Ah!" thought Pahom, "I have made the sides too long; I must make this one shorter." And he went along the third side as he moved faster. He looked at the sun. It was nearly halfway to the horizon, and he had not yet done two miles of the third side of the square. He was still ten miles from his goal.

hollow

horizon

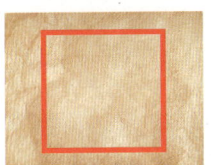
square

Stop & Think
Why did Pahom not lie down at lunch?

CHECK UP True or false?

1. Pahom walked for 100 yards on the first side of the square. _____
2. Pahom did not stop to have lunch. _____
3. Pahom made the first side and the second side of the square too long. _____

GRAMMAR POINT

it would be a pity to ~
- This land here is so nice that **it would be a pity to** lose it.
- **It would be a pity to** leave that out.

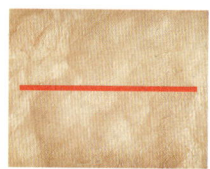
straight line

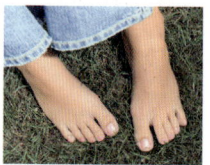
bare feet

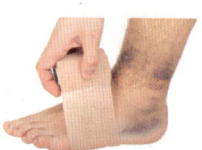
bruised

flask

"I've got to hurry back in a straight line now. I shouldn't go too far," he thought. "Besides, I already have a huge amount of land." So Pahom turned and hurried toward the hill that he had started from.

But he now walked with difficulty. He was done in by the heat, his bare feet were cut and bruised, and his legs began to fail. He longed to rest, but it was impossible if he meant to get back before sunset. The sun waits for no man, and it was sinking lower and lower.

"Oh dear," he thought, "if only I had not blundered by trying for too much. What if I am too late?"

He looked toward the hill and at the sun. He was still far from his goal, and the sun was already near the rim.

Pahom walked on and on. It was very hard to walk, but he went quicker and quicker. He began running. He threw away his coat, his boots, his flask, and his cap and kept only the spade which he used as a support.

Stop & Think
What did Pahom throw away while he was returning to the hill?

KEY WORDS

- **hurry back** to rush to get back
- **bruised** injured; black and blue
- **blunder** to make an error
- **soaking** very wet
- **give way** to fail
- **be done in by** to lose to; to be defeated by
- **long to** to desire; to want to
- **breathless** unable to breathe
- **parched** very dry

Step 4

"What shall I do?" he thought again. "I have grasped too much and ruined the whole affair. I can't get there before the sun sets." This fear made him still more breathless.

Pahom went on running. His soaking shirt and trousers stuck to him, and his mouth was parched. His chest was working like a blacksmith's bellows, his heart was beating like a hammer, and his legs were giving way as if they did not belong to him. Though afraid of death, he could not stop. He gathered the rest of his strength and ran on.

trousers

blacksmith

hammer

Stop & Think
What was Pahom afraid of as he returned to the hill?

Check Up Put the right words.

support   land   heart

1. Pahom thought he had tried for too much _____.
2. Pahom kept his spade and used it as a _____.
3. Pahom's _____ was beating like a hammer.

Grammar Point

-er and -er (double comparatives)
- The sun waits for no man, and it was sinking **lower and lower**.
- It was very hard to walk, but he went **quicker and quicker**.

hold one's sides

The sun was close to the rim. [was near to] Now, yes now, it was about to set. The sun was quite low, but he was also near his aim. [goal] Pahom could already see the people on the hill waving their arms to hurry him up. He could see the fox-fur cap on the ground and the money on it, and the chief sitting on the ground holding his sides. And Pahom remembered his dream.

"There is plenty of land," he thought, "but will God let me live on it? I have lost my life. [died] I shall never reach that spot."

Pahom looked at the sun, which had reached the earth. With all his remaining strength, he rushed on.

Key Words

- **hold one's sides** to laugh badly
- **labor** work
- **take a long breath** to breathe deeply
- **flow** to come from
- **bury** to put a dead person into the ground
- **six feet** about two meters; the depth at which a person is buried
- **lose one's life** to die
- **in vain** for no use; without gain
- **fellow** a person; a guy
- **click one's tongue** to make a clicking noise

Just as he reached the hill, it suddenly grew dark. He looked up—the sun had already set. He gave a cry. "All my labor has been in vain," he thought.

He was about to stop, but he heard the Bashkirs still shouting. He realized that the sun seemed to have set, but the Bashkirs on the hill could still see it. He took a long breath and ran up the hill. It was still light there. He reached the top and saw the cap. He fell forward and reached the cap with his hands.

"Ah, that's a fine fellow!" exclaimed the chief. "He has gained much land."

Pahom's servant came running up and tried to raise him, but he saw that blood was flowing from his mouth. Pahom was dead.

The Bashkirs clicked their tongues to show their pity. His servant picked up the spade and dug a grave long enough for Pahom to lie in and buried him in it. Six feet from his head to his heels was all he needed.

blood

grave

Stop & Think
How much land did Pahom need?

Check Up Choose the right words.
1. The sun set at the bottom of the hill _____ than at the top. (slower | faster)
2. The _____ said that Pahom had gained much land. (chief | interpreter)
3. Pahom's servant saw that he was _____. (alive | dead)
4. Did the Devil win his contest with Pahom? (Yes | No)

Grammar Point

enough ~ to...
- His servant dug a grave long enough for Pahom to lie in.

Super Reading Story Training Book

Step 5

A Christmas Carol
– Charles Dickens

A Christmas Carol

foggy

greedy

beggar

One Christmas Eve, Scrooge sat busy in his office. It was cold and foggy weather. The city clocks had just rung three times, but it was already quite dark.

Scrooge was an old man. He was known by everyone to be mean, miserly, and cold. He was a greedy sinner. No warmth could warm him, and no cold could chill him. Nobody ever stopped Scrooge on the street to say, "My dear Scrooge, how are you?" No beggars implored him to give them some money. Even the dogs seemed to know him, and they avoided him, too. But Scrooge did not care at all. He liked it that way. People avoided him, and he avoided people.

He had worked in the same dark office for many years. Once it had been the office of *Scrooge and Marley*. Scrooge and Marley had been partners for many years. And even now, seven years after Marley had died, those names were still on the door.

It was a very small room with a very small fire. The only other person in the office was Bob Cratchit,

Stop & Think
How did people feel about Scrooge?

KEY WORDS

- **miserly** acting like a miser; refusing to spend money
- **greedy** wanting more money
- **sinner** a person who sins; a bad person
- **implore** to beg; to plead
- **bah, humbug** an expression of unhappiness or disgust

Scrooge's clerk. Bob was very cold. Scrooge did not give Bob much wood for his fire because he did not like to spend money. So the clerk put on his coat and tried to warm himself by the light of a candle.

merry

Scrooge did not like anything. He especially hated Christmas.

"Merry Christmas, Uncle," cried a cheerful voice. It was the voice of Scrooge's nephew Fred.

→ happy, pleasant

≠ niece

"Bah, humbug," said Scrooge.

"Oh, come on, Uncle," said Fred. "I'm sure you don't mean it."

you don't intend to do it

"I do," said Scrooge. "Why are you merry? You're a poor man."

→ happy

"Well, why aren't you merry? You're a very rich man. And it's Christmas!"

"Bah, humbug," said Scrooge again. "You keep Christmas in your own way, and let me keep it in mine."

as you like

Check Up True or false?

1. Scrooge was a greedy man. ____
2. Scrooge and Marley still worked together. ____
3. Bob Cratchit was Scrooge's boss. ____

Grammar Point

no + noun (emphasis)
- **No warmth** could warm him, and **no cold** could chill him.
- **No beggars** implored him to give them some money.

A Christmas Carol

portly

books

bow

"Don't be so angry, Uncle. Come and have dinner with us tomorrow."

Scrooge merely answered, "Goodbye."
→ only, simply

"I don't want to be angry with you, Uncle," said Fred. "So a Merry Christmas, Uncle."

"Goodbye," Scrooge only said.

After Scrooge's nephew left, the clerk let two other people in. They were portly gentlemen. They had books and papers in their hands and bowed to Scrooge.
→ rather fat

"Excuse us. May I ask, are you Mr. Scrooge or Mr. Marley?" said one of the gentlemen.

"Mr. Marley has been dead these seven years. He died seven years ago this very night," answered Scrooge.

"Mr. Scrooge then," said the man. "At this festive season of the year, it is nice for everyone to give something to people who have nothing—no homes, no food."
← Christmas season

"Are there no prisons? Any orphanages?" said Scrooge.
jails ← → places where orphans live

"There are. But they always need a little more. So a few of us are raising funds to buy the poor some meat, drink, and means of warmth. What shall I put you down for?"
→ raising money
→ tools, equipments
→ write down, record

Stop & Think
What did Scrooge's nephew ask him to do?

Key Words

- **portly** overweight; rather fat
- **raise funds** to raise money
- **anonymous** of unknown name (≠ signed)
- **excuse** a reason
- **orphanage** a place where orphans live
- **put down** to write down; to note
- **all day off** not having to work for an entire day
- **pick a man's pocket** to steal money from a man

"Nothing!" answered Scrooge. →*a gift without a name*

"You wish to give an anonymous gift?"

lazy

"No. I wish to be left alone. I don't make merry at Christmas, and I can't afford to make lazy fools merry. I have my work to worry about." →*don't have money to*

After the men left, Scrooge turned to his clerk. "You'll want all day off tomorrow, I suppose?" he asked. →*guess, think*

"If that's convenient, sir," the clerk responded. →*do not go to work* →*suitable, okay*

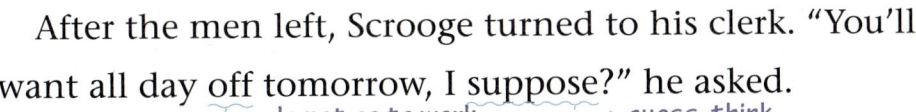
empty

"It's not convenient, and it's not fair. Yet you'll still expect me to pay you a day's wages for no work, won't you?" →*unfair* →*money that is paid for work*

"It's only once a year, sir."

"That's a poor excuse for picking a man's pocket every twenty-fifth of December. But I suppose you must have the whole day. Be here early the next morning." *bad reason* →*stealing money from a man*

The clerk promised that he would arrive early. Scrooge walked out of the office and went back to his empty home. →*≠ full*

> **Stop & Think**
> What did Scrooge give Bob Cratchit for Christmas?

Check Up Put the right words.

> money   wages   died   early

1. Scrooge said that Marley _____ seven years ago.
2. The men asked Scrooge to give them some _____.
3. Scrooge paid Bob Cratchit his day's _____ for Christmas.
4. Bob Cratchit promised to arrive _____ the day after Christmas.

Grammar Point

dead (adjective) / **die** (verb)
- Mr. Marley has **been dead** these seven years.
- He **died** seven years ago this very night.

A Christmas Carol **147**

knocker

dressing gown

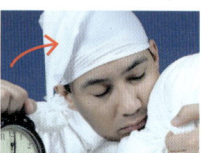
nightcap

drag

cask

When Scrooge got to his building, he put the key into the lock of the door. But when he looked at the knocker, he did not see a knocker but Marley's face. Scrooge stared for a moment, and then it was a knocker again. He said, "Pooh, pooh!" and closed the door with a bang.

Scrooge went up to his room, and carefully locked the door. He checked twice to see if the door was locked and then made a little fire in the fireplace. He put on his dressing gown, slippers, and nightcap, and sat down before the very low fire. As he threw his head back in his chair, he heard something in the house. It was far away, but it was coming closer. It sounded as if some person were dragging a heavy chain over the casks in the wine merchant's cellar. Then, he heard the noise much louder on the floors below. Then, it came up the stairs, and then it came straight toward his door. It came right through the heavy door, and a ghost passed into the room before his eyes. The face! He recognized it right away as Marley's. It was Marley's ghost.

Stop & Think

What went into Scrooge's room?

KEY WORDS

- **knocker** an old-fashioned doorbell
- **drag** to pull something on the ground
- **caustic** sarcastic
- **dreadful** frightening; scary
- **linger** to remain in one place
- **low fire** a fire that is not hot
- **straight toward** directly at something
- **as ever** as usual
- **apparition** a ghost
- **stay away from** to keep away from; to avoid

"How now," said Scrooge, caustic and cold as ever. "What do you want with me?"

"Much." Marley's voice, no doubt about it.

"Who are you?"

"Ask me who I was."

"Who were you then?" said Scrooge, raising his voice.

"In life, I was your partner, Jacob Marley."

"Mercy! Dreadful apparition, why do you trouble me? What do you want?" Scrooge's voice trembled as he spoke.

dreadful

"I have been traveling since I died. Though I am dead, I must walk through the world of the living. I cannot rest. I cannot stay. I cannot linger anywhere."

"Why?" asked Scrooge.

"Because I'm unhappy. I was very bad to people when I was alive. If a man stays away from other people while he is alive, that man becomes like me," said Marley's ghost.

> **Check Up** Answer the questions.

1 What kind of noise did Scrooge hear?
   a. a screaming man   b. a dragging chain   c. a laughing woman
2 What could Marley not do?
   a. rest   b. speak   c. move

> **Grammar Point**
>
> **as if ~ (subjunctive)**
> • It sounded **as if** some person **were dragging** a heavy chain over the casks.

A Christmas Carol 149

escape

chain

bell

wide open

"I am here tonight to warn you that you have yet a chance and hope of escaping my fate," said Marley's ghost.

"This is the chain I made during my lifetime. Every time I refused to help those in need, the chain became longer and heavier. When I died, our chains were about the same, Scrooge, but now, after seven years, yours is much longer than mine. I want to help you not to be unhappy like me when you die."

"How?" asked Scrooge.

"You will be visited by three more ghosts," answered Marley's ghost. "Expect the first tonight when the bell tolls one. Expect the second tomorrow night at the same hour. The third will come the next night, when the last stroke of twelve has rung."

The ghost began floating out the window.

"But wait. Will I see you again? Can't you tell me more?"

"No, Scrooge, you won't see me again. Remember what I told you, for your own sake, or you will soon see your own heavy chain."

The ghost disappeared out the window, which was wide open.

Stop & Think

How many ghosts will visit Scrooge?

KEY WORDS

- **escape** to avoid; to get away from
- **in need** poor; needy
- **float out** to fly out by being carried by the wind
- **be drawn aside** to be opened
- **fate** destiny
- **stroke** a knock; a beat
- **troubled sleep** a restless sleep
- **figure** a form or shape; the human form

As Scrooge went to the window to see where Marley had gone, he suddenly heard some crying down below. Again, Scrooge's heart froze. The voices came not from people, but from ghosts. He quickly closed the window. He tried to say, "Humbug," but he stopped at the first syllable.

flash up

"This couldn't have happened. I will go to sleep, and tomorrow everything will be fine," he thought. Then, he went to bed and fell into a troubled sleep.

figure

When Scrooge awoke, it was still so dark. "Was it all a dream?" he wondered. Just then, the clock tolled a deep, dull, hollow one.

green holly

Light flashed up in the room in an instant, and the curtains of his bed were drawn aside by a strange figure. The ghost was an old man with long white hair. He held a branch of fresh green holly in his hand. From the top of his head, a bright clear jet of light sprang.

"I am the Ghost of Christmas Past," he said.

"Whose past?"

"Your past," answered the ghost.

Stop & Think
What was the first ghost to visit Scrooge?

CHECK UP Choose the right words.

1 Marley said that Scrooge's _____ was longer than his own. (life | chain)
2 The first ghost was going to come at _____ in the morning. (one | three)
3 The first ghost looked like _____. (an old man | a young man)

GRAMMAR POINT

be + p.p. (passive)
- You will **be visited by** three more ghosts.
- The curtains of his bed **were drawn** aside **by** a strange figure.

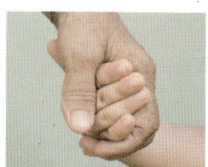
hold one's hand

decoration

tears

"What do you want?"

"Rise and walk with me."

Scrooge got up from his bed. He held the ghost's hand, and they passed through the wall together. Suddenly, they were standing in the country where he had lived as a boy. It was clear enough by the decorations in the shops that there, too, it was Christmastime.

→ Stand up
→ hold–held–held
→ went through

They saw many boys and girls going home across the fields, happily shouting "Merry Christmas" to each other. Scrooge remembered the happiness and joy when he was a child. He could feel tears on his cheek.

"Are you sad?" asked the ghost.

"No, no, I am... happy," said Scrooge.

"They are not real. They are only spirits from Christmas past. They cannot see us."

→ ghosts

But Scrooge knew the spirits, just as he knew the streets, the houses, and the townspeople. Then, they saw Scrooge as a boy, reading on his own in an empty classroom. Seeing himself as he had once been, Scrooge sat down at a desk next to him and began to cry.

→ alone, by himself

Stop & Think
What time of year did the ghost take Scrooge to?

KEY WORDS

- **get up** to rise; to stand up
- **on one's own** alone (≠ together)
- **grow quiet** to become quiet
- **prepare** to get ready; to make something ready
- **decoration** an ornament
- **be left alone** to be by oneself
- **get angry** to become upset
- **apprentice** a person who is learning a skill

"It's me. Once when I was a boy, I was left alone here on Christmas. My father and mother weren't at home. Now, suddenly, I wish I would ..." Scrooge's voice grew quiet.

→ became quiet

apprentice

"What do you wish?" the ghost asked.

"Last night, a young boy came to my office window and sang me a Christmas carol. I just got angry and told him to leave. I wish I'd given some money to that poor boy," said Scrooge with heavy sadness.

→ became upset

The ghost smiled. "Let's see another Christmas," he said.

This time, Scrooge saw the office where he had first worked. He saw Mr. Fezziwig, the man whom he had worked for. Young Scrooge was helping them prepare the office for a Christmas party. Soon,

→ get ready

there were many young people there. They were his fellow apprentices. They were enjoying themselves and dancing. Even he, Scrooge himself, was dancing and enjoying himself.

→ companion
→ learners

CHECK UP Finish the sentences.

1. Scrooge and the ghost
2. The images Scrooge saw
3. Scrooge once worked

a. were not real.
b. in an office for Mr. Fezziwig.
c. passed through the wall together.

GRAMMAR POINT

where (relative adverb)

- Suddenly, they were standing in *the country* **where** he had lived as a boy.
- This time, Scrooge saw *the office* **where** he had first worked.

in pain

shadow

At the end of the party, Mr. and Mrs. Fezziwig said "Merry Christmas" to everybody.

"It's old Mr. Fezziwig's office. He was such a happy, kind boss." → supervisor, head

The ghost looked at Scrooge and asked, "What's the matter?"

"I was thinking of my clerk, Bob Cratchit. I wish I'd said something to him yesterday," said Scrooge.

The ghost smiled again. "Come, my time grows short," said the ghost. "Another Christmas," he said. → becomes

The scene changed. Scrooge again saw himself. He was older now—a man in the prime of life. He was sitting with a young woman. She had once been his girlfriend. She was crying. → view → the best years of life

"No, it's too late. You have another love now," she said.

"What? What other love?" Scrooge asked.

"Money. You love only money now, not me. Goodbye."

"No more! Ghost! Please remove me from this place," Scrooge cried in pain. → take me away from

"No, Scrooge. I told you that these were shadows of the things that have been," said the ghost. "There is one more scene."

Stop & Think
Who did Scrooge see with himself?

KEY WORDS
- **the prime of life** the best years of one's life
- **bear** to stand
- **struggle with** to fight with
- **be interested in** to like; to care about
- **haunt** to follow around
- **drowsiness** sleepiness

Years had passed since the last scene. Scrooge saw a beautiful woman smiling with her children in a warm house. The door opened, and the father came in. His arms were full of Christmas presents. He gave one to each of his children. The children laughed and shouted as they opened the presents.

Scrooge looked at the mother. She was the woman from Scrooge's past. She had left him because he had been more interested in money than in her. Looking at the happy family, Scrooge realized what he had lost.

"No more! Leave me, ghost," shouted Scrooge.

"This was your life. These things happened and cannot be changed. Only the future can be changed," the ghost said.

"Please, ghost, I cannot bear it. Haunt me no longer!" Scrooge shouted sadly.

As Scrooge struggled with the spirit, he suddenly became exhausted. He was overcome by drowsiness and sank into a heavy sleep.

haunt

exhausted

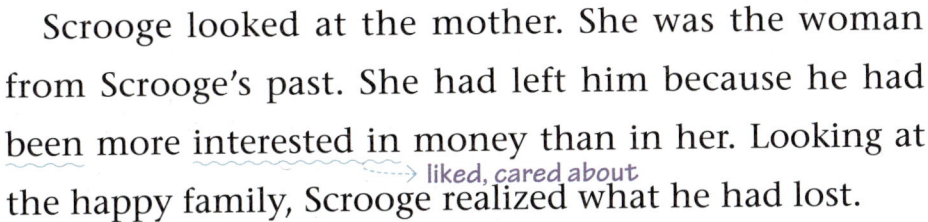
drowsiness

Stop & Think
What did Scrooge tell the ghost?

CHECK UP True or false?

1. Scrooge never had a girlfriend in his entire life. _____
2. Scrooge loved money more than people. _____
3. The beautiful woman Scrooge saw was his mother. _____
4. Scrooge asked the ghost to show him some more scenes. _____

GRAMMAR POINT

I wish ~ (subjunctive)
- **I wish I'd said** something to him yesterday.

A Christmas Carol 155

bowl of punch

couch

torch

robe

Scrooge awoke in his bedroom. It was one in the morning again—time for the second ghost. He looked around his bedroom. There was nobody there. He went to the door of his living room.

"Come in, Ebenezer Scrooge," said a voice.

He opened the door and saw something very surprising. The room looked so different. The walls were covered with Christmas trees. Heaped upon the floor were turkeys, geese, pigs, sausages, plum puddings, chestnuts, apples, and great bowls of punch. Upon the couch in the center of the room sat a happy giant, holding a glowing torch which lit the room.

Heaped upon → Piled
covered with → filled with
glowing → burning
lit the room → light–lit–lit

"Come in. Come in. I am the Ghost of Christmas Present," said the giant.

"Ghost, I learned a lot from the ghost last night. Tonight, if you have something to teach me, take me anywhere you want," said Scrooge.

"Touch my robe," said the giant.

Stop & Think
Who was the second ghost?

KEY WORDS

- **heaped upon** piled on
- **light** to make light
- **crutch** a stick one uses to help one walk
- **gather** to get together
- **couch** a long sofa
- **bless** to say something good about
- **complain** to grumble; to criticize
- **propose** to offer

Scrooge did as he was told. Scrooge found they were walking in a London street on Christmas morning. The ghost took him to the Cratchits' house. At the door, the ghost smiled and stopped to bless Bob Cratchit's dwelling.

→ find–found–found
→ the Cratchit family's
→ ≠ curse

crutch

gather

Mrs. Cratchit, Bob's wife, was preparing their Christmas dinner. Just then Bob Cratchit was coming back from church with the youngest son, Tiny Tim. Tiny Tim was ill and used a crutch to walk.

The family sat down to eat their meal. They had only one goose, some potatoes, and a small Christmas pudding. It seemed very small for such a large family, but nobody complained. Though it was a very simple Christmas meal, they were still as happy as if they had eaten a king's meal. After dinner, all the Cratchit family gathered around the fire. Bob proposed, "A Merry Christmas to us all, my dears. God bless us!"

→ grumbled
→ got together
→ offered

Stop & Think
What did Bob Cratchit's family have to eat?

CHECK UP Put the right words.

| giant   Tiny Tim   touch   enjoyed |

1. There was a _____ sitting in the middle of Scrooge's living room.
2. The ghost told Scrooge to _____ his robe.
3. _____ needed to use a crutch to walk.
4. The Cratchits had a simple meal, but they _____ it.

GRAMMAR POINT

such a/an + adjective + noun (high degree)
- It seemed very small for **such a large family**.

A Christmas Carol   157

"God bless us every one!" said Tiny Tim. Tiny Tim sat very close to his father's side upon his little stool. He was very sick. Bob held his withered little hand in his → thin and dry, shrunken
as if he loved the child and wished to keep him by his side, but he dreaded that Tiny → feared, was afraid
Tim might be taken from him.
→ be taken away from

stool

"Will he be here next Christmas?" Scrooge asked.

"With help," replied the ghost.

Scrooge raised his head when he heard his name spoken.

"Let's drink to Mr. Scrooge," said Bob.
→ turned red
"To Scrooge?" Mrs. Cratchit's face reddened, and she said, "Why should we drink to that old, stingy, unfeeling man?"
miserly ← → unkind
"My dear," was Bob's mild answer, "it's Christmas Day."

"Well, you are right. I'll drink to him. But nothing we do could make that mean old man feel happy or merry," said Mrs. Cratchit.

Stop & Think
Who did Bob Cratchit propose a toast to?

KEY WORDS

- **withered** shrunken
- **stingy** greedy; miserly
- **cast a shadow** to darken; to make dark
- **dig up** to unearth
- **dread** to fear; to be afraid of
- **unfeeling** having no emotions; unkind
- **take away** to remove
- **vanish** to disappear

The mention of his name cast a dark shadow on the party, which lasted for a full five minutes. After some time, the Cratchits became cheerful again. They were not a handsome family. They were not well dressed. But they were happy, grateful, and pleased with one another.

→ made dark
→ happy, pleasant
→ wearing nice clothes
→ thankful
→ happy with

cheerful

The ghost took Scrooge away from the Cratchits' house. The two of them walked through the streets of London. People were going to parties with their friends and families. Suddenly, they were in a cold, dark, empty place. They looked through the window of a small house. Inside, there was a big family in a very small room. Yet they were happy and were singing Christmas carols together.

→ looked into

look through

miner

Scrooge asked, "Who are they?"

"They are poor miners," answered the ghost. "They have hard lives working inside the Earth to dig up coal."

dig up

Slowly, the scene vanished, and Scrooge suddenly heard a hearty laugh. It was his nephew Fred's house. Fred was telling everyone about his visit to his uncle.

→ disappeared
→ cheerful laugh

hearty laugh

Check Up   Answer the questions.

1 How did Mrs. Cratchit feel about drinking to Scrooge?
   a. pleased   b. nervous   c. unhappy

Grammar Point

which (relative pronoun) : referring to a previous clause

• The mention of his name cast a dark shadow on the party, **which** lasted for a full five minutes.

A Christmas Carol

phantom

mist

bend down upon one's knee

"So when I said 'Merry Christmas' to him, he replied 'Bah, humbug!'" said Fred. Everyone laughed.

"He's a strange old man," said Fred. "He is rich, but he doesn't do anything good with his money. He even lives like he's poor. I invite him to have Christmas dinner with us every year, but he never comes. Someday, perhaps he will change his mind. And someday perhaps he will pay poor Bob Cratchit more money as well."

For the rest of the evening, Scrooge and the ghost watched his nephew and friends enjoy their Christmas party. Then, the clock struck twelve. Scrooge looked around for the ghost, but he saw the ghost no more. Then, he remembered Marley's prediction, and he lifted his eyes.

Scrooge saw a solemn phantom coming like a mist along the ground toward him. Unlike the others, he could not see this one's face or body. It was covered from head to toe in a long black garment. The only visible part of the phantom was one outstretched hand.

The phantom moved slowly and silently. As it came near him, Scrooge bent down upon his knee, for the ghost seemed to scatter gloom and mystery as it moved. The ghost did not speak at all.

KEY WORDS

- **prediction** a guess about the future
- **phantom** a ghost
- **garment** a piece of clothing
- **scatter** to spread
- **yet to come** the future
- **solemn** quiet and serious
- **mist** fog
- **outstretched** extended
- **gloom** unhappiness; sadness
- **funeral** a ceremony held for a dead person

"I am in the presence of the Ghost of Christmas Yet to Come," said Scrooge. "You are about to show me the things which have not happened yet, but will happen in the time before us," Scrooge said, looking at the strange ghost. "Is that so, Spirit?"

→ in front of, nearby
→ future

point with one's hand

The ghost silently moved its head a little and pointed with its hand. Scrooge suddenly found himself in the middle of the city. The ghost stopped beside a group of businessmen. Scrooge could hear some of them talking.

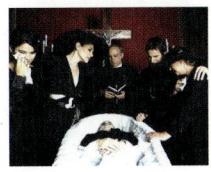
funeral

"I don't know much about it. I only know he's dead," said one great fat man.

"When did he die?" inquired another.

"Last night, I believe."

→ asked

"What has he done with his money?" asked a red-faced gentleman.

"I haven't heard," responded the first man. "He didn't leave it to me though. That's all I know."

"At least his funeral will be very cheap," said one man.

Stop & Think
Who was the third ghost?

CHECK UP Choose the right words.
1. Fred wanted Scrooge to give Bob Cratchit more _____. (money | food)
2. The third ghost wore _____ clothes. (black | white)
3. The third ghost said _____. (many things | nothing)
4. Were the people the ghost showed Scrooge talking about a marriage? (Yes | No)

GRAMMAR POINT

for + S + V (reason) : given as an afterthought
- Scrooge bent down upon his knee, **for** the ghost seemed to scatter gloom and mystery.

A Christmas Carol **161**

old rag

shopkeeper

"That's true. He had no friends. No one liked him, so nobody will go to his funeral."

Scrooge did not understand why the ghost wanted him to listen to this conversation, but he knew the ghost would not answer him, so he did not ask.

They left the busy scene and went to an obscure → little known part of the town. The streets were dark and small. They visited a dirty shop full of horrible old things you can → awful, terrible imagine—iron, old rags, bottles, clothes, and bones. It was a place where people came to sell their things when they needed money.

Scrooge watched as three people brought things to sell to the shopkeeper. They were from the same dead man's house.

"What have you got to sell?" asked the shopkeeper.

One woman took out some towels, silver teaspoons, and other small things, and said, "He doesn't need these now."

"No indeed, ma'am," answered the shopkeeper.
→ certainly, surely

Stop & Think
Where did the three people get the items they were selling?

Key Words

- **obscure** little known
- **in horror** in fear; in disgust
- **pale light** a dim light
- **uncared for** not taken care of
- **tenderness** kindness; mercy
- **be not likely to** be unlikely to
- **bare** having nothing; empty
- **unwept** not mourned
- **as silent as ever** quiet like usual
- **connected with** related to; concerning

"Take a look at these," said the other woman. "Bed curtains and blankets. He isn't likely to catch a cold without them now."
→ doesn't seem to, is unlikely to

blanket

Scrooge listened to this dialogue in horror. "Ghost, I see. The case of this unhappy man might be my own."
→ in fear
→ situation, condition

The scene had suddenly changed, and Scrooge found himself in another terrible room. There was a bare bed with no blankets or curtains around it. A pale light from outside fell straight upon the bed. On it, unwatched, unwept, and uncared for, was the dead body of the unknown man. He was covered by a thin sheet.
→ having nothing, empty
→ dim light
→ not watched
→ not mourned
→ not taken care of

catch a cold

The ghost, as silent as ever, merely pointed at the body. Scrooge realized that the ghost wanted him to look at the face of the dead man, but he could not do it.
→ quiet like usual

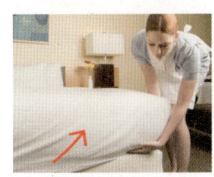
sheet

"I cannot look at his face," cried Scrooge. "Let me see some tenderness connected with this death, or this dark chamber will be forever in my memory."
→ kindness, mercy
→ related to
→ large room

chamber

The scene changed to another home. A woman stood up as her husband entered the room. "Have you gotten any news?" she asked.
→ got up
→ Have you heard

CHECK UP Finish the sentences.

1. The shopkeeper asked the women
2. One woman was selling
3. The ghost pointed at

a. what they had to sell.
b. bed curtains and blankets.
c. a dead body covered by a sheet.

GRAMMAR POINT

be likely to ~ / it is likely that ~

- He **isn't likely to** catch a cold without them now.
 = It **isn't likely that** he will catch a cold without them now.

A Christmas Carol   **163**

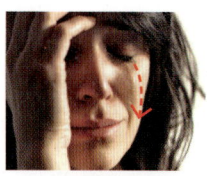
flow down

churchyard

grave

"When I visited him to find out if we could pay the money one week later," he answered, "an old woman told me he was dead."

→ discover, learn

"That's great news," she said. "I'm sorry for saying that. I mean that now we have time to get the money that we have to pay."

"No, ghost! Show me someone who's sorry about a death, not someone who's happy because of a death," shouted Scrooge.

→ feel bad about

The ghost took him to poor Bob Cratchit's house. Scrooge saw the family sitting quietly around the fire. They were talking about Tiny Tim.

"I met Fred, Mr. Scrooge's nephew," said Bob. "And he said that he was very sorry to hear about Tiny Tim."

Bob turned to his family and said, "We must never forget what a good boy Tiny Tim was."

"No, never father," shouted all the children.

Then, Bob Cratchit broke down all at once. He couldn't help it as the tears flowed down his face.

started to cry ← → suddenly
was unable to stop doing it ←

"Ghost," said Scrooge, "something informs me that

→ tells

Stop & Think
Why was the Cratchit family sad?

KEY WORDS

- **be sorry about** to regret; to feel bad about
- **all at once** immediately; suddenly
- **neglected** ignored
- **but for** if not; without
- **break down** to suddenly start crying a lot
- **churchyard** the land around a church
- **lie upon** to rest on
- **assure** to promise; to tell

164   Step 5

our parting moment is at hand. Tell me. Who was the dead man we saw?"

The Ghost of Christmas Yet to Come took Scrooge to a churchyard. The ghost stood among the graves and pointed down to one. Scrooge crept toward it, trembling as he went, and followed the finger to read the name on the neglected grave: EBENEZER SCROOGE.

"Am I that man who lay upon the bed? No, ghost! Oh no, no. I am not the man I was. I will not be the man I must have been but for this evening. Why show me this if I am past all hope? Assure me that I may yet change these shadows."

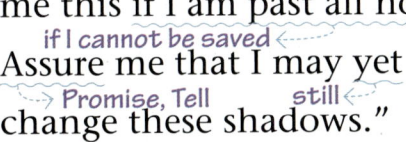

Check Up   True or false?

1 The Ghost of Christmas Yet to Come took Scrooge to a churchyard. _____
2 Scrooge wanted to know who the dead man was. _____
3 The name on the grave was Scrooge's. _____

Grammar Point

relative pronoun

- Now we have time to get *the money* **that** we have to pay.
- Show me *someone* **who**'s sorry about a death, not *someone* **who**'s happy because of a death.
- Who was *the dead man* **(whom)** we saw?
- Am I *that man* **who** lay upon the bed?

A Christmas Carol **165**

butcher's shop

butcher

Scrooge continued, "I will honor Christmas in my heart and try to keep it all the year. I will live in the past, present, and future. I will never forget the lessons that I have been taught."

> keep, remember

> teach–taught–taught

Then, the phantom began to disappear, and Scrooge realized that he was back in his own bedroom. Best and happiest of all, time was before him. He had time to make amends.

> make up for the mistakes

Scrooge heard the church bells ringing loudly. Running to the window, he opened it and put out his head. It was a clear, bright, stirring, golden day.

> exciting, thrilling

"What day is it today?" cried Scrooge to a boy down on the street.

"Today? It's Christmas Day, sir," answered the boy.

"Christmas!" Scrooge was surprised. All of the visits from the ghosts had taken place in one night.

> occurred, happened

"Do you know the butcher's shop down the street?" Scrooge asked. "Please go and tell the butcher I'll buy a big goose. Come back with the man, and I'll give you a nice tip." The boy ran off quickly.

"I'll send it to Bob Cratchit's. He won't know who

Stop & Think
What did Scrooge tell the boy to do?

Key Words
- **honor** to keep; to remember
- **stirring** exciting, thrilling
- **dress oneself** to put on one's clothes
- **a dozen times** 12 times
- **make amends** to make up for a past mistake
- **butcher's shop** a store that sells meat
- **one's Sunday best** one's finest clothes
- **courage** bravery

is sending it. It's twice the size of Tiny Tim," Scrooge thought to himself.

Scrooge then dressed himself in his Sunday best and went out onto the streets. Many people were on the streets, and Scrooge gave each of them a delighted smile. He said, "Good morning, sir," or "A Merry Christmas to you," to everyone he passed.

→ put on his finest clothes
pleased

delighted

knock

Later in the afternoon, he walked toward his nephew's house. He passed the door a dozen times before he had the courage to go up and knock. But he finally did.

→ 12 times
→ bravery

Fred was very surprised to see his uncle. "Uncle, why are you here?" he asked.

↔ aunt

"I have come to dinner. Will you let me in, Fred?" Scrooge asked.

"Of course you may!" cried out Fred.

Fred was very happy, and so were his wife and all their friends. They had a wonderful party together.

Check Up Put the right words.

| the goose | one night | have dinner |

1. Scrooge realized that all three ghosts had visited him in _____.
2. Scrooge sent _____ to Bob Cratchit's house.
3. Scrooge went to his nephew's house to _____.

Grammar Point

So am I.

- You are happy. **So am I.** (= I **am also happy**.)
- Fred was very happy, and **so were** his wife and all their friends.
  = Fred was very happy, and **his wife and all their friends were also very happy**.

A Christmas Carol **167**

salary

assist

The next day, Scrooge went to the office early in the morning. He wanted to be there before Bob got there. Bob was eighteen minutes late. As Bob walked in, Scrooge said, "Hello. What do you mean by coming here at this time of day?"

"I'm very sorry, sir. I'm late," replied Bob.

"Yes, I think you are," said Scrooge.

"Now, I'll tell you what, my friend," said Scrooge. "I'm not going to stand this sort of thing any longer. And therefore... therefore, I am going to pay you more money!"

Scrooge continued, "I'll raise your salary and assist your struggling family. We will discuss your affairs this very afternoon," Scrooge said with a nice smile.

That afternoon, Scrooge took Bob out for a drink and explained how he was going to help him.

> Stop & Think
> What did Scrooge tell Bob Cratchit he was going to do?

Key Words

- **raise salary** to give more money for working
- **struggling** having a hard time
- **this very afternoon** today; now
- **do not mind** to not care
- **ever afterward** forever
- **assist** to aid; to help
- **affairs** personal or business interests
- **laugh at** to make fun of; to tease
- **dealing with** a relationship with

Scrooge was better than his word. He did everything he said he was going to do and more. He became a friend of the Cratchit family, and to Tiny Tim, who did not die, he was like a second father. He became as good a friend, as good a master, and as good a man as the city ever knew.

Some people laughed at him because he had changed. Scrooge did not mind. Scrooge's own heart laughed, and that was quite enough for him. He had no further dealings with ghosts, but he lived happily ever afterward.

laugh at

→ a person who acts like a father
→ did not care
→ spirit
→ relationship with
→ forever

Stop & Think
How did Scrooge act toward Tiny Tim?

Check Up Answer the questions.
1 What did Scrooge promise Bob Cratchit?
   a. a bigger house   b. a healthy family   c. a higher salary
2 What kind of man did Scrooge become?
   a. a greedy man   b. a good man   c. a silly man

Grammar Point
as ~ as ~ ever…
• He became **as good** a friend, **as good** a master, and **as good** a man **as** the city **ever** knew.

A Christmas Carol **169**

Super Reading
Story
Training Book

Step

6

The Last Leaf
– O. Henry

The Last Leaf

In a little district west of Washington Square, the streets have run crazy and broken themselves into small strips called "places." These "places" make strange angles and curves. One street crosses itself a time or two. An artist once discovered a valuable possibility on this street. Suppose a collector with a bill for paints, paper, and canvas should, in taking this route, suddenly meet himself coming back, without a cent having been paid on account.

So, to quaint old Greenwich Village, the art people soon came prowling, hunting for north windows and eighteenth-century gables and Dutch attics and low rents. Then, they imported pewter mugs and a dish or two from Sixth Avenue and became a "colony."

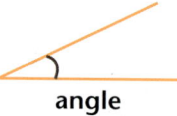
angle

gable

attic

Stop & Think
What kind of people went to old Greenwich Village?

Key Words

- **run crazy** to move in a strange way
- **quaint** old-fashioned
- **colony** an area where a group of similar-minded people live
- **pneumonia** an inflammation of the lungs
- **boldly** bravely
- **victim** someone who has been hurt or killed
- **possibility** a chance; an opportunity
- **prowl** to move around looking for something
- **stride** to walk with quick, long steps
- **scores of** large numbers of (1 score = 20)
- **tread** to walk slowly

At the top of an ugly, three-story brick house, Sue and Johnsy had their studio. "Johnsy" was a nickname for Joanna. One was from Maine; the other from California. They had met at the restaurant Delmonico's on Eighth Street and had found that their tastes in art, food, and clothes were so similar that the joint studio resulted.

That was in May. In November, a cold, unseen stranger, whom the doctors called Pneumonia, visited the colony, touching one here and there with his icy fingers. Over on the east side, this ravager strode boldly, claiming scores of victims, but his feet trod slowly through the maze of the narrow and moss-grown "places."

Mr. Pneumonia was not what you would call a gentleman. A small woman with blood thinned by the warm California zephyrs was no match for the tough

three-story

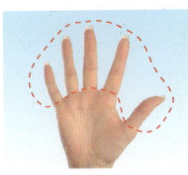
fingers

maze

moss-grown

> **Stop & Think**
> What happened in the colony in November?

Check Up Choose the right words.
1. There were "_____" in Washington Square. (places | attics)
2. People went to old Greenwich Village looking for low _____. (rents | houses)
3. Sue and _____ lived together. (Delmonico | Johnsy)
4. Did many people get pneumonia in May? (Yes | No)

Grammar Point

one / the other
- **One** was from Maine; **the other** from California.

The Last Leaf 173

and deadly illness. But he attacked Johnsy, and she lay, scarcely moving, on her painted iron bedstead, looking through the small Dutch windowpanes at the blank side of the next brick house.
→ empty

One morning, the busy doctor invited Sue into the hallway.

"She has one chance in—let us say, ten," he said, as he shook down the mercury in his clinical thermometer.
→ a ten-percent chance, 1/10
→ shake–shook–shaken

"And that chance is for her to want to live. Sometimes when people give up trying to live, it doesn't matter what medicines I give. Your friend has made up her mind that she's not going to get well. Has she anything on her mind?"
→ quit, stop
→ decided, determined
→ get better
→ Is there anything she cares about?

windowpane

"She... she wanted to paint the Bay of Naples some day," said Sue.
→ nonsense

"Paint? Bosh! Does she have anything on her mind worth thinking about twice, like a man, for instance?"
→ important, valuable

"A man?" said Sue, with a hard sound in her voice.

Stop & Think
What did the doctor say Johnsy needed to do?

KEY WORDS

- **deadly** causing death; lethal
- **one chance in ten** a ten-percent chance, 1/10
- **have on one's mind** to think about something
- **weakness** a weak point; problem (≠ strength)
- **subtract** to take away; to remove
- **swagger** to walk; to stride

- **windowpane** the glass part of a window
- **make up one's mind** to decide
- **bosh** nonsense; pshaw
- **accomplish** to do; to complete
- **one-in-five chance** a twenty-percent chance, 1/5
- **popular tune** a well-known song

"Is a man worth—but, no, Doctor. There is nothing of the kind."

"Well, it is the weakness then," said the doctor. "I will do all that science, so far as it may be employed by me, can accomplish. But whenever my patient begins to count the carriages in her funeral procession, I subtract fifty percent from the power of medicine to cure. If you can get her to ask one question about the new winter styles in cloak sleeves, I will promise you a one-in-five chance for her instead of one in ten."

After the doctor left, Sue went into the workroom and cried a napkin to a pulp. Then, she swaggered into Johnsy's room with her drawing board, whistling a popular tune.

Johnsy lay, scarcely making a move under the bedclothes, with her face toward the window. Sue stopped whistling, thinking she was asleep.

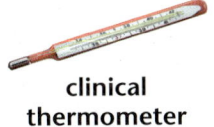
clinical thermometer

carriage

drawing board

Stop & Think
What did the doctor want Sue to do?

Check Up
Put the right words.

> medicine   cried   live

1. The doctor said Johnsy had one chance in ten to _____.
2. _____ is less effective when patients think about death.
3. Sue _____ very hard after the doctor left.

Grammar Point

participle clause
- she lay, **scarcely moving**, … **looking** through the small Dutch windowpanes …
- Johnsy lay, **scarcely making** a move under the bedclothes,…
- Sue stopped whistling, **thinking** she was asleep.

The Last Leaf 175

count backward

ivy vine

skeleton branch

She arranged her board and began a pen-and-ink drawing to illustrate a magazine story. Young artists must pave their way to Art by drawing pictures for the magazine stories that young authors must write to pave their way to literature.

As Sue was sketching a pair of elegant horseshow riding trousers and a monocle on the figure of the hero, an Idaho cowboy, she heard a low sound, several times repeated. She quickly went to the bedside.

Johnsy's eyes were open wide. She was looking out the window and counting backward. "Twelve," she said, and a little later, "eleven"; and then "ten," and "nine"; and then "eight" and "seven" almost together.

Sue looked out the window. What was there to count? There was only a bare, dreary yard to be seen, and the blank side of the brick house twenty feet away. An old, old ivy vine, twisted and decayed at the roots, climbed halfway up the brick wall. The cold breath of autumn had taken most of its leaves from the vine until its skeleton branches clung, almost bare, to the bricks.

"What is it, dear?" asked Sue.

KEY WORDS

- **pave one's way** to make a path
- **bare** having nothing
- **blank** bare; empty
- **cling to** to hold on to
- **ten to one** a ninety-percent chance
- **eyes be open wide** to be wide awake
- **dreary** dark; gloomy
- **skeleton branches** branches that have no leaves
- **have to do with** to be concerned with
- **as good a chance as** very good odds

"Six," said Johnsy, in almost a whisper. "They're falling faster now. Three days ago, there were almost a hundred. It made my head ache to count them. But now it's easy. There goes another one. There are only five left now."

→ gave me a headache

"Five what, dear. Tell your Sudie."

"Leaves. On the ivy vine. When the last one falls, I must go, too. I've known that for three days. Didn't the doctor tell you?"

"Oh, I have never heard of such nonsense," complained Sue, with magnificent scorn. "What have old ivy leaves to do with your getting well? And you used to love that vine so, you naughty girl. Don't be like that. Why, the doctor told me this morning that your chances for getting well real soon were—let's see exactly what he said—he said the chances were ten to one. Why, that's almost as good a chance as we have in New York when we ride on the streetcars or walk past a new building."

→ silliness
→ be concerned with
→ Well, You know
→ ninety percent

streetcar

Stop & Think
What was Johnsy counting?

Check Up True or false?

1 Johnsy was counting backward. _____
2 Johnsy said she would die when the last leaf fell. _____
3 Sue said Johnsy's chances of living were ten to one. _____

Grammar Point

the subject of gerund
- What have old ivy leaves to do with **your/you** getting well?

The Last Leaf 177

broth

pork chop

"Try to have some broth now, and let Sudie go back to her drawing, so she can sell it to the editor. Then, I'll buy port wine for her sick child and pork chops for her greedy self."

"You don't need to get any more wine," said Johnsy, keeping her eyes *fixed* out the window.

"There goes another. No, I don't want any broth. That leaves just four. I want to see the last one fall before it gets *dark*. Then, I'll go, too."

"Johnsy, dear," said Sue, *bending over* her, "will you promise to keep your eyes closed and not to look out the window until I am done working? I must *hand* my drawings *in* by tomorrow. I need the light, or I would pull the *shade* down."

"Couldn't you draw in the other room?" Johnsy asked coldly.

"I'd *rather* be here beside you," said Sue. "Besides, I don't want you to keep looking at those *silly* ivy leaves."

Stop & Think
What did Sue ask Johnsy to do?

Key Words

- **port wine** a type of wine
- **bend over** to lean over
- **be tired of** to be sick of
- **beard** facial hair on a man's chin and cheeks
- **except for** not including
- **fixed** attached to; set on
- **hand in** to turn in; to submit
- **hermit** a man who lives by himself
- **noteworthy** important; remarkable
- **minor** ≠ major

"Tell me as soon as you have finished," said Johnsy, closing her eyes, and lying white and still as a fallen statue, "because I want to see the last one fall. I'm tired of waiting. I'm tired of thinking. I want to turn loose my hold on everything and go sailing down, down, just like one of those poor, tired leaves."

statue

"Try to sleep," said Sue. "I must call Behrman up to be my model for the old hermit-miner. I'll just be gone for a minute. Don't try to move until I come back."

miner

Old Behrman was a painter who lived on the ground floor beneath them. He was past sixty and had a long beard like Michelangelo's Moses curling down from his wide head. Behrman was a failure in art. He had been painting for forty years, but he had never produced anything noteworthy. He had always been about to paint a masterpiece, but he had never yet begun it. For several years, he had painted nothing except for minor advertisements here and there.

beard

Moses

Stop & Think
Who was Behrman?

Check Up Answer the questions.

1. What did Johnsy ask Sue to do?
   a. draw in another room
   b. give her some broth
   c. pull the shade down
2. What kind of an artist was Behrman?
   a. a successful one
   b. an average one
   c. a failed one

Grammar Point

not to + V
- Will you promise **to keep** your eyes closed and **not to look** out the window?

The Last Leaf

juniper berry

canvas

easel

He earned a little by serving as a model for those young artists in the colony who could not pay for a professional. He drank gin to excess and still talked about his coming masterpiece. For the rest, he was a fierce little old man, who made fun of anyone who was soft and who regarded himself as a bulldog ready to protect the two young artists living in the studio above him.

Sue found Behrman smelling strongly of juniper berries in his dimly lit den below. In one corner was a blank canvas on an easel that had been waiting there for twenty-five years to receive the first line of the masterpiece. She told him about Johnsy's fancy and how she feared she would, indeed, light and fragile as a leaf herself, float away when her slight hold upon the world grew weaker.

Old Behrman, with his red eyes plainly streaming, shouted about how silly Johnsy's idea was.

"What!" he cried. "Are there people in this world so foolish to believe that they will die when a leaf falls off

> **Stop & Think**
> What did Behrman drink too much of?

Key Words

- **to excess** too much (≠ in moderation)
- **regard oneself as** to think of oneself as
- **den** a small quiet room
- **float away** to be carried away by the wind
- **stream** to flow
- **horrid** awful; horrible
- **fierce** ≠ meek
- **dimly lit** not bright; dark
- **fragile** easily breakable
- **plainly** clearly; obviously
- **pose as a model** to sit for someone to use as a model
- **lie sick** to be sick in bed

a vine? I have never heard of such a thing. No, I will not pose as a model for you. Why did you allow such a silly thought to enter her head? Oh, that poor little Miss Johnsy."

"She is very ill and weak," said Sue, "and the fever has left her mind filled with thoughts of death and other horrible things. Very well, Mr. Behrman, if you do not care to pose for me, you don't have to. But I think you are a horrid old man."

→ has allowed
→ you don't need to
→ awful, very bad

"You are just like a woman!" yelled Behrman. "Who said I will not pose? Go on. I will go with you. For half an hour, I have been trying to say that I am ready to pose. God, this is not a place in which someone as pretty as Miss Johnsy should lie sick. Someday, I will paint a masterpiece, and we shall all go away. God, yes."

→ be sick in bed
→ leave

pose as a model

Check Up   Finish the sentences.

1. Behrman worked as
2. There was a blank canvas
3. Behrman thought Johnsy's idea
4. Behrman decided to

a. in one corner of Berhman's den.
b. pose as a model for Sue.
c. a model for artists in the colony.
d. was silly.

Grammar Point

relative pronoun : separating a noun from its relative pronoun

- ... for *those young artists* in the colony **who** could not pay for a professional
- ... *a blank canvas* on an easel **that** had been waiting there for twenty-five years ...

windowsill

peer out

serrated

decay

Johnsy was sleeping when they went upstairs. Sue pulled the shade down to the windowsill and motioned Behrman to go into the other room. In there, they fearfully peered out the window at the ivy vine. Then, they looked at each other for a moment without speaking. A persistent, cold rain was falling along with some snow. Behrman, in his old blue shirt, took his seat as the hermit-miner on an upturned kettle for a rock.

→ drew down
→ gave a signal
→ looked out
→ constant
→ sat down
→ upside-down

When Sue awoke from an hour's sleep the next morning, she found Johnsy with dull, wide-open eyes staring at the drawn green shade.

→ draw–drew–drawn

"Pull it up. I want to see," she ordered in a whisper.

→ Open it. / Raise it.

Wearily, Sue obeyed.

→ followed
≠ Energetically

But, incredibly, despite the beating rain and fierce gusts of wind that had lasted throughout the entire night, there still remained one ivy leaf against the wall. It was the last one on the vine. Still dark green near its stem, but, with its serrated edges tinted yellow as it was

→ amazingly
→ in spite of
→ strong winds
→ colored

Stop & Think
What did Johnsy tell Sue to do when she woke up?

KEY WORDS

- **motion** to give a signal; to make a motion
- **peer out** to look out at something
- **upturned** upside-down; turned over
- **gusts of wind** strong winds
- **hang** to hold on to; to cling
- **fearfully** in a scared manner; with fear
- **persistent** constant; continual
- **incredibly** amazingly
- **decay** to rot
- **lean ~ down** to bend down; to bend over

beginning to decay, it hung bravely from a branch some twenty feet above the ground.

rot ← decay
clung *hang-hung-hung

"It is the last one," said Johnsy. "I thought it would surely fall during the night. I heard the wind. It will fall today, and I shall die at the same time."

"Dear, dear!" said Sue, leaning her worn face down to the pillow. "Think of me, if you won't think of yourself. What would I do?"

weary → worn
bending ← leaning

worn face

Stop & Think
What did Johnsy and Sue see outside?

CHECK UP Choose the right words.

1. Sue and Behrman looked out the _____ at the ivy vine. (window | door)
2. There was still _____ left on the vine. (one leaf | two leaves)
3. Johnsy thought the last leaf would fall during the _____. (day | night)
4. Was Johnsy ready to die? (Yes | No)

GRAMMAR POINT

despite (= in spite of)

- **Despite** the beating rain and fierce gusts of wind ... , there still remained one ivy leaf against the wall.

tie

twilight

eave

stir

But Johnsy did not answer. The most lonesome thing in the entire world is a soul when it is making ready to go on its mysterious, far journey. The fancy seemed to possess her more strongly as, one by one, the ties that bound her to friendship and to Earth were loosed.

The day passed, and even in the twilight, they could see the lone ivy leaf clinging to its stem against the wall. And then, with the coming of the night, the north wind again began to blow while the rain still beat against the windows and ran down the eaves.

When it was light enough, Johnsy, the merciless, commanded that the shade be raised.

The ivy leaf was still there.

Johnsy lay for a long time looking at it. And then she called to Sue, who was stirring her chicken broth over the gas stove.

"I've been a bad girl, Sudie," said Johnsy. "Something has made that last leaf stay there to show me how

Stop & Think
What did Sue and Johnsy see the next morning?

KEY WORDS

- **mysterious** strange; unknown
- **twilight** the period of time when the sun goes down
- **command** to order
- **wicked** evil; very bad
- **sit up** to sit while one is in bed
- **be loosed** to be let go; to be freed
- **merciless** without mercy; cruel
- **stir** to mix; to blend
- **sin** a bad deed; a wrong act
- **even chances** a fifty-percent chance

wicked I was. It is a sin to want to die. You may bring me a little broth now and some milk with a little port in it, and… No, bring me a hand-mirror first, and then pack some pillows about me, and I will sit up and watch you cook."

hand-mirror

An hour later, she said, "Sudie, someday I hope to paint the Bay of Naples."

The doctor came in the afternoon, and Sue had an excuse to go into the hallway as he left.

pillow

"Even chances," said the doctor, taking Sue's thin, shaking hand in his. "With good nursing, you'll win. And now I must see another case I have downstairs. Behrman, his name is—some kind of an artist, I believe. Pneumonia, too. He is an old, weak man, and the attack is acute. There is no hope for him, but he goes to the hospital today to be made more comfortable."

Check Up   Put the right words.

| the last leaf | nutrition | pneumonia | wicked |

1. Johnsy looked at _____ for a long time.
2. Johnsy said it was _____ for her to want to die.
3. The doctor told Sue that Behrman had _____.
4. The doctor said that Johnsy needed _____ and care.

Grammar Point

command that + S (+ should) + V

- Johnsy, the merciless, **commanded** that the shade **(should) be raised**.

knit

janitor

The next day, the doctor said to Sue, "She's out of danger. You've won. Nutrition and care now—that's all she needs."

That afternoon, Sue went to the bed where Johnsy lay, contentedly knitting a very blue and very useless woolen shoulder scarf, and she put one arm around her, pillows and all.

"I have something to tell you, my dear," she said. "Mr. Behrman died of pneumonia in the hospital today. He was ill for only two days. The janitor found him on the morning of the first day in his room downstairs helpless

Stop & Think
What happened to Behrman?

Key Words

- **out of danger** safe
- **janitor** a person who looks after a building; a cleaning man
- **helpless** unable to help oneself
- **dreadful** awful; horrible
- **flutter** to move, often because of the wind
- **contentedly** happily
- **be soaked** to be very wet
- **scattered** spread out

with pain. His shoes and clothing were soaked and icy cold. They couldn't imagine where he had been on such a dreadful night. And then they found a lantern, still lit, a ladder that had been dragged from its place, some scattered brushes, and a palette with green and yellow colors mixed on it, and—look out the window, dear, at the last ivy leaf on the wall. Didn't you wonder why it never fluttered or moved when the wind blew? Ah, darling, it's Behrman's masterpiece. He painted it there the night that the last leaf fell."

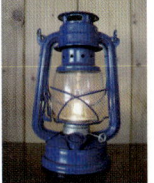
lantern

ladder

palette

Check Up True or false?

1 The janitor saw Behrman painting outside. ____
2 Behrman was found with his shoes and clothes soaking wet. ____
3 Behrman painted the last leaf. ____
4 The last leaf was Behrman's masterpiece. ____

Grammar Point

die of / die from

- Mr. Behrman **died of** pneumonia in the hospital today.
- She **died from** injuries after the car accident.

AMERICAN SCHOOL TEXTBOOK READING KEY
미국교과서 읽는 리딩

▶ **EASY 코스**

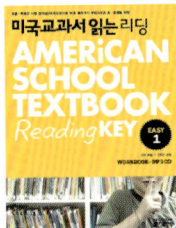 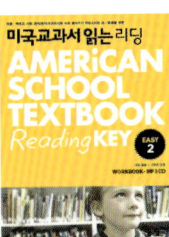 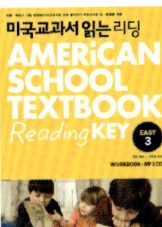

EASY 1   EASY 2   EASY 3

▶ **BASIC 코스**

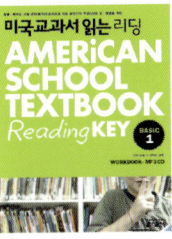 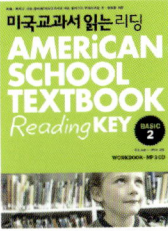 

BASIC 1   BASIC 2   BASIC 3

▶ **CORE 코스**

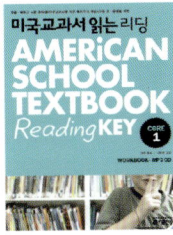 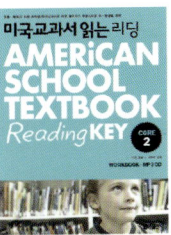 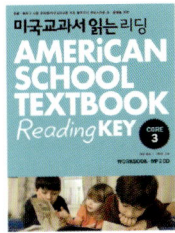

CORE 1   CORE 2   CORE 3

<영어 슈퍼 리딩 훈련>으로 공부한 후 <미국교과서 읽는 리딩> 시리즈의 EASY, BASIC, CORE 코스 원서 읽기에 도전해 보세요. <미국교과서 읽는 영단어>와 함께 공부하면 더욱 효과적입니다.

〈영어 슈퍼 리딩 스토리 훈련〉이면
영어 소설 읽기에 성공할 수밖에 없는 특별한 이유!

〈영어 슈퍼 리딩 스토리 훈련〉은 직독직해를 위한
끊어읽기(/)와 의미단위별 영어표현이 담긴 훈련북이 별도로 제공됩니다.
또한 Close Up과 Grammar Point를 통해 영문의 구조를 명쾌하게 설명합니다.
훈련북을 잘 활용하면 영문에 대한 이해력은 물론이고
어휘와 문장구조 파악 능력까지 근본적으로 향상시킬 수 있습니다.
이제 사전의 도움 없이
〈영어 슈퍼 리딩 스토리 훈련〉으로 행복한 원서 읽기를 시작하세요!
어휘, 문법, 독해, 듣기도 한번에 잡을 수 있습니다.

〈영어 슈퍼 리딩 스토리 훈련〉은
이런 분들께 더욱 효과적입니다!

- 사전 없이 원서를 읽고 싶다.
- 희미하게 잔해만 남아있는 내 영어, 기초부터 차근차근 다시 세우고 싶다.
- 뉴욕타임즈 베스트셀러 소설을 원서 그대로 읽고 싶다.
- 토익, 토플 등 각종 영어시험에서 고득점을 얻고 싶다.
- 영어로만 수업하는 이중언어교육 또는 몰입교육에 대비하고 싶다.
- 해외유학을 준비 중이다.

세계 명작, 유명 단편소설에서 선별한
15편의 스토리로 연습하는 슈퍼 리딩 스토리 6단계 훈련

영어 슈퍼 리딩 스토리 훈련

SUPER READING TRAINING BOOK

Michael A. Putlack | e - Creative Contents 지음

TRAINing BOOK

사전 없이 원서 읽는 영어 실력
〈영어 슈퍼 리딩 스토리 훈련〉으로 하루 30분씩 180일간만 훈련하십시오.
당신도 6개월 후 뉴욕타임즈 베스트셀러를 원서로 읽을 수 있습니다.
원어민 녹음 MP3 무료 다운로드 www.englishbus.kr

교육 R&D에 앞서가는
Key 키출판사

영어슈퍼리딩훈련

사전 없이 영어원서 읽는 공부기술!

사전 없이 원서 읽는 영어 실력, 〈영어 슈퍼 리딩 훈련〉으로
하루 20분씩 180일간만 훈련하십시오.
이제 당신도 6개월 후 교양 지식 분야 원서를 두려움 없이 읽을 수 있습니다.

〈영어 슈퍼 리딩 훈련〉은 이미 수많은 학생들이 경험한 감동의 영어체험,
베스트셀러 〈미국교과서 읽는 영단어〉시리즈의 슈퍼 리딩 훈련북입니다.

www.englishbus.kr
원어민 녹음 MP3 지금 바로 다운로드 받으세요! (무료)

메인북 p.220 + 트레이닝북 p.220

〈영어슈퍼리딩훈련〉시리즈(전2권)
1. 미국교과서편 〈영어슈퍼리딩훈련〉 정가 19,800원
2. 명작편 〈영어슈퍼리딩스토리훈련〉 정가 19,800원

사회·과학·언어·예술 등 미국교과서에서 뽑은
180개의 주요테마로 연습하는 6단계 슈퍼 리딩 훈련북

세계 명작, 유명 단편소설에서 선별한
15편의 스토리로 연습하는 **슈퍼 리딩 스토리 6단계 훈련**

영어 슈퍼 리딩 스토리 훈련

SUPER READING TRAINING BOOK

Michael A. Putlack | e-Creative Contents 지음

TRAINing BOOK

교육 R&D에 앞서가는
key 키출판사

How to Use This Book

훈련북에서는 정답 및 해설뿐만 아니라 직독직해에 필수인 의미단위별 끊어읽기(/)와 구문별 영어표현을 제공합니다. 또한 **Close Up**과 **Grammar Point**에 대한 설명을 추가하여 학습자들이 영문 구조를 제대로 이해할 수 있도록 도와줍니다. 훈련북을 잘 활용하면 영문에 대한 이해력은 물론 어휘와 문장구조 파악 능력까지 근본적으로 향상시킬 수 있으므로 반복학습하도록 합시다.

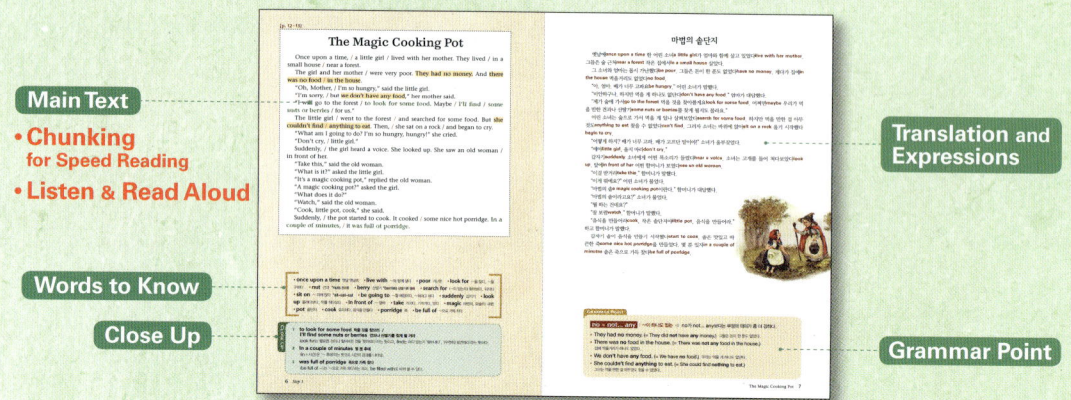

1 우리말 뜻과 영어표현 확인하기 자, 이제 훈련북을 보면서 본책에서 미처 이해하지 못한 어휘와 표현을 확인하고 영문을 완벽하게 소화하도록 합시다. 먼저, 〈Words to Know〉에 있는 단어들을 한번 훑어 봅니다. 그런 다음 위의 영어 본문을 읽으며 한글 번역과 대조해 나갑니다. Close Up과 Grammar Point를 통해 영문구조도 완벽하게 이해하도록 합시다. 또한 번역과 함께 제시된 영어표현은 영문을 의미단위로 이해하는 키워드이므로 반복해서 읽으며 완벽하게 이해하도록 합시다.

2 도전! 직독직해 & 의미 덩어리별 끊어읽기(Chunking) 이제 번역을 보지 말고 위의 영어 본문을 혼자 해석해 봅시다. 이때 의미 덩어리별 끊어읽기(/) 표시를 활용하면 순차적으로 영문을 읽어 나가는 데 많은 도움이 됩니다. 모르는 부분이 있으면 우리말 뜻과 영어표현을 다시 한번 확인하며 완전히 이해될 때까지 반복하도록 합시다.

3 오디오 들으며 따라 읽기 영어는 눈으로만 읽는 것보다 소리와 함께 익히는 것이 기억에 더 오래 남습니다. 이 책의 본문은 모두 원어민의 정확한 발음으로 녹음되어 있습니다. www.englishbus.co.kr에서 MP3파일을 무료로 다운로드 받으세요. 그런 다음 본문을 2회 반복해서 들으며 정확한 발음과 억양을 익힙니다. 스크립트에는 슬래시(/)로 끊어읽기가 표시되어 있습니다. 본문을 들을 때는 끊어읽기를 참고하여 원어민의 발음, 억양, 연음 등에 주의를 기울여 듣습니다. 스크립트 위에 억양, 연음 등을 표시해도 좋습니다. 그런 다음 2회 더 반복해서 들으며 큰 소리로 따라 읽습니다. 이때 원어민을 똑같이 흉내 내어 읽는 것이 중요합니다.

4 오디오 없이 혼자서 소리 내어 읽기 다음은 오디오 없이 본문을 소리 내어 읽으며 원어민처럼 흉내 내어 봅니다. 발음이나 억양이 어색한 부분이 있으면 다시 한번 오디오를 들으며 확인합시다.

5 영어 본문에 다시 한번 도전 이제 다시 본책으로 돌아가 영어 본문을 읽고 문제를 풀어 봅시다. 영어로만 읽어도 아주 쉽게 읽히고 문제를 이해할 수 있게 될 것입니다.

★ 정답은 Training Book의 〈Answers & Translations〉에서 확인하실 수 있습니다.

MP3 무료 다운로드 이 책의 본문은 모두 원어민의 정확한 발음으로 녹음되어 있습니다. www.englishbus.co.kr에서 MP3 파일을 무료로 다운로드 받으세요.

직독직해 훈련을 위한 길잡이

직독직해는 끊어읽기(Chunking)에서 시작

영문을 정확하고 빠르게 읽기 위해서는 영문을 어순 그대로 따라가며 해석할 수 있는 능력이 필요합니다. 그러기 위해서는 우리말과는 다른 영어의 어순과 구조를 익히는 것이 필수입니다.

영어식 어순 감각을 발달시키는 가장 좋은 방법은 의미 덩어리별로 문장을 이해하는 것입니다. 영어의 문장은 의미 덩어리(하나의 의미를 가진 어구)인 청크(chunk)로 이루어져 있습니다. 이 의미 덩어리만 이해하면 아무리 긴 문장도 순차적으로 쭉쭉 읽어 나갈 수 있습니다. 또한 들리는 대로 바로바로 이해해야 하는 영어 리스닝에도 효과적입니다.

> 다음 문장을 봅시다.   They lived in a small house.
> 이 문장을 쪼개어 보면,   They lived / in a small house.
>   그들은 살았다   작은 집에서

이렇게 두 개의 의미 덩어리로 이루어져 있습니다. 아무리 길고 복잡한 문장이라도 그 뼈대는 〈주어+동사〉의 간단한 기본문에서 출발합니다. 거기에 필요에 따라 여러 가지 표현을 추가하여 다양한 뜻을 나타내게 됩니다. 영어에 능통한 사람들의 머릿속에는 영문을 대할 때 자동적으로 기본문과 기타 표현으로 분리해 쭉쭉 읽어 나갈 수 있는 엔진이 들어있습니다. 영문을 읽을 때 어디서 끊어읽기를 하는지만 봐도 대충 그 사람의 '영어 내공'을 짐작할 수 있죠. 좀 더 긴 다른 문장을 살펴 봅시다.

> I know / many people / who look beautiful / but have ugly hearts.
> 나는 알고 있다   많은 사람들을   (겉으로는) 아름다워 보이는   하지만 추한 마음을 가진

이때 굳이 완벽한 우리말을 위하여 뒤에서부터 해석해 오는 것은 금물입니다. 뒤에서부터 해석해 올라오는 습관이 굳어지면 시간도 오래 걸릴 뿐만 아니라 절대 영어의 어순 감각을 키울 수 없습니다.

한 문장을 몇 개로 쪼갤 것인가?

한 문장을 몇 개로 끊어 하나의 의미단위로 삼을 것인가 하는 것은 문장의 요소나 영어 실력에 따라 달라질 수 있지만, 일반적으로 '주어+동사' 다음, 접속사(and, but, or 등) 앞, 관계사(that, who 등) 앞, 부사구, to 부정사 등의 앞뒤에서 끊게 됩니다. 또한 주어가 길 때는 흔히 주어를 구분해 주기 위하여 주어 뒤에서도 끊습니다.

> However, // the news / that interested me the most // was about my master's daughter.
> 하지만   나를 가장 흥미롭게 했던 소식은   주인집 따님에 대한 것이었다
> Her name was Stephanette, // and she was / the most beautiful girl / in the surrounding area.
> 그녀의 이름은 스테파네트였다   그리고 그녀는   가장 아름다운 소녀였다   그 일대에서

초보자의 경우에는 한 문장 안에 슬래시가 많이 들어가게 되지만, 독해실력이 향상될수록 슬래시의 개수가 줄어들고 차츰 문장을 한눈에 해석할 수 있게 됩니다. 본 훈련북에서는 초보 학습자를 고려하여 가능한 한 잘게 의미 덩어리를 나누어 놓았습니다. 차츰 실력이 향상되어 끊어읽기가 거추장스럽게 느껴지는 단계가 되면, 아무런 표시가 되어 있지 않은 본책의 영문을 읽으며 여러분의 독해력을 시험해 보시기 바랍니다. 끊어읽기 연습을 통해 영문의 어순과 구조에 익숙해지고, 놀라우리만치 독해 속도가 빨라진 것을 느끼게 될 것입니다.

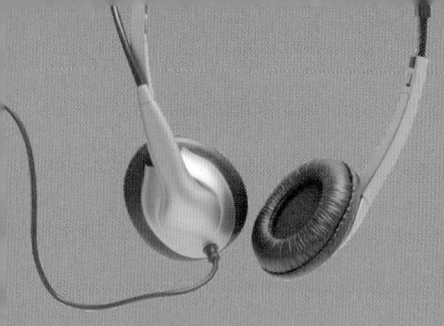

Super Reading Story Training Book

Step 1

The Magic Cooking Pot
•
The Shoemaker and the Elves
•
Jack and the Beanstalk
•
The Ugly Duckling
•
Aesop's Fables

The Magic Cooking Pot

Once upon a time, / a little girl / lived with her mother. They lived / in a small house / near a forest.

The girl and her mother / were very poor. They had no money. And there was no food / in the house.

"Oh, Mother, / I'm so hungry," said the little girl.

"I'm sorry, / but we don't have any food," her mother said.

"I will go to the forest / to look for some food. Maybe / I'll find / some nuts or berries / for us."

The little girl / went to the forest / and searched for some food. But she couldn't find / anything to eat. Then, / she sat on a rock / and began to cry.

"What am I going to do? I'm so hungry, hungry!" she cried.

"Don't cry, / little girl."

Suddenly, / the girl heard a voice. She looked up. She saw an old woman / in front of her.

"Take this," said the old woman.

"What is it?" asked the little girl.

"It's a magic cooking pot," replied the old woman.

"A magic cooking pot?" asked the girl.

"What does it do?"

"Watch," said the old woman.

"Cook, little pot, cook," she said.

Suddenly, / the pot started to cook. It cooked / some nice hot porridge. In a couple of minutes, / it was full of porridge.

- **once upon a time** 옛날 옛날에 • **live with** ~와 함께 살다 • **poor** 가난한 • **look for** ~을 찾다, ~을 구하다 • **nut** 견과 *nuts 견과류 • **berry** 산딸기 *berries 산딸기류 열매 • **search for** (~이 있는지) 찾아보다, 뒤지다 • **sit on** ~ 위에 앉다 *sit-sat-sat • **be going to** ~할 예정이다, ~하려고 하다 • **suddenly** 갑자기 • **look up** 올려다보다, 위를 쳐다보다 • **in front of** ~ 앞에 • **take** 가지다, 가져가다, 받다 • **magic** 마법의, 요술의; 마법 • **pot** 솥단지 • **cook** 요리하다, 음식을 만들다 • **porridge** 죽 • **be full of** ~으로 가득 차다

CLOSE UP

1. **to look for some food** 먹을 것을 찾으러 /
   I'll find some nuts or berries 견과나 산딸기를 찾게 될 거야
   look for는 필요한 것이나 잃어버린 것을 '찾아보다'라는 뜻이고, find는 어디 있는지 '찾아내다', '(우연히) 발견하다'라는 뜻이다.

2. **In a couple of minutes** 몇 분 후에
   〈in+시간〉은 '~ 후에'라는 뜻으로 시간의 경과를 나타냄.

3. **was full of porridge** 죽으로 가득 찼다
   〈be full of ~〉는 '~으로 가득 차다'라는 의미. be filled with로 바꿔 쓸 수 있다.

마법의 솥단지

옛날에**once upon a time** 한 어린 소녀**a little girl**가 엄마와 함께 살고 있었다**live with her mother**. 그들은 숲 근처**near a forest** 작은 집에서**in a small house** 살았다.

그 소녀와 엄마는 몹시 가난했다**be poor**. 그들은 돈이 한 푼도 없었다**have no money**. 게다가 집에**in the house** 먹을거리도 없었다**no food**.

"아, 엄마. 배가 너무 고파요**be hungry**." 어린 소녀가 말했다.

"미안하구나. 하지만 먹을 게 하나도 없단다**don't have any food**." 엄마가 대답했다.

"제가 숲에 가서**go to the forest** 먹을 것을 찾아볼게요**look for some food**. 어쩌면**maybe** 우리가 먹을 만한 견과나 산딸기**some nuts or berries**를 찾게 될지도 몰라요."

어린 소녀는 숲으로 가서 먹을 게 있나 살펴보았다**search for some food**. 하지만 먹을 만한 걸 아무것도**anything to eat** 찾을 수 없었다**can't find**. 그러자 소녀는 바위에 앉아**sit on a rock** 울기 시작했다**begin to cry**.

"어떻게 하지? 배가 너무 고파. 배가 고프단 말이야!" 소녀가 울부짖었다.

"얘야**little girl**, 울지 마라**don't cry**."

갑자기**suddenly** 소녀에게 어떤 목소리가 들렸다**hear a voice**. 소녀는 고개를 들어 쳐다보았다**look up**. 앞에**in front of her** 어떤 할머니가 보였다**see an old woman**.

"이걸 받거라**take this**." 할머니가 말했다.

"이게 뭐예요?" 어린 소녀가 물었다.

"마법의 솥**a magic cooking pot**이란다." 할머니가 대답했다.

"마법의 솥이라고요?" 소녀가 물었다.

"뭘 하는 건데요?"

"잘 보렴**watch**." 할머니가 말했다.

"음식을 만들어라**cook**, 작은 솥단지야**little pot**, 음식을 만들어라." 하고 할머니가 말했다.

갑자기 솥이 음식을 만들기 시작했다**start to cook**. 솥은 맛있고 따끈한 죽**some nice hot porridge**을 만들었다. 몇 분 있자**in a couple of minutes** 솥은 죽으로 가득 찼다**be full of porridge**.

GRAMMAR POINT

no = not... any : ~이 하나도 없는 ⇨ no가 not... any보다는 부정의 의미가 좀 더 강하다.

- They had **no** money. (= They did **not** have **any** money.) 그들은 돈이 한 푼도 없었다.
- There was **no** food in the house. (= There was **not any** food in the house.)
  집에 먹을거리가 하나도 없었다.
- We do**n't** have **any** food. (= We have **no** food.) 우리는 먹을 게 하나도 없단다.
- She could**n't** find **anything** to eat. (= She could find **nothing** to eat.)
  그녀는 먹을 만한 걸 아무것도 찾을 수 없었다.

[p. 14–15]

"Wow!" said the girl. "That's amazing. Let's eat the porridge."
"Wait," said the old woman. "First, / the pot must stop."
Then, / she said to the pot, / "Stop, little pot, stop."
The pot / immediately / stopped cooking.
"You must always say / those words, / or the pot will keep cooking porridge. Now, / you can eat."
"It's delicious!" said the little girl.
"You can have this pot," said the old woman.
"Oh, I am so happy. Thank you so much."
"Just don't forget / the magic words," said the old woman.
The little girl took the pot / and ran back to her home.
"Mother," shouted the little girl.
"Look at / what I have. It's a magic cooking pot."
The girl's mother / looked at the pot.
"Magic? Are you sure?"
"Of course. Watch this," answered the little girl.
"Cook, little pot, cook."
Immediately, / the pot cooked / some nice hot porridge. In a couple of minutes, / it was full of porridge.
"Wait a minute, / Mother," said the little girl.
"We have to say / the magic words / to stop the pot. Stop, little pot, stop," she said.
The pot / immediately / stopped cooking.
The little girl and her mother / ate porridge / every day. They were not hungry / anymore.
One day, / the little girl went out / to play with her friends. She was out / for a long time. Her mother / became very hungry. So she decided to eat / without her daughter.

- **amazing** 아주 놀라운　• **immediately** 즉시, 즉각　• **keep -ing** 계속해서 ~하다 *keep–kept–kept
- **delicious** 맛있는　• **forget** 잊어버리다　• **magic words** 마법의 말, 주문　• **take** 가지다, 가지고 가다 *take–took–taken
- **run back** 뛰어 돌아가다, 뛰어 돌아오다　• **shout** 소리치다, 외치다　• **look at** ~을 쳐다보다
- **anymore** 더 이상　• **go out** 밖에 나가다 *go–went–gone　• **be out** 밖에 나가 있다　• **decide to** ~하기로 결정하다　• **without** ~ 없이　• **daughter** 딸 ≠ son

CLOSE UP

1 **the pot must stop** 솥이 멈춰야 한다 / **You must always say those words** 너는 항상 이 말을 해야 한다 / **We have to say the magic words** 우리는 마법의 주문을 외워야 한다
must와 have to는 '~해야 한다'라는 뜻으로, 필요성이나 의무를 나타냄.

2 **you can eat** 먹어도 된다 / **you can have this pot** 이 솥을 가져도 된다
여기서 can은 '~해도 된다'라는 허가의 의미.

3 **what I have** 내가 가진 것
⟨what+주어+동사⟩는 '~한 것'이라는 의미. *ex*) what I do(내가 하는 것) / what you need(네가 필요한 것)

"와**wow**! 그거 진짜 신기하네요**be amazing**. 같이 이 죽을 먹어요**let's eat the porridge**." 소녀가 말했다.

"기다리거라**wait**. 우선**first** 솥이 멈춰야 한단다**must stop**." 할머니가 말했다.

그런 다음 할머니는 솥에게 말했다. "멈춰라**stop**, 작은 솥단지야, 멈춰라."

솥은 즉시**immediately** 요리를 멈췄다**stop cooking**.

"언제든지**always** 이 말을 해야**say those words** 한단다. 안 그러면**or** 솥이 계속 죽을 만들 게다**keep cooking porridge**. 자, 이제**now** 먹어도 된다**can eat**."

"맛있어요**be delicious**!" 어린 소녀가 말했다.

"이 솥을 가져도**have this pot** 된다." 할머니가 말했다.

"와, 너무 행복해요**be happy**. 정말 고맙습니다**thank you so much**."

"주문**the magic words**을 잊지만 말거라**don't forget**." 할머니가 당부했다.

어린 소녀는 솥을 가지고**take the pot** 집으로 뛰어 돌아왔다**run back to her home**.

"엄마." 어린 소녀가 소리쳤다**shout**.

"제가 뭘 가지고 있는지**what I have** 보세요. 마법의 솥이에요."

소녀의 엄마는 솥을 살펴보았다**look at the pot**.

"마법**magic**이라고? 정말이니**are you sure**?"

"그럼요**of course**. 이거 보세요**watch this**." 어린 소녀가 대답했다.

"음식을 만들어라, 작은 솥단지야, 음식을 만들어라."

솥은 즉시 맛있고 따끈한 죽을 만들었다. 몇 분 있자 솥은 죽으로 가득 찼다**be full of porridge**.

"잠깐만요**wait a minute**, 엄마." 어린 소녀가 말했다.

"주문을 외워서**say the magic words** 솥단지를 멈춰야**stop the pot** 해요. 멈춰라, 작은 솥단지야, 멈춰라." 소녀가 말했다.

솥은 즉시 요리를 멈췄다.

어린 소녀와 엄마는 날마다**every day** 죽을 먹었다**eat porridge**. 그들은 이제 더는 배를 곯지 않았다**be not hungry**.

어느 날**one day** 어린 소녀는 친구들과 놀려고**play with her friends** 밖에 나갔다**go out**. 소녀는 한참 동안**for a long time** 밖에 있었다**be out**. 엄마는 너무 배가 고파졌다**become hungry**. 그래서 딸 없이**without her daughter** 식사하기로 마음먹었다**decide to eat**.

GRAMMAR POINT

stop -ing : ~하는 것을 멈추다   **keep -ing** : 계속 ~하다   **decide to** : ~하기로 결심하다

⇨ 어떤 동사는 동명사를 목적어로 취하고, 어떤 동사는 to부정사를 목적어로 취한다.
이와 같은 동사의 특징은 그때그때 잘 파악해 두는 것이 좋다.

- The pot immediately **stopped** coo**king**. 솥은 즉시 요리하는 것을 멈췄다.
- The pot will **keep** coo**king** porridge. 솥은 계속 죽을 만들 것이다.
- She **decided to** eat without her daughter. 그녀는 딸 없이 식사하기로 마음먹었다.

[p. 16-17]

"Cook, little pot, cook," she said.

The pot started / cooking some porridge. After a few minutes, / the pot was full of porridge. The mother **wanted the pot** / **to stop cooking**.

"No more, little pot, no more," said the mother.

But the pot did not stop cooking. Those were not the magic words.

"Stop cooking, little pot, stop cooking," she cried.

But those were not the magic words / either.

Soon, / the porridge began to overflow / from the pot. It spilled onto the floor. The mother did not know / what to do. She **kept trying** / **to stop the pot**. But she did not remember / how to make it stop.

The kitchen filled with porridge. Then, / the porridge spilled into the street / and went into the next house. The villagers were surprised.

"What's happening?" they asked.

"The magic pot / will not stop cooking," answered the mother.

The villagers / scooped up the porridge / with buckets / and took it away. But the magic pot / continued cooking. Soon, / there was porridge / in every house / in the village.

Just then, / the little girl / came back to her home.

"Stop, little pot, stop," she shouted.

The magic cooking pot / immediately / stopped cooking.

"It's a good little pot. But you must say / the right words!" said the little girl.

- **cry** 외치다 *cry–cried–cried • **either** (부정문에서) ~도 또한 ~아니다 • **overflow** 흘러 넘치다 • **spill** 쏟아지다, 흘러나오다, 넘쳐 나오다 *spill–spilled–spilled • **fill with** ~로 가득 차다, ~로 채워지다 = be filled with • **villager** (시골) 마을 사람 • **be surprised** 놀라다 • **scoop up** 퍼내다, 퍼올리다 • **take away** 없애다, 치우다 • **continue -ing** 계속해서 ~하다 • **come back** 돌아오다

CLOSE UP

1 **wanted the pot to stop cooking** 솥이 요리를 멈추길 바랐다
   〈want ~ to...〉는 '~이 …하기를 바라다/원하다'라는 의미.

2 **kept trying to stop the pot** 솥을 멈추려고 계속 애썼다
   〈try to ~〉는 '~하려고 애쓰다/노력하다'라는 의미.

"음식을 만들어라, 작은 솥단지야, 음식을 만들어라." 엄마가 말했다.

솥이 죽을 만들기**cook some porridge** 시작했다. 몇 분 뒤에**after a few minutes** 솥은 죽으로 가득 찼다. 엄마는 솥이 요리를 멈추길**stop cooking** 바랐다.

"그만해라**no more**, 작은 솥단지야. 그만해라." 엄마가 말했다.

그러나 솥은 요리를 멈추지 않았다. 그건 주문**magic words**이 아니었다.

"요리를 멈춰라, 작은 솥단지야, 요리를 멈춰." 엄마가 외쳤다.

하지만 그것 역시**either** 주문이 아니었다.

얼마 안 있어**soon** 죽이 솥에서 흘러 넘치기**overflow from the pot** 시작했다. 죽은 바닥으로 흘러내렸다**spill onto the floor**. 엄마는 어찌할 바**what to do**를 몰랐다**do not know**. 엄마는 솥을 멈추려고 계속 애썼다**keep trying**. 그러나 그것을 멈추게 하는 법**how to make it stop**이 생각나지 않았다**do not remember**.

부엌이 죽으로 가득 찼다**fill with porridge**. 그러더니 죽은 길거리로 넘쳐서**spill into the street** 옆집으로 흘러 들어갔다**go into the next house**. 마을 사람들**the villagers**이 깜짝 놀랐다**be surprised**.

"무슨 일이죠**what's happening**?" 그들이 물었다.

"마법의 솥이 요리를 멈추질 않아요." 엄마가 대답했다.

마을 사람들이 양동이로**with buckets** 죽을 퍼서**scoop up the porridge** 치웠다**take it away**. 그러나 마법의 솥은 계속해서 요리를 했다**continue cooking**. 곧 마을의**in the village** 집집마다**in every house** 죽 범벅이 되었다**there is porridge**.

바로 그때**just then** 어린 소녀가 집으로 돌아왔다**come back**.

"멈춰라, 작은 솥단지야, 멈춰라." 소녀가 외쳤다.

마법의 솥은 즉시**immediately** 요리를 멈췄다.

"이건 말 잘 듣는 작은 솥단지**a good little pot**예요. 하지만 주문을 제대로 외워야**say the right words** 해요!" 어린 소녀가 말했다.

GRAMMAR POINT

what to ~ : 무엇을 ~해야 할지   **how to ~** : 어떻게 ~해야 할지, ~하는 방법

- The mother did not know **what to** do. 엄마는 무엇을 해야 할지 몰랐다.
- She did not remember **how to** make it stop. 그녀는 그것을 멈추게 하는 법이 생각나지 않았다.

[p. 18-19]

The Shoemaker and the Elves

There was once / an old shoemaker. He owned / an old shoe shop. He worked / on the first floor, / and he and his wife / lived / on the second floor. The shoemaker and his wife / were very poor. Few people / visited his shop, / so he did not make / much money.

One day, / the shoemaker / told his wife.

"One last pair of shoes. That's / all I can make. We don't have any money. What are we going to do?"

"It is late. So we should go to bed. Make the shoes / in the morning," answered the shoemaker's wife. The shoemaker and his wife / went upstairs / and went to bed.

The next morning, / the shoemaker and his wife / went downstairs. There was something / on the table. It was / a pair of shoes.

"Look at these," the shoemaker said. "What beautiful shoes! It's magic."

Just then, / a lady / came into the store. The lady / looked at the shoes / and said, "What beautiful shoes! I'll take them." She gave the shoemaker / three gold coins / for the shoes.

"Three gold coins! Now I can make / two more pairs of shoes," the shoemaker said. So he went out / and bought / some more leather. He came back / and cut the leather.

"It is late. Make them / in the morning," said his wife. The shoemaker and his wife / went upstairs / and went to bed.

- **shoemaker** 구두 만드는 사람, 구두장이　• **own** 가지다, 소유하다　• **work** 일하다, 작업하다　• **first floor** 1층
- **second floor** 2층　• **make money** 돈을 벌다　• **wife** 아내　• **last** 마지막의, 마지막 남은　• **pair** (둘씩 짝을 이룬) 쌍　• **go to bed** 잠자리에 들다　• **go upstairs** 위층으로 올라가다　• **magic** 마법, 요술; 마법의
- **gold coin** 금화　• **leather** 가죽　• **cut the leather** 가죽을 자르다, 재단하다

CLOSE UP

1 **Few people visited his shop** 그의 가게를 찾는 사람들이 별로 없었다
   few는 수가 '많지 않은', '거의 없는'이라는 부정적인 뜻으로 쓰임.

2 **all I can make** 내가 만들 수 있는 전부
   〈all+주어+동사〉는 '~하는 전부' 또는 '~하는 오직 한 가지'라는 의미.
   ex) all I have(내가 가진 전부) / all I want(내가 원하는 모든 것)

3 **a pair of shoes** 구두 한 켤레 / **two more pairs of shoes** 구두 두 켤레 더
   a pair는 둘씩 짝을 이룬 '한 쌍'을 의미함. two pairs는 '두 쌍'이 된다.
   ex) a pair of socks(양말 한 켤레) / a pair of pants(바지 한 벌) / a pair of earrings(귀걸이 한 쌍)

구두장이와 꼬마요정들

옛날에once 구두장이 할아버지an old shoemaker가 있었다. 그는 오래된 구둣방an old shoe shop을 소유하고 있었다own. 그는 1층에서on the first floor 작업을 했고work, 그와 그의 아내는 2층에서on the second floor 살았다live. 구두장이 부부(구두장이 할아버지와 그의 아내)는 몹시 가난했다be poor. 가게를 찾는visit his shop 사람들이 별로 없어서few people 할아버지가 돈을 많이 벌지 못했기do not make much money 때문이다.

어느 날one day 구두장이 할아버지가 할머니(그의 아내)에게 말했다.
"마지막 구두 한 켤레one pair of shoes. 그게 내가 만들 수 있는 전부all I can make요. 우리한테 돈이 한 푼도 없구려don't have any money. 어찌하면 좋겠소?"
"시간이 늦었어요. 그러니 자러 갑시다go to bed. 구두는 아침에 만들도록 해요." 할머니가 대답했다. 구두장이 부부는 위층으로 올라가go upstairs 잠자리에 들었다go to bed.

다음 날 아침the next morning 구두장이 부부는 아래층으로 내려갔다go downstairs. 작업대 위에on the table 뭔가가 있었다there is something. 구두 한 켤레a pair of shoes였다.
"이것 좀 봐요look at these." 구두장이 할아버지가 말했다. "정말 아름다운 구두로군what beautiful shoes! 마법magic이 일어났구려."

바로 그때just then 귀부인 한 명a lady이 가게로 들어왔다come into the store. 귀부인이 그 구두를 보고look at the shoes 말했다. "정말 아름다운 구두네요! 제가 사겠어요I'll take them." 귀부인은 구두장이 할아버지에게 구둣값으로for the shoes 금화 세 닢three gold coins을 주었다give.

"금화 세 닢이라니! 이제 구두를 두 켤레는 더two more pairs of shoes 만들 수 있겠군can make." 구두장이 할아버지가 말했다. 그래서so 할아버지는 나가서go out 가죽을 더 구입했다buy some more leather. 그리고 돌아와서come back 가죽을 재단했다cut the leather.

"시간이 늦었어요. 구두는 아침에 만들도록 해요." 할머니가 말했다. 구두장이 부부는 위층으로 올라가 잠자리에 들었다.

GRAMMAR POINT

What ~! / How ~! (감탄문)

- **What** beautiful shoes! 정말 아름다운 구두로군! (What + 형용사 + 복수명사!)
- **How beautiful** they are! 정말 아름답네요! (How + 형용사 + 주어 + 동사!)

- **What a** wonderful **surprise!** 정말 멋지게 놀라운 일이야! (What a/an + 형용사 + 단수명사!)
- **How fast** it flies! 정말 빨리 날아가네요! (How + 부사 + 주어 + 동사!)

[p. 20–21]

The next morning, / the shoemaker and his wife / came down. They saw / two beautiful pairs of shoes / on the table.

"Look at these," he said. "More magic."

The shoemaker / put the shoes / in the window. A man saw them. He walked into the shop. "How beautiful / they are! I must buy them. Here are / six gold coins."

"Now I can buy / enough leather / to make four pairs of shoes," the shoemaker said. So he went out / and bought / some more leather. He came back / and cut the leather.

"It is late," said his wife. "So we should go to bed." The shoemaker and his wife / went upstairs / and went to bed.

The next morning, / the shoemaker and his wife / came down. They saw / four beautiful pairs of shoes / on the table.

"Look at these," he said. "They're beautiful. Even more magic."

A while later, / two customers / entered the store. They looked at the shoes / and said, "Those shoes are beautiful. We'll take them." They paid the shoemaker / twelve gold coins / for the shoes.

The shoemaker and his wife / were very happy. But they wondered, "Who is making these shoes? We must know."

That night, / the shoemaker / cut the leather / for the shoes. But he and his wife / did not go upstairs. Instead, / they hid downstairs. They waited and waited.

- **come down** 내려오다 • **put** 두다, 놓다 • **walk into** (걸어) 들어오다 • **enough** 충분한 • **go out** 밖으로 나가다, 외출하다 • **even more** 한층 더, 더욱 더 • **a while later** 잠시 후 • **customer** 손님 • **enter** 들어오다, 들어가다 • **pay for** ~에 대한 값을 지불하다 *pay–paid–paid • **wonder** 궁금하다 • **instead** 대신, 대신에 • **hide** 숨다 *hide–hid–hidden • **wait** 기다리다

CLOSE UP

1 **Here are six gold coins.** 여기 금화 여섯 닢이요.
   〈here is/are ~〉는 어떤 것을 주거나 내놓을 때 '여기 ~가 있다'라는 의미로 쓰임.

2 **They paid the shoemaker twelve gold coins for the shoes.**
   그들은 구두장이에게 구둣값으로 금화 열두 닢을 지불했다.
   〈pay + 사람 + 돈〉은 '~에게 …을 지불하다'라는 의미. 무엇에 대한 대가인지를 나타내려면 전치사 for를 사용한다.

다음 날 아침 구두장이 부부가 아래로 내려왔다**come down**. 그들은 아름다운 구두 두 켤레**two beautiful pairs of shoes**가 작업대 위에 놓여 있는 걸 보았다**see**.

"이것 좀 봐요." 할아버지가 말했다. "또 마법**more magic**이 일어났구려."

구두장이 할아버지는 그 구두들을 진열창에 놓았다**put the shoes in the window**. 한 남자**a man**가 그것들을 보았다**see them**. 그는 가게로 들어왔다**walk into the shop**. "정말 멋진**how beautiful** 구두로군요! 제가 꼭 사야겠습니다**must buy**. 금화 여섯 닢**six gold coins**을 드리지요."

"이제 구두 네 켤레**four pairs of shoes**를 만들 가죽을 충분히**enough leather** 살 수 있겠군**can buy**." 구두장이 할아버지가 말했다. 그래서 할아버지는 나가서 가죽을 더 구입했다. 그리고 돌아와서 가죽을 재단했다.

"시간이 늦었어요. 그러니 자러 갑시다." 할머니가 말했다. 구두장이 부부는 위층으로 올라가 잠자리에 들었다.

다음 날 아침 구두장이 부부가 아래로 내려왔다. 작업대 위에 아름다운 구두 네 켤레**four beautiful pairs of shoes**가 보였다.

"이것 좀 봐요." 할아버지가 말했다. "아름답군. 또 다시 마법**even more magic**이 일어났구려."

잠시 후**a while later** 손님 두 명**two customers**이 가게로 들어왔다**enter the store**. 그들은 구두들을 보고 말했다. "저 구두들은 아름답군요. 우리가 사겠습니다." 그들은 구두장이 할아버지에게 구둣값으로 금화 열두 닢을 지불했다**pay twelve gold coins**.

구두장이 부부는 아주 행복했다**be happy**. 하지만 궁금증이 생겼다**wonder**. "누가**who** 이런 구두를 만드는**make these shoes** 걸까? 알아야겠어**must know**."

그날 밤**that night** 구두장이 할아버지는 구두를 만들 가죽을 재단했다. 하지만 부부는 위층으로 올라가지 않았다. 대신에**instead** 아래층에 숨어 있었다**hide downstairs**. 그들은 기다리고 또 기다렸다**wait and wait**.

GRAMMAR POINT

enough ~ to... : …할 정도로 충분한 ~ ⇒ enough의 위치에 주의할 것. 명사 앞, 형용사 뒤에 온다.

- Now I can buy **enough** leather **to** make four pairs of shoes.
  이제 구두 네 켤레를 만들 가죽을 충분히 살 수 있겠군.

- She had **enough** money **to** pay for the clothes. 그녀는 그 옷값을 치를 돈이 충분히 있었다.
- You are old **enough** **to** help your mother with housework.
  너는 엄마가 집안일 하는 걸 도울 수 있을 만한 나이가 되었다.

[p. 22–23]

At midnight, / two elves / came into the shoemaker's shop. They jumped onto the table.

"Look at this leather," one said.

"Let's make / some beautiful shoes / with it," said the other.

The elves / worked hard / all night long. They made / several beautiful pairs of shoes. When the sun rose, / they left.

"Those elves / are very kind," said the shoemaker.

"You're right," answered his wife. "We should do something / for them."

"What can we do?" asked the shoemaker.

"I know," said his wife. "**Their clothes / looked poor.** Let's make some clothes / for them."

So the shoemaker and his wife / made some tiny clothes / for the elves. They sewed / tiny pants, shirts, hats, and boots / for the elves. Then, / they put the new clothes / on the table.

That night, / the shoemaker and his wife / hid again. At midnight, / the elves / came into the shoemaker's shop. When they jumped onto the table, / they saw the clothes.

"What are these?" one said. "Are these clothes / for us?"

"Yes," said the other. "They are for us."

The elves / put their new clothes on. Then, / they danced / with each other.

"We cannot stay here / any longer," said the first elf.

"You're right. They know about us. Now it's time / for us to go," said the second elf.

"Goodbye, / shoemaker," they said.

The elves left / and never came back. But now the shoemaker / could make good shoes. He worked hard, / too. So he and his wife / became very rich. And they lived happily / ever after.

- **midnight** 한밤중 • **elf** (귀가 뾰족하고 마술을 부리는) 요정 *복수형: elves • **jump onto** ~ 위로 뛰어오르다 • **all night long** 밤새(도록) • **several** 몇 개의, 서너 개의 • **rise** (해, 달 등이) 떠오르다 *rise–rose–risen • **leave** 떠나다 • **clothes** 옷 • **look poor** 가난해 보이다, 볼품없어 보이다 • **tiny** 아주 작은 • **sew** 바느질하다, (바느질로 옷을) 만들다 • **put on** (옷 등을) 입다 • **stay** 머무르다 • **any longer** 더 이상 • **happily** 행복하게 • **ever after** 그 후로 계속

CLOSE UP

1 **Their clothes looked poor.** 그들의 옷은 볼품없어 보였어요.
   〈look + 형용사〉는 '~하게 보이다'라는 의미.

2 **The elves put their new clothes on.** 요정들은 그들의 새 옷을 입었다.
   〈put ~ on〉은 옷, 신발, 모자, 안경, 장신구 등을 '입다/쓰다/끼다/걸치다' 등의 의미를 가짐.
   참고로, put on은 입는 동작을 나타내고, wear는 입고 있는 상태를 나타낸다.

자정이 되자at midnight 꼬마요정 둘two elves이 구두장이 할아버지의 가게로 들어왔다come into the shoemaker's shop. 요정들은 작업대 위로 깡충 뛰어올랐다jump onto the table.

"이 가죽 좀 봐look at this leather." 요정 하나가 말했다.

"그걸로 아름다운 구두를 만들자let's make some beautiful shoes." 다른 요정이 말했다.

꼬마요정들은 밤새all night long 열심히 작업했다work hard. 그들은 아름다운 구두를 몇 켤레several beautiful pairs of shoes 만들었다. 동이 트자the sun rises 그들은 떠나갔다leave.

"저 요정들은 마음씨가 아주 곱구려be kind." 구두장이 할아버지가 말했다.

"그러게나 말이에요. 그들에게 뭔가 해 줘야do something for them겠어요." 할머니가 대답했다.

"뭘 해 줄 수 있을까?" 구두장이 할아버지가 물었다.

"나한테 맡겨요. 그들의 옷their clothes이 볼품없어 보였어요look poor. 그들에게 옷을 지어make some clothes 줍시다." 할머니가 말했다.

그래서 구두장이 부부는 꼬마요정들을 위해 자그마한 옷을 몇 개some tiny clothes 만들었다. 그들은 요정들을 위해 자그마한 바지와 셔츠, 모자, 부츠pants, shirts, hats, and boots를 바느질해서 만들었다sew. 그런 다음then 그 새 옷가지들the new clothes을 작업대 위에 올려놓았다put on the table.

그날 밤 구두장이 부부는 다시 숨어 있었다hide again. 자정이 되자 꼬마요정들이 구두장이 할아버지의 가게로 들어왔다. 그들이 작업대 위로 깡충 뛰어오르자 옷가지들이 보였다see the clothes.

"이게 뭐지? 이 옷들은 우리한테 주는for us 건가?" 요정 하나가 말했다.

"그런가 본데yes. 우리한테 주는 거야." 다른 요정이 말했다.

꼬마요정들은 그들의 새 옷을 입었다put their new clothes on. 그리고는 서로 춤을 추었다dance with each other.

"우리는 더는any longer 여기에 머물면 안 돼cannot stay here." 첫 번째 요정이 말했다.

"맞아. 그들이 우리에 대해 알고 있어know about us. 이제 우리가 떠나야 할for us to go 때가 됐군it's time." 두 번째 요정이 말했다.

"구두장이 할아버지, 안녕히 계세요goodbye." 꼬마요정들이 인사했다.

꼬마요정들은 떠나갔고leave 다시는 돌아오지 않았다never come back. 그러나 이제but now 구두장이 할아버지는 좋은 구두를 만들make good shoes 수 있었다. 작업도 열심히 했다. 그래서 구두장이 부부는 매우 큰 부자가 되었다become very rich. 그리고 그 후로 계속ever after 행복하게 살았다live happily.

GRAMMAR POINT

it's time for ~ to... : ~가 …해야 할 때이다

- Now **it's time for** us **to** go. 이제 우리가 떠나야 할 때가 됐군.
- **It's time for** you **to** do something for your family. 네가 가족을 위해 뭔가 해야 할 때가 됐어.

The Shoemaker and the Elves

[p. 24-25]

Jack and the Beanstalk

Long ago, / there lived / a mother and her son. The son's name / was Jack. They lived / in a small cottage. They were very poor. Their only valuable possession / was an old cow.

One day, / the mother said to Jack.

"We've got no money, / Jack. Go and sell the cow."

So Jack took the cow / and walked toward the town. On his way to the town, / he met / a strange old man. He asked Jack, "Where are you going / with that cow?"

"I'm going to town / to sell the cow / so that we can buy some food," said Jack.

"Ah ... / but the town is / so very far away ... I will gladly / buy the cow / from you," the old man said.

"Take a look at these." The old man showed Jack / some beautiful beans. "These are magic beans. I will give you / five magic beans / for your cow," he offered.

Jack was impressed / by the magic beans. So he sold the cow / to the old man / for five beans. Jack was very proud of himself.

But when he got home, / his mother was angry.

"What? Beans!" she cried. "You sold our cow / for five beans? You fool! Only a fool / would exchange a cow / for five beans. No supper / for you. Go to bed / right now," she told him. Then, / Jack's mother / threw the beans / out the window.

The next morning, / Jack looked out the window / and saw an amazing sight. There was / an enormous beanstalk / growing next to the window. It rose so high / that he could not see / where it ended.

"The old man was right," said Jack. "They were magic beans." Jack started / climbing up the beanstalk. He climbed / for hours and hours. Finally, / he got to the top of the beanstalk.

- **cottage** 작은 집, 오두막   • **valuable** 값어치 있는, 값나가는   • **possession** 소유, 소유물   • **strange** 이상한, 낯선   • **far away** 아주 먼, 멀리 있는   • **gladly** 기꺼이, 즐거운 맘으로   • **take a look at** ~을 (살펴)보다   • **offer** 제안하다   • **be impressed by** ~에 감동받다, ~에 깊은 인상을 받다, ~에 반하다   • **be proud of** ~을 자랑스럽게 여기다   • **fool** 바보   • **exchange** 교환하다, 바꾸다   • **throw** 던지다 *throw–threw–thrown   • **amazing** 놀라운, 믿을 수 없는   • **sight** 눈에 보이는 광경, 모습   • **enormous** 거대한   • **beanstalk** 콩나무   • **climb up** (기어) 올라가다 ≠ climb down   • **get to** ~에 도착하다, ~에 다다르다

CLOSE UP

1. **On his way to the town** 읍내로 가는 길에
   〈on one's way to ~〉는 '~로 가는 길에'라는 의미.

2. **Jack was very proud of himself.** 잭은 자기 자신이 아주 자랑스러웠다.(잭은 아주 뿌듯했다.)
   〈be proud of ~〉는 '~을 자랑스럽게 여기다'라는 의미.

3. **would exchange a cow for five beans** 암소를 콩 다섯 알과 바꿀 것이다
   〈exchange ~ for...〉는 '~을 …와 맞바꾸다'라는 의미.

잭과 콩나무

옛날에**long ago** 어머니와 아들**a mother and her son**이 살고 있었다. 아들의 이름**the son's name**은 잭**Jack**이었다. 두 사람은 작은 오두막에서 살았다**live in a small cottage**. 그들은 몹시 가난했다**be poor**. 유일하게 값나가는 재산**valuable possession**이라곤 늙은 암소**an old cow**뿐이었다.

어느 날**one day** 어머니가 잭에게 말했다.

"잭, 돈이 하나도 없구나**have got no money**. 가서 암소를 팔아라**sell the cow**."

그래서 잭은 암소를 끌고 읍내를 향해 걸었다**walk toward the town**. 읍내로 가는 길에**on his way to the town** 잭은 낯선 노인**a strange old man**을 만났다**meet**. 노인이 잭에게 물었다. "그 암소를 끌고 **with that cow** 어디로 가는 게냐?"

"식량을 좀 사려고**buy some food** 이 암소를 팔러 읍내에 가는**go to town** 길이에요." 잭이 대답했다.

"아…… 그렇지만 읍내는 아주아주 멀리**so very far away** 있단다…… 내가 기꺼이**gladly** 너한테서 **from you** 그 암소를 사 주마**buy the cow**." 노인이 말했다.

"이것들 좀 봐라**take a look at these**." 노인은 잭에게 아름다운 콩 몇 알**some beautiful beans**을 보여 주었다. "이것들은 마법의 콩**magic beans**이란다. 너한테 암소 값으로 **for your cow** 마법의 콩 다섯 알 **five magic beans**을 주마." 노인이 제안했다**offer**.

잭은 마법의 콩에 **by the magic beans** 반했다(감탄했다)**be impressed**. 그래서 콩 다섯 알을 받고 암소를 노인에게 팔았다. 잭은 아주 뿌듯했다**be proud of himself**.

그러나 잭이 집에 돌아오자**get home** 어머니는 화를 냈다**be angry**.

"뭐라고**what**? 콩이라고**beans**!" 어머니가 소리쳤다. "우리 암소를 콩 다섯 알에 팔았다고? 이 멍청한 녀석아**you fool**! 바보나**only a fool** 암소를 콩 다섯 알과 맞바꿀**exchange a cow for five beans** 게다. 네가 먹을 저녁밥은 없다**no supper**. 당장**right now** 가서 잠이나 자거라**go to bed**."

어머니는 잭을 나무랐다. 그리고 나서 잭의 어머니는 콩알들을 창밖으로 던져 버렸다**throw the beans out the window**.

다음 날 아침**the next morning** 잭이 창밖을 내다보니**look out the window** 놀라운 광경**an amazing sight**이 보였다. 창가에**next to the window** 어마어마한 콩나무 한 그루**an enormous beanstalk**가 자라나 있었던 것이다. 콩나무는 아주 높이 뻗어 올라가서**rise so high** 잭은 그 끝이 어디인지**where it ends** 보이지도 않았다**cannot see**.

"그 영감님 말이 맞았어. 그것들은 마법의 콩이었던 거야." 잭은 중얼거렸다. 잭은 콩나무를 오르기**climb up the beanstalk** 시작했다. 몇 시간이나**for hours and hours** 기어올랐다. 마침내**finally** 잭은 콩나무 꼭대기에 이르렀다**get to the top**.

GRAMMAR POINT

so that... : …하기 위해서, …하도록   **so ~ that...** : 아주 ~해서 …하다

- I'm going to town to sell the cow **so that** we can buy some food.
  우리가 음식을 좀 살 수 있도록 이 암소를 팔러 읍내에 가고 있어요.

- It rose **so high that** he could not see where it ended.
  그것은 아주 높이 뻗어 올라가서 그는 그 끝이 어디인지 보이지도 않았다.

[p. 26-27]

There, / high in the clouds, / was a huge castle.

"I wonder / who lives there," thought Jack / as he walked / toward the castle. When Jack got to the castle, / he tripped over an enormous foot. **It belonged to / the biggest woman / he had ever seen.**

"You, boy," said the woman. "What are you doing here? My husband / is a giant. He loves to eat / little boys like you."

"Please / **don't let him eat me**," answered Jack. "I just came here / because I smelled breakfast, / and I am so hungry."

The giant's wife / was kindhearted, / so she gave Jack / some food. All of a sudden, / the ground / began to shake. "Hide, boy," said the woman. "My husband is coming."

"Fee, fi, fo, fum, / I can smell a little boy," said the giant / when he walked into the kitchen. "Are you cooking a boy / for me / for breakfast?"

"No, dear," she answered. "You probably smell the boy / you ate last week."

The giant sat down / and ate his breakfast. Then, / he took out a huge bag. It was filled with gold. After a while, / he fell asleep / at the table. Then, / Jack came out / quietly. He took the bag of gold / and **ran out of the castle**. He climbed down the beanstalk / and showed his mother the gold. She was very pleased with him.

Jack and his mother / lived happily. But they soon / **ran out of gold**. Jack decided / to climb the beanstalk again. He got to the top of the beanstalk / and walked to the castle.

"Oh, it's you again?" said the giant's wife. "Go away! You're a bad boy. Didn't you take / my husband's gold?"

"That wasn't me. That was another boy," answered Jack.

The giant's wife / believed Jack. She gave him / some food. Then, / the ground / began to shake. "He's coming," said the woman. "Hide, / or he will find you."

- **huge** 아주 큰, 거대한 • **castle** 성 • **trip over** ~에 걸려 넘어지다 • **belong to** ~에 속하다, ~의 것이다
- **husband** 남편 ≠ wife • **giant** 거인 • **kindhearted** 마음씨 착한 ≠ mean • **all of a sudden** 갑자기
- **shake** 흔들리다 • **probably** 아마도, 필시 • **sit down** 앉다 • **take out** (속에 있던 것을) 꺼내다, 내놓다
- **be filled with** ~로 가득 차다 • **fall asleep** 잠들다 ≠ wake up • **take** 잡다, 가져가다 *take–took–taken
- **run** 뛰다, 달아나다 • **out of** ~의 밖으로 • **run out** (~이) 다 떨어지다, (~을) 다 써버리다 • **be pleased with** ~에 기뻐하다, ~에 만족하다 • **go away** 가 버리다, 사라지다 • **find** 찾다, 찾아내다 ≠ hide

CLOSE UP

1. **It belonged to the biggest woman he had ever seen.** 그것은 그가 지금껏 본 중에 몸집이 가장 큰 여자의 것이었다.
   〈최상급+주어+have/had ever seen〉은 '지금까지 본 중에 가장 ~한'이라는 의미.

2. **don't let him eat me** 그가 나를 잡아먹게 하지 말아 주세요
   〈let+목적어+동사원형〉은 '~가 …하게 놔두다/허락하다'라는 의미.

3. **ran out of the castle** 성 밖으로 도망쳤다
   〈run+out of〉로 '~ 밖으로 도망치다/달아나다'라는 의미.

4. **ran out of gold** 황금이 다 떨어졌다
   〈run out+of〉로 '~이 다 떨어지다/바닥나다'라는 의미.

Step 1

구름 속 높은 곳에**high in the clouds** 거대한 성이 한 채**a huge castle** 있었다.

"저기에 누가 사는지**who lives there** 궁금한걸**wonder**." 잭은 성을 향해 걸어가며**walk toward the castle** 이런 생각을 했다. 잭은 성에 도착해서**get to the castle** 거대한 발에 걸려 넘어졌다**trip over an enormous foot**. 그것은 잭이 지금껏 본 중에 몸집이 가장 큰 여자**the biggest woman**의 발이었다.

"꼬마야**you, boy**. 여기에서 뭘 하고 있는 거니? 내 남편**my husband**은 거인**a giant**이란다. 그이는 너같이 작은 사내아이들**little boys like you**을 즐겨 잡아먹지**love to eat**." 여자가 말했다.

"남편이 저를 잡아먹게 하지 말아 주세요**don't let him eat me**." 잭이 대답했다. "저는 아침식사 냄새를 맡고**smell breakfast** 여기 온**come here** 것뿐이고, 배가 너무 고파요**be so hungry**."

거인의 아내**the giant's wife**는 마음씨가 고와서**be kindhearted** 잭에게 먹을 것을 좀 주었다**give some food**. 갑자기**all of a sudden** 바닥**the ground**이 흔들리기 시작했다**begin to shake**. "얘야, 숨어라**hide**. 남편이 오고 있어**be coming**." 여자가 말했다.

"흠, 흠, 쿵, 쿵. 작은 사내아이 냄새가 난다**smell a little boy**." 거인은 부엌으로 들어서며**walk into the kitchen** 말했다. "내 아침식사로**for breakfast** 사내아이를 요리하고**cook a boy** 있는 건가?"

"아니에요, 여보**no, dear**. 아마 당신이 지난주에 먹은 사내아이 냄새일 거예요." 여자가 대답했다.

거인은 자리에 앉아**sit down** 아침을 먹었다**eat his breakfast**. 그런 다음 거대한 자루를 하나 꺼냈다**take out a huge bag**. 자루에는 황금이 가득 들어 있었다**be filled with gold**. 잠시 후**after a while** 거인은 식탁에서**at the table** 잠이 들었다**fall asleep**. 그러자 잭이 살금살금 나왔다**come out quietly**. 잭은 금이 든 자루를 가지고**take the bag of gold** 성 밖으로 도망쳤다**run out of the castle**. 잭은 콩나무를 내려와**climb down the beanstalk** 어머니에게 황금을 보여 주었다**show the gold**. 어머니는 잭에게 크게 만족했다(기뻐했다)**be pleased with him**.

잭과 어머니는 행복하게 살았다**live happily**. 그러나 그들은 곧 황금이 다 떨어졌다**run out of gold**. 잭은 다시**again** 콩나무에 올라가기로 마음먹었다**decide to climb**. 잭은 콩나무 꼭대기에 이르자 성으로 걸어갔다.

"아니, 또 너구나**you again**?" 거인의 아내가 말했다. "썩 사라지거라**go away**! 넌 나쁜 아이**a bad boy**다. 네가 내 남편의 황금을 가져가지**take my husband's gold** 않았느냐?"

"그건 제가 아니었어요**not me**. 다른 아이**another boy**였어요." 잭이 대답했다.

거인의 아내는 잭의 말을 믿었다**believe Jack**. 그녀는 잭에게 먹을 것을 주었다. 그때 바닥이 흔들리기 시작했다. "남편이 온다. 몸을 숨기거라**hide**. 안 그러면**or** 남편이 널 찾아낼**find you** 거야." 여자가 말했다.

GRAMMAR POINT

명령문 + or... : ~해라. 안 그러면…

- **Hide, or** he will find you. 숨어라. 안 그러면 그가 널 찾아낼 거야. (= **If you don't hide,** he will find you.)

- **Hurry up, or** you'll be late. 서둘러. 안 그러면 늦을 거야. (= **If you don't hurry up,** you'll be late.)

[p. 28-29]

"Fee, fi, fo, fum, / you have a boy / for me / today, / don't you?" said the giant.

"Sorry, dear. I don't. But here are / some bacon and eggs / for you," she said.

After breakfast, / the giant said, "Wife, / bring me my hen. I want / some golden eggs." So she brought the hen / to the table. "Lay," said the giant. The hen / laid a golden egg.

After a while, / the giant fell asleep / at the table. Then, / Jack came out of his hiding place. He grabbed the hen / and ran out of the castle. He climbed down the beanstalk / and showed his mother the hen. They became very rich.

But **Jack got bored** / one day, / so he climbed up the beanstalk / again. He went to the castle, / but he hid from the giant's wife / this time.

"Fee, fi, fo, fum, / I can smell a little boy," roared the giant.

"Can you? Maybe / it's that thief / again," said the giant's wife. "Let's find that boy."

They looked in the kitchen, / but they could not find Jack. Soon, / they gave up / and ate breakfast. Then, / the giant got his harp. "Play," he said. The harp / began to play / some beautiful music.

After a while, / the giant fell asleep / at the table. Then, / Jack came out of his hiding place. He grabbed the harp / and ran out of the castle. But the harp called out, "Master, save me! The boy is stealing me!"

The giant woke up / and chased Jack. Jack ran to the beanstalk / and began climbing down it. The giant / started climbing down, / too.

"Mother, / **get the axe**. Quick! The big giant is coming," shouted Jack. When he reached the bottom, / he grabbed the axe. He cut down the beanstalk.

The beanstalk fell, / and the giant fell down / with it. His head / hit the ground. Thump! He was dead. Jack never went back / to the giant's castle.

- **bring** 가져오다 *bring–brought–brought • **hiding place** 숨는 곳, 은신처 • **grab** 움켜쥐다 • **get bored** 지루해지다, 심심해지다 ≠ excited • **roar** 고함치다, 으르렁거리다 • **thief** 도둑 • **give up** 포기하다 • **call out** 소리치다, 외치다 • **master** (하인, 노예 등의) 주인 • **steal** 훔치다 • **wake up** (잠에서) 깨다 ≠ fall asleep • **chase** 뒤쫓다 • **cut down** 베어 버리다, 잘라 내다 • **fall down** (땅에) 떨어지다 • **be dead** 죽다

CLOSE UP

1. **Jack got bored** 잭은 따분해졌다
   〈get+형용사〉는 '~하게 되다'라는 뜻으로 상태의 변화를 나타냄.
2. **get the axe** 도끼 가져오세요
   get은 어떤 것을 '가져오다'라는 뜻으로도 쓰임.

"흠, 흠, 쿵, 쿵. 오늘 내게 줄 사내아이가 있군have a boy for me. 그렇지?" 거인이 말했다.

"미안해요, 여보sorry, dear. 아니에요. 하지만 여기 당신한테 줄 베이컨과 달걀some bacon and eggs이 있어요." 여자가 말했다.

아침식사를 마친 뒤after breakfast 거인이 말했다. "마누라, 내 암탉을 가져와bring my hen. 황금 알이 몇 개 필요해want some golden eggs." 그래서 여자는 암탉을 식탁으로 가져왔다. "알을 낳아라lay." 거인이 말했다. 암탉은 황금 알을 하나 낳았다lay a golden egg.

잠시 후 거인은 식탁에서 잠이 들었다. 그러자 잭이 숨어 있던 곳his hiding place에서 나왔다. 잭은 암탉을 움켜잡고grab the hen 성 밖으로 달아났다. 잭은 콩나무를 내려와 어머니에게 암탉을 보여 주었다show the hen. 그들은 큰 부자가 되었다become very rich.

그러나 어느 날 잭은 따분해져서get bored 다시 콩나무를 올라갔다. 잭은 성으로 갔지만go to the castle, 이번에는this time 거인의 아내한테서 몸을 숨겼다hide from the giant's wife.

"흠, 흠, 쿵, 쿵. 작은 사내아이 냄새가 난다." 거인이 으르렁거리는 소리로 말했다roar.

"그래요? 아마 또 그 도둑놈that thief again인가 봐요." 거인의 아내가 말했다. "그 꼬맹이를 찾아냅시다let's find that boy."

그들은 부엌을 살펴보았지만look in the kitchen 잭을 찾아낼 수 없었다cannot find Jack. 이내 그들은 포기하고give up 아침을 먹었다. 그런 다음 거인은 그의 하프를 집어 들었다get his harp. "연주해라play." 거인이 말했다. 하프가 아름다운 음악을 연주하기play some beautiful music 시작했다.

잠시 후 거인은 식탁에서 잠이 들었다. 그러자 잭이 숨어 있던 곳에서 나왔다come out of his hiding place. 잭은 하프를 움켜잡고grab the harp 성 밖으로 달아났다. 하지만 하프가 소리쳤다call out. "주인님master, 저를 구해 주세요save me! 이 사내아이가 저를 훔쳐 가요steal me!"

거인은 잠에서 깨어나wake up 잭을 뒤쫓았다chase Jack. 잭은 콩나무로 달려가서run to the beanstalk 나무를 내려가기climb down it 시작했다. 거인도 내려가기 시작했다.

"엄마, 도끼를 가져오세요get the axe. 빨리요quick! 큰 거인이 오고 있어요." 잭이 소리쳤다. 잭은 바닥에 도달하자reach the bottom 도끼를 움켜쥐었다grab the axe. 잭은 콩나무를 찍어 넘어뜨렸다cut down the beanstalk.

콩나무가 쓰러지자fall 거인도 함께 떨어졌다fall down. 거인의 머리가 땅에 부딪쳤다hit the ground. 쿵thump! 거인은 숨이 끊어졌다be dead. 잭은 결코never 다시 거인의 성으로 가지go back to the giant's castle 않았다.

> **GRAMMAR POINT**
>
> **부가의문문** ⇨ 앞 문장이 긍정이면 부정으로, 앞 문장이 부정이면 긍정으로 묻는다.
>
> - You have a boy for me today, **don't you?** 오늘 내게 줄 사내아이가 있군. 그렇지?
> - You are cooking a boy for me, **aren't you?** 내게 줄 사내아이를 요리하고 있군. 그렇지?
> - You don't have much money, **do you?** 돈이 별로 없군. 그렇지?
> - You are not the thief, **are you?** 넌 그 도둑이 아니야. 그렇지?

The Ugly Duckling

One summer / in a country farmyard, / Mother Duck / was sitting on her new eggs. She sat on them / for a long time. Finally, / the eggs / began to crack. Six little ducklings / popped out / and started to cry out, / "Quack, quack!" Mother Duck was very pleased. "My little ducklings!" she said.

She looked inside her nest. One egg / had not opened.

"That's strange," she thought. "This egg is bigger / than the other ones."

Mother Duck / **couldn't recall** / **laying that seventh egg**. How did it get there? "Did I count the eggs / wrongly?" Mother Duck wondered.

An old duck / came by / to see the ducklings.

"Hello, / Mother Duck. I see / your eggs / have hatched. How are the ducklings?" the old duck asked.

"Almost all of them / have hatched. **There is** / **only one egg left**," Mother Duck answered.

"That egg / looks strange. It looks like / a turkey egg. Leave it alone," said the old duck.

"No, / I can't do that. It's my egg, / so **I must wait for it**," said Mother Duck. She got back into her nest / and sat on the big egg. After a while, / the egg finally hatched.

They looked at the last baby duckling / with great surprise. He looked nothing like / the other ducks. In fact, / he did not look like / much of a duck / at all. He was big, gray, ugly, and strange looking.

"Well, / he certainly is / an unusual-looking duckling," said the old duck.

"Hmm," said Mother Duck, "he was in the egg / for so long, / so **he must be** / **so big**. I am sure / he will become / a proper-looking duck."

- **farmyard** 농가의 뜰, 농장 앞마당 • **crack** 금이 가다 • **duckling** 새끼 오리 • **pop out** 튀어나오다
- **nest** 둥지 • **recall** 기억하다, 상기하다 • **wrongly** 잘못되게, 틀리게 • **wonder** 의아하다, 궁금하다
- **hatch** 알에서 깨다, 부화하다 • **look like** ~처럼 보이다 • **with great surprise** 아주 놀라서 • **in fact** 사실, 실은 • **ugly** 못생긴, 못난 • **unusual-looking** 이상하게 생긴, 특이하게 생긴 • **proper-looking** 제대로 생긴

CLOSE UP

1. **couldn't recall laying that seventh egg** 그 일곱 번째 알을 낳은 기억이 안 났다
   recall은 '기억해 내다'라는 의미. can't recall 하면 '기억이 안 난다'라는 뜻이 됨.

2. **There is only one egg left** 딱 한 개의 알만 남았어요
   〈there is/are ~ left〉는 '~이 남아 있다'라는 의미.

3. **I must wait for it** 그것을 기다려야 해요 / **he must be so big** 저렇게 커진 게 틀림없어요
   must는 '~해야 한다(의무, 필요)' 또는 '~임에 틀림없다(추측)'라는 의미. 문맥에 따라 적절한 의미를 파악하자.

미운 오리 새끼

어느 여름one summer 시골의 농장 뜰에서in a country farmyard 어미 오리Mother Duck가 새로 낳은 알들을 품고sit on her new eggs 있었다. 어미는 오랫동안for a long time 그 알들을 품었다. 마침내finally 알들이 금이 가기 시작했다begin to crack. 작은 새끼 오리 여섯 마리six little ducklings가 튀어나와pop out 큰 소리로 울기cry out 시작했다. "꽥꽥quack, quack!" 어미 오리는 무척 기뻤다be pleased. "내 귀여운 새끼들my little ducklings!" 어미가 말했다.

어미는 둥지 안을 살펴보았다look inside her nest. 알 한 개가 부화하지 않았다.

"그거 이상하네be strange. 이 알은 다른 알들보다 더 크잖아be bigger." 하고 어미는 생각했다.

어미 오리는 그 일곱 번째 알을 낳은lay that seventh egg 기억이 안 났다cannot recall. 그 알이 어떻게how 거기 있게 된get there 걸까? "내가 알들을 잘못 세었나count the eggs wrongly?" 어미 오리는 의아해했다wonder.

늙은 오리 한 마리an old duck가 새끼 오리들을 보러see the ducklings 잠깐 들렀다come by.

"안녕하시오hello, 오리 엄마Mother Duck. 당신 알들your eggs이 부화했구려hatch. 새끼들은 좀 어떤가?" 늙은 오리가 물었다.

"거의 다almost all of them 부화했어요. 딱 한 개의 알만only one egg 남았네요left." 어미 오리가 대답했다.

"그 알은 이상해 보이는군look strange. 마치 칠면조 알처럼 보이는걸look like a turkey egg. 그냥 내버려 둬요leave it alone." 늙은 오리가 말했다.

"안 돼요no. 그럴 수 없어요can't do that. 이건 내 알my egg이니까 기다려야wait for it 해요." 어미 오리가 말했다. 어미는 둥지로 돌아가서get back into her nest 그 커다란 알을 품었다sit on the big egg. 얼마 뒤after a while 알이 마침내 부화했다finally hatch.

그들은 마지막으로 나온 새끼 오리the last baby duckling를 기절초풍하며with great surprise 바라보았다. 녀석은 다른 오리들과 조금도 닮지 않았던look nothing like the other ducks 것이다. 사실in fact 그 새끼 오리는 전혀 오리처럼 보이지 않았다do not look like much of a duck. 그 오리는 몸집이 크고big 회색인데다gray 못생기고ugly 이상해 보였다strange looking.

"음well, 확실히certainly 특이하게 생긴unusual-looking 녀석이로군." 늙은 오리가 말했다.

"흠hmm, 쟤는 알 속에in the egg 너무 오래for so long 있어서 저렇게 커진be so big 게 틀림없어요. 분명히 제대로 생긴proper-looking 오리가 될 거예요." 어미 오리가 말했다.

GRAMMAR POINT

look + 형용사 : ~하게 보이다   **look like + 명사** : ~처럼 보이다, ~을 닮다

- That egg **looks** strange. 그 알은 이상해 보이는군.
- It **looks like** a turkey egg. 그것은 칠면조 알처럼 보이는걸.
- He **looked** nothing **like** the other ducks. 그는 다른 오리들과 조금도 닮지 않았다.
- He did not **look like** much of a duck at all. 그는 전혀 오리의 모습을 닮지 않았다.

[p. 32–33]

　　Mother Duck / took her children / to the pond. They all / jumped into the pond / one by one. The ugly duckling / swam very well. Actually, / he swam even better / than the others. Mother Duck was pleased.
　　All of the animals / gathered around / Mother Duck and her ducklings. "What a beautiful family!" they all said. Then, / they noticed / the ugly duckling. "What is wrong / with that big duckling? He's very ugly," they said. One of the ducks / even pecked at the ugly duckling. This made the ugly duckling / very sad.
　　Mother Duck and her ducklings / went swimming / in the pond / every day. And, / every day, / the ducks and other animals / laughed at the ugly duckling. Even the farm girl / disliked the ugly duckling. "Go away," she said. "You are an ugly duckling."
　　The ugly duckling / felt very sad. "Nobody loves me. They all tease me! Why am I different / from my brothers?"
　　One night, / he ran away / from the farm. He traveled / a long, long way / until he finally found / a huge field. He soon fell asleep. When he woke up, / he was by a lake. He looked up in the sky / and saw two geese.
　　"You look very strange," they said. "But we like you. Do you want / to fly with us?" they asked the ugly duckling.
　　The ugly duckling agreed, / but he suddenly heard / a loud noise. "Bang! Bang!"
　　The two geese / fell to the ground. They were dead. In the distance, / the ugly duckling / saw some men / with hunting rifles. He got very scared. He ran away / from the hunters. He ran and ran / until he was very far away.

- **pond** 연못　• **swim** 헤엄치다 *swim-swam-swum　• **better than** ~보다 더 나은　• **gather around** ~ 주위에 모여들다　• **notice** 알아채다, 주목하다　• **peck at** (부리 등으로) ~을 쪼다　• **laugh at** ~을 비웃다, ~을 놀리다　• **dislike** 싫어하다　• **tease** 놀리다　• **run away from** ~에서 도망치다　• **wake up** (잠에서) 깨어나다　• **goose** 기러기 *복수형: geese　• **fly** 날다　• **agree** 동의하다　• **loud** 시끄러운　• **noise** 시끄러운 소리, 잡음　• **in the distance** 멀리서　• **rifle** 소총, 엽총, 장총　• **get scared** 겁이 나다, 두렵다　• **hunter** 사냥꾼　• **far away** 멀리

CLOSE UP

1. **This made the ugly duckling very sad.** 이것은 미운 오리 새끼를 매우 서글프게 했다.
   〈make+목적어+형용사〉의 형식으로 쓰면 '~을 …하게 만들다'라는 의미.
2. **went swimming in the pond** 연못으로 헤엄치러 갔다
   〈go+V-ing〉는 '~하러 가다'라는 의미. ex) go fishing(낚시하러 가다) / go climbing(등산 가다)
3. **Why am I different from my brothers?** 왜 나는 내 형제들과 다른 걸까?
   〈be different from ~〉은 '~와 다르다'라는 의미.
4. **ran away from the farm** 농장에서 뛰쳐나갔다 / **ran away from the hunters** 사냥꾼들을 피해 달아났다
   〈run away from ~〉은 '~에서 달아나다/도망가다'라는 의미.

어미 오리는 새끼들을 연못으로 데려갔다**take her children to the pond**. 새끼들은 모두 한 마리씩 **one by one** 연못으로 뛰어들었다**jump into the pond**. 미운 오리 새끼**the ugly duckling**는 헤엄을 매우 잘 쳤다**swim very well**. 정말로**actually** 다른 새끼 오리들보다 헤엄을 훨씬 더 잘**even better** 쳤다. 어미 오리는 흐뭇했다.

모든 동물들**all of the animals**이 어미 오리와 새끼 오리들 주위에 모여들었다**gather**. "참으로 보기 좋은 가족**a beautiful family**이야!" 다들 입을 모아 말했다. 그리고는 미운 오리 새끼에게 주목했다**notice the ugly duckling**. "저 덩치 큰 오리 새끼는 뭐가 잘못된 거지**what is wrong**? 정말 못생겼군**be ugly**." 동물들이 말했다. 오리들 중 한 마리**one of the ducks**는 심지어 미운 오리 새끼를 쪼기까지 했다**peck at the ugly duckling**. 이것은 미운 오리 새끼를 몹시 서글프게 했다**make the ugly duckling very sad**.

어미 오리와 새끼 오리들은 날마다**every day** 연못에**in the pond** 헤엄치러 갔다**go swimming**. 그리고 날마다 오리들과 다른 동물들은 미운 오리 새끼를 놀려 댔다**laugh at the ugly duckling**. 농장 주인의 딸**the farm girl**까지도 미운 오리 새끼를 싫어했다**dislike the ugly duckling**. "저리 가**go away**. 넌 미운 오리 새끼야." 주인집 딸은 이렇게 말했다.

미운 오리 새끼는 무척 슬펐다**feel sad**. "아무도**nobody** 날 사랑하지**love me** 않아. 다들 나를 못살게 군다고**tease me**! 왜**why** 나는 내 형제들과 다른**be different** 걸까?"

어느 날 밤**one night** 미운 오리 새끼는 농장에서 뛰쳐나갔다(도망쳤다)**run away from the farm**. 미운 오리 새끼는 먼먼 길을 이동한**travel a long, long way** 끝에 마침내 드넓은 들판을 발견했다**find a huge field**. 그리고 곧 잠이 들었다**fall asleep**. 잠에서 깨어**wake up** 보니 미운 오리 새끼는 호숫가에**by lake** 있었다. 하늘을 올려다보니**look up in the sky** 기러기 두 마리가 보였다**see two geese**.

"넌 참 이상하게 생겼구나." 그들이 말했다. "하지만 우린 네가 마음에 든다**like you**. 우리와 함께 날지**fly with us** 않을래?" 그들이 미운 오리 새끼에게 물었다.

미운 오리 새끼가 그러겠노라고**agree** 했는데, 갑자기**suddenly** 큰 소음 **a loud noise**이 들렸다. "탕**bang**! 탕!"

두 기러기가 땅에 떨어졌다**fall to the ground**. 그들은 숨이 끊어졌다**be dead**. 미운 오리 새끼는 멀리서**in the distance** 몇몇 사내들**some men**이 엽총을 들고 있는**with hunting rifles** 모습을 보았다. 미운 오리 새끼는 너무 겁이 났다**get scared**. 그래서 사냥꾼들을 피해 달아났다**run away from the hunters**. 아주 먼 곳에**very far away** 이를 때까지 달리고 또 달렸다**run and run**.

GRAMMAR POINT

비교급 + than... : ···보다 더 ~한 / ~하게

⇨ 비교급은 형용사나 부사에 -er을 붙이며, 3음절 이상일 경우는 그 앞에 **more**를 붙인다.

- He swam even **better than** the others. 그는 다른 애들보다 헤엄을 훨씬 더 잘 쳤다.
- This egg is **bigger than** the other ones. 이 알은 다른 것들보다 더 크다.
- He is **more beautiful than** any other bird. 그는 다른 어떤 새보다 더 아름답다.

[p. 34-35]

    Finally, / he found an old hut / in the forest. He entered the hut. There were / a woman, a cat, and a hen. The woman was very old. "What are you? A duck?" she asked. "How wonderful! You can stay here / and lay eggs for me."
    The next day, / the cat asked the ugly duckling, "Where are your eggs?"
    "I don't have any eggs," he answered.
    "Then you are useless. You must leave," the hen said.
    The ugly duckling / left the hut. **The weather / was getting colder.**
    One day / at sunrise, / he saw / something beautiful and strange / overhead. It was / a flight of beautiful birds / —three swans! They had long necks / and soft white wings. They were migrating south.
    "Oh, what beautiful birds!" he thought. He called to them. "Who are you? Take me with you." But they did not hear him.
    Winter came, / and the water in the lake / froze. **The poor ugly duckling / could not even swim / in the water.** He was cold / and had no food to eat.
    A farmer / walked by the lake. He saw the ugly duckling / lying on the ice. "You poor bird," he said. "I will take you home / and help you." He picked up the ugly duckling / and took him home. The man had / a wife, a son, and a daughter. **They took good care of / the ugly duckling.** Slowly, / **he started to get better.** Thanks to them, / the ugly duckling / was able to survive / the cold winter.
    However, / by springtime, / he had grown so big. The farmer **decided / to set the ugly duckling free** / by the pond.

• **hut** 오두막   • **lay an egg** 알을 낳다   • **useless** 소용없는, 쓸데없는   • **get colder** 추워지다   • **overhead** 머리 위로, 머리 위에   • **flight** (함께 나는 새의) 떼, 비행 편대   • **migrate** (새, 동물이 계절에 따라) 이동하다   • **freeze** (얼음이) 얼다 *freeze–froze–frozen   • **lie** 눕다, 누워 있다 *lying은 lie의 현재분사형   • **poor** 불쌍한, 가엾은   • **pick up** 집어 들다, 집어 올리다   • **take good care of** ~을 잘 돌보다   • **be able to** ~할 수 있다   • **survive** 살아남다, ~을 견뎌 내다   • **set free** 놓아주다, 석방하다

CLOSE UP

1. **The weather was getting colder.** 날씨가 점점 추워지고 있었다. / **he started to get better** 그는 나아지기 시작했다 (그는 회복되기 시작했다)
〈get + 비교급〉은 '점점 더 ~하게 되다'라는 의미.

2. **They took good care of the ugly duckling.** 그들은 미운 오리 새끼를 잘 보살폈다.
〈take care of ~〉는 '~을 돌보다/보살피다'라는 의미. '잘 돌본다'고 강조하려면 take good care of와 같이 good을 넣으면 된다.

3. **decided to set the ugly duckling free** 미운 오리 새끼를 놓아주기로 결정했다
〈decide to ~〉는 '~하기로 결정하다'라는 의미. 〈set ~ free〉는 '~을 (자유롭게) 놓아주다'라는 의미.

마침내 미운 오리 새끼는 숲 속에서in the forest 낡은 오두막 한 채를 발견했다find an old hut. 미운 오리 새끼는 그 오두막으로 들어갔다enter the hut. 여자a woman와 고양이a cat와 암탉a hen이 있었다. 여자는 나이가 매우 지긋한 할머니였다be very old. "너는 뭐냐what are you? 오리냐a duck?" 할머니가 물었다. "잘됐구나how wonderful! 여기에 머물면서stay here 내게 알을 낳아 주면lay eggs 되겠다."

다음 날the next day 고양이가 미운 오리 새끼에게 물었다. "네 알들your eggs은 어디에where 있니?" "나는 알이 없어요don't have any eggs." 미운 오리 새끼가 대답했다.

"그럼 넌 쓸모가 없구나be useless. 떠나 줘야겠다must leave." 암탉이 말했다.

미운 오리 새끼는 오두막을 떠났다leave the hut. 날씨the weather가 점점 더 추워지고get colder 있었다.

어느 날one day 해가 뜰 무렵at sunrise, 미운 오리 새끼는 무언가 아름답고 낯선 것something beautiful and strange이 머리 위로overhead 지나가는 걸 보았다. 그것은 아름다운 새 떼a flight였다. 바로 세 마리의 백조three swans였다! 백조들은 기다란 목long necks과 부드럽고 하얀 날개soft white wings를 가지고 있었다. 그들은 남쪽으로 이동하는migrate south 중이었다.

"아, 정말 아름다운 새들이다what beautiful birds!" 미운 오리 새끼는 생각했다. 녀석은 백조들에게 소리쳤다call to them. "당신들은 누구죠who are you? 나를 데려가 줘요take me with you." 그러나 백조들한테는 녀석의 소리가 들리지 않았다do not hear him.

겨울이 와서winter comes 호수의 물the water in the lake이 얼었다freeze. 가엾은poor 미운 오리 새끼는 물에서 헤엄도 칠 수 없게 되었다cannot even swim. 미운 오리 새끼는 추웠고be cold 먹을 만한 먹이도 없었다have no food to eat.

한 농부a farmer가 호숫가를 지나갔다walk by the lake. 그는 미운 오리 새끼가 얼음 위에 쓰러져 있는lie on the ice 걸 보았다. "가엾은 새로구나you poor bird." 그가 말했다. "내가 널 집으로 데려가서 take you home 도와주마help you." 농부는 미운 오리 새끼를 집어 들고pick up 집으로 데려갔다. 그 남자에게는 아내와 아들과 딸이 있었다. 그들은 미운 오리 새끼를 잘 보살폈다take good care of the ugly duckling. 미운 오리 새끼는 차츰slowly 회복되기get better 시작했다. 그들 덕분에thanks to them 미운 오리 새끼는 추운 겨울을 견뎌 낼survive the cold winter 수 있었다.

그렇지만 봄이 될 무렵by springtime 미운 오리 새끼는 몸집이 아주 크게 자라grow so big 있었다. 농부는 미운 오리 새끼를 연못가에by the pond 놓아주기로set free 결정했다.

GRAMMAR POINT

can : ~할 수 있다 ⇨ 어떤 것을 할 수 있는 능력을 나타내며, 과거형은 could이다.

be able to : ~할 수 있다 ⇨ can과 같은 의미이며, 과거형은 was/were able to이다.

- The poor ugly duckling **could** not even swim in the water.
  가엾은 미운 오리 새끼는 물에서 헤엄도 칠 수 없게 되었다.
- Thanks to them, the ugly duckling **was able to** survive the cold winter.
  그들 덕분에 미운 오리 새끼는 추운 겨울을 견뎌 낼 수 있었다.

[p. 36-37]

　　The ugly duckling / was alone again. He was swimming alone / in the pond. Then, suddenly, / he started to flap his wings / and flew into the sky. "I can fly. I can fly!" shouted the ugly duckling. "This is amazing."
　　The ugly duckling / flew all around the land. Then, / he looked down / and saw a garden. It was a garden / with a pond. "That's a beautiful garden," he thought. "I will go there."
　　He landed in the pond / in the garden. He looked over / and saw three swans. They were the three swans / he had seen in winter. "Oh, they are so beautiful," he thought. "I have to / speak to them."
　　But the ugly duckling / did not know / what to say. He suddenly felt shy. He looked down / into the water. Then, / he saw his reflection / in the water. He looked / just like the swans. He was not / an ugly duckling. He was a swan. "I'm a swan!" he cried.
　　"Mother, look," some children shouted. "There's a new swan. Isn't he beautiful? He's the most beautiful / of all the swans."
　　The children / threw some bread / into the pond / for him to eat. He was so pleased. All his life, / people had thought / he was ugly. Now, / they told him / how beautiful he was. It was / the happiest moment / of his life.

- **alone** 혼자, 혼자서   • **flap one's wings** 날개를 퍼덕이다   • **fly into** ~로 날다, ~로 날아가다   • **garden** 정원   • **land** 내려앉다, 상륙하다   • **look over** 주위를 둘러보다   • **shy** 부끄러운   • **look down into** ~ 속을 내려다보다   • **reflection** (거울, 물 등에) 비친 모습, 반영   • **the most beautiful** 가장 아름다운   • **throw** 던지다   *throw–threw–thrown   • **pleased** 기쁜, 만족한   • **the happiest moment** 가장 행복한 순간

CLOSE UP

1. **The ugly duckling was alone** 미운 오리 새끼는 혼자가 되었다 /
   He was swimming alone 그는 혼자 헤엄치고 있었다
   alone은 '혼자'라는 뜻의 형용사 또는 부사로 쓰인다. 하지만 명사 앞에는 쓰지 않는다. *ex*) the alone ugly duckling (×)

2. **They were the three swans he had seen in winter.** 그들은 녀석이 겨울에 보았던 그 세 마리 백조들이었다.
   기준이 되는 시제는 과거(were)인데, 겨울에 백조를 보았던 것은 이보다 먼저 발생한 일이므로 대과거임을 나타내는 과거완료(had seen) 시제를 썼다.

3. **for him to eat** 그가 먹을 수 있도록
   to부정사의 의미상 주어는 to부정사 앞에 〈for+목적격〉으로 나타낸다.

4. **All his life** 평생
   all one's life는 '평생', '태어나서부터 줄곧'이라는 의미. *ex*) all my life(내 평생)

30　Step 1

미운 오리 새끼는 다시 혼자가 되었다be alone. 녀석은 연못에서 혼자 헤엄치고swim alone 있었다. 그러다 갑자기 날개를 퍼덕이기flap his wings 시작하더니 하늘로 날아올랐다fly into the sky. "내가 날 수 있어can fly. 날 수 있다고!" 미운 오리 새끼는 소리쳤다. "정말 놀라운 일이야be amazing."

미운 오리 새끼는 땅을 빙 돌며 날았다fly all around the land. 그리고는 아래를 내려다보니look down 정원이 하나 보였다see a garden. 연못이 있는with a pond 정원이었다. "아름다운 정원a beautiful garden이구나. 저곳에 가go there 봐야지." 녀석은 생각했다.

미운 오리 새끼는 정원에 있는 연못에 내려앉았다land in the pond. 살펴보니look over 백조 세 마리가 보였다see three swans. 녀석이 겨울에 보았던see in winter 그 세 마리 백조들이었다. "아, 저들은 참으로 아름답구나. 저들에게 말을 걸어speak to them 봐야겠다." 하고 미운 오리 새끼는 생각했다.

그러나 미운 오리 새끼는 무슨 말을 해야 할지what to say 몰랐다do not know. 미운 오리 새끼는 갑자기 수줍어졌다feel shy. 녀석은 물 속을 내려다보았다look down into the water. 그때 물에 비친 자기 모습his reflection in the water이 보였다. 미운 오리 새끼는 꼭 그 백조들처럼 보였다look just like the swans. 미운 오리 새끼가 아니었다. 녀석은 백조였던 것이다. "내가 백조로구나!" 하고 녀석은 외쳤다.

"엄마, 보세요look." 어린아이들 몇 명이 소리쳤다. "새로운 백조a new swan가 있어요. 아름답지 않아요? 저 모든 백조들 중에서도of all the swans 가장 아름다워요be the most beautiful."

아이들은 연못에 빵을 던져서throw some bread 녀석이 먹을 수 있도록 했다. 녀석은 무척 기뻤다be pleased. 태어나서부터 줄곧all his life 사람들은 녀석이 못생겼다be ugly고 생각해 왔다. 하지만 이제는 now 녀석이 참으로 아름답다how beautiful he was고 말하는 것이 아닌가. 녀석의 삶에서of his life 가장 행복한 순간the happiest moment이었다.

GRAMMAR POINT

the + 최상급 : 가장 ~한 / ~하게

⇨ 최상급은 형용사나 부사에 -est를 붙이며, 3음절 이상일 경우는 그 앞에 most를 붙인다.

- He's **the most beautiful** of all the swans. 그는 모든 백조들 중에서 가장 아름답다.
- It was **the happiest** moment of his life. 그의 인생에서 가장 행복한 순간이었다.

The Ant and the Grasshopper

One summer day, / a grasshopper / hops into a field. He sings happily / because it is / a beautiful summer day. He sees an ant / pass by. The ant is working hard. It is carrying some corn / to its home.

"Why don't you stay and chat / with me?" asks the grasshopper. "That corn looks heavy. Why are you carrying it?"

"I'm saving food / for the winter," answers the ant. "I recommend / that you do the same thing. Then, / you will have / plenty of food / for the winter."

"Winter?" says the grasshopper. "Why worry about that? We have lots of food / right now. And winter is / a long time away."

The ant leaves the grasshopper. The ant works hard / every day, / so it gathers / lots of food. After a while, / the ant completely / fills its house / with food.

Meanwhile, / the grasshopper / stays in the field. But he does not work / at all. Instead, / he plays and sings / every day.

Soon, / summer turns to fall, / and fall turns to winter. When the weather gets colder, / the food starts to disappear. The grasshopper discovers / that he has no food / to eat. He looks over / at the ant's house. The ant has plenty of food / and a nice, warm house. The grasshopper realizes / how foolish he was.

That winter, / there is / lots of snow. Later, / when spring arrives, / the ant comes out of its house. The ant had enough food / during winter. Now, / it is ready / to start gathering food / for the next winter. When the ant looks around the field, / there is / no sign of the grasshopper.

- Moral: Work hard today / to prepare for tomorrow.

- **hop** 깡충깡충 뛰다 • **pass by** 지나가다 • **carry** (실어) 나르다 • **stay** 머물다 • **save** 저장하다, 모으다
- **recommend** 권하다 • **plenty of** 많은, 충분한 • **a long time away** 아직 먼 • **gather** 모으다
- **completely** 완전히, 온전히 • **meanwhile** 한편 • **get colder** 추워지다 • **disappear** 사라지다
- **discover** 발견하다, 알게 되다 • **look over** 둘러보다 • **realize** 깨닫다 • **foolish** 어리석은 • **be ready to** ~할 준비가 되다 • **sign** 징후, 조짐, 기색, 흔적 • **prepare for** ~을 준비하다, ~에 대비하다

CLOSE UP

1. **Why don't you stay and chat with me?** 나와 함께 머물며 이야기나 나누지 않을래?
   〈Why don't you ~?〉는 '~하는 게 어때?', '~하지 않을래?'라는 뜻으로 권유나 제안을 나타냄.

2. **plenty of food** 많은 식량 / **lots of food** 많은 식량 / **lots of snow** 많은 눈
   〈plenty of ~〉와 〈lots of ~〉는 둘 다 '많은 ~'이라는 의미.

3. **fills its house with food** 그의 집에 식량을 가득 장만한다
   〈fill ~ with...〉는 '~을 …로 가득 채우다'라는 의미.

4. **it is ready to start gathering food** 그것은 식량을 모으기 시작할 준비가 되어 있다
   〈be ready to ~〉는 '~할 준비가 되어 있다', '언제라도 ~할 수 있다'라는 의미.

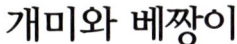

개미와 베짱이

어느 여름날one summer day 베짱이 한 마리a grasshopper가 들판으로 톡 뛰어 들어간다hop into a field. 때는 화창한 여름날a beautiful summer day이어서 베짱이는 행복하게 노래를 부른다sing happily. 베짱이 눈에 개미 한 마리an ant가 지나가는pass by 게 보인다. 개미는 열심히 일을 하고work hard 있다. 낟알을 집까지 운반하는carry some corn to its home 중이다.

"나와 함께with me 머물며 이야기나 나누지stay and chat 않을래?" 베짱이가 물어본다. "그 낟알that corn은 무거워 보이는구나look heavy. 그걸 왜 나르고 있는 거니?"

"겨울을 대비해for the winter 식량을 비축하는save food 거야." 개미가 대답한다. "너도 똑같이 하는 do the same thing 게 좋을 거야. 그러면 겨울에 먹을 식량이 풍부해have plenty of food지거든."

"겨울이라고?" 베짱이가 말한다. "왜why 그런 걱정을 하니worry about that? 당장right now 먹을 게 많이 있는데have lots of food. 게다가 겨울은 아직 멀었잖아a long time away."

개미는 베짱이를 떠난다leave the grasshopper. 개미는 날마다every day 열심히 일해서 먹이를 많이 모은다gather lots of food. 얼마 뒤after a while 개미는 집에다 식량을 하나 가득 장만한다fill its house with food.

한편meanwhile 베짱이는 들판에 머물러 있다stay in the field. 그러나 일은 전혀 하지 않는다. 대신에 날마다 놀면서 노래를 부른다play and sing.

얼마 안 있어soon 여름이 가을이 되고turn to fall, 가을은 겨울이 된다turn to winter. 날씨the weather가 더 추워지자get colder 먹이the food가 사라지기disappear 시작한다. 베짱이는 먹을 식량이 없다have no food to eat는 사실을 알게 된다discover. 베짱이는 개미네 집을 기웃거린다look over at the ant's house. 개미한테는 식량도 많고, 멋지고 따뜻한 집a nice, warm house도 있다. 베짱이는 자신이 얼마나 어리석었는지how foolish 깨닫는다realize.

그해 겨울that winter, 눈이 많이lots of snow 내린다. 나중에later 봄이 오자spring arrives 개미가 집 밖으로 나온다come out of its house. 개미는 겨울 동안during winter 먹이를 충분히 먹었다have enough food. 이제 이듬해 겨울을 나기 위해for the next winter 식량을 모으기gather food 시작할 준비가 되어 있다. 개미가 들판을 둘러보는데look around the field, 베짱이의 흔적은 없다no sign of the grasshopper.

- 교훈: 오늘 열심히 일해서 내일을 대비하라prepare for tomorrow.

GRAMMAR POINT

see + 목적어 + 동사원형 : ~가 …하는 것을 보다

⇨ see(보다), hear(듣다)와 같은 지각동사는 목적어 다음에 동사원형이 온다.

- He **sees** an ant **pass** by. 그는 개미 한 마리가 지나가는 것을 본다.

- All the animals **heard** the hare **brag** many times. 모든 동물들이 토끼가 자랑하는 것을 여러 번 들었다.

[p. 40-41]

The Hare and the Tortoise

One day, / a hare was bragging about / how fast he could run. "I am / the fastest animal / in the entire forest," he said. All the animals / were tired of hearing / the hare brag. They had heard his bragging / many times before.

The hare started / to make fun of the tortoise. "You are so slow," laughed the hare. "A snail could run faster / than you."

The tortoise smiled at the hare / and replied, "Yes, I am slow. But I bet / I can reach / the end of this field / before you. Let's run a race."

"Oh, really? It's a bet," said the hare. "All right, / everyone. Let's find out / who the faster animal is."

The tortoise and the hare / went to the starting line. All the animals / in the forest / gathered to watch. "Ready. Go," shouted the fox.

The hare raced off / and left the tortoise behind. The tortoise / simply kept moving / as fast as he could.

When the hare was halfway / across the field, / he looked back. The tortoise was / far behind him. "Ha," thought the hare. "It will take the tortoise all day / to finish. I'm going to / get some rest here." The hare rested, / but he soon fell asleep / in the warm sunshine.

The tortoise, / in the meantime, / walked and walked. He never stopped / until he got to the finish line.

A few hours later, / the hare woke up. "Oh, no!" the hare thought. He looked ahead / toward the finish line. The tortoise / was about to cross it. The hare ran / as fast as he could, / but it was too late. The tortoise / crossed the finish line / first. The tortoise had won.

• *Moral: Slow and steady / wins the race.*

• **brag** 뻐기다, 자랑하다 • **entire** 전체의, 모든 • **forest** 숲 • **tired of** ~이 지겨운, ~에 질린 • **make fun of** ~을 놀리다 • **bet** 장담하다, 내기하다; 내기 • **run a race** 경주를 하다 • **find out** 알아내다 • **race off** 빨리 달려 나가다 • **leave ~ behind** ~을 훨씬 앞서다 • **halfway** 절반쯤, 중간에 • **across** ~을 가로질러 • **look back** 뒤돌아보다 • **far behind** ~보다 훨씬 뒤에 • **get some rest** 휴식을 취하다, 쉬다 • **fall asleep** 잠들다 • **in the meantime** 한편, 그사이에 • **wake up** (잠에서) 깨다 • **finish line** 결승선 • **be about to** 막 ~하려고 하다 • **cross** 건너다, 지나다 • **steady** 꾸준한, 한결같은

CLOSE UP

1. **were tired of hearing the hare brag** 토끼가 자랑하는 것을 듣는 데 신물이 났다
   〈be tired of ~〉는 '~에 넌더리가 나다', '~에 신물이 나다'라는 의미.

2. **It will take the tortoise all day to finish.** 거북이는 끝나려면 온종일 걸릴 거야.
   〈it takes (+A)+시간+to...〉는 '(A가) …하는 데 시간이 ~만큼 걸린다'라는 의미.

3. **was about to cross it** 그것을 넘으려는 참이었다
   〈be about to ~〉는 '막 ~하려는 참이다'라는 의미.

토끼와 거북이

어느 날one day 토끼a hare가 자신이 얼마나 빨리how fast 달릴 수 있는지can run 자랑하고brag 있었다. "숲을 통틀어서in the entire forest 내가 가장 빠른 동물the fastest animal이야." 토끼가 말했다. 동물들은 모두all the animals 토끼가 자랑하는 것을 듣는 데 신물이 났다be tired of hearing. 전에도 수없이many times 그의 자랑his bragging을 들었기hear it 때문이다.

토끼가 거북이를 놀리기make fun of the tortoise 시작했다. "넌 너무 느려be slow." 토끼가 조롱하며 말했다. "달팽이a snail도 너보다는 빨리faster than you 달릴 수 있을 거야."

거북이가 토끼에게 미소를 지으며smile at the hare 대답했다. "맞아, 난 느려. 하지만 내가 너보다 먼저before you 이 들판 끝에 도착할reach the end of this field 수 있을걸. 경주해run a race 보자."

"어, 정말이지oh, really? 내기a bet 하는 거다." 토끼가 말했다. "자, 여러분all right, everyone. 누가 더 빠른 동물the faster animal인지 알아봅시다find out."

거북이와 토끼는 출발선the starting line으로 갔다. 숲 속 동물들이 모두 구경하려고 모였다gather. "준비ready, 출발go." 여우가 소리쳤다.

토끼는 쏜살같이 달려 나가서race off 거북이를 훨씬 앞섰다leave the tortoise behind. 거북이는 그저 최대한 빨리as fast as he can 꾸준히 나아갔다keep moving.

토끼가 들판을 반쯤 가로질러halfway across the field 가서 뒤를 돌아보았다look back. 거북이는 토끼보다 한참 뒤처져far behind him 있었다. 토끼는 생각했다. "하ha, 거북이는 끝나려면to finish 온종일 걸릴take all day 거야. 나는 여기서 조금 쉬어야겠다get some rest." 토끼는 휴식을 취했다rest. 하지만 따뜻한 햇볕 속에서in the warm sunshine 곧 잠들어 버렸다fall asleep.

그 사이에in the meantime 거북이는 걷고 또 걸었다walk and walk. 거북이는 결승선the finish line에 도착할 때까지 결코 멈추지 않았다never stop.

몇 시간 뒤a few hours later 토끼가 잠에서 깨어났다wake up. "아뿔싸oh, no!" 하고 토끼는 생각했다. 토끼는 결승선 쪽으로 앞을 내다보았다look ahead. 거북이가 결승선을 넘으려는 참이었다be about to cross it. 토끼는 최대한 빨리 달렸지만, 때는 이미 너무 늦었다be too late. 거북이가 먼저 결승선을 넘었다cross the finish line. 거북이가 이긴win 것이다.

교훈: 천천히 꾸준히 하면slow and steady 경주에서 승리한다win the race.

GRAMMAR POINT

as ~ as one can/could : 최대한 ~하게 ⇒ as ~ as possible로 바꿔 쓸 수 있다.

- The tortoise simply kept moving **as** fast **as he could.**
  거북이는 그저 최대한 빨리 꾸준히 나아갔다. (= **as fast as possible**)

- The hare ran **as** fast **as he could.** 토끼는 최대한 빨리 달렸다. (= **as fast as possible**)

- Try **as** hard **as you can.** 최대한 열심히 노력해라. (= **as hard as possible**)

[p. 42-43]

The Sick Lion

Once, / there was / a very old lion. As he got older, / he became weak and slow. He could no longer / hunt animals. So he was not able to / eat any food.

The lion was sure / he would soon die. He was very sad. As he slowly walked home, / the lion told a bird / about his sad situation. Soon, / all of the animals / in the forest / heard about the lion.

The other animals / felt sorry for the lion. "That's terrible," they said. "We should visit the lion / and see / how he is doing." So, / one by one, / they went to visit the lion / in his cave.

The lion was old and weak, / but he was also very wise. As each animal came into his cave, / they were easy / to catch and eat. Soon, / the old lion / became fat.

Still, / he kept pretending / to be sick. And the animals / kept going / into the lion's cave. After a while, / many of the animals / of the forest / had disappeared.

One day, / early in the morning, / the fox went to the lion's cave. The fox was very wise, / too. He slowly walked / close to the cave. Standing outside the cave, / the fox called out, "Hello. How are you feeling now?"

The lion answered, "I am not doing / very well. Why don't you come in? I can't see you / very well. Come closer / and tell me / some kind words. I am old / and will die soon."

While the lion was talking, / the fox was looking closely / at the ground. The fox suddenly realized / what the lion was doing.

Finally, / the fox looked up / and answered, "No thank you. I can see many footprints / entering your cave. But I cannot see any footprints / leaving your cave."

• Moral: A wise person learns / from the misfortunes of others.

- **weak** 약한 ≠ strong • **hunt** 사냥하다 • **die** 죽다 • **situation** 상황, 처지 • **feel sorry for** ~을 불쌍하게 여기다 • **terrible** 심한, 지독한 • **one by one** 하나씩, 차례로 • **cave** 동굴 • **wise** 현명한 • **pretend** ~인 체하다 • **disappear** 사라지다 • **stand** 서다 • **call out** 외치다 • **closer** 더 가까이 • **closely** 자세히, 주의 깊게 • **realize** 깨닫다 • **footprint** 발자국 • **misfortune** 불운, 불행

CLOSE UP

1. **could no longer hunt animals** 동물 사냥을 더는 할 수 없었다
   no longer는 '더는 ~ 아니다', '이제는 ~ 아니다'라는 의미.
2. **felt sorry for the lion** 사자에게 연민을 느꼈다
   〈feel sorry for ~〉는 '~을 가엾게 여기다', '~에게 연민을 느끼다'라는 의미.
3. **footprints entering your cave** 굴에 들어간 발자국 / **footprints leaving your cave** 굴에서 나온 발자국
   entering...과 leaving...은 각각 footprints를 수식하며, 서로 의미 대조를 이루고 있다.

병든 사자

옛날에once 아주 늙은 사자 한 마리a very old lion가 있었다. 사자는 나이가 들면서get older 약해지고 느려졌다become weak and slow. 동물 사냥도 더는 할 수 없었다. 그래서 먹이도 먹을 수가 없었다.

사자는 자기가 곧 죽을will soon die 거라고 확신했다be sure. 몹시 슬펐다be sad. 사자는 천천히 집으로 걸어가면서walk home 어느 새한테 자신의 서글픈 처지his sad situation에 대해 이야기했다. 곧 숲속의in the forest 모든 동물들all of the animals이 사자의 소식을 듣게hear about the lion 되었다.

다른 동물들은 사자에게 연민을 느꼈다feel sorry for the lion. "참 안됐어that's terrible. 우리가 사자를 찾아가서visit the lion 어떻게 지내는지how he is doing 살펴보는 게 좋겠다." 동물들이 말했다. 그래서 동물들은 한 마리씩one by one 사자 굴로in his cave 사자를 방문하러 갔다go to visit the lion.

사자는 늙고 기운이 없었지만be old and weak 매우 지혜롭기도 했다be wise. 동물들이 하나씩each animal 자신의 굴로 들어오면come into his cave 잡아먹기catch and eat가 수월했다. 얼마 안 가서soon 늙은 사자는 살이 쪘다become fat.

그런데도still 사자는 계속 아픈 시늉을 했다pretend to be sick. 그리고 동물들은 계속 사자 굴로 들어갔다go into the lion's cave. 얼마 뒤after a while 숲 속 동물 다수가 자취를 감추었다disappear.

어느 날one day 아침 일찍early in the morning 여우the fox가 사자 굴로 갔다go to the lion's cave. 여우 역시 매우 지혜로웠다. 여우는 천천히 굴에 가까이 다가갔다walk close to the cave. 여우는 굴 밖에 서서stand outside the cave 큰 소리로 외쳤다call out. "안녕하세요hello. 지금은 좀 어떠신가요how are you feeling?"

사자가 대답했다. "썩 좋지는 않아I am not doing very well. 들어오는 게 어떤가why don't you come in? 자네가 잘 안 보이는군can't see you. 좀 더 가까이 와서come closer 내게 위로의 말some kind words이라도 해 주게. 난 늙어서 오늘내일 한다네."

사자가 말하는 동안 여우는 땅바닥을 유심히 살피고look closely at the ground 있었다. 여우는 문득suddenly 사자가 무슨 짓을 벌이고 있는지what the lion is doing 깨달았다realize.

마침내finally 여우가 고개를 들고look up 대답했다. "사양하겠어요no thank you. 어르신의 굴에 들어간enter your cave 발자국이 많이 보이네요can see many footprints. 하지만 굴에서 나온leave your cave 발자국은 보이질 않는군요cannot see any footprints."

- 교훈: 현명한 사람a wise person은 타인의 불행 the misfortunes of others으로부터 배운다.

GRAMMAR POINT

as (접속사) : ~하면서/~할 때/~하니까 ⇨ 상황에 따라 다양한 의미로 쓰임.

- **As** he got older, he became weak and slow. 나이가 들면서 그는 약해지고 느려졌다. (~하면서)
- **As** he slowly walked home, the lion told a bird about his sad situation.
  사자는 천천히 집으로 걸어가면서 어느 새한테 자신의 서글픈 처지에 대해 이야기했다. (~하면서)
- **As** each animal came into his cave, they were easy to catch and eat.
  동물들이 하나씩 자신의 굴로 들어오면 잡아먹기가 수월했다. (~할 때, ~하면)

- **As** it's raining, we should stay at home. 비가 오니까 집에 있는 게 좋겠다. (~하니까)

[p. 44-45]

The Boy Who Cried Wolf

There once was / a shepherd boy. He watched / a flock of sheep / at the bottom of a mountain. The shepherd boy / was bored / watching the sheep / all day / by himself. So he sometimes / talked to his dog / or played his pipe.

One day, / he became very bored. So he thought of a plan / to have some fun. He decided / to play a trick on the villagers. He ran down / toward the village / and cried out, "Wolf! Wolf!"

The villagers / heard the shepherd boy. The kind villagers / ran up the mountain / to help him. But when they arrived, / they found no wolf.

"Where is the wolf?"

The boy laughed / at the sight of / their angry faces.

"Ha, ha, ha! I fooled all of you," he said.

"Don't cry 'wolf,' / shepherd boy," said the villagers, "when there's no wolf!" They went back / down the mountain.

A few days later, / the shepherd boy / was bored again. So the boy / cried out again, "Wolf! Wolf!" When the villagers arrived, / the shepherd boy / was laughing at them / again.

One day / while the boy was watching the sheep, / a wolf really did come. It started / attacking his sheep. The frightened boy / ran toward the village / and shouted even louder / than before.

"Wolf! Wolf! A wolf / is killing my sheep!"

But the villagers thought / he was fooling them / again. So they didn't come. "He will not trick us / again," they said. Because none of them / went to help the boy, / the wolf killed / many of the sheep. And the flock scattered.

• Moral: No one / believes liars / even when they tell the truth.

• **shepherd** 양치기 • **flock of sheep** 양 떼 • **at the bottom of** ~의 아래에 • **bored** 지루한 • **by oneself** 혼자서 • **pipe** 피리 • **play a trick on** ~에게 장난하다, ~에게 속임수를 쓰다 • **villager** 마을 사람 • **run down** 달려 내려가다 ≠ run up • **fool** 장난하다, 속이다 • **cry** 외치다 • **laugh at** ~을 보고 웃다, ~을 비웃다 • **while** ~하는 동안에 • **attack** 공격하다 • **frightened** 놀란, 겁먹은 • **louder** 더 큰 소리로 • **kill** 죽이다 • **trick** 장난하다, 속이다 • **scatter** 흩어지다 • **liar** 거짓말쟁이 • **truth** 진실, 사실

CLOSE UP

1 **The Boy Who Cried Wolf** 늑대가 나타났다고 외친 소년
Who Cried Wolf는 The Boy를 수식하는 관계사절.

2 **decided to play a trick on the villagers** 마을 사람들을 속이기로 마음먹었다
⟨play a trick on ~⟩은 '~을 속이다', '~에게 장난 치다'라는 의미. 동사 fool과 trick도 같은 의미로 함께 알아 두자.

3 **at the sight of their angry faces** 그들의 화난 얼굴을 보고
⟨at the sight of ~⟩는 '~을 보고'라는 의미. sight(보기, 봄)는 동사 see(보다)의 명사형이다.

4 **a wolf really did come** 정말로 늑대 한 마리가 나타났다
여기서 did come은 came의 의미를 강조한 형태. 이처럼 do는 긍정문에서 동사의 의미를 강조할 수 있다.
ex) I do love you.(나 정말로 너 사랑해.) / She does look happy.(그녀는 정말 행복해 보여.)

늑대가 나타났다고 외친 소년 (양치기 소년과 늑대)

옛날에**once** 양치기 소년**a shepherd boy**이 살았다. 소년은 산기슭에서**at the bottom of a mountain** 양 떼**a flock of sheep**를 지켰다**watch**. 양치기 소년은 온종일**all day** 혼자서**by himself** 양들을 지키자니 **watch the sheep** 따분했다**be bored**. 그래서 간간이**sometimes** 자신의 개에게 말을 걸거나**talk to his dog** 피리를 불었다**play his pipe**.

어느 날**one day** 양치기 소년은 몹시 지루해졌다**become bored**. 그래서 재미를 좀 보려고**have some fun** 계획을 하나 생각했다**think of a plan**. 마을 사람들을 속여 먹기로**play a trick on the villagers** 결심한 것이다. 소년은 마을로**toward the village** 달려 내려가서**run down** 소리쳤다**cry out**. "늑대다**wolf**! 늑대가 나타났다**wolf**!"

마을 사람들이 양치기 소년의 소리를 들었다**hear the shepherd boy**. 마음씨 좋은 마을 사람들은 소년을 도우려고**help him** 산 위로 달려 올라갔다**run up the mountain**. 그러나 그들이 도착해**arrive** 보니 늑대는 하나도 보이지 않았다**find no wolf**.

"늑대가 어디에 있느냐?"

소년은 그들의 화난 얼굴을 보고**at the sight of their angry faces** 웃었다**laugh**.

"하하하**ha, ha, ha**! 제가 여러분 모두를 속인**fool all of you** 거예요." 소년이 말했다.

"이 양치기 녀석아, 늑대도 하나 없는데**there's no wolf** '늑대가 나타났다'고 외치지 마라**don't cry wolf**." 마을 사람들은 이렇게 말했다. 그리고 되돌아서 산을 내려갔다**go back down the mountain**.

며칠 뒤**a few days later** 양치기 소년은 다시 따분했다**be bored again**. 그래서 소년은 또 크게 소리쳤다**cry out again**. "늑대다! 늑대가 나타났다!" 마을 사람들이 도착해 보니 양치기 소년은 또 그들을 보고 웃고**laugh at them** 있었다.

어느 날 소년이 양들을 지키고 있는데, 정말로**really** 늑대 한 마리**a wolf**가 나타났다**come**. 늑대는 그의 양들을 공격하기**attack his sheep** 시작했다. 겁에 질린 소년**the frightened boy**은 마을로 달려가서 **run toward the village** 전보다 훨씬 더 큰 소리로 외쳤다**shout even louder**.

"늑대예요! 늑대가 나타났어요! 늑대 한 마리가 내 양들을 죽이고**kill my sheep** 있어요!"

그러나 마을 사람들은 소년이 또 자기들을 속이고**fool them again** 있다고 생각했다. 그래서 오지 않았다. "녀석이 또 다시 우리를 속이지는**trick us again** 못할걸." 하고 그들은 말했다. 그들 중 아무도**none of them** 소년을 도우러 가지**go to help the boy** 않았기 때문에 늑대가 양 여러 마리를 죽였다**kill many of the sheep**. 그리고 양 떼는 뿔뿔이 흩어져 버렸다**scatter**.

- 교훈: 거짓말쟁이**liars**는 진실을 말하더라도**tell the truth** 아무도**no one** 믿지**believe** 않는다.

GRAMMAR POINT

to부정사 (목적) : ~하기 위해서, ~하려고

- He thought of a plan **to have** some fun. 그는 재미를 좀 보려고 계획을 하나 생각했다.
- The kind villagers ran up the mountain **to help** him.
  마음씨 좋은 마을 사람들은 그를 도우려고 산 위로 달려 올라갔다.
- None of them went **to help** the boy. 그들 중 아무도 소년을 도우러 가지 않았다.

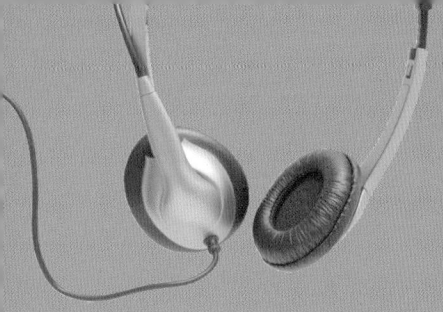

Super Reading Story Training Book

Step 2

The Little Mermaid

– Hans Christian Andersen

[p. 48-49]

The Little Mermaid

Deep beneath the sea, / the Sea King lived. He lived with his six daughters, / very beautiful mermaids, / in a palace. His wife died / many years ago. Their grandmother / took care of the mermaid princesses.

Each princess was beautiful, / but **the youngest was the loveliest / of all**. **Her skin was like a rose.** Her eyes were deep sea-blue. Her long hair flew smoothly / in the sea. And **she had / the most beautiful singing voice / in the world.** When she sang, / the fish flocked / from all over the sea / to listen to her. **She seemed like / other girls on land.** But, **like all mermaids**, / she had no legs. She had a tail / **like a fish.**

The Little Mermaid / had a wonderful life. She played and sang / with her sisters / all day long. She also liked / to spend her time / in her wonderful sea garden. The seahorses kept her company, / and sometimes / a dolphin would come and play.

But the Little Mermaid was happiest / when her grandmother told her stories. Her grandmother told her / all about the world above the sea. She told her / about beautiful ships, villages, and the people above.

The Little Mermaid / never went out of the sea.

"Oh, how I'd love to go up there / and see the sky at last!"

"You're still too young," said her grandmother.

"When you are fifteen, / you can swim to the top of the ocean / and see the wonderful things / for yourself," said her grandmother.

The Little Mermaid / **could hardly wait**. Every night, / she stood by the window / and looked up through the water. She often dreamed of the land / above the water.

- **beneath** ~아래, ~밑에 • **mermaid** 인어 • **palace** 궁전, 성 • **take care of** ~을 돌보다, ~을 보살피다 • **princess** 공주 • **loveliest** 가장 아름다운, 가장 사랑스러운 • **flock** (떼를 지어) 모여들다 • **tail** 꼬리 • **wonderful** 멋진, 신나는 • **spend time** 시간을 보내다 • **seahorse** 해마 • **keep ~ company** ~와 친구하다, ~와 놀다 • **dolphin** 돌고래 • **ship** 배 • **I'd love to** ~하고 싶다 • **for oneself** 혼자서 • **stand by** ~옆에 서다 • **look up** 올려다보다 • **dream of** ~의 꿈을 꾸다

CLOSE UP

1. **Her skin was like a rose.** 그녀의 피부는 장미꽃 같았다. /
   She seemed like other girls on land. 그녀는 육지에 사는 여느 소녀들과 비슷해 보였다.
   여기서 like는 '~와 비슷한'이라는 의미. ⟨be like ~⟩는 '~와 같다/비슷하다', ⟨seem like ~⟩는 '~와 비슷하게 보이다'라는 뜻이다.

2. **like all mermaids** 모든 인어들처럼 / **like a fish** 물고기처럼
   여기서 like는 '~처럼', '~와 똑같이', '~와 마찬가지로'라는 의미.

3. **could hardly wait** 도저히 기다리기가 힘들었다
   hardly는 '거의 ~ 아니다'라는 의미. can과 함께 쓰이면 '~하기 힘들다', '도저히 ~할 수 없다'의 뜻이 된다.

인어공주

바닷속 깊은 곳에**deep beneath the sea** 바다의 왕**the Sea King**이 살았다**live**. 왕은 매우 아름다운 인어들**beautiful mermaids**인 여섯 딸과 함께**with his six daughters** 궁전에서**in a palace** 살고 있었다. 그의 아내**his wife**는 여러 해 전에**many years ago** 세상을 떠났다**die**. 그래서 그들의 할머니**their grandmother**가 인어 공주들**the mermaid princesses**을 돌보았다**take care of**.

공주들은 하나같이**each princess** 아름다웠지만**be beautiful**, 그 중에서도 막내**the youngest**가 가장 사랑스러웠다**be the loveliest**. 그녀의 피부**her skin**는 장미꽃 같았다**be like a rose**. 두 눈**her eyes**은 바다처럼 짙은 푸른색**deep sea-blue**이었다. 긴 머리카락**her long hair**은 바닷속에서 하늘하늘 일렁거렸다**fly smoothly**. 게다가 막내는 세상에서**in the world** 가장 고운**the most beautiful** 노래하는 목소리**singing voice**를 가지고 있었다. 막내가 노래하면 물고기들**the fish**이 바다 곳곳에서**from all over the sea** 떼 지어 몰려와**flock** 그녀의 노래를 들었다**listen to her**. 막내는 육지에 사는 여느 소녀들과 비슷해 보였다**seem like other girls**. 하지만 모든 인어들처럼**like all mermaids** 그녀에게는 다리가 없었다**have no legs**. 물고기처럼**like a fish** 꼬리가 달려 있었다**have a tail**.

인어공주**the Little Mermaid**는 아주 신나는 삶을 살았다**have a wonderful life**. 온종일**all day long** 언니들과**with her sisters** 놀며 노래를 불렀다**play and sing**. 또한 그녀의 아주 멋진 바다 정원**sea garden**에서 즐겨 시간을 보냈다**spend her time**. 해마들**the seahorses**이 그녀의 친구가 되어 주었고**keep her company**, 때로는 돌고래**a dolphin**가 와서 놀기도**come and play** 했다.

그러나 인어공주는 할머니가 여러 가지 이야기를 해 줄**tell her stories** 때가 가장 행복했다. 할머니는 그녀에게 바다 위의 세상**the world above the sea**에 관해 전부 이야기해 주었다. 아름다운 배**ships**와 마을**villages**과 바깥세상 사람들**the people above**에 관해 이야기해 주었다.

인어공주는 바다 밖으로 나가 본 적이 없었다**never go out of the sea**.

"아, 저 위로 올라가서**go up there** 꼭 하늘을 보고**see the sky** 싶다!"

"넌 아직 너무 어리단다**be too young**." 할머니가 타일렀다.

"열다섯 살이 되면**be fifteen** 너 혼자서**for yourself** 바다 꼭대기까지 헤엄쳐 올라가**swim to the top of the ocean** 근사한 것들을 볼**see the wonderful things** 수 있을 게다." 할머니가 말했다.

인어공주는 도저히 기다리기가 힘들었다**can hardly wait**. 매일 밤**every night** 창가에 서서**stand by the window** 바닷물을 올려다보았다**look up through the water**. 종종 물 밖의 육지가 나오는 꿈도 꿨다**dream of the land**.

GRAMMAR POINT

최상급 + 범위 ⇨ 최상급 다음에는 대개 of all, in the world와 같이 범위를 나타내는 어구가 나옴.

- The youngest was **the loveliest of all**. 그 중에서도 막내가 가장 사랑스러웠다.
- She had **the most beautiful** singing voice **in the world**. 그녀는 세상에서 가장 고운 노래하는 목소리를 가졌다.
- He is **the richest** man **in the country**. 그는 그 나라에서 가장 부자였다.

[p. 50–51]

At last, / the Little Mermaid / turned fifteen.

"There, / now you can go to the surface," said her father.

The Little Mermaid / was so excited. She combed / her long golden hair. She polished / the scales on her tail. She kissed her grandmother goodbye.

In a second, / the Little Mermaid swam up / toward the surface of the sea. She swam so fast / that even the fish / could not keep up with her.

Suddenly, / she popped out of the water. How wonderful! For the first time, / she saw the great sky. It was full of / red and orange clouds. The sun was setting. "It's so lovely!" she exclaimed happily.

In front of her / was a big ship. She swam close to the ship / and looked inside. There was / a big party. There were / many handsome gentlemen, / but the finest of all / was a prince. He was laughing / and shaking hands with everyone. She had never seen / anyone like him / before. She could not take her eyes off him.

All of a sudden, / the weather changed. The sky became dark, / and heavy rain started to fall. The waves became very rough. Lightning flashed, / and thunder boomed / throughout the sky. The ship rolled up and down / on the waves. Then, / the ship broke apart / and started to sink.

The Little Mermaid / saw the prince / fall into the sea. "People cannot breathe / underwater," she thought. "I must save him." The Little Mermaid / went diving down / to look for him. He was sinking / deep into the ocean. She seized his shoulder / and took him to the surface.

When she got to land, / she pushed the prince's body / onto the shore. The prince was still not awake. The Little Mermaid / looked into his handsome face / all night long.

By the morning, / the storm was finished, / and the warm sun appeared. In the sunlight, / the prince looked more handsome. His eyes were still closed. "Wake up. Please don't die," she whispered.

- **turn** ~이 되다   • **comb** (머리를) 빗다   • **polish** 광을 내다, 윤이 나게 하다   • **in a second** 순식간에
- **keep up with** (처지지 않고) ~을 따라가다   • **pop out of** (갑자기) ~에서 밖으로 나오다   • **set** (해가) 지다
- **finest** 가장 멋진   • **shake hands with** ~와 악수하다   • **rough** 거친, 드센   • **lightning** 번개
- **flash** (섬광이) 번쩍이다   • **thunder** 천둥   • **boom** 쾅 소리를 내다   • **roll up and down** 오르락내리락 하다, 이리저리 흔들리다   • **break apart** 부서지다, 쪼개지다   • **sink** 가라앉다, 침몰하다   • **breathe** 숨을 쉬다
- **dive down** (물속으로) 뛰어들다, 잠수해 들어가다   • **seize** 잡다, 움켜잡다   • **get to land** 육지에 다다르다
- **shore** 해안   • **be awake** 깨다, 눈을 뜨다   • **all night long** 밤새도록   • **storm** 폭풍우   • **appear** 나타나다   • **whisper** 속삭이다

CLOSE UP

1. **There was a big party.** 큰 파티가 있었다. /
   There were many handsome gentlemen 잘생긴 신사들이 많이 있었다
   〈there is/are ~〉는 '~가 있다'라는 의미. 뒤에 오는 명사가 단수이면 is, 복수이면 are를 쓴다. 과거일 때는 was/were를 쓴다.

2. **She could not take her eyes off him.** 그녀는 그에게서 눈을 뗄 수 없었다.
   〈take one's eyes off ~〉는 '~에서 눈(길)을 떼다'라는 의미. 보통 cannot과 함께 쓰여 어떤 매력에 감탄했음을 나타낸다.

마침내at last 인어공주가 열다섯 살이 되었다turn fifteen.

"자, 이제 수면으로 가도go to the surface 좋다." 아버지가 말했다.

인어공주는 몹시 신이 났다be excited. 긴 금발her long golden hair에 빗질을 했다comb. 꼬리에 난 비늘들the scales on her tail은 윤이 나게 닦았다polish. 인어공주는 할머니에게 작별 키스를 했다.

인어공주는 금세 해수면을 향해toward the surface of the sea 헤엄쳐 올라갔다swim up. 헤엄치는 속도가 너무 빨라서swim so fast 물고기들도 그녀를 따라갈keep up with her 수 없을 정도였다.

별안간suddenly 인어공주는 물 밖으로 튀어나왔다pop out of the water. 참으로 근사하구나how wonderful! 난생 처음으로for the first time 인어공주는 드넓은 하늘the great sky을 보았다. 하늘에는 붉은빛과 주황빛 구름들red and orange clouds이 가득했다. 석양이 지고 있었다. "정말 아름답다it's so lovely!" 인어공주는 기쁨에 겨워 소리쳤다exclaim happily.

그녀 앞에in front of her 커다란 배 한 척a big ship이 있었다. 그녀는 배 가까이close to the ship 헤엄쳐 가서 안을 들여다보았다look inside. 성대한 파티a big party가 열리고 있었다. 잘생긴 신사들handsome gentlemen이 많았지만, 그 중에서 가장 멋진the finest 사람은 왕자a prince였다. 왕자는 웃으며 모든 이들과 악수를 나누고 있었다. 인어공주는 전에 그와 같은 사람anyone like him을 한 번도 본 적이 없었다never see. 그녀는 왕자한테서 눈을 뗄take her eyes off him 수가 없었다.

갑자기all of a sudden 날씨the weather가 바뀌었다change. 하늘the sky이 컴컴해지더니become dark 폭우heavy rain가 쏟아지기fall 시작했다. 파도the waves는 몹시 거칠어졌다become rough. 번개lightning가 번쩍하고flash, 하늘에 온통 천둥thunder이 울려 퍼졌다boom. 배가 파도에 밀려 너울거렸다roll up and down. 그러더니 배는 산산조각이 나서break apart 가라앉기sink 시작했다.

인어공주는 왕자가 바다로 떨어지는fall into the sea 걸 보았다. "사람들은 물속에서underwater 숨을 쉴 수가 없어cannot breathe. 내가 저 사람을 구해save him 줘야만 해." 하고 인어공주는 생각했다. 인어공주는 왕자를 찾으러look for him 물속으로 뛰어들었다go diving down. 왕자는 바다 깊은 곳으로deep into the ocean 가라앉고 있었다. 인어공주는 왕자의 한쪽 어깨를 잡고seize his shoulder 그를 수면으로 데려갔다take him to the surface.

육지에 다다르자get to land 인어공주는 왕자의 몸the prince's body을 해안으로 밀었다push onto the shore. 왕자는 여전히 깨어나지 않았다be not awake. 인어공주는 밤새all night long 왕자의 잘생긴 얼굴을 들여다보았다look into his handsome face.

아침 무렵by the morning 폭풍the storm이 그치고be finished 따사로운 태양the warm sun이 모습을 나타냈다appear. 햇빛이 비치니in the sunlight 왕자는 더 잘생겨 보였다look more handsome. 그의 두 눈his eyes은 여전히 감겨 있었다be closed. "깨어나세요wake up. 죽으면 안 돼요don't die." 인어공주가 속삭였다.

GRAMMAR POINT

so ~ that... : 아주 ~해서 …하다

- She swam **so** fast **that** even the fish could not keep up with her.
  그녀는 아주 빨리 헤엄쳐서 물고기들도 그녀를 따라갈 수 없었다.

- The prince was **so** handsome **that** she could not take her eyes off him.
  왕자가 너무 잘생겨서 그녀는 그에게서 눈을 뗄 수 없었다.

[p. 52-53]

Now, / she could see / dry land ahead. She took the prince / onto a pretty beach / with calm water. She laid the prince / on the warm sand. At that moment, / she saw some girls / walking along the sand. Quickly, / she swam away / and hid behind some rocks. She watched the prince. "I must stay here / until someone comes / to save him," she thought.

After a while, / a pretty girl / came along the beach. She saw the prince / and ran to him. At that moment, / the prince opened his eyes / and smiled at the girl. The girl called for help. Soon, / some people came / and took the prince away.

The Little Mermaid / felt so sad / because she could not see him / anymore. She swam back home / full of sorrow.

"What did you see?" her sisters asked. But she told them nothing. She was too sad / to speak. She was quiet / all day long.

Days and weeks / went by. The Little Mermaid / could only think about the prince. She missed him / so much. At night, / she often swam to the beach. She looked for the prince, / but she did not see him.

One day, / she finally told her sisters / her story. One of the sisters / took her to his palace. He lived in a great palace / by the sea. She could see the prince / looking out his window. She was so happy. Every night, / she swam near the palace / and watched the prince.

The Little Mermaid / loved the world above the sea / more and more. Now / she had only one wish / —to become a human.

"Grandmother," she asked one day. "Can humans live forever?"

"No, they can't," said her grandmother. "Humans die. They live shorter lives / than we do. Mermaids live for 300 years, / and then we become / foam on the sea. But humans have souls. Their souls live forever."

- **dry land** 마른 땅 • **ahead** 앞으로, 앞에 • **calm** 잔잔한, 고요한 • **lay** 내려놓다, 눕히다 • **swim away** 헤엄쳐 가 버리다 • **hide** 숨다 • **smile at** ~을 보고 웃다 • **call for** ~을 부르다, ~을 요청하다 • **take away** 데려가다, 가져가 버리다 • **full of sorrow** 슬픔에 가득 찬, 슬픔에 가득 차서 • **quiet** 조용한 ≠ loud • **all day long** 하루 종일 • **go by** (시간 등이) 지나다, 지나가다 • **miss** 그리워하다 • **finally** 마침내, 드디어 • **look out** (~의 밖을) 내다보다 • **wish** 바람, 소망 • **human** 인간 • **forever** 영원히 • **life** 생명; 생애, 삶 *pl. lives • **foam** 거품 • **soul** 영혼

CLOSE UP

1. **took the prince onto a pretty beach** 왕자를 예쁜 해변 위로 데려갔다 / **took the prince away** 왕자를 데려갔다 / **took her to his palace** 그녀를 그의 궁전으로 데려갔다
   여기서 take는 '(사람을) 데리고 가다'라는 의미.

2. **She was too sad to speak.** 그녀는 너무 슬퍼서 말도 할 수 없었다.
   ⟨too ~ to...⟩는 '너무 ~해서 …할 수 없다', '…하기에는 너무 ~하다'라는 의미.
   ex) You are too young to go up there.(넌 너무 어려서 저 위로 올라갈 수 없어.)

이제 인어공주 앞에 마른 땅이 보였다see dry land. 공주는 왕자를 잔잔한 물이 있는with calm water 예쁜 해변 위로onto a pretty beach 데려갔다. 공주는 따뜻한 모래밭에on the warm sand 왕자를 눕혔다lay the prince. 바로 그때at that moment 인어공주는 소녀 몇 명some girls이 모래밭을 따라 걷고walk along the sand 있는 모습을 보았다. 인어공주는 재빨리 헤엄쳐 달아나swim away 바위들 뒤로 숨었다hide behind some rocks. 인어공주는 왕자를 지켜봤다watch the prince. "누군가 그를 구하러 올come to save him 때까지 여기 머물러stay here 있어야 해." 하고 인어공주는 생각했다.

얼마 후after a while 예쁜 소녀 한 명a pretty girl이 해변을 따라 왔다come along the beach. 소녀는 왕자를 보더니see the prince 그에게 달려왔다run to him. 바로 그때 왕자가 눈을 뜨고open his eyes 소녀에게 미소를 지었다smile at the girl. 소녀는 도움을 요청했다call for help. 곧 사람들이 몇 명some people 와서 왕자를 데려갔다take the prince away.

인어공주는 이제 왕자를 볼 수 없었기cannot see him anymore 때문에 무척 슬펐다feel sad. 공주는 슬픔에 젖은 채full of sorrow 집으로 헤엄쳐 돌아갔다swim back home.

"뭘 봤니?" 언니들이 물었다. 그러나 인어공주는 언니들에게 아무 말도 하지 않았다tell them nothing. 너무 슬퍼서too sad 말이 나오지 않았다to speak. 인어공주는 온종일all day long 말이 없었다be quiet.

며칠이 가고 몇 주가 지났다. 인어공주는 오직 왕자에 대한 생각밖에only think about the prince 할 수 없었다. 왕자가 너무 보고 싶었다miss him so much. 밤에는at night 자주 해변으로 헤엄쳐 갔다swim to the beach. 왕자를 찾아봤지만look for the prince 보이지 않았다do not see him.

어느 날one day 인어공주는 드디어finally 언니들에게 사연을 들려주었다tell her story. 언니들 중 하나one of the sisters가 인어공주를 왕자가 사는 궁전으로 데려갔다take her to his palace. 왕자는 바닷가에 있는by the sea 커다란 궁전에 살고 있었다live in a great palace. 인어공주는 왕자가 창밖을 내다보고look out his window 있는 모습을 볼 수 있었다. 인어공주는 너무 기뻤다. 매일 밤every night 인어공주는 궁전 근처에서 헤엄치며swim near the palace 왕자를 지켜봤다.

인어공주는 점점 더more and more 바다 위의 세상the world above the sea을 좋아하게 되었다. 이제 그녀에게는 한 가지 소원밖에only one wish 없었다. 바로 인간이 되는become a human 것이었다.

"할머니, 인간humans은 영원히 살live forever 수 있나요?" 어느 날 인어공주가 물었다.

"아니, 그렇지 않단다." 할머니가 대답했다. "인간은 죽는단다die. 우리들보다 수명이 더 짧지live shorter lives. 인어들은 300년을 살고live for 300 years, 그러고 나면 바다의 물거품foam on the sea이 된단다. 하지만 인간에게는 영혼이 있어have souls. 그들의 영혼은 영원히 살지."

GRAMMAR POINT

see + 목적어 + 동사원형/현재분사 ⇨ 지각동사는 목적어 다음에 동사원형이나 현재분사가 온다.

- The Little Mermaid **saw** the prince **fall** into the sea. 인어공주는 왕자가 바다로 떨어지는 것을 보았다.
- She **saw** some girls **walking** along the sand. 그녀는 소녀 몇 명이 모래밭을 따라 걷고 있는 것을 보았다.
- She could **see** the prince **looking** out his window. 그녀는 왕자가 창밖을 내다보고 있는 모습을 볼 수 있었다.

[p. 54-55]

"I want to be like a person. Can I get a human soul?" asked the Little Mermaid.

"Don't say that," said her grandmother.

"Is there any way / that I can get a soul?" she asked / over and over again.

At last, / her grandmother replied.

"There is / only one way. If a man loves you / with all his heart / and marries you, / then his soul can enter your body. Then, / you would have a soul / and would live forever," she continued. "But that will never happen / because we have tails. Humans think / tails are ugly. They prefer legs. No man will want / to marry a mermaid."

The Little Mermaid / looked at her tail / and thought.

"I want to have two legs. I must win the prince's love / and marry him. I love him. I will do anything / for him. Maybe the sea witch / can help me."

She swam off / to see the sea witch. The sea witch / lived in a horrible, scary place. Her house was made / from the bones of dead sailors. And there were sea snakes / everywhere. The Little Mermaid / felt very afraid. She almost left. Then, she thought, "The prince! And my soul! I must not be afraid."

The Little Mermaid / swam up to the sea witch. When the witch saw the Little Mermaid, / she said, "I know / what you want. I can give you / a pair of human legs. Then, / you will be able to / walk on land. Come in."

The Little Mermaid / followed the witch / into the bone house.

"You are a stupid girl. You will be sorry. But I will grant your wish," the witch said.

"I will make a magic drink / for you. Tomorrow morning, / before sunrise, / you must swim to land / and drink it. Then your tail will split in two, / and you will have two legs. But it will be very painful. It will hurt / every time you walk. Can you bear the pain?"

- **over and over again** 자꾸, 거듭해서 • **with all one's heart** 진심으로, 극진히 • **marry** 결혼하다
- **continue** 계속하다 • **ugly** 흉한, 보기 싫은, 못생긴 • **prefer** 더 좋아하다 • **sea witch** 바다 마녀
- **swim off** 헤엄쳐 가다 • **horrible** 끔찍한 • **scary** 무서운, 겁나는 • **be made from** ~로 만들어지다
- **sailor** 선원, 뱃사람 • **sea snake** 바다 뱀 • **swim up to** ~로 헤엄쳐 가다 • **a pair of** 한 쌍의 • **be able to** ~할 수 있다 • **stupid** 어리석은, 멍청한 • **grant one's wish** ~의 소원을 들어주다 • **magic drink** 마법의 음료 • **sunrise** 일출, 해돋이, 동틀녘 • **split in** ~로 나뉘다, ~로 갈라지다 • **painful** 고통스러운, 아픈 • **hurt** 아프다; 아프게 하다, 다치게 하다 • **every time** ~할 때마다 • **bear pain** 고통을 참다

CLOSE UP

1 **you would have a soul and would live forever** 네게 영혼이 생겨서 영원히 살게 될 거다
   여기서 would(~일 것이다)는 실현 불가능하다고 생각되는 미래의 일을 나타냄.

2 **was made from the bones of dead sailors** 죽은 뱃사람들의 뼈로 만들어졌다
   〈be made from ~〉은 '~으로 만들어지다'라는 의미. ex) Cheese is made from milk.(치즈는 우유로 만든다.)

3 **what you want** 네가 원하는 것
   〈what+주어+동사〉는 '~한 것'이라는 의미. ex) what you have (네가 가진 것)

"저는 인간처럼 되고**be like a person** 싶어요. 제가 인간의 영혼을 가질**get a human soul** 수 있나요?" 인어공주가 물었다.

"그런 말 하면 못쓴다**don't say that**." 할머니가 타일렀다.

"제가 영혼을 얻을**get a soul** 수 있는 방법이 없나요?" 인어공주는 거듭**over and over again** 물었다.

마침내 할머니가 대답했다.

"방법이 딱 한 가지**only one way** 있기는 하지. 만약 인간 남자**a man**가 진심으로**with all his heart** 너를 사랑해서**love you** 너와 결혼한다면**marry you**, 그의 영혼**his soul**이 네 몸에 들어갈**enter your body** 수 있단다. 그러면**then** 네게 영혼이 생겨서 **have a soul** 영원히 살게**live forever** 될 거다." 할머니는 계속 말을 이었다. "하지만 우리에게는 꼬리가 있기 때문에 그런 일은 절대로 일어나지 않을**never happen** 거다. 인간들은 꼬리가 추하다**be ugly**고 생각하지. 그들은 다리를 더 좋아한단다**prefer legs**. 어떤 남자도 **no man** 인어와 결혼하고**marry a mermaid** 싶어 하지는 않을 게다."

인어공주는 자신의 꼬리를 바라보며**look at her tail** 생각했다.

"나는 두 다리를 갖고**have two legs** 싶어. 왕자님의 사랑을 얻고**win the prince's love** 그와 결혼해야 **marry him** 해. 난 그를 사랑해**love him**. 그를 얻기 위해서라면 무슨 일이라도 할**do anything for him** 테야. 어쩌면**maybe** 바다마녀**the sea witch**가 날 도와줄**help me** 수 있을지도 몰라."

인어공주는 바다마녀를 만나러**see the sea witch** 헤엄쳐 갔다**swim off**. 바다마녀는 끔찍하고 무서운 곳**a horrible, scary place**에 살고 있었다. 바다마녀의 집은 죽은 뱃사람들의 뼈**the bones of dead sailors**로 만들어져 있었다. 그리고 사방에**everywhere** 바다뱀들**sea snakes**이 득실댔다. 인어공주는 너무 무서웠다**feel afraid**. 하마터면 떠나 버릴 뻔했다**almost leave**. 그때 이런 생각이 들었다. "왕자님은 **the prince**! 그리고 내 영혼은**my soul**! 절대로 무서워하면 안 돼**must not be afraid**."

인어공주는 바다마녀에게 헤엄쳐 갔다**swim up to the sea witch**. 마녀는 인어공주를 보자 이렇게 말했다. "네가 원하는 것**what you want**을 안다. 나는 너에게 인간의 다리 한 쌍**a pair of human legs**을 줄 수 있지. 그러면 육지에서 걸을**walk on land** 수 있게 될 거다. 들어오너라**come in**."

인어공주는 마녀를 따라**follow the witch** 해골 집으로**into the bone house** 들어갔다.

"넌 어리석은 아이**a stupid girl**로구나. 후회하게 될 거다**will be sorry**. 그래도 네 소원을 들어주마 **grant your wish**." 마녀가 말했다.

"네게 마법의 물약**a magic drink**을 만들어 주마. 내일 아침**tomorrow morning** 해 뜨기 전에**before sunrise** 육지로 헤엄쳐 가서**swim to land** 그것을 마셔야**drink it** 한다. 그러면 꼬리가 둘로 갈라져서**split in two** 두 다리가 생길 거다. 하지만 매우 고통스러울**be painful** 게다. 걸을 때마다**every time you walk** 아플**hurt** 것이다. 그 고통을 참을**bear the pain** 수 있겠느냐?"

GRAMMAR POINT

will be able to : ~할 수 있을 것이다   **must be able to** : ~할 수 있어야 한다

⇨ will can(×), must can(×)과 같이 두 개의 조동사를 연달아 쓸 수는 없다. 이때는 can을 be able to로 대체한다.

- You **will be able to** walk on land. 너는 육지에서 걸을 수 있게 될 거야.
- I **must be able to** talk to the prince. 나는 왕자님께 말을 할 수 있어야 해.

The Little Mermaid

[p. 56-57]

"Yes," replied the Little Mermaid. "It doesn't matter!" whispered the Little Mermaid / with tears in her eyes. "As long as I can go back to him!"

"But remember / one more thing," the sea witch added. "Once you become a human, / you can never become a mermaid again. You will never return / to your father's palace. And if the prince marries another girl, / you will turn into foam on the sea."

"I will do it," the Little Mermaid said.

"Ah, / but there is / one more thing," said the sea witch. "You must pay me. I want your voice. You have the prettiest voice / in the world."

"My voice? Then how can I speak?" the Little Mermaid asked. "How will I make the prince / fall in love with me? I must be able to / talk to him."

"You are beautiful," said the sea witch. "You can dance. You can smile at him. Your deep blue eyes / will speak for you. You do not need to talk."

"All right," the Little Mermaid / agreed to the price. Instantly, / her voice was gone.

The sea witch / made the magic drink / for her. The Little Mermaid / took the drink / and swam to land. She reached the beach / and then / drank the magic drink. Suddenly, / she felt a horrible pain. It was like / a knife in her body. She passed out / in the sand.

The next morning, / the Little Mermaid / woke up. She looked at her body. Her tail was gone. She had the prettiest legs / on Earth. Then, / she saw a shadow. She looked up. The prince was standing over her / and looking down at her.

- **with tears in one's eyes** 눈물을 글썽이며 • **as long as** ~하기만 한다면, ~하는 한 • **remember** 기억하다 • **once** 일단 ~하면 • **return** (되)돌아가다 • **turn into** ~로 바뀌다 • **pay** 지불하다 • **fall in love with** ~와 사랑에 빠지다 • **instantly** 즉각, 즉시 • **knife** 칼 • **pass out** 실신하다, 기절하다 • **shadow** 그림자 • **look up** 올려다보다 • **look down at** ~을 내려다보다

CLOSE UP

1. **will turn into foam on the sea** 바다의 물거품으로 변할 것이다
   〈turn into ~〉는 모습이나 성질이 '~으로 변하다', '~으로 바뀌다'라는 의미.

2. **make the prince fall in love with me** 왕자가 나와 사랑에 빠지게 만들다
   〈make+목적어+동사원형〉은 '~을 …하게 만들다'라는 의미. 〈fall in love with ~〉는 '~와 사랑에 빠지다', '~에게 반하다'라는 의미.

3. **her voice was gone** 그녀의 목소리가 사라졌다 / **Her tail was gone.** 그녀의 꼬리가 사라지고 없었다.
   〈be gone〉은 어떤 것이 사라지거나, 더는 남아 있지 않은 상태를 나타냄.

"네." 인어공주가 대답했다. "상관없어it doesn't matter! 왕자님한테 돌아갈go back to him 수만 있다면." 인어공주는 두 눈에 눈물을 글썽이며with tears in her eyes 속삭였다.

"그런데 한 가지 더one more thing 기억할remember 게 있다." 바다마녀가 덧붙였다. "일단once 인간이 되면become a human 결코 다시는 인어가 될 수 없다never become a mermaid again. 네 아버지의 궁전에도to your father's palace 결코 돌아오지 못한다never return. 그리고 만약 왕자가 다른 여자와 결혼하게marry another girl 되면 넌 바다의 물거품으로 변할turn into foam on the sea 거다."

"그래도 하겠어요." 인어공주가 말했다.

"아, 그런데 한 가지가 더 있지." 바다마녀가 말했다. "내게 값을 치러야pay me 한다. 네 목소리를 다오want your voice. 너는 세상에서 가장 예쁜 목소리the prettiest voice를 지녔잖니."

"제 목소리를요my voice? 그럼 저는 어떻게how 말을 할 수 있죠can speak?" 인어공주가 물었다. "어떻게 왕자님이 저와 사랑에 빠지게fall in love with me 하겠어요? 왕자님한테 말을 할talk to him 수 있어야 해요."

"넌 아름답잖니be beautiful." 바다마녀가 말했다. "춤도 출dance 수 있지. 왕자에게 미소도 지을smile at him 수 있고. 네 짙은 파란 눈동자your deep blue eyes가 네 마음을 전해 줄speak for you 거다. 말은 필요하지 않아do not need to talk."

"좋아요all right." 인어공주가 값을 치르는 데 동의했다agree to the price. 그 즉시instantly 그녀의 목소리her voice는 사라져 버렸다be gone.

바다마녀는 인어공주에게 마법의 물약을 만들어 주었다make the magic drink. 인어공주는 그 물약을 가지고take the drink 육지로 헤엄쳐 갔다. 공주는 해변에 도착한reach the beach 다음 마법의 물약을 마셨다drink the magic drink. 갑자기 끔찍한 고통이 느껴졌다feel a horrible pain. 마치 몸속에 칼이 있는 a knife in her body 것 같았다. 인어공주는 모래밭에서in the sand 정신을 잃었다pass out.

다음 날 아침the next morning 인어공주가 깨어났다wake up. 공주는 자기 몸을 살펴보았다look at her body. 꼬리her tail가 사라지고 없었다be gone. 세상에서on Earth 가장 예쁜 다리the prettiest legs가 생겼다. 그때 웬 그림자가 보였다see a shadow. 인어공주는 위를 쳐다보았다look up. 왕자가 인어공주 옆에 지키고 서서stand over her 그녀를 내려다보고look down at her 있었다.

GRAMMAR POINT

as long as : ~하기만 하면   **once** : 일단 ~하면

- **As long as** I can go back to him! 그에게 돌아갈 수만 있다면!
- **Once** you become a human, you can never become a mermaid again.
  일단 인간이 되면, 결코 다시는 인어가 될 수 없다.

The Little Mermaid 51

[p. 58-59]

"Who are you? Where did you come from?" asked the prince.
But the Little Mermaid / could not speak. She just looked deeply / into his eyes / with her sad blue eyes. At that moment, / the prince had very strong feelings / for her.
"I'll take you to the castle / and look after you," he said. The prince took the Little Mermaid / inside his castle. **Every step / felt like sharp knives.** But she was with the prince, / so she was happy.
In the days that followed, / the Little Mermaid / started a new life. The prince gave the Little Mermaid / her own room. He gave her / beautiful clothes and jewelry to wear, / too. She was the most beautiful girl / in the kingdom. But the Little Mermaid / could not say anything / to the prince. **All she could do / was smile at him.**
The prince held many parties. One night, / some girls / sang for the prince. They sang well, / but the Little Mermaid was sad. "**I used to sing / much better than that**," she thought. "**I wish / the prince could hear / my singing voice.**"
Then, / the girls started to dance. Now, / the Little Mermaid could dance / for the prince. She danced and danced. She suffered terrible pain / throughout her body, / but she danced so beautifully. Everyone was amazed / by the Little Mermaid's dancing. The prince could not stop watching her.
After the party, / the Little Mermaid and prince / did everything together. They had picnics / on the beach. They went riding together. They walked / beside the calm ocean. The Little Mermaid's feet ached, / but she did not care. She was happy / to be with the prince.
Sometimes at night, / she went to the ocean. She put her feet / into the cool water. **It always felt so good.** At those times, / she thought of her family. She missed them / so much. "I hope / they are well. I hope / they understand me," she thought.

- **deeply** 깊이, 그윽하게　・**feeling** 느낌, 감정; 동정심, 연민　・**look after** ~을 돌보다　・**sharp** 날카로운
- **in the days that follow** 그 후로, 그다음 날부터　・**jewelry** 보석(류)　・**kingdom** 왕국　・**hold a party** 파티를 열다　・**suffer** (고통을) 겪다, 시달리다　・**be amazed by** ~에 아주 놀라다　・**have a picnic** 소풍을 가다　・**go riding** 승마하러 가다　・**ache** 아프다　・**do not care** 상관하지 않다, 신경 쓰지 않다　・**put A into B** A를 B 안으로 넣다, A를 B에 담그다　・**at those times** 그럴 때면　・**hope** 바라다, 희망하다

CLOSE UP

1. **Every step felt like sharp knives.** 걸음을 옮길 때마다 날카로운 칼로 찌르는 것 같았다. / **It always felt so good.** 그것은 항상 느낌이 너무 좋았다.
   feel의 주어로 사람이 아닌 사물이 오면, 그 사물의 '촉감/느낌이 ~하다'라는 의미.

2. **All she could do was (to) smile at him.** 그녀가 할 수 있는 거라곤 왕자에게 미소를 짓는 것뿐이었다.
   ⟨all ~ can do is (to)...⟩는 '~가 할 수 있는 것은 오직 …하는 것뿐이다'라는 의미. 이때 to는 써도 되고 안 써도 된다.

3. **I used to sing much better than that.** 나는 예전에 저보다 훨씬 더 노래를 잘했는데.
   ⟨used to + 동사원형⟩은 '예전에 ~했다'라는 의미로, '지금은 그렇지 않다'는 뜻을 포함한다.

"당신은 누구죠? 어디서 왔나요?" 왕자가 물었다.

그러나 인어공주는 말을 할 수 없었다**cannot speak**. 슬픔에 찬 파란 눈으로**with her sad blue eyes** 왕자의 눈을 그윽이 쳐다볼**look deeply into his eyes** 뿐이었다. 그 순간 왕자는 인어공주에게 아주 강한 연민을 느꼈다**have strong feelings**.

"당신을 성으로 데려가서**take you to the castle** 돌봐 주겠소**look after you**." 왕자가 말했다. 왕자는 인어공주를 성 안으로 데려갔다. 걸음을 옮길 때마다**every step** 날카로운 칼로 찌르는 것 같았다**feel like sharp knives**. 하지만 인어공주는 왕자와 함께 있어서**be with the prince** 행복했다**be happy**.

그다음 날부터**in the days that followed** 인어공주는 새로운 삶을 시작했다**start a new life**. 왕자는 인어공주에게 그녀만의 방**her own room**을 마련해 주었다. 입고 치장할 아름다운 옷과 보석**beautiful clothes and jewelry**도 주었다. 인어공주는 왕국에서**in the kingdom** 제일 아름다운 아가씨**the most beautiful girl**였다. 그러나 인어공주는 왕자에게 아무런 말도 할 수 없었다**cannot say anything**. 그녀가 할 수 있는 거라곤**all she can do** 왕자에게 미소를 짓는**smile at him** 것뿐이었다.

왕자는 파티를 많이 열었다**hold many parties**. 어느 날 밤**one night** 소녀 몇 명**some girls**이 왕자를 위해 노래를 불렀다**sing for the prince**. 그들은 노래를 잘했지만**sing well**, 인어공주는 슬펐다**be sad**. "예전에 나는 저것보다 훨씬 더 노래를 잘했는데**sing much better**." 하고 인어공주는 생각했다. "왕자님이 내가 노래하는 목소리를 들을**hear my singing voice** 수 있다면 좋으련만."

그때 소녀들이 춤을 추기 시작했다. 이제는 인어공주도 왕자를 위해 춤을 출**dance for the prince** 수 있었다. 공주는 춤을 추고 또 추었다**dance and dance**. 온몸이**throughout her body** 끔찍한 통증에 시달렸지만**suffer terrible pain**, 공주는 매우 아름답게 춤을 췄다**dance beautifully**. 모두**everyone**가 인어공주의 춤 솜씨에 놀라움을 금치 못했다**be amazed**. 왕자도 인어공주를 쳐다보는 걸 그만둘 수가 없었다(눈길을 뗄 수 없었다)**cannot stop watching**.

파티 이후**after the party** 인어공주와 왕자는 모든 걸 함께했다**do everything together**. 둘은 해변에서**on the beach** 소풍을 즐겼다**have picnics**. 함께 말도 타러 갔다**go riding**. 잔잔한 바닷가를 거닐기도 했다**walk beside the ocean**. 인어공주의 발은 아팠지만**ache**, 그녀는 개의치 않았다**do not care**. 왕자와 함께 있어서 행복하기만 했다.

인어공주는 밤에 가끔씩**sometimes at night** 바다로 갔다**go to the ocean**. 시원한 물에 발을 담갔다**put her feet into the cool water**. 그러면 언제나 기분이 너무 좋았다**feel so good**. 그럴 때면**at those times** 가족 생각이 났다**think of her family**. 인어공주는 식구들이 너무 보고 싶었다**miss them so much**. "다들 건강하셔야**be well** 할 텐데. 날 이해해 주시면**understand me** 좋겠어." 하고 인어공주는 생각했다.

Grammar Point

I wish ~ (가정법) : ~라면 좋겠는데

⇨ I wish 뒤에 나오는 종속절에 '가정법 과거' 동사가 쓰이면 현재 사실과 반대되는 소망을 나타냄.

- **I wish** the prince **could hear** my singing voice. 왕자님이 내 노래하는 목소리를 들을 수 있다면 좋으련만.
- **I wish** I **had** two legs and **walked** on the beach every day.
  내게 두 다리가 있어서 날마다 해변을 걷는다면 좋겠는데.
- **I wish** I **were** a human. 내가 인간이라면 얼마나 좋을까. (가정법 과거에서 be동사는 항상 **were**로 씀.)

The Little Mermaid

[p. 60-61]

Day by day, / the prince loved the Little Mermaid / more and more. But he loved her / like a sister. He did not think of / marrying her.

One day, / the prince told the Little Mermaid, "You are the sweetest girl / I know. You remind me of a girl. This girl saved my life / when my ship sank. I almost drowned. I only saw her once, / but I cannot forget her. She is the only girl / I can ever love."

"I wish / I could tell him / it was me!" the Little Mermaid thought. "I saved you. But you don't know me." She felt so sad.

One day, / the king ordered the prince / to visit the next kingdom. The king wanted the prince / to marry the princess of the kingdom.

"I must go there / because my father ordered me," said the prince, "but no one can make me / marry this princess. You remind me / more of my lost love. If I must get married, / I will marry you." He kissed the Little Mermaid. "Will you come with me? I want you / to sail with me," he asked.

The prince, the Little Mermaid, and many others / got on a ship / and sailed across the sea. At last, / they arrived at a beautiful town. Many people came to the ship / and welcomed the prince. And there was / the princess. She had deep blue eyes, / just like the Little Mermaid.

"It is you," cried the prince. "My true love! You are the girl / who saved my life. Let us get married / tonight."

The prince / turned to the Little Mermaid. He said, "My wish has come true. I am so happy. I have found my true love. And I know / you will be happy for me / because you love me."

The Little Mermaid's heart / was broken. She would never marry the prince now. His wedding / meant one thing. She must die.

- **day by day** 나날이, 날이 갈수록 • **sweetest** 가장 사랑스러운 • **remind** 상기시키다, 생각나게 하다 • **save one's life** ~의 목숨을 구하다 • **drown** 물에 빠져 죽다, 익사하다 • **forget** 잊어버리다 • **I wish I could ~** ~할 수만 있다면 (좋을 텐데) • **order** 명령하다, 명하다 • **lost** 잃어버린 • **sail** (배로) 항해하다 • **get on a ship** 배에 오르다, 배를 타다 • **welcome** 환영하다, 맞이하다 • **turn to** ~을 향하다, ~을 돌아보다 • **come true** 실현되다, 이루어지다 • **be broken** 부서지다, (마음이) 무너지다 • **wedding** 결혼, 결혼식

CLOSE UP

1. **You remind me of a girl.** 너를 보면 어떤 소녀가 생각나. /
   You remind me more of my lost love. 너를 보면 잃어버린 내 사랑이 더 생각나.
   〈~ remind me of...〉는 '~을 보면 …이 생각나다'라는 의미.

2. **ordered the prince to visit the next kingdom** 왕자에게 이웃 나라를 방문하라고 분부했다
   〈order ~ to...〉는 '~에게 …하라고 명령하다'라는 의미.

3. **make me marry this princess** 나를 이 공주와 결혼하게 만들다 /
   If I must get married, I will marry you. 내가 결혼을 해야 한다면 너와 결혼하겠어. /
   Let us get married tonight. 오늘 밤에 결혼합시다.
   일반적으로, 그냥 '결혼하다'라고 할 때는 get married를 쓰고, '~와 결혼하다'라고 할 때는 marry를 쓴다. 이때 marry 뒤에 전치사 with를 붙이지 않도록 주의하자.

날이 갈수록**day by day** 왕자는 점점 더**more and more** 인어공주를 사랑하게**love the Little Mermaid** 되었다. 하지만 왕자는 인어공주를 여동생처럼**like a sister** 사랑하는 것이었다. 왕자는 인어공주와 결혼할 생각이 없었다.

어느 날 왕자가 인어공주에게 말했다. "너는 내가 아는 가장 사랑스런 소녀**the sweetest girl**다. 너를 보면 어떤 소녀가 생각나**remind me of a girl**. 그 소녀는 내 배가 침몰했을 때 내 생명을 구해 주었단다 **save my life**. 난 물에 빠져서 죽을 뻔했지**almost drown**. 그녀를 딱 한 번 보았을**see her once** 뿐이지만 잊혀지지가 않는구나**cannot forget her**. 그녀만이 내가 사랑할 수 있는 유일한 여자**the only girl**야."

"그게 바로 나**it is me**라는 걸 왕자님께 말할 수만 있다면**I wish I could**!" 하고 인어공주는 생각했다. "제가 왕자님을 구했어요**save you**. 하지만 저를 몰라 보시네요**don't know me**." 인어공주는 몹시 슬펐다 **feel so sad**.

어느 날 왕이 왕자에게 이웃 나라를 방문하라고**visit the next kingdom** 분부했다**order**. 왕은 왕자가 그 나라의 공주와 결혼하기를**marry the princess of the kingdom** 바랐다.

"아버지께서 내게 명하시니**order me** 거기 가야**go there** 하겠지만, 아무도**no one** 나를 이 공주와 결혼하게 만들**make me marry this princess** 수는 없어." 왕자가 말했다. "너를 보니 잃어버린 내 사랑**my lost love**이 더 생각나는구나. 만약 내가 결혼해야 한다면**must get married** 너랑 결혼하겠어**will marry you**." 왕자는 인어공주에게 입을 맞췄다**kiss the Little Mermaid**. "나와 함께 가겠니**come with me**? 나와 함께 항해**sail with me**해다오." 왕자가 부탁했다.

왕자와 인어공주, 그리고 다른 많은 사람들이 배에 올라**get on a ship** 바다를 가로질러 항해했다**sail across the sea**. 마침내 그들은 아름다운 도시에 도착했다**arrive at a beautiful town**. 많은 사람들이 배로 와서**come to the ship** 왕자를 환영했다**welcome the prince**. 그리고 그 공주도 있었다. 그녀는 꼭 인어공주처럼**just like the Little Mermaid** 짙은 파란색 눈을 갖고 있었다**have deep blue eyes**.

"당신이로군요**it is you**!" 왕자가 소리쳤다. "내 진정한 사랑**my true love**! 바로 당신이 내 생명을 구한 소녀로군요. 오늘 밤이라도 결혼식을 올립시다**let us get married**."

왕자는 인어공주를 돌아보며**turn to the Little Mermaid** 말했다. "내 소원**my wish**이 이뤄졌어**come true**. 너무 행복하구나. 내 진정한 사랑을 찾다니**find my true love**. 너는 나를 사랑하니까 나를 위해 기뻐해 주겠지."

인어공주의 마음**the Little Mermaid's heart**이 무너져 내렸다 **be broken**. 이제는 결코 왕자와 결혼하지 못하게 되었다. 왕자의 결혼 **his wedding**은 한 가지를 뜻했다**mean one thing**. 인어공주가 죽어야만 **must die** 하는 것이다.

GRAMMAR POINT

who / whom (관계대명사)

⇨ 앞에 나온 사람 명사(선행사)를 대신 받음. who 또는 whom이 이끄는 관계절은 그 명사를 수식하며, 목적격인 whom은 생략할 수 있다.

- You are *the girl* **who** saved my life. 당신이 내 생명을 구한 소녀로군요.
- You are *the sweetest girl* **(whom)** I know. 너는 내가 아는 가장 사랑스러운 소녀야.
- She is *the only girl* **(whom)** I can ever love. 그녀만이 내가 사랑할 수 있는 유일한 여자야.

The Little Mermaid

[p. 62-63]

That night, / the prince and the princess / got married / on his ship. The wedding was beautiful. There was joyful music / everywhere. But the Little Mermaid / did not hear the music.

"This is / my last night on Earth," she said to herself. "Tomorrow, / I will die / and become foam on the sea."

At the wedding, / the Little Mermaid danced / for the last time. She moved / like an angel. **She danced / more beautifully than ever.** But her feet and heart / were in pain. After that night, / she would not see the prince again.

At midnight, / the music stopped, / and the prince led his bride away. All was silent, / yet **the Little Mermaid stayed awake**. She went out / to look at the water / by herself.

Just then, / the Little Mermaid's sisters / swam up to the ship. They looked different. Their beautiful hair / was gone.

"Little sister!" they cried. "We gave our hair / to the sea witch. In return, / she gave us a knife. Before the sun rises, / you must kill the prince. When his blood splashes on you, / your tail will return. You will become a mermaid again. Hurry up / and do it. You must kill him / before the sun rises, / or it will be too late."

The Little Mermaid **took the knife / from her sisters**. It was very sharp. She sneaked into the prince's room. The prince and the princess / were sleeping peacefully. The Little Mermaid / **took the knife out**. She looked at the knife. Then, / she looked at the prince. No, / she could not do it. She loved him. She threw the knife / into the sea. Then, / she jumped into the sea. The sun was rising.

- **joyful** 즐거운, 행복한 • **be in pain** 아프다, 고통스럽다, 괴로워하다 • **midnight** 한밤중, 자정 • **bride** 신부
- **silent** 고요한, 조용한 • **stay awake** (자지 않고) 깨어 있다 • **by oneself** 혼자 • **in return** 대신에, 답례로
- **rise** (해, 달 등이) 뜨다, 솟아오르다 • **blood** 피 • **splash** 튀기다 • **sneak into** ~에 몰래 숨어들다
- **peacefully** 평화로이, 고이 • **take out** 꺼내다, 꺼내 들다 • **throw** 던지다 • **jump into** ~로 뛰어들다

CLOSE UP

1 **She danced more beautifully than ever.** 그녀는 그 어느 때보다 더 아름답게 춤췄다.
   〈비교급+than ever〉는 '그 어느 때보다 더 ~하다'라는 의미.

2 **the Little Mermaid stayed awake** 인어공주는 (자지 않고) 깨어 있었다
   〈stay+형용사〉는 '~한 상태를 유지하다'라는 의미. ex) stay healthy(건강을 유지하다) / stay young(젊음을 유지하다)

3 **took the knife from her sisters** 언니들한테서 칼을 받았다 / **took the knife out** 칼을 꺼냈다
   여기서 take의 기본 의미는 '손에 잡다'라는 뜻이다. 따라서 문맥상 첫 번째 표현은 '받다'가 되고, 두 번째 표현은 밖으로 잡아 빼는 거니까 '꺼내다'의 뜻이 된다.

그날 밤that night 왕자와 이웃 나라 공주the prince and the princess는 배 위에서on his ship 결혼했다get married. 결혼식은 아름다웠다. 사방에 흥겨운 음악joyful music이 울렸다. 그러나 인어공주는 음악 소리가 들리지 않았다do not hear the music.

"이게 내가 세상에서 보내는 마지막 밤my last night on Earth이로구나." 인어공주는 혼잣말로 중얼거렸다. "내일이면tomorrow 나는 죽어서die 바다의 물거품이 될become foam on the sea 거야."

결혼식에서at the wedding 인어공주는 마지막으로for the last time 춤을 추었다dance. 인어공주는 천사 같이 몸을 움직였다move like an angel. 그 어느 때보다 더 아름답게more beautifully than ever 춤췄다. 하지만 그녀의 발과 마음her feet and heart은 고통으로 괴로웠다be in pain. 그날 밤이 지나면 인어공주는 왕자를 다시는 보지 못할 터였다.

자정이 되자at midnight 음악이 멈추고 왕자는 신부를 데려갔다lead his bride away. 사방이 고요했다be silent. 하지만 인어공주는 자지 않고 깨어 있었다stay awake. 인어공주는 혼자서by herself 바다를 보러look at the water 나갔다go out.

바로 그때just then 인어공주의 언니들the Little Mermaid's sisters이 배로 헤엄쳐 다가왔다swim up to the ship. 그들은 달라진 모습을 하고 있었다look different. 아름다웠던 머리카락their beautiful hair이 하나도 남아 있지 않았다be gone.

"막내야little sister!" 언니들이 소리치며 말했다. "우리가 바다마녀에게to the sea witch 우리 머리카락을 줬어give our hair. 그 대가로in return 마녀가 칼을 하나 주었단다give a knife. 해가 뜨기 전에 넌 왕자를 죽여야kill the prince 해. 왕자의 피his blood가 네 몸에 튀면splash on you 네 꼬리your tail가 되돌아올return 거야. 넌 다시 인어가 될become a mermaid again 거야. 서둘러서hurry up 그렇게 해라do it. 해 뜨기 전에 왕자를 죽여야 한다. 안 그러면or 때를 놓치게be too late 돼."

인어공주는 언니들한테서from her sisters 칼을 받았다take the knife. 아주 날카로웠다be sharp. 인어공주는 왕자의 방으로 몰래 들어갔다sneak into the prince's room. 왕자와 이웃 나라 공주가 고이 자고sleep peacefully 있었다. 인어공주는 칼을 꺼냈다take the knife out. 칼을 살펴보았다look at the knife. 그리고는 왕자를 바라보았다look at the prince. 안 돼no. 인어공주는 그렇게 할 수 없었다cannot do it. 그녀는 왕자를 사랑했다. 인어공주는 칼을 바다에 던져 버렸다throw the knife into the sea. 그런 다음 바다로 뛰어들었다jump into the sea. 해가 떠오르고 있었다.

Grammar Point

give A to B (= give B A) : A를 B에게 주다 (= B에게 A를 주다)

- We **gave** our hair **to** the sea witch. (= We **gave** the sea witch our hair.)
  우리는 바다마녀에게 우리 머리카락을 줬어.
- She **gave** us a knife. (= She **gave** a knife **to** us.) 그녀가 우리에게 칼을 하나 줬어.
- ※ She gave us it. (X) / She **gave** it **to** us. (O) → 목적어가 둘 다 대명사일 경우, 항상 후자와 같은 형식으로 쓴다.

[p. 64–65]

The Little Mermaid felt cold water. "I am dying," she thought.

But the Little Mermaid / did not turn into foam. Suddenly, / she felt her body / rising into the air. She saw / other lovely floating children. They were singing / around her.

"Where am I? Who are you?" asked the Little Mermaid. She could speak again! She had a new voice. It was even more beautiful / than before.

"You're with us / in the sky. We are / the fairies of the air," they responded. "You are now / a fairy of the air. There are many ways / to win a soul. We can get souls / by doing good deeds," they continued.

"Mermaids only get souls / if humans love them. But the fairies of the air / can live for 300 years. If we do good deeds / for 300 years, / we can earn souls. You tried so hard / to earn a soul. You loved the prince / so much / that you gave your life / for him. We will help you / get a soul. Your soul will live forever."

"I can earn a soul? This is wonderful."

The Little Mermaid / looked down at the ship. She saw / the prince and the bride. The prince was looking sadly / into the ocean. He seemed to have guessed / what had happened to her.

She flew down to them. Of course, / they could not see the Little Mermaid. She moved her body / around them. They felt the cool air / move around them. The Little Mermaid / kissed the prince and his bride. Then, she smiled / and flew up into the sky.

"In 300 years, / I will have a soul," she said. "And I will see my prince / in heaven."

- **turn into** ~이 되다, ~으로 변하다 • **rise** 올라가다, 솟아오르다 • **lovely** 사랑스러운 • **floating** 떠다니는
- **fairy** 요정 • **win a soul** 영혼을 얻다 • **deed** 행위, 행동 • **earn a soul** 영혼을 얻다 • **sadly** 슬프게, 슬프게도 • **guess** 추측하다, 짐작하다 • **fly down** 날아 내려오다 • **fly up** 날아 오르다 • **heaven** 천국

CLOSE UP

1. **It was even more beautiful than before.** 그것은 전보다 훨씬 더 아름다웠다.
   비교급 앞에 쓰인 even은 '훨씬'이라는 뜻으로 비교급을 강조한다. 이 밖에 much, far, still, a lot 등도 비교급을 수식할 수 있다.

2. **We can get souls by doing good deeds.** 우리는 착한 일을 해서 영혼을 얻을 수 있어.
   〈by+V-ing〉는 '~함으로써'라는 뜻으로 수단 및 방법을 나타냄.

3. **We will help you (to) get a soul.** 우리는 네가 영혼을 얻을 수 있게 도와줄 거야.
   〈help+목적어+(to) 동사원형〉은 '~가 …하는 것을 돕다'라는 의미. 이때 to는 써도 되고 안 써도 된다.
   ex) I'll help you (to) find it.(네가 그것을 찾도록 도와줄게.)

4. **He seemed to have guessed what had happened to her.** 그는 그녀에게 무슨 일이 생긴 건지 짐작한 것 같았다.
   〈seem to have p.p.〉는 '~한 것처럼 보이다'라는 의미.
   what had happened to her(그녀에게 무슨 일이 생겼는지)는 대과거이므로 과거완료 시제를 썼다.

인어공주는 차가운 바닷물을 느꼈다**feel cold water**. "이제 죽는구나**be dying**." 하고 인어공주는 생각했다.

그러나 인어공주는 물거품으로 바뀌지 않았다**do not turn into foam**. 갑자기 인어공주는 자신의 몸이 공중으로 올라가고**rise into the air** 있는 게 느껴졌다. 공중에 떠다니는 다른 사랑스러운 아이들**other lovely floating children**이 보였다. 그들은 인어공주 주위에서 노래하고**sing around her** 있었다.

"여기가 어디지**where am I**? 너희들은 누구니?" 인어공주가 물었다. 인어공주는 다시 말을 할 수 있었다**can speak again**! 목소리가 새로 생긴**have a new voice** 것이다. 전보다 훨씬 더 아름다운**even more beautiful** 목소리였다.

"넌 우리와 함께**with us** 하늘에**in the sky** 있는 거야. 우리는 공기의 요정들**the fairies of the air**이란다." 그들이 대답했다. "너도 이제 공기의 요정**a fairy of the air**이야. 영혼을 얻는**win a soul** 방법은 많이 **many ways** 있단다. 우리는 착한 일을 해서**do good deeds** 영혼을 얻을**get souls** 수 있어." 그들이 계속 말했다.

"인어들은 인간이 사랑을 해 주어야만 영혼을 얻지. 하지만 공기의 요정들은 300년을 살**live for 300 years** 수 있단다. 우리는 300년 동안 착한 일을 하면 영혼을 얻을**earn souls** 수 있어. 넌 영혼을 얻으려고 무척 애썼지**try so hard**. 왕자를 너무 사랑한 나머지 그를 위해**for him** 네 목숨까지 바쳤어**give your life**. 네가 영혼을 얻을 수 있게 우리가 도와줄게. 네 영혼**your soul**은 영원히 살게**live forever** 될 거야."

"내가 영혼을 얻을 수 있다고? 정말 멋지구나."

인어공주는 배를 내려다보았다**look down at the ship**. 왕자와 신부가 보였다**see the prince and the bride**. 왕자는 슬퍼하며 바다를 들여다보고**look into the ocean** 있었다. 인어공주에게 무슨 일이 생긴 건지**what happens** 짐작한 것 같았다**seem to guess**.

인어공주는 날아서 두 사람에게 내려갔다**fly down to them**. 당연히 두 사람에게는 인어공주가 보이지 않았다. 인어공주는 두 사람 주위에서 **around them** 몸을 움직였다**move her body**. 두 사람은 서늘한 바람**the cool air**이 그들 주위를 맴도는**move around them** 걸 느꼈다. 인어공주는 왕자와 신부에게 입을 맞췄다**kiss**. 그런 다음 미소를 지으며**smile** 하늘로 날아 올라갔다**fly up into the sky**.

"300년이 지나면**in 300 years** 내게 영혼이 생길**have a soul** 거야." 하고 인어공주는 말했다. "그러면 천국에서**in heaven** 나의 왕자님을 만나겠지**see my prince**."

GRAMMAR POINT

feel + 목적어 + 동사원형/현재분사 ⇒ feel도 지각동사이므로 목적어 다음에 동사원형이나 현재분사가 온다.

- They **felt** the cool air **move** around them. 그들은 서늘한 바람이 그들 주위를 맴도는 걸 느꼈다.
- Suddenly, she **felt** her body **rising** into the air. 갑자기 그녀는 자신의 몸이 공중으로 올라가고 있는 게 느껴졌다.

The Little Mermaid

Super Reading Story Training Book

Step 3

Beauty and the Beast
– Beaumont, Madame de

•

The Stars
– Alphonse Daudet

[p. 68-69]

Beauty and the Beast

Once, / there was / a rich merchant / who had many ships. He bought and sold / things from around the world. He lived in a big house / by the sea. He had three daughters. The daughters were all very beautiful, / but the youngest was the most beautiful / of all. In fact, / she was so beautiful / that everyone called her "Beauty."

Beauty was not only pretty / but also kind and smart. She loved reading. Her two sisters / were not very nice / though. They were selfish and greedy. They liked to go to parties / and to wear nice dresses. They were always mean to Beauty. They laughed at her / when she read books. They only thought about / marrying rich men.

One day, / there was a terrible storm / at sea. All the merchant's ships sank, / so he lost everything. The man had to sell his big house / and move into a small house / in the countryside.

"I'm sorry, my children. All my ships sank," said the man. "We have no money, / so we have to work / to earn money."

"But, Father," said the eldest daughter, "we have never worked / in our lives. We don't know / how to work."

"We can't work. No rich man / will want to marry us!" the middle daughter cried.

The family moved / to the small country house.

"This house is so tiny," said the eldest daughter.

"How are we supposed to live here?" the middle daughter cried.

- **rich** 부유한, 부자의 ≠ poor • **merchant** 상인 • **youngest** 가장 어린; 막내 • **in fact** 사실 • **not only ~ but also...** ~뿐만 아니라 …도 • **kind** 친절한, 마음씨 고운 • **smart** 똑똑한, 영리한 • **though** (문장 끝에 와서) 그렇지만, 하지만 • **selfish** 이기적인 • **greedy** 탐욕스러운, 욕심 많은 • **go to a party** 파티에 가다 • **mean** 비열한, 심술궂은, 못된 • **laugh at** ~을 비웃다, ~을 조롱하다 • **marry** 결혼하다 • **terrible** 아주 심한, 지독한, 끔찍한 • **storm** 폭풍우 • **sink** 가라앉다 • **lose** 잃다 • **countryside** 시골 (지역) • **earn money** 돈을 벌다 • **eldest** 가장 나이가 많은 • **cry** 소리치다, 외치다, 울부짖다 • **tiny** 아주 작은 • **be supposed to** ~해야 한다, ~하기로 되어 있다

CLOSE UP

1. **she was so beautiful that everyone called her "Beauty"**
   그녀는 너무 아름다워서 모두가 그녀를 '뷰티'라고 불렀다
   〈so ~ that...〉은 '아주 ~해서 …하다'라는 의미. 〈call A B〉 하면 'A를 B라고 부르다'라는 의미.

2. **The man had to sell his big house** 그 남자는 자신의 저택을 팔아야 했다 /
   we have to work to earn money 우리 돈을 벌기 위해 일해야 한다
   〈have to ~〉는 '~해야 한다'라는 의미. 과거일 땐 〈had to ~〉로 쓴다.

3. **How are we supposed to live here?** 우리가 어떻게 여기서 산다는 말인가요?
   〈be supposed to ~〉는 '~하기로 되어 있다', '~해야 한다'라는 의미.

미녀와 야수

옛날에once 배를 여러 척 소유한have many ships 부유한 상인a rich merchant이 있었다. 상인은 세계 도처에서 온 물건들things from around the world을 사고팔았다buy and sell. 그는 바닷가에 있는by the sea 저택에서 살았다live in a big house. 상인에게는 딸이 셋 있었다have three daughters. 딸들은 모두 무척 아름다웠지만, 그 중에서도 막내the youngest가 가장 아름다웠다be the most beautiful. 사실in fact 막내딸은 몹시 아름다워서 모두들 그녀를 '뷰티(미녀)'라고 불렀다call her "Beauty".

뷰티는 예쁠be pretty 뿐만 아니라 마음씨도 곱고 영리했다be kind and smart. 뷰티는 책 읽기를 무척 좋아했다love reading. 하지만 두 언니들her two sisters은 그다지 착하지 않았다be not very nice. 언니들은 이기적이고 욕심이 많았다be selfish and greedy. 파티에나 다니며go to parties 근사한 옷을 입는wear nice dresses 걸 좋아했다. 언니들은 항상 뷰티에게 못되게 굴었다be mean to Beauty. 뷰티가 책을 읽고 있으면 비웃었다laugh at her. 그 둘은 돈 많은 남자와 결혼할 생각밖에 하지 않았다.

어느 날one day 바다에at sea 심한 폭풍a terrible storm이 불었다. 상인의 배가 전부all the merchant's ships 침몰해서sink 상인은 모든 걸 잃고lose everything 말았다. 그는 자신의 저택을 팔고sell his big house 시골의in the countryside 작은 집으로 이사 가야만move into a small house 했다.

"얘들아my children, 미안하구나. 내 배가 전부all my ships 가라앉았단다sink." 상인이 말했다. "우리 한테 돈이 한 푼도 없으니have no money, 돈을 벌려면earn money 일을 해야 한단다have to work."

"하지만 아버지, 우리는 생전in our lives 일이라곤 해 본 적이 없어요never work. 우리는 일을 할 줄 모른다고요don't know how to work." 첫째 딸이 말했다.

"저희는 일 못해요can't work. 부유한 남자는 아무도no rich man 우리와 결혼하고marry us 싶어 하지 않을 거예요!" 둘째 딸이 소리쳤다.

가족은 작은 시골집으로 이사 갔다move to the country house.

"이 집은 너무 작아요be tiny." 첫째 딸이 말했다.

"우리가 어떻게 여기서 산다는 말인가요?" 둘째 딸이 울부짖었다.

GRAMMAR POINT

not only ~ but also... : ~뿐만 아니라 …도

- Beauty was **not only** pretty **but also** kind and smart. 뷰티는 예쁠 뿐만 아니라 마음씨도 곱고 영리했다.
- She loved **not only** reading **but also** cooking. 그녀는 독서뿐만 아니라 요리도 무척 좋아했다.

[p. 70-71]

The two sisters / did not stop complaining. But Beauty did not complain / at all. Instead, / she tried to be happy / and to make everyone else happy.

"I will clean the house, / Father," she said. "This house is small, / but we can be happy here."

Beauty worked hard / every day. She woke up / early in the morning / and cleaned the house. She cooked / breakfast, lunch, and dinner / for her family. But her sisters / never did any work. They sat around / and complained / all the time.

One day, / Beauty's father / received a letter. He read the letter / and instantly cheered up.

"Children, / I just heard some good news," he said. "One of my ships / did not sink. It is bringing back / lots of gold and silver / for us. We are rich again. I must go to the port now."

Beauty's sisters / jumped for joy. "We are rich! We are rich!" they cried.

"Oh, Father, / you must buy us / some new dresses," said the two older sisters.

"Yes, my dears, / I will," said their father.

"And you, Beauty, / what would you like me / to get you?" asked her father.

Beauty did not want anything. She was happy / just because she could see her father happy. "Please bring me a rose, / Father," said Beauty. "There are no roses / in our garden."

Beauty's father / hurried to the port. When he arrived there, / he heard some bad news.

"The gold and silver / are gone," his friend told him. "Pirates stole it. There is your ship. It has many holes in it, / so you must fix the holes / before the ship can sail again."

Beauty's father / fell to the ground.

"Without any gold or silver, / I cannot afford / to fix my ship," said Beauty's father sadly. "I will leave the ship there / for now / and return to the countryside."

- **complain** 불평하다 • **wake up** (잠에서) 깨다 • **sit around** 빈둥거리다 • **receive** 받다 • **instantly** 즉각, 즉시 • **cheer up** 기운이 나다 • **bring back** 가지고 돌아오다 • **port** 항구 • **jump for joy** 뛸 듯이 기뻐하다 • **garden** 정원 • **hurry** 서두르다, 서둘러 가다 • **be gone** 가 버리다, 없다, 사라지다 • **pirate** 해적 • **steal** 훔치다 • **fix** 수선하다, 고치다 • **fall to the ground** 땅에 주저앉다 • **afford to** ~할 여유가 있다, ~할 수 있다

CLOSE UP

1 **she tried to be happy and to make everyone else happy**
그녀는 행복해지려고 했고 다른 사람들도 모두 행복하게 해 주려고 애썼다
〈try to ~〉는 '~하려고 노력하다'라는 의미. 여기서는 to be와 to make가 tried의 목적어임.

2 **I cannot afford to fix my ship** 나는 배를 수리할 형편이 안 돼
〈cannot afford to ~〉는 시간적 또는 금전적으로 '~할 여유가 없다'라는 의미.

두 언니들은 불평을 그치지 않았다do not stop complaining. 그러나 뷰티는 전혀 불평하지 않았다do not complain. 대신 행복해지려고 했고 다른 사람들도 모두 행복하게 해 주려고make everyone else happy 애썼다.

"아버지, 제가 집을 청소할게요clean the house." 뷰티가 말했다. "이 집은 작지만be small, 우린 여기서 행복하게 지낼be happy here 수 있어요."

뷰티는 날마다every day 열심히 일했다work hard. 아침 일찍 깨어나wake up early 집을 청소했다. 식구들을 위해 아침, 점심, 저녁을 지었다cook breakfast, lunch, and dinner. 그러나 언니들은 절대 아무 일도 하지 않았다never do any work. 항상all the time 빈둥거리며sit around 투덜대기만 했다.

어느 날 뷰티의 아버지Beauty's father가 편지 한 통을 받았다receive a letter. 그는 편지를 읽고read the letter 즉시 기운이 났다cheer up.

"얘들아, 내가 방금 좋은 소식을 들었다hear some good news." 아버지가 말했다. "내 배들 중 한 척one of my ships이 가라앉지 않았다는구나do not sink. 그 배가 우리에게 줄 금과 은을 잔뜩lots of gold and silver 싣고 돌아오는bring back 중이란다. 우린 다시 부자가 된be rich again 거야. 내가 지금 항구에 나가go to the port 봐야겠구나."

뷰티의 언니들은 뛸 듯이 기뻐했다jump for joy. "우린 부자다! 우린 부자야!" 하고 그들은 소리쳤다.

"오, 아버지, 저희한테 새 드레스 사 주셔야buy us some new dresses 해요." 두 언니들이 말했다.

"그래, 얘들아. 그러도록 하마." 아버지가 말했다.

"그리고 너 뷰티야, 너한테는 뭘 사다 주면 좋겠니?" 아버지가 물었다.

뷰티는 아무것도 바라지 않았다do not want anything. 그저 아버지가 행복해하는 모습을 볼see her father happy 수 있는 것만으로도 기뻤다. "제게는 장미 한 송이 갖다 주세요bring me a rose, 아버지." 뷰티가 말했다. "우리 정원에in our garden 장미가 하나도 없으니까요no roses."

뷰티의 아버지는 서둘러 항구로 갔다hurry to the port. 그런데 그곳에 도착해서arrive there 나쁜 소식을 들었다hear some bad news.

"금과 은the gold and silver은 없어졌다네be gone." 그의 친구가 그에게 말했다. "해적들pirates이 훔쳐 갔어steal it. 자네의 배는 있네. 배에 구멍이 많이 나서have many holes in it 배가 다시 출항할sail again 수 있으려면 그 전에 구멍들을 때워야fix the holes 하지만 말일세."

뷰티의 아버지는 땅바닥에 주저앉았다fall to the ground.

"금이나 은이 없으면without any gold or silver 내 배를 수리할 형편이 안 돼cannot afford to fix." 뷰티의 아버지가 서글프게 말했다. "당분간은for now 배를 저기에 남겨 두고leave the ship there 시골로 돌아가야겠구나return to the countryside."

GRAMMAR POINT

would like ~ to... : ~가 …하기를 바라다 ⇨ would like는 보통 줄여서 'd like로 쓴다.

- What **would** you **like** me **to** get you? 내가 너한테 뭘 사다 주면 좋겠니?

- I **would like** you **to** buy me some new dresses. 제게 새 드레스를 사 주시면 좋겠어요.
  (= I'**d like** you **to**...)

Beauty and the Beast

[p. 72-73]

Then he remembered his daughters. He looked in his pockets / and **found only a few coins**. "I don't have enough money / to buy any dresses." Sadly, / he started to walk back home.

Suddenly, / the weather became terribly cold. It began to snow, / and the wind blew heavily. Soon, / he was lost / in a forest.

"This is very strange," he said to himself. "I have never seen this forest / before. I must be lost."

He heard wolves / howling loudly. He began to feel very afraid. "**I must find some shelter. There is no way / I will get home tonight**," he said.

He looked around / and saw a light / at some distance. "What is that? Is there a house / there?"

Beauty's father / followed the light. After a few minutes, / he found a castle.

"I wonder / who lives here," he said. He went to the door of the castle.

"Hello?" he called. But there was no answer. The door was open, / so he walked inside. He saw no one. It was cold, / and he was tired. He entered a large hall. It was a dining room. A huge fire was burning / in the fireplace. And the dining table / was full of food. There was a single plate / on the table / with a knife and fork beside it.

"**This must be / someone's dinner**," he thought. He **waited / for the person to arrive**, / but no one came. Finally, / after he had waited / for a couple of hours, / he sat down at the table / and ate the food. Because he was starving, / he ate all of the food. Then, / he found a bedroom / and fell asleep immediately.

- **remember** 기억하다, 생각해 내다 • **coin** 동전 • **terribly** 아주, 심하게 • **heavily** 강하게, 심하게 • **be lost** 길을 잃다 • **wolf** 늑대 • **howl** (늑대 등이) 길게 울다, 울부짖다 • **shelter** 쉴 곳, 피난처 • **look around** 둘러보다, 두리번거리다 • **at some distance** 좀 떨어진 곳에 • **wonder** 궁금하게 여기다 • **dining room** 식사하는 방, 식당 • **burn** (불이) 타오르다, 불타다 • **fireplace** 벽난로 • **dining table** 식탁 • **be full of** ~으로 가득 차다 • **plate** 접시 • **dinner** 저녁식사 • **a couple of** 둘의, 두서너 개의, 몇 개의 • **starving** 몹시 배가 고픈 • **fall asleep** 잠들다, 잠에 끓어떨어지다 • **immediately** 즉시, 즉각

CLOSE UP

1. **found only a few coins** 동전 몇 푼밖에 없었다
   a few는 '몇 개라는 의미로, 뒤에 복수명사가 온다. only a few 하면 '몇 개밖에 안 되는', '근소한'이라는 의미.

2. **I must be lost.** 내가 길을 잃은 게 틀림없군. / **I must find some shelter.** 피신할 곳을 찾아야겠어. / **This must be someone's dinner.** 이건 누군가의 저녁식사가 틀림없어.
   must는 '~해야 한다(의무, 필요)' 또는 '~임에 틀림없다(추측)'라는 의미. 문맥에 따라 적절한 의미를 파악하자.

3. **There is no way (that) I will get home tonight.** 오늘 밤에 집에 가기는 글렀어.
   〈there is no way (that) ~〉는 '~할 방법이 없다', '절대로 ~ 아니다/안 되다'라는 의미.

4. **waited for the person to arrive** 그 사람이 도착하기를 기다렸다
   〈wait for ~ to...〉는 '~가 …하기를 기다리다'라는 의미.

그때 그는 딸들 생각이 났다remember his daughters. 그가 호주머니 속을 살펴보니look in his pockets 동전 몇 푼밖에only a few coins 없었다. "드레스를 살 만한 돈이 없군." 그는 안타까워하며sadly 집으로 걸어 돌아가기walk back home 시작했다.

갑자기 날씨the weather가 엄청나게 추워졌다become cold. 눈이 내리기snow 시작하고, 바람the wind도 심하게 불었다blow heavily. 곧 그는 숲에서in a forest 길을 잃었다be lost.

"이거 참 이상하군be strange." 그는 혼잣말을 했다. "이 숲은 전에 한 번도 본 적이 없는데never see this forest before. 내가 길을 잃은 게 틀림없어."

늑대들wolves이 큰 소리로 울부짖는howl loudly 소리가 들렸다. 그는 몹시 두려워지기feel afraid 시작했다. "피신할 곳을 찾아야겠군find some shelter. 오늘 밤에 집에 가기는get home 글렀어no way." 그가 말했다.

주위를 둘러보니look around 좀 떨어진 곳에서at some distance 불빛이 하나 보였다see a light. "저게 뭘까? 저기에 인가a house가 있나?"

뷰티의 아버지는 그 빛을 따라갔다follow the light. 몇 분 뒤after a few minutes 그는 성을 한 채 발견했다find a castle.

"이곳에 누가 사는 걸까I wonder." 그는 이렇게 말하며 성문the door of the castle으로 갔다.

"여보세요hello?" 그가 외쳤다. 그러나 아무런 대답이 없었다no answer. 문이 열려 있길래 그는 안으로 들어갔다walk inside. 아무도 보이지 않았다see no one. 날씨는 추웠고, 그는 피곤했다. 그는 커다란 홀로 들어갔다enter a hall. 그곳은 식당a dining room이었다. 벽난로에in the fireplace 큰 불a huge fire이 활활 타고burn 있었다. 게다가 식탁the dining table에는 음식이 가득 차려져 있었다be full of food. 식탁 위에on the table 접시가 한 개a single plate 놓여 있고, 그 옆에beside it 나이프와 포크a knife and fork가 있었다.

"이건 누군가의 저녁식사someone's dinner가 틀림없어." 하고 그는 생각했다. 그 사람이 도착하길 for the person to arrive 기다렸지만wait 아무도no one 오지 않았다come. 결국finally 두 시간을 기다린 끝에 그는 식탁에 앉아sit down at the table 음식을 먹었다eat the food. 그는 몹시 배가 고팠기 be starving 때문에 음식을 전부 먹어 버렸다eat all of the food. 그런 다음 침실을 발견하고는find a bedroom 즉시 곯아떨어졌다fall asleep.

GRAMMAR POINT

have/has + p.p. (현재완료: 경험) ⇨ 지금까지의 경험을 나타낼 수 있음.

- I **have** never **seen** this forest before. 이 숲은 전에 한 번도 본 적이 없는데.
- We can't work. We **have** never **worked** in our lives. 우리는 일 못해요. 생전 일이라곤 해 본 적이 없잖아요.
- You look familiar. I'm sure we **have met** before. 당신은 낯이 익어요. 우리 분명 전에 만난 적 있어요.

[p. 74-75]

In the morning, / Beauty's father woke up. He looked around the room. He saw some breakfast / on the table. But he did not see anybody. He sat down at the table / and enjoyed breakfast. While he ate, / he looked outside. He saw **a beautiful garden / full of flowers**.

"That's strange," he thought. "Last night, / there was a huge snowstorm, / but the sun is shining now, / and the flowers are blooming."

Just then, / he remembered the promise / that he had made to Beauty.

"A rose!" he said aloud. "==I promised Beauty / I would bring her a rose.==" He went out to the garden / and found a rose bush. **It was full of / beautiful red roses.** He picked one. But **as soon as he picked the rose**, / he heard a loud roar. And he saw a frightful, angry beast / coming toward him.

"You dirty thief!" cried the Beast.

"I saved your life / and gave you food and a bed. But, in return, / you are stealing my flowers. **Now you're going to / pay for it. I'm going to / kill you.**"

Beauty's father fell to the ground / and cried out, "Forgive me. I only wanted a single rose / for my daughter. ==I promised to bring a rose / to my youngest daughter, Beauty.== Please do not kill me."

The Beast looked down at him angrily / and said, "All right. You may go home. But you have to / send me your daughter. She must come here / and live in this castle / with me. If not, / then you must return here / and die. Go back to your bedroom. There is a box of gold / there. Take it and go."

- **huge** 거대한, 커다란, 엄청난 • **snowstorm** 눈보라 • **shine** 빛나다 • **bloom** 꽃이 피다 • **promise** 약속; 약속하다 • **rose bush** 장미 나무, 장미 덤불 • **pick** (꽃 등을) 꺾다, 따다 • **as soon as** ~하자마자 • **roar** 으르렁거리는 소리 • **frightful** 무시무시한, 겁나는 • **dirty** 더러운 • **thief** 도둑 • **save one's life** ~의 목숨을 구하다 • **in return** 그 대가로, 그 보상으로 • **steal** 훔치다 • **pay for** ~에 대한 대가를 치르다 • **forgive** 용서하다 • **angrily** 노하여, 성나서

CLOSE UP

1. **a beautiful garden full of flowers** 꽃들이 가득한 아름다운 정원 /
   It was full of beautiful red roses. 그것은 아름다운 장미꽃들로 가득했다.
   〈full of ~〉는 '~로 가득한'이라는 의미.

2. **as soon as he picked the rose** 그가 장미를 꺾자마자
   〈as soon as + 주어 + 동사〉는 '~하자마자'라는 의미.

3. **Now you're going to pay for it.** 이제 넌 그 대가를 치러야겠다. /
   I'm going to kill you. 너를 죽여 버리겠다.
   〈be going to ~〉는 '~할 것이다'라는 뜻으로, 현재의 상황으로 보아 앞으로 곧 일어나게 될 일, 또는 이미 계획하거나 결정해서 앞으로 하게 될 일을 말할 때 쓰임.

아침이 되자in the morning 뷰티의 아버지는 잠에서 깨어났다wake up. 그는 방을 둘러보았다look around the room. 탁자에on the table 아침식사가 차려져 있는 게 보였다see some breakfast. 그러나 사람은 아무도 보이지 않았다do not see anybody. 그는 탁자에 앉아서 아침식사를 맛있게 먹었다enjoy breakfast. 식사를 하면서 그는 밖을 내다보았다look outside. 꽃들이 가득한full of flowers 아름다운 정원이 보였다see a garden.

"그거 이상하군." 그는 생각했다. "어젯밤에는last night 엄청난 눈보라a huge snowstorm가 몰아쳤는데, 지금은 태양the sun이 빛나고shine 있고, 꽃들the flowers이 피어나고bloom 있네."

바로 그때just then 그는 뷰티에게 한 약속이 떠올랐다remember the promise. "장미a rose!" 그는 큰 소리로 말했다. "내가 뷰티한테 장미를 갖다 주겠다고bring her a rose 약속했지."

그는 정원으로 나가go out to the garden 장미 덤불을 찾았다find a rose bush. 아름다운 빨간 장미들이 한가득 있었다. 그는 한 송이를 꺾었다pick one. 그러나 그가 장미를 꺾자마자 크게 으르렁거리는 소리가 들렸다hear a loud roar. 그리고 무시무시하게 생긴 성난 야수a frightful, angry beast가 자신에게 다가오고come toward him 있는 게 보였다.

"이 더러운 도둑놈you dirty thief!" 야수가 소리쳤다.

"난 네 목숨을 구해 주고save your life, 네게 음식과 잠자리를 주었다give food and a bed. 그런데 그 보답으로in return 넌 내 꽃들을 훔치고steal my flowers 있는 것이냐. 이제 넌 그 대가를 치러야pay for it 되겠다. 네 놈을 죽여kill you 버리겠다."

뷰티의 아버지는 땅에 주저앉아fall to the ground 큰 소리로 외쳤다. "용서해 주십시오forgive me. 딸아이에게 줄 장미 딱 한 송이만 얻고 싶었을want a single rose 뿐입니다. 제 막내딸my youngest daughter 뷰티에게 장미를 갖다 주기로 약속했거든요. 부디 목숨만은 살려 주십시오do not kill me."

야수는 성난 표정으로angrily 그를 내려다보며look down at him 말했다. "좋아all right. 집에 가도go home 좋다. 하지만 네 딸을 내게 보내야send me your daughter 한다. 네 딸은 여기로 와서come here 이 성에서in this castle 나와 함께with me 살아야 한다. 안 그러면if not 네가 여기로 돌아와서return here 죽어야 한다must die. 네 침실로 돌아가라go back to your bedroom. 거기에 금 한 상자a box of gold가 있다. 그걸 가지고take it 가라."

GRAMMAR POINT

promise의 용법

- I **promised** Beauty **(that)** I would bring her a rose. 나는 뷰티에게 장미 한 송이를 갖다 주겠다고 약속했다.
- I **promised to** bring a rose to my youngest daughter, Beauty.
  나는 내 막내딸 뷰티에게 장미 한 송이를 갖다 주기로 약속했다.
- I **promised** my daughter Beauty **to** bring her a rose. 나는 내 딸 뷰티에게 장미 한 송이를 갖다 주겠다고 약속했다.

[p. 76-77]

Beauty's father / hurried away from the castle / as fast as he could. When he got home, / he told his children / what had happened.

"I must return to the castle," he said. "I just wanted to say goodbye / to all of you."

Beauty's sisters / suddenly became angry at her.

"Beauty, / what have you done?" they shouted. "It's your fault. You wanted the rose, / and now Father must die. You stupid girl!"

"Father, / I'll go to the Beast. I'm not afraid. I will go / and live with the Beast," Beauty said quietly.

"No, Beauty, no."

"There is no choice," she said. "The Beast will kill you and our family / if I do not go."

Beauty's father was very sad. He went to his bedroom. Beauty followed him there.

"What is the Beast like, / Father? Is he very ugly?" she asked.

"Yes, the Beast is ugly, / but he can also be kind. Look. He gave me / this box of gold. But do not tell your sisters / about it. They will only want / to spend it on new dresses."

"Father, / please give the money / to them," Beauty told her father. "While you were away, / two men came here. My sisters are going to marry them, / so they will have to / buy many things. They need that money."

The next morning, / Beauty said goodbye to her family / and left for the castle. She was very sad, / but she did not cry. Late in the evening, / she finally arrived at the Beast's castle. The door was open, / so she walked up to it. She saw nobody. "Hello?" she yelled, / but no one answered.

"What a weird place!" thought Beauty. But she was very brave. She walked around the castle / and found the dining room. There was a table / with lots of food on it. All her favorite foods / were on the table. There were / two plates, two glasses, two forks, and two knives. Beauty sat down / and ate the food.

- **say goodbye** 작별인사를 하다, 작별을 고하다 • **angry at** ~에게 화내는 • **fault** 잘못 • **stupid** 어리석은, 바보 같은 • **afraid** 두려워하는, 겁내는 • **quietly** 조용히, 침착하게 • **ugly** 추한, 못생긴 • **spend** (돈 등을) 쓰다 • **be away** 멀리 가 있다, 부재 중이다 • **cry** 울다 • **arrive at** ~에 도착하다 • **walk up to** ~에 다가가다 • **yell** 소리치다, 외치다 • **weird** 이상한 • **brave** 용감한 • **favorite** (제일) 좋아하는 • **sit down** 앉다

CLOSE UP

1 **as fast as he could** 최대한 빨리 (할 수 있는 한 빨리)
⟨as ~ as one can/could⟩는 '최대한 ~하게'라는 의미. ⟨as ~ as possible⟩로 바꿔 쓸 수 있다.

2 **What is the Beast like** 야수는 어떤 사람이에요
⟨What is ~ like?⟩는 '~는 어떤 사람이니?'라는 의미.

3 **spend it on new dresses** 새 드레스를 사는 데 그것을 쓴다
spend는 '(돈을) 쓰다', '(시간을) 보내다'라는 의미. ⟨spend+돈+on ~⟩하면 '~에 돈을 쓰다'의 뜻이 된다.

뷰티의 아버지는 되도록 빨리as fast as he can 허겁지겁 성에서 벗어났다hurry away from the castle. 그는 집에 도착해서get home 자식들에게 무슨 일이 있었는지what happens 들려주었다.

"나는 성으로 돌아가야return to the castle 한단다." 아버지가 말했다. "그저 너희 모두에게to all of you 작별인사를 하고say goodbye 싶었단다."

뷰티의 언니들이 갑자기 뷰티에게 화를 냈다become angry at her.

"뷰티야, 네가 무슨 짓을 한 거니?" 언니들이 언성을 높였다. "네 잘못(책임)your fault이야. 네가 장미를 원하는want the rose 바람에 이제 아버지께서 돌아가시게 생겼어must die. 멍청한 계집애 같으니you stupid girl!"

"아버지, 제가 야수한테 갈게요go to the Beast. 저는 두렵지 않아요. 제가 가서 야수와 함께 살겠어요live with the Beast." 뷰티가 조용히 말했다.

"안 된다, 뷰티야. 안 돼."

"선택의 여지가 없어요no choice." 뷰티가 말했다. "제가 가지 않으면 야수가 아버지와 우리 가족을 죽일kill you and our family 거예요."

뷰티의 아버지는 몹시 슬펐다be sad. 그는 자기 침실로 갔다go to his bedroom. 뷰티가 거기로 아버지를 따라갔다follow him.

"아버지, 야수는 어떤 사람이에요? 아주 흉하게 생겼나요be ugly?" 뷰티가 물었다.

"그래, 야수는 흉하게 생겼단다. 하지만 친절할 수도 있을can be kind 것 같구나. 봐라look. 야수가 내게 이 금 상자this box of gold를 줬단다. 하지만 네 언니들한테는 이것에 대해 말하지 마라do not tell. 그 애들은 오로지 새 드레스를 사는 데다 이걸 쓰려고spend it on new dresses 할 테니 말이다."

"아버지, 그 돈은 언니들에게 주세요." 뷰티가 아버지에게 말했다. "아버지가 안 계신be away 동안 두 남자two men가 여기 왔었어요come here. 언니들은 그 남자들과 결혼할marry them 테니 많은 것을 사야buy many things 할 거예요. 언니들한테는 그 돈이 필요해요need that money."

다음 날 아침the next morning 뷰티는 식구들에게 작별인사를 하고say goodbye 성을 향해 떠났다leave for the castle. 뷰티는 무척 슬펐지만 울지 않았다. 저녁 늦게late in the evening 뷰티는 드디어 야수의 성에 도착했다arrive at the Beast's castle. 성문the door이 열려 있어서be open 뷰티는 그 문으로 다가갔다walk up to it. 아무도 보이지 않았다see nobody. "여보세요hello?" 뷰티가 소리쳐 불러 봤지만 아무도no one 대답하지answer 않았다.

"참 이상한 곳a weird place이구나." 하고 뷰티는 생각했다. 그렇지만 뷰티는 매우 용감했다be brave. 그녀는 성을 돌아다니다가walk around the castle 식당을 발견했다find the dining room. 음식이 푸짐하게 차려진 식탁이 하나a table with lots of food on it 있었다. 뷰티가 제일 좋아하는 음식들her favorite foods이 전부 식탁 위에 있었다. 접시 두 개two plates와 유리잔 두 개two glasses, 포크 두 개two forks, 나이프 두 개two knives가 있었다. 뷰티는 앉아서sit down 음식을 먹었다eat the food.

GRAMMAR POINT

had + p.p. (과거완료: 대과거) ⇨ 과거의 어느 시점보다 먼저 일어난 일을 말할 때 쓰임.

- When he <u>got</u> home, he <u>told</u> his children what **had happened.**
  그는 집에 도착해서 자식들에게 무슨 일이 있었는지 말했다. (집에 와서 자식들에게 말한 것보다 무슨 일이 생긴 게 먼저임.)

- He <u>remembered</u> the promise that he **had made** to Beauty. 그는 뷰티에게 한 약속이 떠올랐다.
  (약속이 떠오른 것보다 뷰티에게 약속을 한 게 먼저임.)

[p. 78-79]

After supper, / Beauty started / to look around the castle. It was a beautiful castle / with many fine rooms. When Beauty got to one room, / she looked at the door. There was a sign / on the door. **It read "Beauty's Room."**

"Is this my room? Well, if he gives me a special room, / maybe he will not kill me," she thought.

Beauty opened the door / and went inside. It was the most beautiful room / she had ever seen. It was full of / flowers, books, and beautiful clothes. She picked up one book / and opened it. Inside, / there was a note. It read:

> Welcome, Beauty.
> Do not be afraid.
> You will be safe and happy / here.
> I will do anything / you want.
> You may have all of this.

"He must be very kind," Beauty thought. Beauty was very tired. She went to bed / and fell asleep instantly.

Beauty spent the next day / alone. In the evening, / Beauty put on the most beautiful dress / and went to the dining room. All of her favorite foods / were on the table. Beauty sat down. Suddenly, / she heard a gentle growl, / and the Beast came in. He was wearing fine clothes, / but he had as much hair as a lion.

Beauty said, "Thank you for my present, / sir."

"Call me Beast," said the Beast.

"Tell me, / Beauty. Am I very ugly? **Are you afraid of me?**"

"Yes, Beast, / you are ugly," said Beauty slowly. "But **you seem to be very gentle. I'm not afraid of you** / because you're nice to me."

"Thank you for saying that," said the Beast.

That evening, / Beauty and the Beast / had dinner together. They talked about many topics. By the end of the dinner, / Beauty thought / that the Beast was not so frightening.

- **supper** 저녁 • **look around** 둘러보다 • **fine** 좋은, 비싼 • **sign** 표지판 • **read** (~라고) 적혀 있다 • **kill** 죽이다 • **pick up** 집어 들다 • **safe** 안전한 • **alone** 혼자서 • **put on** (옷을) 입다 • **gentle** 부드러운, 친절한, 온화한 • **growl** 으르렁거리는 소리 • **topic** 주제 • **frightening** 무서운, 겁나는

CLOSE UP

1 **It read "Beauty's Room."** 거기에는 '뷰티의 방'이라고 적혀 있었다.
   read의 주어로 편지나 쪽지, 표지판 등이 오면 '~라고 쓰여 있다'라는 의미.

2 **Are you afraid of me?** 내가 무섭소? / **I'm not afraid of you** 난 당신이 무섭지 않아요
   〈be afraid of ~〉는 '~을 무서워하다', '~을 두려워하다'라는 의미.

3 **you seem to be very gentle** 당신은 무척 온화하게 보여요
   〈seem to ~〉는 '~인 것처럼 보이다'라는 의미.

저녁식사 후after supper 뷰티는 성을 둘러보기look around the castle 시작했다. 훌륭한 방들이 많이 있는with many fine rooms 아름다운 성a beautiful castle이었다. 뷰티는 한 방에 이르러서get to one room 방문을 살펴보았다look at the door. 문 위에on the door 표지판a sign이 붙어 있었다. 거기에는 '뷰티의 방Beauty's Room'이라고 적혀 있었다.

"여기가 내 방my room이라고? 음, 야수가 내게 특별한 방a special room을 주는 거라면, 아마도 maybe 날 죽이지는 않겠구나." 하고 뷰티는 생각했다.

뷰티는 방문을 열고open the door 안으로 들어갔다go inside. 뷰티가 그때까지 본 중에 가장 아름다운 방the most beautiful room이었다. 방에는 꽃과 책과 아름다운 옷들flowers, books, and beautiful clothes이 가득했다. 뷰티는 책 한 권을 집어서pick up one book 펼쳐 보았다. 안쪽에inside 쪽지a note 가 하나 있었다. 내용은 이러했다.

> 뷰티여, 환영하오welcome.
> 두려워하지 마시오do not be afraid.
> 당신은 이곳에서 안전하고 행복해질be safe and happy 거요.
> 당신이 원하는 건 무엇이든지anything you want 내가 해 주겠소.
> 당신은 이 모든 걸 누려도have all of this 좋소.

"야수는 마음씨가 무척 고운 게 틀림없어." 하고 뷰티는 생각했다. 뷰티는 몹시 피곤했다be tired. 그래서 잠자리에 들어go to bed 곧 잠들었다fall asleep.

뷰티는 그다음 날을 혼자서 보냈다spend the next day alone. 저녁 때in the evening 뷰티는 가장 아름다운 드레스를 입고put on the most beautiful dress 식당으로 갔다go to the dining room. 뷰티가 가장 좋아하는 음식들이 전부 식탁에 차려져 있었다. 뷰티는 자리에 앉았다. 갑자기 부드럽게 그르렁거리는 소리가 들리더니hear a gentle growl 야수가 들어왔다come in. 야수는 좋은 옷을 입고wear fine clothes 있었지만 사자처럼 털이 많았다have as much hair as a lion.

뷰티가 말했다. "선물을 주셔서 감사합니다thank you for my present, 나으리sir."

"야수라고 불러요call me Beast." 야수가 말했다.

"말해 보시오tell me, 뷰티. 내가 아주 흉하게 생겼소? 내가 무섭소?"

"네, 야수님. 당신은 보기 싫게 생겼어요." 뷰티가 천천히 말했다. "그렇지만 무척 온화하게 보이세요seem to be gentle. 제게 잘해 주셔서be nice to me 저는 당신이 무섭지 않아요."

"그렇게 말해 주니 고맙소thank you for saying that." 야수가 말했다.

그날 저녁 뷰티와 야수Beauty and the Beast는 함께 저녁식사를 했다have dinner together. 둘은 여러 가지 주제에 관해 얘기를 나눴다talk about many topics. 저녁식사가 끝날 무렵by the end of the dinner 뷰티는 야수가 그다지 무섭지 않다be not so frightening고 생각하게 되었다.

GRAMMAR POINT

as much/many ~ as... : …만큼 많은 ~

⇨ 셀 수 없는 명사 앞에는 much, 셀 수 있는 명사 앞에는 many를 쓴다.

- He had **as much** hair **as** a lion. 그는 사자만큼 많은 털이 있었다.

- The garden had **as many** flowers **as** I had expected. 정원에는 기대했던 만큼 많은 꽃들이 있었다.

[p. 80-81]

The next day, / Beauty went downstairs. There, / she saw the Beast / waiting for her.

"There is a mirror / in your bedroom," the Beast said. "It is a magic mirror. When you want to see your father, / look into that mirror."

"That is very generous / of you. Thank you," replied Beauty.

"Beauty, / I know / that I am ugly," said the Beast. "I must be stupid / as well / because I cannot think of / anything smart / to say to you."

Beauty felt bad. "I know many people / who look beautiful / but have ugly hearts," she said. "I like you better / than those people, / Beast."

"Then will you marry me?" asked the Beast.

"Marry you? Oh, no. I'm sorry, / but I cannot do that," she said.

Beauty lived in the castle / with the Beast, / and they were very happy. Every night / at nine o'clock, / Beauty and the Beast / had dinner together / and chatted. At the end of every dinner, / the Beast always proposed, "Will you marry me?" And Beauty always answered, "I like you, / but I cannot marry you."

For three months, / Beauty lived at the castle. She was happy there. She read books / and walked through the garden / every day. But, one day, / she looked into the magic mirror. She saw her father. He was sick in bed / and was all by himself.

"I must go / and see my father. I must talk to the Beast / at dinner," Beauty thought.

At nine o'clock, / Beauty and the Beast / had dinner together. The Beast said, "If you will not marry me, / then will you be my friend? I want you / to stay with me / forever."

"Of course I will," Beauty answered. "You are kind to me. I will stay here with you, / but there is a problem. I looked into the magic mirror / and saw my father. He is sick in bed / and all by himself. Will you please / let me go to visit him?"

- **go downstairs** 아래층으로 내려가다 • **mirror** 거울 • **look into** ~을 들여다보다 • **generous** 후한, 너그러운, 관대한 • **feel bad** 가엽게 여기다, 미안한 마음이 들다 • **chat** 이야기하다 • **propose** 청혼하다 • **sick** 아픈 • **sick in bed** 아파서 몸져눕다 • **all by oneself** 혼자서 • **stay** 머물다, 남아 있다 • **forever** 영원히

CLOSE UP

1. **I know many people who look beautiful but have ugly hearts.**
   아름다워 보여도 추한 마음을 지닌 사람들을 많이 알아요.
   〈who ~ hearts〉 부분은 many people을 수식하는 관계절이다.

2. **all by himself** 홀로
   all by oneself는 '혼자서'라는 의미. *ex)* all by myself(나 혼자서) / all by herself(그녀 혼자서)

Step 3

다음 날 뷰티가 아래층으로 내려갔다go downstairs. 거기서 야수가 그녀를 기다리고wait for her 있는 게 보였다.

"당신 침실에in your bedroom 거울이 하나a mirror 있소." 야수가 말했다. "마법 거울a magic mirror 이라오. 아버지가 보고see your father 싶으면 그 거울을 들여다보시오look into that mirror."

"참으로 관대한be generous 분이세요. 고맙습니다." 뷰티가 대답했다.

"뷰티, 나도 내가 흉하게 생겼다는 걸 알아요." 야수가 말했다. "또한 어리석은be stupid 것도 틀림없 소. 당신에게 말하려면 어떤 영리한 말도anything smart 생각나지 않으니cannot think of 말이오."

뷰티는 안됐다는 생각이 들었다feel bad. "겉으로는 아름다워 보이지만look beautiful 추한 마음을 지닌have ugly hearts 사람들을 많이 알고 있어요." 뷰티가 말했다. "그런 사람들보다는 당신이 더 좋아요 like you better, 야수님."

"그럼 나와 결혼해marry me 주겠소?" 야수가 물었다.

"당신과 결혼이요? 오, 아뇨oh, no. 미안하지만 그렇게 할 수는 없어요cannot do that." 뷰티가 말했다.

뷰티는 성에서in the castle 야수와 함께with the Beast 지냈고, 두 사람은 무척 행복했다. 매일 밤 every night 9시에at nine o'clock 뷰티와 야수는 함께 만찬을 먹고have dinner together 담소를 나눴 다chat. 매번 저녁식사가 끝날 때마다at the end of every dinner 야수는 언제나 청혼을 했다always propose. "나와 결혼해 주겠소?" 그리고 뷰티는 언제나 이렇게 대답했다always answer. "당신을 좋아하 지만like you 당신과 결혼할 수는 없어요cannot marry you."

뷰티는 3개월 동안for three months 성에서 지냈다live at the castle. 그곳에서 뷰티는 행복했다. 날마다every day 책을 읽고read books 정원 을 거닐었다walk through the garden. 그러던 어느 날 뷰티는 마법 거 울을 들여다보았다look into the magic mirror. 아버지가 보였다see her father. 아버지는 아파서 몸져누운be sick in bed 채 홀로all by himself 계셨다.

"가서 아버지를 뵈어야go and see my father 해. 저녁식사 때at dinner 야수에게 말해야겠어talk to the Beast." 하고 뷰티는 생각했다.

9시에 뷰티와 야수는 함께 만찬을 먹었다. 야수가 말했다. "나와 결 혼하지 못하겠다면 내 친구가 되어be my friend 주겠소? 당신이 영원히 forever 내 곁에 머물면stay with me 좋겠소."

"당연히of course 그러겠어요." 뷰티가 대답했다. "당신은 제게 친절하시잖아요. 이곳에서 당신과 함께 있겠어요stay here with you. 하지만 한 가지 문제a problem 가 있어요. 제가 마법 거울을 들여다보니 아 버지의 모습이 보였어요. 아파서 몸져누운 채 홀로 계셨어요. 아버지를 찾아뵈러 갈go to visit him 수 있 게 허락해 주시겠어요?"

GRAMMAR POINT

want + 목적어 + to부정사 : ~가 …하기를 원하다
let + 목적어 + 동사원형 : ~가 …하도록 허락하다

⇨ want 뒤에는 to부정사가 오고, let 뒤에는 동사원형이 온다는 점에 주의할 것.

- I **want** you **to stay** with me forever. 당신이 영원히 내 곁에 머물면 좋겠소.
- Will you please **let** me **go** to visit him? 아버지를 찾아뵈러 갈 수 있게 허락해 주시겠어요?

[p. 82-83]

"If you leave, / you will not come back," the Beast said.

"I promise to come back," said Beauty. "But let me go there / for one week."

The Beast thought for a moment / and then said, "Okay. You may go."

He gave Beauty a ring / and said, "Take this. Put on this ring / and go to bed. Tomorrow, / you will wake up / in your father's home. After seven days, / take the ring off / and put the ring by your bed. You'll wake up / in this castle."

"Goodbye, Beauty. Don't forget your promise. Come back / in seven days."

Beauty thanked the Beast. She put the ring on / and went to sleep. In the morning, / when she woke up, / she was in her father's home. She got up / and ran to her father.

"Father, / I'm home," she said.

"Oh, Beauty," he cried, "you have returned. I thought / the Beast ate you. I'm so ill, / and I am all alone. Your sisters are married, / and they never visit me."

"Father, / I am only here / for one week, / but I will take good care of you. You will feel better soon," Beauty responded.

Beauty's father looked at her. "You look beautiful," he said. "Your dress looks very nice. Is the Beast good to you?"

"Yes, he is very kind to me. I like him very much. Perhaps I almost love him," Beauty said.

Her older sisters heard / that Beauty was back. They came to visit her / with their husbands. Both sisters were unhappy. One had a very handsome husband, / but he was unkind. The other had a very smart husband, / but he talked too much. When they saw Beauty / in her beautiful dress, / they both became angry.

"Why is she always happy?" said one.

"I can't stand this. Let's keep Beauty here / longer than a week. Then, / the Beast will become angry with her. Maybe the Beast will eat her / then." The other sister agreed.

- **for a moment** 잠시 • **ring** 반지 • **put on** (반지 등을) 끼다 • **ill** 아픈 • **take care of** ~을 돌보다, ~을 보살피다 • **feel better** 나아지다, 회복되다 • **respond** 대답하다 • **be good to** ~에게 잘해 주다 • **perhaps** 어쩌면, 아마도 • **almost** 거의 • **unhappy** 불행한 • **handsome** 잘생긴 • **unkind** 불친절한, 잘해 주지 않는 • **can't stand** 참을 수 없다 • **keep** (사람을) 붙들어 두다 • **agree** 동의하다

CLOSE UP

1 **Put on this ring** 이 반지를 껴요 / **take the ring off** 반지를 빼요
옷을 입거나 장신구를 몸에 착용하는 것은 put on, 벗는 것은 take off라고 함.

2 **Beauty in her beautiful dress** 아름다운 드레스를 입고 있는 뷰티
in 다음에 의류가 나오면 '~을 입은/착용한/쓴' 등의 의미가 됨.

"당신은 떠나면leave 돌아오지 않을 거요will not come back." 야수가 말했다.
"돌아오겠다고 약속할게요promise to come back." 뷰티가 말했다. "그렇지만 일주일만for one week 집에 보내 주세요let me go there."
야수는 잠시 생각한think for a moment 뒤에 말했다. "좋소okay. 가도 좋아요you may go."
야수는 뷰티에게 반지 한 개를 주며give Beauty a ring 말했다. "이걸 받아요take this. 이 반지를 끼고 put on this ring 잠자리에 드시오go to bed. 그러면 내일tomorrow 당신 아버지 집에서in your father's home 깨어날wake up 거요. 이레가 지나면after seven days 반지를 빼서take the ring off 침대 옆에by your bed 두시오. 그럼 이 성에서 잠을 깨게wake up in this castle 될 거요."
"뷰티, 잘 다녀오시오goodbye. 약속을 잊으면 안 돼요don't forget your promise. 7일 뒤에in seven days 돌아오는come back 거요."
뷰티는 야수에게 감사했다thank the Beast. 그녀는 반지를 끼고put the ring on 잠을 잤다go to sleep. 아침이 되어in the morning 잠에서 깨었을 때 뷰티는 아버지의 집에in her father's home 있었다. 뷰티는 일어나서get up 아버지에게 달려갔다run to her father.
"아버지, 저 왔어요I'm home." 뷰티가 말했다.
"오, 뷰티야. 네가 돌아왔구나return." 아버지가 소리쳤다. "야수가 널 잡아먹은 줄 알았다. 내가 너무 아픈데 혼자 있단다. 네 언니들your sisters은 결혼하더니 나를 한번도 찾지 않는구나never visit me."
"아버지, 제가 이곳에 일주일밖에 못 있지만, 잘 보살펴 드릴게요take good care of you. 곧 나아지실 feel better 거예요." 뷰티가 대답했다.
뷰티의 아버지가 딸을 바라보았다look at her. "아름다워 보이는구나look beautiful." 아버지가 말했다. "드레스가 무척 좋아 보여look nice. 야수가 너한테 잘 대해 주니?"
"네, 저한테 아주 자상해요be very kind. 저는 그를 아주 많이 좋아해요like him very much. 어쩌면 거의 사랑하는지도almost love him 모르겠어요." 뷰티가 대답했다.
뷰티의 언니들이 뷰티가 돌아왔다는 소식을 들었다. 그들은 남편들과 함께with their husbands 뷰티를 보러 왔다come to visit her. 언니들은 둘 다 불행했다be unhappy. 한 언니one는 아주 잘생긴 남편을 두었지만have a handsome husband 자상하지 않은be unkind 사람이었다. 다른 언니the other는 아주 영리한 남편을 두었지만have a smart husband 말이 너무 많은talk too much 사람이었다. 언니들은 뷰티가 아름다운 드레스를 입은 걸 보자 둘 다 화가 났다become angry.
"쟤는 왜 만날 행복한 거지?" 한 언니가 말했다.
"이런 일은 참을 수가 없어can't stand this. 뷰티를 일주일 이상longer than a week 이곳에 잡아 두자keep Beauty here. 그러면 야수가 쟤한테 화나게 될become angry with her 거야. 그럼 야수는 어쩌면 쟤를 잡아먹을eat her지도 몰라." 다른 언니도 동의했다.

GRAMMAR POINT

one / the other ⇨ 두 개 중에서 '하나'는 one, '나머지 하나'는 the other로 표현한다.

- **One** had a very handsome husband. **The other** had a very smart husband.
  한 명은 아주 잘생긴 남편을 두었다. 다른 한 명은 아주 영리한 남편을 두었다.

- There are two roses. **One** is red, and **the other** is pink.
  장미가 두 송이 있다. 하나는 빨간색이고, 다른 하나는 분홍색이다.

[p. 84-85]

So they said to Beauty, "Oh, Beauty, / we are so happy / to see you. Please stay here / for a few more days."

Beauty disliked / seeing them sad. So a week passed, / but Beauty did not go back to the castle.

Then, one night, / Beauty had a dream. In her dream, / she saw the Beast. The Beast was lying / on the grass. He was very sick and sad. He seemed to be dying. Beauty heard the Beast saying, "Oh, Beauty! Beauty, / why haven't you come back yet? I am dying."

Beauty woke up / and jumped out of bed. It was the middle of the night.

"I'm coming back, / Beast!" she said. She removed the ring quickly / and put it beside her bed. Then, / she went back to sleep.

Beauty woke up / in the castle. She jumped up / and went looking for the Beast. She tried every room / in the castle, / but she could not find the Beast / anywhere.

Then, / she remembered her dream. She ran into the garden / and saw the Beast.

"Wake up, / Beast. Wake up," she cried. "I'm back. I'm so sorry."

The beast slowly lifted his head. "I waited for you, / Beauty. But you didn't come. Now it is too late. I'm going to die soon."

"No, Beast, / you cannot die. I need you," said Beauty.

"I love you, / Beast. Please don't die. I want to marry you." Beauty kissed his ugly face.

- **dislike** 싫어하다 • **pass** (시간이) 지나다, 흐르다 • **have a dream** 꿈을 꾸다 • **lie** 눕다, 누워 있다 • **seem to** ~인 것처럼 보이다 • **die** 죽다 • **jump out of bed** 침대에서 벌떡 일어나다/뛰어내리다 • **the middle of the night** 한밤중 • **remove** 제거하다, 빼다 • **go looking for** ~을 찾으러 가다 • **be back** 돌아오다 • **lift** (위로) 들다, 올리다 • **wait for** ~을 기다리다

CLOSE UP

1 **I am dying.** 나는 죽어 가고 있소. / **I'm coming back, Beast!** 돌아갈게요, 야수님!
현재진행 시제는 문맥에 따라 현재 진행 중인 일(~하고 있다)을 나타낼 수도 있고, 예정되어 있는 가까운 미래(~할 것이다)를 나타낼 수도 있다.

2 **She tried every room** 그녀는 모든 방을 다 뒤져 보았다
〈try+명사〉는 '~을 해 보다'라는 의미. 어떤 명사가 오느냐에 따라 다양한 의미를 가진다.
ex) Try this soup.(이 수프 먹어 봐.) / Try these shoes.(이 신발 신어 봐.)

그래서 두 사람은 뷰티에게 말했다. "오, 뷰티야, 널 보니 정말 반갑구나. 며칠만 더**for a few more days** 여기 머물러 있으렴**stay here**."

뷰티는 언니들이 슬퍼하는 모습을 보는**see them sad** 게 싫었다**dislike**. 그래서 한 주**a week**가 흘러갔지만**pass** 뷰티는 성으로 돌아가지 않았다**do not go back**.

그러던 어느 날 밤**one night** 뷰티는 꿈을 꾸었다**have a dream**. 꿈에**in her dream** 야수가 보였다**see the Beast**. 야수는 풀밭에 누워**lie on the grass** 있었다. 몹시 아프고 슬픈 모습이었다**be sick and sad**. 야수는 죽어 가고 있는 것처럼 보였다**seem to be dying**. 뷰티는 야수가 하는 말을 들었다. "아, 뷰티! 뷰티, 어째서 아직도 돌아오지 않은 거요? 나는 죽어 가고 있소."

뷰티는 잠에서 깨어 침대에서 벌떡 일어났다**jump out of bed**. 한밤중**the middle of the night**이었다. "돌아갈게요, 야수님!" 뷰티가 말했다. 뷰티는 재빨리 반지를 빼서**remove the ring** 침대 옆에 놓았다**put it beside her bed**. 그리고는 다시 잠이 들었다**go back to sleep**.

뷰티는 성에서 잠을 깼다**wake up in the castle**. 뷰티는 벌떡 일어나**jump up** 야수를 찾으러 갔다**go looking for the Beast**. 성에 있는 모든 방을 다 뒤져 보았지만**try every room** 어디에서도**anywhere** 야수를 찾을 수 없었다**cannot find the Beast**.

그때 뷰티는 꿈이 생각났다**remember her dream**. 뷰티가 정원으로 달려갔더니**run into the garden** 야수가 보였다.

"야수님, 정신 차리세요**wake up**. 깨어나세요." 뷰티가 소리치며 말했다. "제가 돌아왔어요**I'm back**. 정말 미안해요."

야수가 천천히**slowly** 고개를 들었다**lift his head**. "뷰티, 당신을 기다렸소**wait for you**. 하지만 당신은 오지 않더군. 이제는 너무 늦었소**it is too late**. 나는 곧 죽을**die soon** 거요."

"안 돼요, 야수님. 죽으면 안 돼요**cannot die**. 제게는 당신이 필요해요**need you**." 뷰티가 말했다.

"야수님, 사랑해요**love you**. 제발 죽지 마세요. 당신과 결혼하고 싶어요**want to marry you**." 뷰티는 야수의 흉한 얼굴에 입을 맞추었다**kiss his ugly face**.

GRAMMAR POINT

dislike -ing : ~하는 걸 싫어하다 **go -ing** : ~하러 가다

- Beauty **dislike**d **see**ing them sad. 뷰티는 그들이 슬퍼하는 모습을 보는 게 싫었다.
- She jumped up and **went** look**ing** for the Beast. 그녀는 벌떡 일어나 야수를 찾으러 갔다.

[p. 86-87]

At that moment, / something magical / happened. The sky was filled with bright light. In a moment, / Beauty found herself / inside the castle. The room was filled with flowers. But the Beast was not there. Next to Beauty / was a very handsome young man. He was dressed / like a prince.

"What's going on here? Where is Beast?" Beauty asked.

"I am here, / Beauty," said the prince, "I am the Beast. Well, I was the Beast."

"A long time ago," said the prince, "I was selfish and unkind. A fairy touched me / with her magic wand / and put a spell on me. She turned me / into a beast. She cursed me / to be a beast forever / until someone loved me. You broke the spell, / Beauty. I became a man again / because you love me."

Then, / the fairy suddenly appeared / and said, "Yes, Beauty, / you understand / that kindness is more important / than looks. Your sisters don't understand that. So now they are unhappy / with their husbands. But you will be happy / with your prince. You are the most beautiful couple / in the world. I will marry you / and give you happiness / for the rest of your lives. And I will grant you / many beautiful children, / too."

Beauty and the prince / married soon. They had a wonderful wedding. Beauty invited her father / to live in the castle / with her. Beauty and the prince / lived happily / ever after.

- **at that moment** 바로 그 순간 • **magical** 마술의, 요술 같은 • **happen** 일어나다, 발생하다 • **be filled with** ~으로 가득 차다 • **bright** 밝은 • **be dressed like** ~처럼 옷을 입다 • **prince** 왕자 • **fairy** 요정 • **put a spell on** ~에게 마법을 걸다, ~에게 주문을 걸다 • **turn ~ into...** ~을 …로 변하게 하다 • **curse** 저주하다, 저주를 내리다 • **break a spell** 마법을 풀다, 주문을 풀다 • **appear** 나타나다 • **kindness** 친절함, 다정함, 호의 • **looks** 외모 • **grant** 승인하다, 주다 • **wonderful** 멋진 • **invite** 초대하다, 요청하다

CLOSE UP

1. **Beauty found herself inside the castle** 뷰티는 자신이 성 안에 있는 걸 알았다
   〈find oneself ~〉는 '자기가 ~한 상황에 처했음을 알게 되다'라는 의미.

2. **I will grant you many beautiful children** 너희가 예쁜 자녀를 많이 낳게 해 주마
   〈grant A B〉 하면 'A에게 B를 주다/허락하다/승인하다'라는 의미.

3. **invited her father to live in the castle with her** 아버지에게 자기와 함께 성에서 살자고 청했다
   〈invite ~ to...〉는 '~에게 …해 달라고 (정중히) 청하다'라는 의미.

그 순간at that moment 마법 같은 일something magical이 벌어졌다happen. 하늘the sky에 밝은 빛이 가득했다be filled with bright light. 순식간에in a moment 뷰티는 자신이 성 안에 있게 된 걸 알았다find herself inside the castle. 그 방에는 꽃이 하나 가득 있었다be filled with flowers. 그러나 야수는 그곳에 없었다. 뷰티 옆에는next to Beauty 아주 잘생긴 청년a handsome young man이 있었다. 그는 왕자 같은 옷차림을 하고 있었다be dressed like a prince.

"여기서 무슨 일이 벌어진 거죠what's going on? 야수님은 어디에 있나요?" 뷰티가 물었다.

"뷰티, 난 여기에 있소." 왕자가 말했다. "내가 야수요. 아니, 야수였소."

왕자가 말했다. "오래 전에a long time ago 나는 이기적이고 못되게 굴었소be selfish and unkind. 그래서 어떤 요정a fairy이 마술 지팡이로with her magic wand 나를 건드려touch me 내게 주문을 걸었지put a spell on me. 요정은 나를 야수가 되게 했소turn me into a beast. 누군가 나를 사랑할 때까지 영원히 야수로 살도록 저주를 내린 거요curse me. 당신이 그 주문을 풀었소break the spell, 뷰티. 당신이 나를 사랑하기 때문에 내가 다시 사람이 된become a man again 거요."

그때 요정이 갑자기 나타나서suddenly appear 말했다. "그렇단다, 뷰티야. 너는 다정한 마음kindness이 외모보다 더 중요more important than looks하다는 걸 알고 있지. 네 언니들은 그걸 알지 못한단다. 그래서 지금 네 언니들은 남편들과 행복하지 못한 거야. 하지만 너는 왕자와 행복하게 살be happy with your prince 거다. 너희들은 세상에서 가장 아름다운 한 쌍the most beautiful couple이다. 내가 너희를 결혼시켜서 여생을for the rest of your lives 행복하게 살도록 해 주마give you happiness. 그리고 예쁜 자녀들도 많이many beautiful children 낳게 해 주마."

뷰티와 왕자Beauty and the prince는 곧 결혼했다marry soon. 그들은 아주 멋진 결혼식a wonderful wedding을 올렸다. 뷰티는 아버지에게 자기와 함께 성에서 살자고 청했다. 뷰티와 왕자는 그 후로 계속ever after 행복하게 살았다live happily.

GRAMMAR POINT

-thing + 형용사 ⇨ -thing을 수식하는 형용사는 -thing 뒤에 온다.

- At that moment, **something magical** happened. 그 순간 마법 같은 일이 벌어졌다.
- I cannot think of **anything smart** to say to you. 당신에게 말하려면 어떤 영리한 말도 생각나지 않소.
- There was **nothing interesting** in the castle. 그 성에는 흥미로운 것이 아무것도 없었다.

The Stars

I used to be a shepherd / in the Luberon region / of France. It was a very isolated place, / so I was often all alone / in the pasture. Sometimes, / I did not see many people / for weeks. During those weeks, / I only had my dog / and the flocks of sheep / to accompany me.

From time to time, / I saw a loner / who lived on Mount Lure. He would come down / to hear some news / of the outside world. Also, / I sometimes saw coal miners. They worked in the coal mines / near my field, / so I spoke with them / as they went back and forth / to the coal mines.

Once every two weeks, / I got a visitor / from the farm. This person was usually the farm boy / or an old woman / who worked at the farm. They were sent / to bring me supplies / on a mule. I was always happy / to see them. They would tell me / all of the news / from the lowlands.

However, / the news that interested me the most / was about my master's daughter. Her name was Stephanette, / and she was the most beautiful girl / in the surrounding area. Without seeming to take too much interest, / I would ask / how Stephanette was doing. I asked / if there were any young men / who wanted to marry her.

Of course, / I was just a lowly shepherd / who worked for her father. I had to remind myself / that there was no way / that Stephanette would be interested in me. After all, / there were / many wealthy and handsome young men / in the area.

One Sunday, / I was waiting / for the delivery boy / to arrive. It had been two weeks / since my last delivery, / so I was running out of supplies. By ten o'clock, / no one had arrived yet.

- **used to be** 한때 ~이었다 • **shepherd** 양치기 • **isolated** 외떨어진, 고립된 • **pasture** 초원, 목초지
- **flock** (동물의) 떼 • **accompany** 동반하다, 어울리다, ~와 함께 있다 • **loner** 혼자 있기를 즐기는 사람, 외톨이, 은둔자 • **coal miner** 광부 • **coal mine** 탄광 • **go back and forth** 왔다 갔다 하다 • **visitor** 방문객
- **farm** 농장 • **supplies** 보급품, 일용품, 비축곰 • **mule** 노새 • **lowlands** 저지대, 아랫마을 • **master** 주인
- **surrounding area** 주변 지역, 인근 지역 • **take much interest** 큰 관심을 갖다 • **lowly** 미천한, 하찮은 • **remind oneself** 자신에게 상기시키다 • **be interested in** ~에 관심이 있다 • **wealthy** 부유한
- **delivery boy** 배달 소년 • **run out of** ~이 (거의) 바닥나다

CLOSE UP

1. **Once every two weeks** 두 주에 한 번씩
   every는 '매 ~', '~마다'라는 뜻으로 빈도를 나타낼 수 있다. *ex)* every seven years(7년마다)

2. **Without seeming to take too much interest** 너무 큰 관심은 가지지 않는 척하면서
   〈without+V-ing〉는 '~하지 않고', 〈seem to ~〉는 '~하는 것처럼 보이다'라는 의미. 따라서 without seeming to는 '~하는 기색/내색 없이', '~하지 않는 척하면서'의 뜻이 되겠다.

3. **there was no way that Stephanette would be interested in me**
   스테파네트가 나한테 관심을 가질 일은 절대로 없었다
   〈there is no way (that) ~〉은 '절대로 ~ 아니다/안 되다', '~할 방법이 없다'라는 의미.

별

나는 예전에 프랑스 뤼브롱 지역의in the Luberon region 양치기a shepherd였다. 그곳은 매우 고립된 지역a very isolated place이라 나는 초원에in the pasture 혼자all alone 있을 때가 많았다. 때로는 몇 주씩for weeks 사람 구경을 많이 하지 못했다do not see many people. 그런 주가 계속되는 동안(그럴 때) 내 곁에 있는accompany me 건 내 개my dog와 양 떼the flocks of sheep뿐이었다.

이따금씩from time to time 나는 뤼르 산에서 사는 은둔자를 보았다see a loner. 그는 바깥세상the outside world 소식을 들으려고hear some news 산에서 내려오곤 했다would come down. 또한 나는 가끔씩 광부들도 보았다see coal miners. 그들은 내가 양을 치는 들판 근처near my field 탄광에서 일했기work in the coal mines 때문에, 나는 그들이 탄광을 오갈 때go back and forth 그들과 이야기를 나눴다speak with them.

두 주에 한 번씩once every two weeks 나는 농장에서 오는from the farm 방문객을 맞았다get a visitor. 이 사람은 보통 농장 머슴the farm boy이거나 농장에서 일하는 나이 든 아주머니an old woman였다. 그들은 노새에 실은on a mule 물품을 내게 갖다 주도록bring me supplies 보내졌다. 그들을 보면see them 나는 항상 반가웠다be happy. 내게 저지대의from the lowlands 소식을 전부 들려주곤 했기would tell me 때문이다.

하지만 나를 가장 흥미롭게 했던interest me the most 소식은 주인집 딸my master's daughter에 관한 것이었다. 그녀의 이름her name은 스테파네트Stephanette였는데, 그 일대에서in the surrounding area 가장 아름다운 아가씨the most beautiful girl였다. 나는 너무 큰 관심은 가지지 않는 척하면서without seeming to 스테파네트 아가씨가 어떻게 지내는지how Stephanette is doing 묻곤 했다would ask. 혹시 아가씨와 결혼하고 싶어 하는 청년들이 있는지도 물어봤다.

물론of course 나는 아가씨의 아버지 밑에서 일하는work for her father 한낱 비천한 양치기a lowly shepherd에 지나지 않았다. 스테파네트 아가씨가 나 따위에게 관심을 가질be interested in me 일은 절대로 없다no way는 걸 스스로 상기해야remind myself 했다. 어쨌든after all 그 지역에는in the area 부유하고 잘생긴wealthy and handsome 청년들이 많았many young men으니 말이다.

어느 일요일one Sunday, 나는 배달 소년the delivery boy이 도착하기를 기다리고wait 있었다. 지난번 배달 이후since my last delivery 두 주two weeks가 지나서 물품이 다 떨어져run out of supplies 가고 있었다. 10시가 될 때까지by ten o'clock 아직 아무도 도착하지 않았다no one arrives.

GRAMMAR POINT

would : ~하곤 했다 ⇨ 과거에 자주 반복됐던 일이나 습관을 나타냄.

- He **would** come down to hear some news of the outside world.
  그는 바깥세상 소식을 들으려고 내려오곤 했다.
- They **would** tell me all of the news from the lowlands. 그들은 내게 저지대의 소식을 전부 들려주곤 했다.
- I **would** ask how Stephanette was doing. 나는 스테파네트가 어떻게 지내는지 묻곤 했다.

[p. 90-91]

"That's odd," I thought. "There must be a problem / at my master's house."

I continued to wait, / but no one came / by noon. "They must have forgotten / to send my supplies," I said to myself.

Around noon, / I noticed / that a big storm was coming. In the distance, / some dark clouds / were gathering. Soon, / heavy rain / began to pour down. "Now I understand," I said to myself. "The bad weather / has delayed the delivery person. The roads must be muddy / by now. I should not expect him / to arrive yet."

A few hours later, / the storm was over. The sun shone / high in the sky, / and its warm rays / spread bright light / all over the fields.

All of a sudden, / I heard the familiar sound / of the mule's bells. I eagerly looked / to see if it was the farmhand / or the old woman. However, / it was neither the farmhand / nor the old woman. It was the beautiful Stephanette! Oh, / what a wonderful surprise / that was!

She got off the mule, / and then she said to me, "I got lost / on my way up the hill."

"Are you all right, / mistress?" I asked.

She smiled / and nodded at me.

"The farmhand is sick," said Stephanette, "and the old woman is visiting her children / to spend the holiday with them. So my father sent me instead."

I could not take my eyes off her. She looked so beautiful / in that fresh afternoon air. In fact, / I had never seen her so close / before. And I had never spoken to her. I had only ever seen her / from a distance.

When I returned to the lowlands / in the winter, / her father would invite me to dinner / at his farm. At those times, / she would walk silently / across the room / and not say a word / to any of the servants. She had always looked very proud / during those times. And now / she was standing / in front of me.

- odd 이상한 • notice 알아차리다 • gather 모이다, 모여들다 • pour down 내리 퍼붓다 • delay 지연시키다 • muddy 진흙투성이의 • shine 빛나다 • ray 광선 • spread 퍼트리다 • all of a sudden 갑자기 • familiar 익숙한, 친숙한 • eagerly 열심히 • farmhand 농장 일꾼, 머슴 • get off (탈것에서) 내리다 • get lost 길을 잃다 • mistress 여주인, 아씨 • nod 고개를 끄덕이다 • instead 대신에 • from a distance 멀리서 • invite 초대하다 • silently 조용히 • servant 하인 • proud 도도한

CLOSE UP

1. **They must have forgotten to send my supplies.** 그들은 내 물품을 보내는 걸 잊은 게 틀림없어.
   〈must have p.p.〉는 '~했음에 틀림없다'라는 의미. 과거의 일에 대해 확신을 가지고 추측할 때 쓰인다.

2. **I should not expect him to arrive yet.** 아직 그가 도착하길 기대하면 안 되겠군.
   〈expect ~ to...〉는 '~가 …하기를 (당연히) 기대하다'라는 의미.

3. **I could not take my eyes off her.** 나는 그녀에게서 눈길을 뗄 수 없었다.
   〈take one's eyes off ~〉는 '~에서 눈(길)을 떼다'라는 의미. 보통 cannot과 함께 쓰여 어떤 매력에 감탄했음을 나타낸다.

4. **I had never seen her so close before** 이전에 그렇게 가까이 그녀를 본 적이 한 번도 없었다 /
   I had never spoken to her 그녀에게 말을 걸어 본 적이 전혀 없었다
   〈had never p.p.〉는 '(과거 그 이전에) ~해 본 적이 전혀 없었다'라는 의미. 과거완료의 경험을 나타내는 용법이다.

84 Step 3

"그거 이상하군." 나는 생각했다. "주인집에at my master's house 무슨 일a problem이 생긴 게 틀림없어."

나는 계속 기다렸지만continue to wait, 정오가 될 때까지by noon 아무도 오지 않았다. "보나마나 내 물품을 보내는send my supplies 걸 깜빡 잊은forget 모양이야." 나는 속으로 생각했다.

정오 무렵around noon 나는 큰 폭풍a big storm이 닥치고 있다는 걸 알아차렸다. 멀리서in the distance 먹구름some dark clouds이 모여들고gather 있었기 때문이다. 이윽고 폭우heavy rain가 쏟아지기pour down 시작했다. "이제 알겠군." 나는 속으로 생각했다. "날씨가 나빠서the bad weather 배달부가 지체된delay the delivery person 거야. 보나마나 지금쯤by now 길the roads이 진창이 되었을걸be muddy. 아직 배달부가 도착하기를 기대하면 안 되겠군."

몇 시간 뒤a few hours later 폭풍우the storm가 그쳤다be over. 태양the sun이 하늘 높이high in the sky 빛났고shine, 따뜻한 햇살its warm rays이 온 들판에all over the fields 밝은 빛을 퍼뜨렸다spread bright light.

별안간all of a sudden 친근한 노새의 워낭 소리the sound of the mule's bells가 들렸다. 나는 농장 머슴인지 나이 든 아주머니인지 보려고 열심히 살펴보았다. 하지만 그 사람은 농장 머슴도 아니고neither the farmhand 나이 든 아주머니도 아니었다nor the old woman. 바로 아름다운 스테파네트 아가씨the beautiful Stephanette였! 아, 이렇게 깜짝 놀랄 정도로 황홀한 일what a wonderful surprise이 생기다니!

아가씨는 노새에서 내리더니get off the mule 내게 말했다. "언덕을 올라오다가on my way up the hill 길을 잃었어요get lost."

"괜찮으세요are you all right, 아가씨mistress?" 내가 물었다.

아가씨는 미소를 지으며smile 내게 고개를 끄덕였다nod at me.

"농장 머슴이 아파요be sick." 스테파네트 아가씨가 말했다. "그리고 나이 든 아주머니는 휴일을 함께 보내기 위해 자식들한테 갈 거고요visit her children. 그래서 아버지가 나를 대신 보내셨어요send me instead."

나는 아가씨한테서 눈길을 뗄 수 없었다cannot take my eyes off her. 그 싱그러운 오후의 대기 속에서in that fresh afternoon air 아가씨는 너무 아름다워 보였다look beautiful. 사실in fact 나는 이전에 그렇게 가까이 아가씨를 본 적이 한 번도 없었다never see her so close. 또 아가씨에게 말을 걸어 본 적도 전혀 없었다never speak to her. 그저 멀리서만from a distance 바라봤을 뿐이다.

내가 겨울에in the winter 저지대로 돌아가면return to the lowlands, 아가씨의 아버지가 나를 농장의 만찬에 초대하곤 했다would invite me to dinner. 그럴 때면at those times 아가씨는 조용히silently 방을 가로질러 가며walk across the room 하인들 어느 누구에게도to any of the servants 한마디도 하지 않았다not say a word. 그러는 동안during those times 아가씨는 항상 매우 도도해 보였다look proud. 그런데 지금 그 아가씨가 내 앞에 서 있는stand in front of me 것이었다.

GRAMMAR POINT

neither ~ nor... : ~도 아니고 …도 아니다

- It was **neither** the farmhand **nor** the old woman. 그 사람은 농장 머슴도 아니고 나이 든 아주머니도 아니었다.

- **Neither** he **nor** I will be there. 그도 나도 그곳에 가지 않을 것이다.

[p. 92–93]

After she took my supplies off the mule, / Stephanette looked around the area. She seemed curious / about the pasture and the small barn.

"So this is / where you live, / shepherd?" she asked. She noticed my bed / in the barn. It was a simple bed / made of straw and sheepskin. There were / a cape and a stick / hanging on the wall / above my bed.

"You must be lonely and bored / because you are always alone," she continued. "What do you do / all day long?"

I wanted to answer, "I only think about you, / Stephanette," but I did not. As a matter of fact, / I could not say a single word / to her. How embarrassed / I was.

Stephanette must have noticed / my embarrassment. She started to tease me.

"Do the fairies come to see you / sometimes?" She was laughing / with a twinkle in her eyes. I thought / she was like a fairy, / but I did not say those words. Instead, / I said nothing.

"Well, I must leave now," she said. Stephanette got back on the mule / and said goodbye to me. Then, / the mule led her back / toward the farm. I watched her / as she disappeared down the hill. The sound of the mule's footsteps / continued for a while. The sound of those footsteps / remained with me / for a long time.

Later in the evening, / I brought the flock of sheep back in / from the fields. As I was completing my chores, / I heard a voice / calling my name. It was Stephanette. She had returned. But she was not smiling anymore. Now, / she was soaking wet / and shivering from the cold.

"At the bottom of the mountain, / there is a river / as you know. The rain from the storm / caused the river / to flood. The water has risen very high. I tried to cross the river, / but I almost drowned / in the water. I was so scared / and didn't know what to do. So I just returned here," she said / in a trembling voice.

- **take ~ off...** ~을 …에서 내리다 • **curious** 호기심 어린, 호기심 많은 • **barn** 헛간 • **notice** 알아차리다, 보다 • **straw** 지푸라기 • **sheepskin** 양가죽 • **cape** 망토 • **hang** 걸다; 걸려 있다 • **lonely** 외로운 • **bored** 심심한, 따분한 • **alone** 혼자, 혼자서 • **as a matter of fact** 사실, 실은 • **embarrassed** 당황한, 부끄러운 • **embarrassment** 당황, 쩔쩔맴, 쑥스러움 • **tease** 놀리다 • **with a twinkle in one's eyes** 눈을 반짝이며 • **disappear** 사라지다 • **footstep** 발소리, 발자국 • **remain** 남다, 남아 있다 • **complete** 완전하게 하다, 끝마치다 • **chore** 잡일, 허드렛일 • **soaking** 완전히 젖은 • **shiver** 떨다 • **cause** ~하게 만들다 • **flood** 홍수가 나다; 홍수 • **rise** 오르다, 솟아오르다 • **cross** 건너다 • **drown** 물에 빠져 죽다 • **be scared** 겁나다 • **tremble** 떨다

CLOSE UP

1. **The rain from the storm caused the river to flood.** 폭우 때문에 강에 홍수가 났어요.
   cause는 원인을 나타낸다. 〈~ cause A to...〉하면 '~ 때문에 A가 …하다'라는 의미.
2. **I almost drowned in the water** 하마터면 물에 빠져 죽을 뻔했어요
   동사 앞에 almost 또는 nearly를 쓰면 '(하마터면) ~할 뻔하다'라는 의미가 될 수 있음.

스테파네트 아가씨는 노새에서 내 물품을 내리고take my supplies off the mule 나서 그 일대를 둘러보았다look around the area. 초원the pasture과 조그만 헛간the small barn에 호기심이 동하는 듯했다seem curious.

"그러니까 여기가 당신이 지내는 곳where you live이로군요, 양치기 씨?" 아가씨가 물었다. 아가씨는 헛간에 있는 내 침대를 보았다notice my bed. 지푸라기와 양가죽straw and sheepskin으로 만든 소박한 침대a simple bed였다. 침대 위쪽 벽에는on the wall 망토와 지팡이a cape and a stick가 걸려hang 있었다.

"항상 혼자always alone라서 틀림없이 외롭고 따분하겠네요be lonely and bored." 아가씨가 말을 이었다. "온종일all day long 뭘 하세요?"

나는 "스테파네트 아가씨, 당신 생각만 합니다only think about you."라고 대답하고 싶었지만 그러지 않았다. 사실as a matter of fact 나는 아가씨에게 한마디도a single word 건넬 수 없었다cannot say. 얼마나 쑥스러웠던지how embarrassed.

스테파네트 아가씨는 분명 내 쑥스러움을 눈치챘을notice my embarrassment 것이다. 아가씨는 나를 놀리기tease me 시작했다.

"가끔 요정들the fairies이 당신을 보러 오나요come to see you?" 아가씨는 두 눈을 반짝이며with a twinkle in her eyes 웃고 있었다. 나는 아가씨가 요정 같다be like a fairy고 생각했지만, 그런 말은 하지 않았다. 그러기는커녕instead 아무런 말도 하지 않았다say nothing.

"자, 이제 가야겠어요must leave." 아가씨가 말했다. 스테파네트 아가씨는 다시 노새에 올라타더니get back on the mule 내게 작별인사를 했다say goodbye. 그리고는 노새가 아가씨를 다시 농장으로 태우고 갔다lead her back toward the farm. 나는 아가씨의 모습이 언덕 아래로 사라지는disappear down the hill 동안 지켜보았다. 노새의 발소리the sound of the mule's footsteps가 한동안for a while 계속 이어졌다continue. 그 발소리는 오랫동안for a long time 내게 남아 있었다remain with me.

나중에 저녁이 되자later in the evening 나는 들판에서from the fields 양 떼를 다시 모아들였다bring the flock of sheep back in. 내가 허드렛일을 마치고complete my chores 있는데, 내 이름을 부르는call my name 목소리가 들렸다hear a voice. 스테파네트 아가씨였다. 아가씨가 돌아온 것이다. 그러나 아가씨는 이제 미소 짓고 있지 않았다. 지금은 흠뻑 젖은soaking wet 채로 추위에 떨고shiver from the cold 있었다.

"알다시피as you know 산기슭에at the bottom of the mountain 강a river이 있잖아요. 폭우the rain from the storm로 강에 홍수가 났어요cause the river to flood. 수위the water가 무척 높아졌더군요rise high. 강을 건너려고cross the river 하다가 하마터면 물에 빠져 죽을 뻔했어요almost drown. 너무 무서웠고be scared 어찌해야 할지what to do 몰랐어요don't know. 그래서 그냥 여기로 돌아온return here 거예요." 아가씨는 떨리는 목소리로in a trembling voice 말했다.

GRAMMAR POINT

현재분사 ⇒ be동사와 함께 진행 시제를 만들기도 하고, 분사구를 이끌어 명사를 수식하거나 보충 설명해 주기도 한다.

- There were a cape and a stick **hanging** on the wall above my bed.
  내 침대 위쪽 벽에는 망토와 지팡이가 걸려 있었다. (현재분사구)
- She was **laughing** with a twinkle in her eyes. 그녀는 두 눈을 반짝이며 웃고 있었다. (진행 시제)
- As I was **completing** my chores, I heard a voice **calling** my name.
  내가 허드렛일을 마치고 있는데, 내 이름을 부르는 목소리가 들렸다. (진행 시제 / 현재분사구)

[p. 94-95]

I was not sure / what to do. It was not right / for her / to spend the night on the mountain. I also could not leave / the flock of sheep / to take her home. But then I thought, "The nights in July / are short. It's only one night."

I immediately made a fire / so that she could dry / her feet and clothes. Then, / I gave her / some milk and cheese, / but Stephanette was not interested in eating. She burst into tears. And I almost felt like crying, / too. It was completely dark / outside. I took her to the barn, / and I prepared a bed for her. I laid out a new sheepskin / on the fresh straw / so that she could rest. I said goodnight / and went outside.

I sat down / in front of the door. I tried not to think of the young lady / who was resting in my house. But all that I could think of / was her. I was proud / because I had assisted her. Tonight, / it was my responsibility / to keep her safe. In happiness, / I looked up in the sky. The stars shone / more beautifully than ever / that night.

A while later, / the barn door opened, / and Stephanette came out.

"I cannot sleep," she said. "Do you mind / if I sit next to the fire?"

She sat down / by the fire. I gave her a goatskin / to wrap around herself. We sat by the fire / in silence. That night, / every creature / seemed to come alive. The frogs in the pond / croaked louder / than normal. The insects sang loudly / as well. The fire made a brilliant bright light / as it burned through the night. Even the night air / seemed to be fresher / than normal.

Some noises in the night / frightened her. She moved / closer to me. Just then, / a shooting star / passed in the sky / above us. It was the most beautiful shooting star / I had ever seen.

- **leave** 떠나다, 두고 가다 · **dry** 말리다 · **burst into tears** 울음을 터뜨리다 · **completely** 완전히
- **prepare** 준비하다 · **lay out** 깔다, 펼치다 · **rest** 쉬다 · **be proud** 자랑스럽다 · **assist** 돕다
- **responsibility** 책임 · **keep ~ safe** ~을 안전하게 지키다, ~을 보호하다 · **in happiness** 행복하게 · **Do you mind if ~?** ~해도 될까요? · **wrap around oneself** 몸을 감싸다 · **in silence** 조용히, 말 없이
- **creature** 생물, 피조물 · **croak** 개굴개굴 울다 · **normal** 보통, 평균; 정상의 · **brilliant** 아주 밝은, 눈부신
- **noise** 시끄러운 소리, 잡음 · **frighten** 놀라게 하다 · **shooting star** 별똥별

CLOSE UP

1. **so that she could dry her feet and clothes** 그녀가 발과 옷을 말릴 수 있도록 / **so that she could rest** 그녀가 쉴 수 있도록
   〈so that ~〉은 '~하도록', '~하기 위해서'라는 의미.

2. **I almost felt like crying, too** 나도 거의 울고 싶은 심정이었다
   〈feel like+V-ing〉는 '~하고 싶다'라는 의미.

3. **seemed to come alive** 활기를 띤 것 같았다 / **seemed to be fresher** 더 신선한 것 같았다
   〈seem to ~〉는 '~인 것처럼 보이다'라는 의미.

4. **It was the most beautiful shooting star I had ever seen.** 그것은 내가 지금껏 본 중에 가장 아름다운 별똥별이었다.
   〈최상급+주어+have/had ever seen〉은 '지금까지 본 중에 가장 ~한'이라는 의미.

나는 어찌해야 할지 확신이 서지 않았다. 아가씨가 산에서on the mountain 밤을 보내는spend the night 건 당치도 않은be not right 일이었다. 그렇다고 내가 양 떼를 남겨 두고leave the flock of sheep 아가씨를 집에 데려다 줄take her home 수도 없는 노릇이었다. 하지만 그때 이런 생각이 들었다. "7월의 밤the nights in July은 짧아be short. 딱 하룻밤only one night인데 뭐 어때."

나는 아가씨가 발과 옷을 말릴dry her feet and clothes 수 있도록 즉시 불을 피웠다make a fire. 그런 다음 아가씨에게 우유와 치즈를 좀some milk and cheese 주었으나, 스테파네트 아가씨는 먹는 데 관심이 없었다. 아가씨는 갑자기 울음을 터뜨렸다burst into tears. 그래서 나 역시 거의 울고 싶은 심정이었다feel like crying. 밖은 아주 캄캄했다. 나는 아가씨를 헛간으로 데려가서take her to the barn 잠자리를 마련해prepare a bed 주었다. 신선한 지푸라기 위에on the fresh straw 새 양가죽을 깔아서lay out a new sheepskin 아가씨가 쉴 수 있게 해 주었다. 나는 잘 자라고 인사하고say goodnight 밖으로 나갔다go outside.

나는 문 앞에in front of the door 앉았다sit down. 내 집에서 쉬고 있는 젊은 숙녀를 생각하지think of the young lady 않으려고 애썼다. 하지만 내가 생각할 수 있었던 건 전부all that I can think of 아가씨뿐이었다(온통 아가씨 생각밖에 나지 않았다). 나는 아가씨를 도와줬기assist her 때문에 마음이 뿌듯했다be proud. 오늘 밤엔 아가씨를 안전하게 지키는keep her safe 게 내 책무my responsibility였다. 행복한 마음으로in happiness 나는 하늘을 우러러보았다look up in the sky. 그날 밤에는 별들the stars이 여느 때보다 더 아름답게 빛났다shine more beautifully.

얼마 뒤a while later 헛간 문이 열리더니 스테파네트 아가씨가 밖으로 나왔다come out.

"잠이 안 와요cannot sleep." 아가씨가 말했다. "모닥불 옆에 앉아도sit next to the fire 될까요?"

아가씨는 모닥불 옆에 앉았다sit down by the fire. 나는 아가씨에게 몸에 두르도록wrap around herself 양가죽a goatskin을 주었다. 우리는 잠자코in silence 모닥불 옆에 앉아 있었다sit by the fire. 그날 밤에는 모든 생물every creature이 활기를 띤come alive 것 같았다. 연못의 개구리들the frogs in the pond은 평소보다than normal 더 요란하게 울었다croak louder. 벌레들the insects도 역시 큰 소리로 노래했다sing loudly. 모닥불은 밤새도록through the night 타오르며burn 아주 밝고 환한 빛을 냈다make a brilliant bright light. 밤공기the night air조차 평소보다 더 신선한be fresher 것 같았다.

밤에 들리는 어떤 소리들some noises이 아가씨를 흠칫 놀라게 했다frighten her. 아가씨는 내게 더 가까이 다가왔다move closer to me. 바로 그때 우리 머리 위above us 하늘에서in the sky 별똥별 하나a shooting star가 지나갔다pass. 내가 지금껏 본 중에서 가장 아름다운 별똥별이었다.

GRAMMAR POINT

가주어 it, 진주어 to부정사

⇨ to부정사가 문장의 주어일 때는 대개 가주어 it을 문장 앞에 두고, to부정사구는 문장 뒤로 보낸다.

- Tonight, **it** was my responsibility **to keep** her safe. 오늘 밤에는 그녀를 안전하게 지키는 게 내 책무였다.
- **It** was not right **for** her **to spend** the night on the mountain.
  그녀가 산에서 밤을 보내는 것은 당치 않은 일이었다.
  (여기서 for her는 to spend의 의미상 주어. to부정사의 의미상 주어는 to부정사 앞에 〈for+목적격〉으로 쓴다.)

[p. 96-97]

"What is that?" asked Stephanette.
"A soul / that has entered Heaven," I responded.
Stephanette looked at me / and said, "You are not like / the other young men / I know."
I answered, "I am probably like / most other men, / but my life in the field / is very different from theirs. Here, / I live close to the stars. I know / what happens up there / better than people from the plains."
Stephanette looked up into the sky / and said, "Look! There is / another shooting star." She pointed to a shooting star / streaking across the sky.
"It's so beautiful. I have never seen / so many beautiful stars / in my life. Do you know / the names of the stars?"
"Of course, mistress, / I do," I answered. "Look up there. Do you see / the streak of light / that travels across the sky? That is the Milky Way. The Milky Way / stretches all across France / and goes into Spain. Soldiers often use / the Milky Way / to find their way home."
I continued to point out / some of the stars / to her. I explained constellations / to her.
"Many stars combine / to form constellations. They are like / pictures in the sky. Can you see / that group of stars? That is the Big Dipper. The three stars in front / are the Three Animals. And there is / Orion the Hunter / up there."
"Did you know / that we shepherds / are able to use the sky / like a clock? I can tell the time / by looking at the stars. For instance, / right now, / it is almost midnight." I kept talking.

- **soul** 영혼 • **probably** 아마도, 필시 • **plains** 평원 • **streak** 휙 지나가다, 기다란 자국을 내다 • **a streak of light** 한 줄기의 광선, 빛줄기 • **the Milky Way** 은하수 • **stretch** 뻗어 있다, 펼쳐지다 • **find one's way home** 집으로 가는 길을 찾다 • **point out** ~을 가리키다 • **constellation** 별자리 • **combine** 합치다; 결합하다 • **form** 형성하다, 만들어 내다 • **tell the time** 시간을 말하다, 시간을 맞추다

CLOSE UP

1. **You are not like the other young men** 당신은 다른 청년들과 다르군요 /
   I am probably like most other men 저도 아마 대다수 다른 남자들과 비슷할 거예요 /
   They are like pictures in the sky. 그들은 하늘의 그림과 같지요.
   ⟨be like ~⟩는 '~와 같다', '~와 비슷하다'라는 의미.

2. **my life in the field is very different from theirs** 들에서의 내 생활은 그들의 생활과 아주 달라요
   ⟨be different from ~⟩은 '~와 다르다'라는 의미. 여기서 theirs는 their lives를 의미함.

3. **I can tell the time by looking at the stars.** 저는 별들을 봄으로써 시간을 알 수 있어요.
   ⟨can tell the time⟩은 '지금 몇 시인지 안다', '시계를 볼 줄 안다'라는 의미.
   ⟨by + V-ing⟩는 '~함으로써'라는 뜻으로 수단 및 방법을 나타냄.

"저게 뭐죠?" 스테파네트 아가씨가 물었다.

"천국에 들어간enter Heaven 영혼a soul입니다." 내가 대답했다.

스테파네트 아가씨는 나를 보고 말했다. "당신은 내가 아는 다른 청년들과 다르군요."

내가 대답했다. "저도 아마 대다수 다른 남자들과 비슷할be like most other men 겁니다. 하지만 들에서의 제 생활my life in the field은 그들의 생활과 매우 다르죠be different. 여기서 저는 별들 가까이에 삽니다live close to the stars. 저 위에서up there 무슨 일이 생기는지what happens는 평원에 사는 사람들보다 더 잘 알죠know better."

스테파네트 아가씨는 하늘을 우러러보며look up into the sky 말했다. "보세요look! 별똥별이 하나 더another shooting star 있어요." 아가씨는 쏜살같이 휙 하늘을 가로지르는streak across the sky 별똥별을 가리켰다point to a shooting star.

"정말 아름다워요. 살아오면서in my life 아름다운 별을 이렇게 많이so many beautiful stars 본 적은 한 번도 없었어요never see. 별들의 이름the names of the stars을 알고 있나요?"

"물론이죠, 아가씨. 알고 말고요." 나는 대답했다. "저 위를 보세요look up there. 하늘을 가로질러 가는travel across the sky 빛줄기the streak of light가 보이시죠? 저게 은하수the Milky Way입니다. 은하수는 프랑스 전역을 가로질러 나가stretch all across France 스페인까지 뻗어 있어요go into Spain. 병사들soldiers은 흔히 은하수를 이용해서use the Milky Way 집으로 가는 길을 찾지요find their way home."

나는 계속해서 아가씨에게 몇몇 별들을 가리켰다point out some of the stars. 나는 아가씨에게 별자리를 설명해 주었다explain constellations.

"많은 별들many stars이 결합하여combine 별자리를 이루지요form constellations. 하늘에 있는 그림pictures in the sky이라고나 할까요. 저기 무리 지어 있는 별들that group of stars이 보이시죠? 저건 북두칠성the Big Dipper입니다. 앞에 있는 별 세 개the three stars는 '세 마리 동물the Three Animals'이고요. 그리고 저 위에는up there '사냥꾼 오리온Orion the Hunter'이 있지요."

"우리 양치기들we shepherds이 하늘을 시계처럼 활용할use the sky like a clock 수 있다는 걸 알고 계셨나요? 저는 별들을 보는look at the stars 것으로 시간을 알 수 있어요can tell the time. 가령for instance 지금은right now 거의 자정almost midnight이 다 되었군요." 나는 계속 말을 이었다.

GRAMMAR POINT

to부정사 (목적) : ~하기 위해

- Soldiers often use the Milky Way **to find** their way home.
  병사들은 집으로 가는 길을 찾기 위해 흔히 은하수를 이용한다. (= 은하수를 이용해서 집으로 가는 길을 찾는다)

- Many stars combine **to form** constellations.
  많은 별들이 별자리를 이루기 위해 결합한다. (= 결합하여 별자리를 이룬다)

[p. 98-99]

"All of the stars / are beautiful. But the most beautiful star of all / is the Evening Star. It comes out first / every night. It is the shepherd's friend. She lights our way / at dawn / when we take our flocks out to the fields / and also in the evening / when we return. We call her Maguelonne. Maguelonne chases Saturn in the sky / and marries him / every seven years."

"What? The stars can marry?" she exclaimed.

"Oh, sure. The stars can get married," I told her.

I was just about to explain / how the stars get married. Then, / I felt / as Stephanette laid her head / on my shoulder / and fell asleep. In the cool breeze, / the ribbons in her hair / danced, / and I felt the touch of her curls / against my neck. It was the most enchanting feeling.

We stayed like that / until the stars began to fade / and the first rays of dawn / appeared. I wanted that night / to last forever.

All above us, / the stars continued their march / across the night sky. I imagined / that one of the stars, / the finest and the most brilliant, / had lost her way / and was resting her head / on my shoulder.

- **the Evening Star** (저녁 무렵 서쪽 하늘에 보이는) 금성, 개밥바라기, 저녁별, 샛별 • **dawn** 새벽, 동이 틀 무렵
- **take ~ out** ~을 데리고 나가다 • **chase** 뒤쫓다, 쫓아가다 • **exclaim** 소리치다, 외치다 • **be just about to** 막 ~하려고 하다 • **lay** (살며시 조심스럽게) 놓다, 두다, 얹다 • **shoulder** 어깨 • **fall asleep** 잠들다
- **breeze** 미풍 • **ribbon** 리본 • **curls** 곱슬곱슬한 머리카락 • **enchanting** 황홀한, 고혹적인 • **march** 행진, 행군 • **imagine** 상상하다 • **finest** 가장 멋진, 가장 훌륭한, 가장 아름다운 • **rest** 쉬다, 자다; (어떤 것에) 받치다, 기대다

CLOSE UP

1 **I was just about to explain** 내가 막 설명하려는 참이었다
   〈be about to ~〉는 '막 ~하려고 하다'라는 의미.

2 **the touch of her curls against my neck** 그녀의 곱슬머리가 내 목에 닿는 감촉
   여기서 〈against ~〉는 '~의 가까이에', '~의 곁에', '~에 붙여'라는 의미.

"별들은 모두all of the stars 아름다워요be beautiful. 하지만 그 중에서도 가장 아름다운 별the most beautiful star은 '개밥바라기the Evening Star'입니다. 매일 밤every night 제일 먼저 나타나지요come out first. 양치기의 친구the shepherd's friend인 셈이죠. 개밥바라기는 우리가 새벽에at dawn 양 떼들을 들판으로 몰고 나갈take our flocks out to the fields 때는 물론이고, 저녁에in the evening 돌아올 때도 길을 비춰 주거든요light our way. 우리는 그 별을 '목동의 별'이라고 부릅니다call her Maguelonne. 목동의 별은 하늘에서 토성을 쫓아다니며chase Saturn 7년마다every seven years 토성과 결혼하지요marry him."

"뭐라고요what? 별들이 결혼을 할 수 있다고요?" 아가씨가 소리쳤다.

"아, 그럼요. 별들도 결혼할 수 있지요." 나는 아가씨에게 말했다.

별들이 어떻게 결혼하는지 내가 막 설명하려는 참이었다be about to explain. 그때 스테파네트 아가씨가 내 어깨에 살며시 머리를 기대고lay her head on my shoulder 잠든fall asleep 게 느껴졌다. 서늘한 산들바람에in the cool breeze 아가씨의 머리에 달린 리본the ribbons in her hair이 춤추듯 나부꼈고dance, 나는 아가씨의 곱슬머리가 내 목에 닿는her curls against my neck 감촉을 느꼈다feel the touch. 더할 나위 없이 황홀한 느낌the most enchanting feeling이었다.

우리는 별빛the stars이 희미해지기fade 시작하고 첫 새벽빛the first rays of dawn이 나타날appear 때까지 그렇게 있었다stay like that. 나는 그 밤이 영원히 지속되기last forever를 바랐다.

우리 위에서는 별들이 밤하늘을 가로지르는across the night sky 행군을 계속했다continue their march. 나는 그 별들 중 가장 아름답고the finest 가장 밝은the most brilliant 별 하나가 길을 잃고lose her way 내 어깨에 머리를 기대고 쉬고 있다rest her head on my shoulder고 상상했다imagine.

GRAMMAR POINT

the + 최상급 : 가장 ~한

⇒ 최상급은 형용사나 부사에 -est를 붙이며, 3음절 이상일 경우는 그 앞에 most를 붙인다.

- It was **the most enchanting** feeling. 더할 나위 없이 황홀한 느낌이었다.
- One of the stars, **the finest** and **the most brilliant**, had lost her way.
  별들 중에서 가장 아름답고 가장 밝은 별 하나가 길을 잃었다.

Super Reading Story Training Book

Step

4

What Men Live By
– Leo Tolstoy

•

How Much Land Does a Man Need?
– Leo Tolstoy

[p. 102-103]

What Men Live By

There was once / a poor shoemaker / named Simon. He had no house or land. He lived in a hut / with his wife and children. One morning, / he went to the village / to buy some sheepskins / for a winter coat. He had only three rubles, / but he planned / to visit some of his customers / on the way. They owed him five rubles / for work / he had already done.

Simon visited several customers' houses, / but he could not collect any money. He went to the store / and asked if he could buy the sheepskins / on credit. But the shopkeeper refused / to give them to Simon.

Simon felt downhearted / and started walking homeward. "Though I have no sheepskin coat, / I don't care. I can live / without a coat. Yet my wife will surely fret," he thought.

While he was walking home, / he passed by a church / at the bend in the road. Simon saw something white / behind the church. He did not know / what it was. He came closer, / and, to his surprise, / it was a naked man. He was sitting against the church / without any clothes on.

Suddenly, / Simon felt afraid. "Robbers must have killed him / and stolen his clothes. If I interfere, / I will have a big problem," Simon thought.

Simon continued walking, / but when he looked back, / he saw / the man was moving. Simon felt more frightened.

"If I go there, / he might kill me / for my clothes. Even if he doesn't attack me, / what can I do for him?" thought Simon.

He ran down the road. But he suddenly stopped.

- **hut** 오두막 • **sheepskin** 양가죽 • **ruble** 루블 (러시아의 화폐 단위) • **customer** 손님 • **on the way** 도중에 • **owe** 빚지다 • **collect** 수금하다, 모으다 • **on credit** 외상으로 • **refuse** 거절하다 • **feel downhearted** 낙담하다, 기가 죽다 • **pass by** ~을 지나가다 • **naked** 벌거벗은, 나체의 • **robber** 강도 • **interfere** 간섭하다, 간여하다 • **have a big problem** 큰일에 휘말리다, 곤란한 일을 겪다 • **look back** 뒤돌아보다 • **frightened** 겁나는, 무서운 • **attack** 공격하다

CLOSE UP

1. **owed him five rubles** 그에게 5루블을 빚지고 있었다
   〈owe+사람+돈〉은 '~에게 …을 빚지고 있다', '~에게 …을 지불해야 한다'라는 의미.

2. **to his surprise** 놀랍게도
   to one's surprise는 '놀랍게도', '뜻밖에도'라는 의미. *ex)* To my surprise, he was alive.(놀랍게도 그는 살아 있었다.)

3. **must have killed him and (must have) stolen his clothes** 그를 죽이고 그의 옷을 훔쳐 간 게 분명하다
   〈must have p.p.〉는 '~했음에 틀림없다'라는 의미. 과거의 일에 대해 확신을 가지고 추측할 때 쓰인다.

사람은 무엇으로 사는가

옛날에once 세몬이라는named Simon 가난한 제화공a poor shoemaker이 있었다. 그는 집도 땅도 없었다have no house or land. 아내와 자녀들을 데리고with his wife and children 오두막에서 살았다live in a hut. 어느 날 아침one morning 세몬은 겨울 외투를 만들 양가죽을 좀 사러buy some sheepskins 마을에 갔다go to the village. 가진 돈이라곤 3루블밖에only three rubles 없었지만, 세몬은 가는 길에on the way 고객 몇 명some of his customers을 찾아갈 생각이었다plan to visit. 그들이 세몬에게 그가 이미 마친 작업 비용으로for work 5루블을 지불해야 할 게 있었기owe him five rubles 때문이다.

세몬은 몇몇 고객의 집을 찾아갔으나 한 푼도 수금할 수 없었다cannot collect any money. 세몬은 가게에 가서go to the store 외상으로on credit 양가죽을 살 수 있는지 물어보았다. 그러나 가게 주인the shopkeeper은 세몬에게 양가죽 주는 것을 거절했다refuse to give.

세몬은 낙담한feel downhearted 채 집으로 걸어가기walk homeward 시작했다. "양가죽 외투가 없어도have no sheepskin coat 난 개의치 않아don't care. 외투가 없어도without a coat 난 살 수 있어can live. 하지만 집사람my wife은 분명히 속을 태울will fret 텐데." 하고 세몬은 생각했다.

세몬은 집으로 걸어가는 동안 도로가 굽은 곳에(커브 길에)at the bend 있는 한 교회를 지나가게pass by a church 되었다. 교회 뒤에behind the church 뭔가 하얀 물체something white가 보였다. 무엇인지는 알 수 없었다. 세몬이 좀 더 가까이 가 보니come closer 놀랍게도to his surprise 벌거숭이 사내a naked man였다. 사내는 아무 옷도 걸치지 않은 채without any clothes on 교회에 기대어 앉아sit against the church 있었다.

갑자기suddenly 세몬은 두려움을 느꼈다feel afraid. "강도들robbers이 이 사람을 죽이고kill him 옷을 훔쳐 간steal his clothes 게 분명해. 내가 끼어들면interfere 큰 봉변을 당하게have a big problem 될 거야." 하고 세몬은 생각했다.

세몬은 계속 길을 걸었으나continue walking 뒤를 돌아보니 look back 그 사내가 움직이는 게 보였다. 세몬은 더욱 겁을 먹었다feel frightened.

"내가 저기에 가면go there 그 사람이 내 옷을 뺏으려고for my clothes 나를 죽일지도kill me 몰라. 설령 나를 공격하지attack me 않는다 해도 내가 그 사람한테 뭘 해 줄 수 있겠어?" 하고 세몬은 생각했다.

세몬은 길을 뛰어 내려갔다run down the road. 그러나 갑자기 멈춰섰다suddenly stop.

GRAMMAR POINT

though : 비록 ~해도   **if** : 만약 ~한다면   **even if** : 비록 ~해도, 설사 ~해도

- **Though** I have no sheepskin coat, I don't care.   비록 양가죽 외투가 없어도 난 개의치 않아.
- **If** I interfere, I will have a big problem.   내가 끼어들면 큰 봉변을 당하게 될 거야.
- **Even if** he doesn't attack me, what can I do for him? (**even if = even though**)
  설령 그가 나를 공격하지 않는다 해도 내가 그를 위해 뭘 할 수 있지?

What Men Live By

[p. 104–105]

"What am I doing? The man could be dying!" He felt guilty, / so he turned around / and went back to the church.

When Simon went behind the church, / he saw / that the stranger was a young man. He was freezing and frightened. Simon immediately took off his coat / and put it around the man. Then, / he put boots on the man. Simon had / an extra pair of boots.

"Can you walk?" asked Simon. "It's too cold / to stay here. I will take you / to my home. Here is a stick for you / to lean on / while you walk."

The man stood up / and looked kindly at Simon. But he did not speak. As they walked to Simon's home, / Simon asked him / where he was from / and how he got to the church. The man replied / with a calm voice, "I'm not from around here. God has punished me."

Simon was surprised by the response. But he said, "Well, God rules all men. Come home with me / and at least / make yourself warm." As Simon walked with the stranger, / he felt glad / to help another person.

Simon's wife was preparing dinner / when Simon and the man / came into the house. Matryna noticed / that the man had no hat / and was wearing felt boots. And he was wearing her husband's coat. Simon had no sheepskins. Her heart was ready to break / with disappointment. "He has been out drinking, / and now he has brought another drunk home / with him," she thought.

Simon took off his hat / and sat down on the bench / as if things were all right. Then, he said, "Have a seat, my friend, / and let us have some dinner."

Matryna became very angry / and said, "I cooked dinner, / but not for you. You went out / to buy some sheepskins / but bring a strange man home / instead. He doesn't even have / any clothes of his own. You must have spent / all our money / on vodka. I have no supper / for drunkards like you."

- **feel guilty** 꺼림직하다, 죄책감을 느끼다　• **turn around** 몸을 돌리다, 돌아서다　• **go back** 되돌아가다
- **stranger** 낯선 사람, 나그네, 이방인　• **freezing** 얼어붙을 듯이 추운　• **take off** (옷을) 벗다　• **extra** 여분의
- **stick** 막대기, 지팡이　• **lean on** ~에 기대다　• **stand up** 일어서다　• **calm** 조용한, 차분한　• **punish** 처벌하다, 벌하다　• **be surprised by** ~에 깜짝 놀라다　• **response** 대답, 반응　• **at least** 적어도, 최소한
- **notice** 알아차리다　• **felt boots** 펠트 부츠　• **disappointment** 실망, 낙담　• **bring** 데려오다
- **drunk** 술주정뱅이, 술주정꾼　• **supper** (가벼운) 저녁식사　• **drunkard** 술주정뱅이

CLOSE UP

1. **Her heart was ready to break** 그녀의 마음은 무너질 지경이었다
   〈be ready to ~〉는 '~할 준비가 되어 있다'라는 뜻도 되고, '당장 ~할 것 같다'라는 뜻도 된다. 문맥에 따라 파악하자.
2. **as if things were all right** 마치 모든 게 괜찮다는 듯이
   〈as if ~〉는 '(실제는 그렇지 않은데) 마치 ~인 것처럼'이라는 의미.
3. **any clothes of his own** 자기 소유의 옷도
   of one's own은 '자기 소유의'라는 의미. *ex*) a shop of my own(내 소유의 가게)

"내가 뭘 하는 거지? 그 사람은 죽어 가고be dying 있을 수도 있어!" 세몬은 죄책감이 들어서feel guilty 몸을 돌려turn around 교회로 돌아갔다go back to the church.

세몬이 교회 뒤로 가서go behind the church 보니 그 낯선 이the stranger는 젊은이a young man였다. 그는 몸이 꽁꽁 언 채 겁에 질려freezing and frightened 있었다. 세몬은 즉시 외투를 벗어take off his coat 사내에게 둘러 주었다put it around the man. 그런 다음 사내에게 장화를 신겨 주었다put boots on the man. 세몬에게는 여벌의 장화an extra pair of boots가 있었던 것이다.

"걸을 수 있겠소?" 세몬이 물었다. "날씨가 너무 추워서 여기에 계속 있지는 못해요. 당신을 우리 집으로 데려가take you to my home 주겠소. 여기 지팡이a stick가 있으니 걷는 동안 기대시오lean on."

사내는 일어서서stand up 세몬을 상냥하게 바라보았다look kindly at Simon. 그러나 말은 하지 않았다do not speak. 그들이 세몬의 집으로 걸어가는walk to Simon's home 동안 세몬은 사내에게 어디서where 왔는지be from, 어떻게how 교회에 오게 됐는지get to the church 물어봤다. 사내는 차분한 목소리로with a calm voice 대답했다. "저는 이 근방 사람from around here이 아닙니다. 하느님께서God 저에게 벌을 내리셨지요punish me."

세몬은 그 대답에by the response 깜짝 놀랐다be surprised. 하지만 이렇게 말했다. "음, 하느님께서는 만인을 다스리시지요rule all men. 나와 함께 집에 가서come home with me 최소한at least 몸이라도 녹여요make yourself warm." 그 낯선 이와 함께 걷는walk with the stranger 동안 세몬은 다른 사람을 도왔다는help another person 사실이 기뻤다feel glad.

세몬과 사내가 집에 들어왔을come into the house 때 세몬의 아내Simon's wife는 저녁을 준비하는prepare dinner 중이었다. 마트료나Matryna는 사내가 모자도 없이have no hat 펠트 장화를 신고 있는wear felt boots 걸 눈치챘다. 게다가 사내는 남편의 외투까지 입고wear her husband's coat 있었다. 세몬에게는 양가죽도 없었다have no sheepskins. 마트료나의 마음her heart은 실망감으로with disappointment 무너져 내릴break 지경이었다. "이 사람이 밖에서 술을 마시다가be out drinking 이젠 다른 술주정뱅이another drunk까지 집으로 데려왔군." 하고 그녀는 생각했다.

세몬은 모자를 벗고take off his hat 모든 게 괜찮다는 듯이 의자에 앉았다sit down on the bench. 그리고는 이렇게 말했다. "자리에 앉아요have a seat, 친구여. 저녁을 먹읍시다have some dinner."

마트료나가 몹시 화를 내며become angry 말했다. "저녁을 짓긴cook dinner 했지만 당신 것은 없어요not for you. 양가죽을 산다고 나가서는go out 도리어 낯선 사람을 집에 데려오다니bring a strange man home. 심지어 이 사람은 자기 옷도 변변히any clothes of his own 없잖아요. 당신은 틀림없이 보드카에다on Vodka 우리 돈을 다 써 버렸을spend all our money 거예요. 당신들 같은 술주정뱅이들drunkards like you한테 줄 저녁식사는 없어요have no supper."

GRAMMAR POINT

간접의문 ⇨ 〈의문사＋주어＋동사〉의 어순이 된다.

- Simon asked him **where he was** from and **how he got** to the church.
  세몬은 그에게 어디서 왔는지, 어떻게 교회에 오게 됐는지 물었다.

- He saw something white. He did not know **what it was**.
  그는 뭔가 하얀 것을 보았다. 그는 그게 뭔지 몰랐다.

[p. 106-107]

Simon tried to explain / to his wife / how he had met the man, / but she did not listen. She angrily walked out the door, / but then she stopped undecided; she wanted to work off her anger, / but she also wanted to learn / what sort of a man / the stranger was. **She was curious about the man.**

"**If he were a good man, / he would not be naked.** Where is he from?" she asked.

"That's just / what I'm trying to tell you," answered Simon. "When I passed the church, / I saw him sitting there / naked and frozen. **God made me / go to help him, / or he would have died.** What should I have done? So I helped him get up, / gave him my coat, / and brought him here. Don't be so angry with me. Anger is a sin."

As Matryna listened to her husband, / she looked closely at the man. He sat on the bench / without moving. His hands were folded / on his knees, / and he looked down at the floor. His eyes were closed / as if he were in pain.

"Matryna, / don't you love God?" asked Simon.

Suddenly, / her heart softened / toward the stranger. She went back into the kitchen. She set the table / and served dinner. While they were eating, / Matryna **felt pity for the stranger**. She did not feel angry / anymore. She even began to like him. At that moment, / the man looked at Matryna / and smiled at her. A light seemed to / come from his face.

When they had finished supper, / she asked the man / where he was from. But the man said / he did not know. All he said / was, "God punished me. I was naked and freezing cold. Then, Simon saw me, / **took pity on me**, / and brought me here. You have fed me / and **pitied me**, too. God will reward you."

- **undecided** 결정하지 못한, 주저하는 • **work off** ~을 풀다, ~을 해소하다 • **anger** 화, 분노 • **frozen** (추워서) 꽁꽁 언 • **sin** 죄 • **be folded** 포개지다, 접히다 • **be in pain** 괴로워하다, 아파하다 • **soften** 부드러워지다, 누그러지다 • **serve** (음식 등을) 서빙하다, 제공하다 • **feel pity for** ~을 불쌍하게 여기다 • **seem to** ~하는 것처럼 보이다 • **take pity on** ~을 동정하다 • **feed** 먹이다, 먹을 것을 주다 • **reward** 보상하다, 보답하다

CLOSE UP

1 **She was curious about the man.** 그녀는 그 사내에 대해 궁금해졌다.
   〈be curious about ~〉은 '~에 대해 궁금하게 여기다', '~에 대해 호기심이 생기다'라는 의미.

2 **felt pity for the stranger** 그 낯선 이에게 연민을 느꼈다 / **took pity on me** 나를 불쌍히 여겼다 / **pitied me** 나를 가엾게 여겼다
   〈feel pity for ~〉, 〈take pity on ~〉, 〈pity ~〉는 모두 '~을 불쌍히/가엾게 여기다'라는 의미.

100　Step 4

세몬이 아내에게 어떻게 그 사내를 만났는지 설명하려고 했지만try to explain, 아내는 듣지 않았다do not listen. 마트료나는 화가 나서angrily 문 밖으로 걸어 나갔지만walk out of the door, 확신이 안 선 듯undecided 걸음을 멈췄다stop. (밖으로 나가) 화풀이를 하고도work off her anger 싶었지만, 한편으로는 그 낯선 이가 어떤 사람what sort of a man인지 알고 싶기도 했던 것이다. 그 사내에 대해 궁금해진 be curious about the man 것이었다.

"그가 선한 사람이라면 벌거숭이로 있지는 않을 거예요. 저 사람 어디서 왔대요?" 마트료나가 물었다.

"그게 바로 내가 당신한테 하려던 얘기what I'm trying to tell you요." 세몬이 대답했다. "내가 교회를 지나고 있는데, 저 사람이 알몸으로 꽁꽁 언 채naked and frozen 거기에 앉아 있는 게 보이지 뭐요. 하느님께서 나로 하여금 가서 그 사람을 돕도록go to help him 했기에 망정이지, 안 그랬으면 그는 죽었을 거요. 내가 어찌해야 했겠소? 그래서 그가 일어나도록 도와주고help him get up, 내 외투를 주고give him my coat, 여기로 데려온bring him here 거라오. 내게 그렇게 화내지 마오don't be so angry. 분노anger 는 죄악a sin이오."

마트료나는 남편의 말을 들으며listen to her husband 사내를 유심히 살펴보았다look closely at the man. 사내는 움직이지 않고without moving 의자에 앉아 있었다sit on the bench. 그의 손his hands 은 무릎 위에on his knees 포개어져 있었고be folded, 그는 바닥을 내려다보고 있었다look down at the floor. 그의 눈his eyes은 고통스러운be in pain 듯 감겨져 있었다be closed.

"마트료나, 당신은 하느님을 사랑하지love God 않소?" 세몬이 물었다.

갑자기 그 낯선 이를 향한 그녀의 마음이 누그러졌다soften. 마트료나는 다시 부엌으로 들어갔다go back into the kitchen. 식탁을 차리고set the table 저녁식사를 내왔다serve dinner. 그들이 식사를 하는 동안 마트료나는 그 낯선 이에게 연민을 느꼈다feel pity for the stranger. 이제 더는 화가 나지 않았다. 심지어 그가 마음에 들기like him 시작했다. 그 순간at that moment 사내가 마트료나를 바라보며look at Matryna 미소를 지었다smile at her. 마치 얼굴에서from his face 광채a light 가 나오는 것 같았다.

그들이 저녁식사를 마치자 마트료나는 사내에게 어디에서 왔는지 물었다. 그러나 사내는 모른다고 했다. 다만 이렇게만 말했다. "하느님께서 제게 벌을 내리셨습니다. 저는 벌거벗고 추위에 꽁꽁 얼었지요freezing cold. 그때 세몬이 저를 보고 불쌍히 여겨서take pity on me 여기 데려온bring me here 겁니다. 당신도 제게 음식을 주고feed me 저를 불쌍히 여겨 줬지요pity me. 하느님께서 당신들에게 보답해 주실reward you 겁니다."

GRAMMAR POINT

if ~ (가정법) ⇨ '가정법 과거'와 '가정법 과거완료'가 있다.

- **If** he **were** a good man, he **would** not **be** naked. 만일 그가 선한 사람이라면 벌거숭이로 있지는 않을 거예요.
  (가정법 과거: 현재 사실과 반대되는 가정. if절의 be동사는 항상 were로 씀.)

- God made me go to help him, or he **would have died**.
  (= **If** God **had** not **made** me go to help him, he **would have died**.)
  하느님께서 나로 하여금 가서 그를 돕게 했소. 그렇지 않았다면 그는 죽었을 거요.
  (가정법 과거완료: 과거 사실과 반대되는 가정)

[p. 108-109]

Matryna gave the man some clothes, / and he went to get some sleep. Then, / she and Simon went to bed, too, / but Matryna could not sleep. She could not get the stranger / out of her mind. Then, / she suddenly remembered / that they had eaten / their last piece of bread, / so there was nothing left / for tomorrow. She felt grieved.

"Simon, / what will we do tomorrow?"

"As long as we are alive, / we will find something to eat," Simon answered.

The next morning, / Simon and Matryna woke up / and saw / that the stranger was already awake. He looked much better / than the day before.

Simon said, "Well, friend, / we have to work / for a living. What work do you know?"

"I do not know anything," answered the man.

Surprised, / Simon said, "A man / who wants to learn / can learn anything."

"Then I will learn / how to work."

"What is your name?" asked Simon.

"Michael."

"Well, Michael, / if you work with me, / I will give you food and shelter," offered Simon.

"May God reward you," answered Michael. "Show me / what to do."

Simon showed Michael / how to make boots. Michael learned quickly / and was very skilled. He ate little food / and almost never went anywhere.

He made boots so well / that many people came to Simon's shop. Soon, / Simon began to make a lot of money.

A year passed. Michael lived and worked / with Simon. One day, / Simon and Michael / were working hard / when a carriage / drawn by three horses / drove up to the hut. A servant opened the door, / and a gentleman / wearing a fur coat / got out. He strode into the hut / and asked, "Which of you / is the master bootmaker?"

- **get ~ out of one's mind** ~을 마음에서 몰아내다, ~을 생각하지 않다 • **feel grieved** 슬퍼하다, 한탄하다
- **wake up** 잠에서 깨다 • **awake** 깨어 있는 • **surprised** 놀란 • **shelter** 은신처, 숙소 • **skilled** 숙련된, 능숙한, 솜씨가 좋은 • **carriage** 마차 • **drawn by** ~가 끄는 • **drive up to** (차, 마차 등이) ~로 달려가다
- **servant** 하인 • **stride into** ~로 성큼성큼 걸어 들어오다 • **master bootmaker** 구두 직공장, 제화공의 장

CLOSE UP

1. **how to work** 일하는 법 / **what to do** 무엇을 해야 할지 / **how to make boots** 장화를 만드는 법
   〈how to ~〉는 '어떻게 ~해야 할지(~하는 법)', 〈what to ~〉는 '무엇을 ~해야 할지'라는 의미.

2. **May God reward you.** 하느님께서 보답하시기를.
   〈May+주어+동사원형〉은 '~하기를 기원하다'라는 의미. ex) May God be with you.(신이 함께 하시기를.)

3. **He made boots so well that many people came to Simon's shop.**
   그가 장화를 너무 잘 만들어서 많은 사람들이 세몬의 가게를 찾아왔다.
   〈so ~ that...〉은 '아주 ~해서 …하다'라는 의미.

마트료나는 사내에게 옷가지를 내주었고give the man some clothes, 사내는 잠을 자러get some sleep 갔다. 그러고 나서 마트료나와 세몬도 잠자리에 들었다go to bed. 하지만 마트료나는 잠을 이룰 수가 없었다cannot sleep. 낯선 이에 대한 생각을 마음에서 떨쳐 버릴 수 없었기cannot get the stranger out of her mind 때문이다. 그때 마트료나는 문득 자신들이 마지막 남은 빵 조각their last piece of bread을 먹어 버려서 내일 먹을 게 하나도 남아 있지 않다nothing left는 사실이 떠올랐다. 마트료나는 슬펐다feel grieved.

"세몬, 우리 내일 어떻게 하죠?"

"살아 있는be alive 한 먹을 것이야 구하게find something to eat 되겠지." 세몬이 대답했다.

다음 날 아침the next morning 세몬과 마트료나가 잠에서 깨어wake up 보니 낯선 이는 이미 깨어나 있었다be awake. 그는 전날보다 훨씬 더 좋아 보였다look much better.

세몬이 말했다. "자, 친구. 먹고 살려면for a living 일을 해야만 하네have to work. 어떤 일을 할 줄 아는가?"

"저는 아무것도 모릅니다do not know anything." 사내가 대답했다.

깜짝 놀란surprised 세몬이 말했다. "배우려는 마음이 있는want to learn 사람은 뭐든지 배울learn anything 수 있네."

"그럼 일하는 법how to work을 배우겠습니다."

"이름your name이 뭔가?" 세몬이 물었다.

"미하일Michael입니다."

"좋네, 미하일. 자네가 나와 일을 한다면work with me 내가 음식과 거처food and shelter를 주겠네." 세몬이 제안했다offer.

"하느님께서 보답하시기를 기원합니다may God reward you." 미하일이 대답했다. "무엇을 하면 될지 what to do 알려 주십시오show me."

세몬은 미하일에게 장화 만드는 법how to make boots을 알려 주었다. 미하일은 배우는 속도가 빨랐고learn quickly 솜씨도 매우 좋았다be very skilled. 그는 음식도 별로 먹지 않고eat little food 거의 아무 데도 가지 않았다never go anywhere.

미하일이 장화를 매우 잘 만들어서make boots so well 많은 사람들many people이 세몬의 가게를 찾아왔다come to Simon's shop. 곧 세몬은 돈을 많이 벌기make a lot of money 시작했다.

1년a year이 지났다pass. 미하일은 세몬과 함께 지내며 일을 했다live and work with Simon. 어느 날one day 세몬과 미하일이 열심히 일하고work hard 있는데, 말 세 필이 끄는drawn by three horses 마차 한 대a carriage가 오두막으로 달려왔다drive up to the hut. 하인a servant이 마차 문을 여니open the door 모피 외투를 입은wearing a fur coat 신사a gentleman가 밖으로 나왔다get out. 신사는 오두막 안으로 성큼성큼 걸어 들어오더니stride into the hut 이렇게 물었다. "자네들 중 누가which of you 제화공 장the master bootmaker인가?"

GRAMMAR POINT

능동의 현재분사 / 수동의 과거분사

⇨ 분사는 명사를 수식할 수 있다. 현재분사(-ing형)는 능동, 과거분사(-ed형)는 수동의 의미를 가진다.

- *A gentleman* **wearing** a fur coat got out. 모피 외투를 입은 신사가 밖으로 나왔다.

- *A carriage* **drawn** by three horses drove up to the hut. 세 필의 말이 이끄는 마차 한 대가 오두막으로 달려왔다.

[p. 110-111]

"I am, sir," Simon answered.
Then the gentleman said, "Do you see this leather here?"
"Yes, it is good leather, sir."
"You fool," laughed the gentleman. "It is the finest leather. It comes from Germany / and is extremely expensive. I want you to make me / **a pair of boots / that will last for years**. If they lose their shape / or fall apart, / I will throw you into prison. After one year, / if the boots are still good, / I will pay you ten rubles / for them," said the rich man.
Simon was terrified, / but Michael **advised him / to make the boots**. So Simon agreed, / and then he measured the gentleman's feet. While he was doing that, / Simon saw / Michael was gazing behind the rich man / as if someone were there. Suddenly, / Michael smiled, / and his face turned bright.
"What are you grinning at, / you fool?" shouted the man. "**You had better make these boots / on time**. I will come back / in two days."
"They will be ready," answered Michael.
After he left, / Simon looked at Michael / and said, "Michael, / we must be cautious / with this expensive leather. We cannot make a single mistake."
Michael started cutting the leather, / but he did not cut it / for boots. Instead, / he started to make soft slippers. Simon saw / what Michael was doing, / and he was shocked.
"What are you doing, / Michael? The gentleman ordered boots, / not slippers. You've ruined that leather. What's going to happen to me now?"

- **fool** 바보, 멍청이 • **extremely** 지극히, 아주 • **last** 유지하다, 지속되다 • **lose one's shape** 모양이 망가지다, 모양이 변하다 • **fall apart** 허물어지다, 부서지다, 해어지다 • **throw ~ into prison** ~을 감옥에 쳐 넣다 • **terrified** 겁나는 • **advise** 조언하다 • **measure** (자로) 재다 • **gaze** 응시하다, 바라보다 • **grin at** ~을 보고 싱긋 웃다 • **on time** 제시간에 • **cautious** 주의 깊은 • **make a mistake** 실수하다 • **ruin** 망치다

CLOSE UP

1 **a pair of boots that will last for years** 몇 년이고 오래갈 장화 한 켤레
   여기서 last는 동사로 '오래가다', '(기능이) 지속되다'라는 의미.
   that will last for years는 a pair of boots를 수식하는 관계절이다.

2 **advised him to make the boots** 그에게 장화를 만들라고 조언했다
   〈advise ~ to...〉는 '~에게 …하라고 조언하다/충고하다'라는 의미.

3 **You had better make these boots on time.** 이 장화를 제시간에 만드는 게 좋을 거야.
   〈had better+동사원형〉은 '~하는 게 좋을 거다'라는 뜻으로, 그렇게 하지 않으면 뭔가 안 좋은 일이 생길 거라는 경고를 나타낸다.
   〈on time〉은 '제시간에', '시간을 어기지 않고'라는 의미.

"접니다, 나으리." 세몬이 대답했다.
그러자 신사가 말했다. "여기 이 가죽이 보이나see this leather?"
"네. 좋은 가죽good leather이로군요, 나으리."
"바보 같으니라고you fool." 신사는 비웃으며 말했다. "이건 최고급 가죽the finest leather이란 말일세. 독일제인데come from Germany 매우 비싸지be expensive. 몇 년이고 오래갈last for years 장화를 한 켤레 만들어 make a pair of boots 주게. 만약 장화가 모양이 망가지거나lose their shape 해어지면fall apart 자네를 감옥에 쳐 넣을 throw you into prison 거야. 1년 뒤에도after one year 장화가 여전히 멀쩡하면be still good 장화 값으로 10루블을 지불하지pay you ten rubles." 그 부자 신사가 말했다.

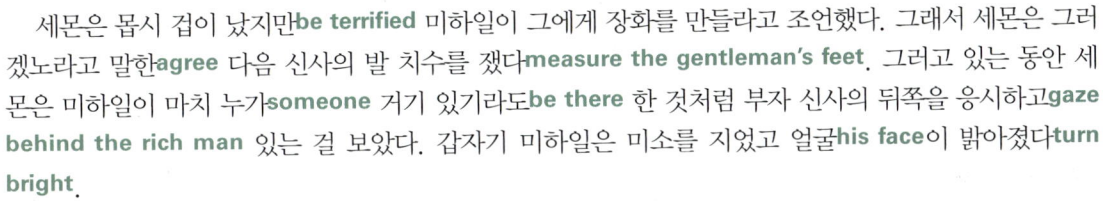

세몬은 몹시 겁이 났지만be terrified 미하일이 그에게 장화를 만들라고 조언했다. 그래서 세몬은 그러겠노라고 말한agree 다음 신사의 발 치수를 쟀다measure the gentleman's feet. 그러고 있는 동안 세몬은 미하일이 마치 누가someone 거기 있기라도be there 한 것처럼 부자 신사의 뒤쪽을 응시하고gaze behind the rich man 있는 걸 보았다. 갑자기 미하일은 미소를 지었고 얼굴his face이 밝아졌다turn bright.

"바보 같으니라고, 뭘 보고 히죽거리는grin at 거야?" 신사가 소리쳤다. "이 장화를 제시간에on time 만드는 게 좋을 거야. 내가 이틀 뒤에in two days 다시 올come back 테니까."

"준비해 놓겠습니다be ready." 미하일이 대답했다.

신사가 떠난 후 세몬이 미하일을 보고 말했다. "미하일, 이 비싼 가죽this expensive leather은 조심해서be cautious 다뤄야만 하네. 한 치의 실수a single mistake도 해서는 안 돼cannot make."

미하일이 가죽을 자르기cut the leather 시작했다. 하지만 장화용으로 자른 게 아니었다. 대신에 그는 부드러운 슬리퍼를 만들기make soft slippers 시작했다. 세몬은 미하일이 하는 짓what Michael is doing을 보고 깜짝 놀랐다be shocked.

"미하일, 뭘 하고 있는 건가? 그 신사는 장화를 주문했다고order boots. 슬리퍼가 아니란not slippers 말일세. 자네가 그 가죽을 망가뜨렸군ruin that leather. 이제 난 어떻게 된단 말인가?"

GRAMMAR POINT

as if ~ (가정법) : 마치 ~인 것처럼 ⇨ 실제는 그렇지 않은데도 마치 그런 것 같다는 의미.

- Michael was gazing behind the rich man **as if** someone **were** there.
  미하일은 마치 누가 거기 있기라도 한 것처럼 부자 신사의 뒤쪽을 응시하고 있었다. **(가정법 과거)**

- Michael was staring at the girls **as if** he **had known** them before.
  미하일은 마치 그들을 전부터 알고 있었던 것처럼 그 여자아이들을 응시하고 있었다. **(가정법 과거완료)**

[p. 112-113]

At that very moment, / the gentleman's servant / rushed into the hut.

"My master does not need boots anymore," he announced. "He is dead. He did not even make it home alive / as he died in the carriage. My master's wife / sent me here / to cancel the order for boots. Instead, / she wants you to quickly make / a pair of soft slippers / for his corpse."

Simon was amazed. Michael took / the pair of soft slippers / he made / and handed them to the servant.

More time passed, / and Michael had now lived with Simon / for six years. He never went anywhere, / and he was always quiet. He had only smiled / two times in six years: / once / when Matryna gave him food / and a second time / when the rich man was in their hut. Simon adored Michael / and was afraid / that Michael would leave him.

One day, / one of Simon's sons / came running to Michael. "Uncle Michael," he cried, "Look! A lady / with two little girls / is coming, / and one of the girls / is lame."

Michael immediately stopped work / and looked out the window. Simon was surprised / since Michael never looked outside. Simon also looked out / and saw / that a well-dressed woman / with two little girls / was coming to his hut. One of the girls / was crippled / in her left leg.

The woman came in / and said, "I want leather shoes / for these two girls / for spring."

Simon answered, "I have never made / such small shoes, / but my assistant Michael / is a master at making shoes, / so he can do it."

Michael was staring at the girls / as if he had known them before. Simon was confused, / but he began to measure the girls' feet. The woman mentioned / that the girls were twins.

Simon asked, "How did it happen to her? Was she born this way?"

"No," the woman answered. "Her mother crushed her leg. Their father died / one week before they were born. And their mother died / right after she gave birth to them."

- **rush** 서둘러 오다/가다 • **cancel** 취소하다 • **corpse** 시체 • **amazed** (대단히) 놀란 • **hand** 건네다, 넘겨주다 • **adore** 흠모하다, 아주 좋아하다 • **be afraid** 겁내다, 두려워하다 • **lame** 절름발이의, 다리를 저는 • **crippled** 불구의, 절름발이의 • **assistant** 조수 • **master** 달인, 명수 • **stare at** ~을 응시하다 • **confused** 혼란스러운, 어리둥절한 • **mention** 언급하다, 말하다 • **twins** 쌍둥이 • **crush** 으스러뜨리다, 짓눌러 뭉개다

Close UP

1. **did not even make it home alive** 살아서 집에 가지도 못했다
   〈make it to ~〉는 '~에 가다', '~에 (간신히) 시간 맞춰 가다'라는 의미. 여기서 home(집으로)은 부사이므로 to 없이 쓰였다.

2. **is a master at making shoes** 신발 만드는 데 도가 텄다
   master는 어떤 일에 통달한 '달인'을 뜻한다. 〈be a master at +V-ing〉하면 '~하는 데 도가 텄다', '~의 달인이다'라는 의미.

3. **Was she born this way?** 그 아이는 이렇게 태어난 건가요? / **she gave birth to them** 그녀는 그들을 낳았다
   〈be born〉은 '태어나다'이고, 〈give birth to ~〉는 '(아이를) 낳다'라는 의미.

바로 그 순간at that very moment, 그 신사의 하인the gentleman's servant이 다급하게 오두막으로 들어왔다rush into the hut.

"우리 주인님한테my master 이제는 장화가 필요 없게 됐습니다do not need boots." 하인이 알렸다. "그분이 돌아가셨어요be dead. 마차 안에서 돌아가시는die in the carriage 바람에 살아서 집에 가시지도 못했습니다. 주인마님my master's wife께서 장화 주문을 취소하려고cancel the order 저를 이곳에 보내셨어요send me here. 대신 시신에게 신길for his corpse 부드러운 슬리퍼 한 켤레a pair of soft slippers를 빨리 만들어quickly make 달라고 하십니다."

세몬은 크게 놀랐다be amazed. 미하일은 자기가 만든 부드러운 슬리퍼 한 켤레를 가져와서 하인에게 건네주었다hand them to the servant.

세월이 더more time 흘러서pass, 미하일은 이제 세몬과with Simon 6년간for six years 함께 지냈다. 미하일은 결코 아무 데도 가지 않았고never go anywhere 언제나 말이 없었다be quiet. 6년 동안in six years 겨우 두 차례two times 미소를 지은smile 게 다였다. 한번은once 마트료나가 그에게 음식을 주었을give him food 때였고, 두 번째는a second time 부자 신사the rich man가 오두막에 왔을be in their hut 때였다. 세몬은 미하일을 아꼈고adore Michael 미하일이 자기를 떠날까 봐 염려했다.

어느 날 세몬의 아들 중 한 명이 미하일에게 달려왔다. "미하일 아저씨Uncle Michael." 아이가 소리치며 말했다. "보세요look! 어떤 부인a lady이 어린 여자아이 둘을 데리고with two little girls 오고 있는데, 그 아이들 중 하나one of the girls가 절름발이예요be lame."

미하일은 즉시 일을 멈추고stop work 창밖을 내다봤다look out the window. 세몬은 깜짝 놀랐다. 미하일은 밖을 내다본 적이 한 번도 없었기 때문이다. 세몬 역시 밖을 내다보니 잘 차려 입은 여인a well-dressed woman이 어린 여자아이 둘을 데리고 오두막으로 오고come to his hut 있는 게 보였다. 한 여자아이는 왼쪽 다리를in her left leg 절었다be crippled.

여인이 들어와서 말했다. "이 두 아이가for these two girls 봄에 신을 가죽 신발을 맞추고 싶어요want leather shoes."

세몬이 대답했다. "저는 그렇게 작은 신발을 만들어 본 적이 없지만, 제 조수my assistant 미하일이 신발 만드는 데 도가 텄으니a master at making shoes 그가 할 수 있을 겁니다."

미하일은 마치 전부터 그들을 알고know them before 있었던 것처럼 그 여자아이들을 뚫어지게 바라보고stare at the girls 있었다. 세몬은 어리둥절했지만be confused 여자아이들의 발 치수를 재기measure the girls' feet 시작했다. 여인은 그 아이들이 쌍둥이twins라고 말했다.

세몬이 물었다. "이 아이는 어쩌다 이렇게 되었습니까? 태어날 때부터 이랬나요be born this way?"

"아뇨." 여인이 대답했다. "그 아이의 엄마her mother가 아이의 다리를 짓누르는crush her leg 바람에 그렇게 됐답니다. 아이들의 아버지는 애들이 태어나기 일주일 전에 세상을 떠났어요. 애들 엄마도 이 애들을 낳고give birth to them 바로 죽었고요."

> **GRAMMAR POINT**
>
> **시제 일치** ⇨ 주절의 시제가 과거일 땐 종속절의 will도 would로 써서 시제를 일치시킨다.
>
> - Simon **was** afraid that Michael **would** leave him. 세몬은 미하일이 자기를 떠날까 봐 염려했다.
>
> - I **thought** the crippled baby **would** die soon. 저는 불구가 된 아기가 곧 죽을 거라 생각했지요.

[p. 114-115]

She continued, "My husband and I / were their neighbors. When I visited their hut, / I found / that the mother, / when dying, / had rolled on this child / and crushed her leg. The babies were left alone. What could I do? I was the only woman / in the village / with a baby, / so I took both girls / and nursed them / as well.

"I thought / the crippled one / would die, / so I did not feed her / at first. But I had so much milk / that I could feed my son and both girls. Then, / my own son died / when he was two." She sighed.

"I **thank God** / **for giving me these two girls**. I would be very lonely / without them. They are precious to me."

She wiped some tears / from her face / as she told the story.

Then, Matryna said, "The old proverb is true. 'One may live / without father or mother, / but one cannot live / without God.'"

As they talked, / suddenly a bright light / filled the room. They looked at Michael, / who was the source of this light. He was smiling / and looking up at the heavens.

After the woman left / with the girls, / Michael **bowed low** / **to Simon and Matryna**. "Farewell," he said. "God has forgiven me. I ask your forgiveness, too, / for anything / I have done wrong."

They saw / a light was shining from Michael. Simon **bowed to Michael** / and said, "I see / that you are not an ordinary man. But please tell me. When I first met you / and brought you home, / you were quite gloomy. But you smiled at my wife / after she gave you some food. Then, / when the rich man came / and ordered boots, / you smiled again. Finally, / when the woman brought the girls, / you smiled a third time. And now / you **have become** / **as bright as day**. Why is your face shining like that, / and why did you smile / those three times?"

- **neighbor** 이웃, 이웃 사람   - **roll on** ~ 위로 뒹굴다   - **nurse** 간호하다, 젖을 먹이다   - **sigh** 한숨을 쉬다
- **lonely** 외로운   - **precious** 소중한, 귀중한   - **wipe tears** 눈물을 닦다   - **proverb** 격언, 속담   - **source** 원천   - **look up** 올려다보다   - **the heavens** 하늘   - **bow** 절하다, 고개를 숙여 인사하다   - **farewell** (작별인사로) 안녕   - **forgive** 용서하다   - **shine** 빛나다   - **ordinary** 보통의, 일반의, 평범한   - **gloomy** 우울한, 음울한
- **three times** 세 번

CLOSE UP

1. **thank God for giving me these two girls** 하느님께 이 두 아이를 주신 데 대해 감사드려요
   〈thank ~ for...〉는 '~에게 …에 대해 감사하다'라는 의미.

2. **bowed low to Simon and Matryna** 세몬과 마트료나에게 깊이 허리 굽혀 절했다 / **bowed to Michael** 미하일에게 고개 숙여 인사했다
   〈bow to ~〉는 '~에게 (허리를 굽혀) 절하다', '~에게 고개를 숙이다'라는 의미. bow low 하면 '깊이 허리 굽혀 절하다'라는 뜻이 된다.

3. **have become as bright as day** 대낮처럼 환해졌다
   〈as bright as day〉는 '대낮처럼 환한'이라는 의미.

여인이 계속 말했다. "제 남편과 저my husband and I는 그들의 이웃their neighbors이었어요. 제가 그들 오두막을 찾아갔을visit their hut 때, 애들 엄마가 죽으면서 이 아이 위로 구르는 바람에 아이의 다리를 깔아뭉갠 걸 알게 되었지요. 갓난애들the babies만 홀로 남겨져 있었죠be left alone. 제가 어쩔 수 있었겠어요? 마을에서는in the village 애 있는with a baby 여자가 저밖에 없던the only woman 터라 제가 두 아이를 모두 데려다가take both girls 젖도 먹였지요nurse them.

저는 불구가 된 아이the crippled one가 죽을 거라 생각해서 처음에는at first 애한테 젖도 주지 않았어요do not feed her. 하지만 제가 젖이 아주 많이 나와서have so much milk 제 아들과 두 여자아이들까지 먹일feed my son and both girls 수 있었죠. 그러다가 제 아들my own son이 두 살be two 때 죽었어요die." 여인은 한숨을 내쉬었다sigh.

"저는 이 두 아이를 주신 데 대해 하느님께 감사드려요thank God. 이 아이들이 없다면without them 제가 무척 외로울be lonely 거예요. 제게는 소중한be precious 애들이죠."

여인은 사연을 들려주며tell the story 얼굴에서from her face 눈물을 닦았다wipe some tears.

그때 마트료나가 말했다. "옛말the old proverb이 틀린 게 하나도 없어요be true. '아버지나 어머니 없이는without father or mother 살 수 있어도may live 하느님 없이는without God 살 수 없다cannot live'고 했잖아요."

그들이 얘기하고 있는데, 갑자기 밝은 빛a bright light이 방 안을 가득 채웠다fill the room. 그들은 미하일을 쳐다보았다look at Michael. 미하일에게서 그 빛이 나오고 있었던the source of this light 것이다. 미하일은 미소를 지으며 하늘을 우러러보고look up at the heavens 있었다.

여인이 여자아이들을 데리고 떠난 뒤, 미하일은 세몬과 마트료나에게 깊이 허리 굽혀 절했다bow low. "안녕히 계십시오farewell." 미하일이 말했다. "하느님께서 저를 용서해 주셨습니다forgive me. 혹시 제가 잘못한do wrong 일이 있다면 역시 두 분의 용서도 구합니다ask your forgiveness."

부부는 미하일한테서from Michael 광채a light가 빛나고shine 있는 걸 보았다. 세몬이 미하일에게 고개 숙여 인사하며bow to Michael 말했다. "자네가 평범한 사람이 아니라는not an ordinary man 걸 알고 있네. 그런데 말해 주게tell me. 내가 처음 자네를 만나서first meet you 집으로 데려왔을bring you home 때 자네는 무척 침울한 상태였네be gloomy. 하지만 아내가 자네에게 음식을 주자give you some food 자넨 아내한테 미소를 지었지smile at my wife. 그다음에는 부자 신사the rich man가 와서 장화를 주문했을order boots 때 다시 미소 지었네smile again. 마지막으로, 그 여인the woman이 여자애들을 데려왔을bring the girls 때 세 번째로 미소 지었지smile a third time. 그리고 이제는 대낮처럼 환하게as bright as day 빛이 나는군. 자네 얼굴이 왜 그렇게 빛나는shine like that 건가? 그리고 왜 세 번 미소 지은smile those three times 건가?"

GRAMMAR POINT

may : ~할 수도 있다, ~일지도 모른다 (가능성) / ~해도 된다 (허락)

- One **may** live without father or mother. 사람은 아버지나 어머니 없이 살 수도 있다.
- When you learn all three things, you **may** return to Heaven. 세 가지를 다 배우면 하늘로 돌아와도 좋다.

What Men Live By

[p. 116-117]

Michael answered, "Light is shining from me / because I was punished, / but now God has forgiven me. I smiled three times / because God sent me here / to learn three truths, / and I have learned them. I learned the first / when your wife pitied me, / so I smiled then. I learned the second / when the rich man ordered the boots, / so I smiled again. And I learned the third / when I saw the little girls, / so I smiled for the third time."

Simon asked, "Michael, / why did God punish you? And what are the three truths? I would like to learn them / for myself."

Michael answered, "God punished me / because I disobeyed him. I was an angel in Heaven, / but I disobeyed God. God sent me / to take the soul of a woman. I came down to Earth / and saw a sick woman / lying alone. She had just given birth to twin girls. The woman saw me / and said, 'Angel of God, / my husband has just died, / and there is no one / to look after my girls. Do not take my soul. Let me live / to care for my babies. Children cannot live / without father or mother.'"

Michael continued, "I put one child at her breast / and put the other in her arms. Then, / I returned to Heaven. I told God, 'I could not take the mother's soul. Her husband died, / and the woman has twins / and prays to stay alive.'

"But God said, 'Go back / and take the woman's soul, / and learn three truths: Learn / what dwells in man. Learn / what is not given to man. And learn / what men live by. When you learn all three things, / you may return to Heaven.'

- **be punished** 벌을 받다 • **truth** 진실 • **the third time** 세 번째 • **disobey** 불복종하다, 거역하다 • **Heaven** 천국, 천당, 하늘나라 • **take a soul** 영혼을 거두다 • **lie alone** 혼자 누워 있다 • **care for** ~를 돌보다 • **breast** 가슴 • **pray** 기도하다 • **stay alive** 살아 있다 • **dwell** 깃들다, 살다 • **live by** ~에 의해 살다

CLOSE UP

1. **sent me here to learn three truths** 세 가지 진리를 배우라고 나를 이곳에 보냈다 / **sent me to take the soul of a woman** 어떤 여인의 영혼을 거두라고 나를 보냈다
 ⟨send ~ to...⟩는 '~을 …하라고 보내다'라는 의미.

2. **I would like to learn them** 나는 그것들을 배우고 싶네
 ⟨I would like to ~⟩는 '~하고 싶다'라는 의미.

3. **look after my girls** 내 딸아이들을 돌보다 / **care for my babies** 내 아기들을 돌보다
 ⟨look after ~⟩와 ⟨care for ~⟩는 '~을 돌보다/보살피다'라는 의미.

미하일이 대답했다. "제게서 빛이 나는 이유는, 제가 벌을 받았으나be punished 하느님께서 이제 저를 용서해 주셨기forgive me 때문입니다. 세 번 미소 지은 이유는, 하느님께서 저를 여기로 보내셔서send me here 세 가지 진리를 배우도록learn three truths 하셨는데, 제가 그것들을 깨달았기learn them 때문이지요. 첫 번째the first 진리는 당신 아내가 저를 불쌍히 여겼을pity me 때 깨달았기 때문에 그때 미소 지었던 겁니다. 두 번째the second 진리는 부자 신사가 장화를 주문했을order the boots 때 깨달았기 때문에 또 미소 지은 것이지요. 그리고 세 번째the third 진리는 제가 그 어린 여자아이들을 보았을see the little girls 때 깨달았기 때문에 세 번째로 미소 지었던 겁니다."

세몬이 물었다. "미하일, 왜 하느님께서 자네를 벌하신 건가? 그리고 그 세 가지 진리란 게 뭔가? 나도 내 자신을 위해 그것들을 배우고 싶네."

미하일이 대답했다. "하느님께서는 제가 그분을 거역했기disobey him 때문에 저를 벌하신 겁니다. 저는 하늘의 천사an angel in Heaven였지만 하느님을 거역했지요. 하느님께서 어떤 여인의 영혼을 거둬 오라고take the soul of a woman 저를 보내셨습니다. 저는 지상으로 내려와come down to Earth 병든 여인a sick woman이 홀로 누워lie alone 있는 걸 보았습니다. 여인은 쌍둥이 여자아이들을 갓 낳은 just give birth to twin girls 상태였지요. 여인은 저를 보자see me 이렇게 말하더군요. "하느님의 천사여 Angel of God, 제 남편my husband이 방금 죽어서just die 제 딸아이들을 돌볼look after my girls 사람이 없습니다no one. 제 영혼을 거둬 가지 말아 주세요. 제 아기들을 돌볼care for my babies 수 있게 살려 주십시오let me live. 아이들은 아버지나 어머니가 없으면 살지 못합니다.""

미하일이 계속 말을 이어갔다. "저는 한 아이one child를 여인의 가슴에at her breast 놓고, 다른 아이 the other를 여인의 팔에in her arms 놓아 주었습니다. 그리고는 하늘로 돌아갔지요return to Heaven. 저는 하느님께 이렇게 말씀드렸습니다. '그 어머니의 영혼을 거둘 수 없었습니다. 남편이 죽었고, 여인에게는 쌍둥이가 있어서have twins 살려 달라고 빌어서요pray to stay alive.'

하지만 하느님께서는 이렇게 말씀하셨지요. '돌아가서 go back 그 여인의 영혼을 거두고 세 가지 진리를 배워 learn three truths 오거라. 사람의 내면에 무엇이 깃들어 있는지what dwells in man 배우거라. 사람에게 주어지지 않은 게 무엇인지(사람이 갖추고 있지 못한 것)what is not given to man 배우거라. 그리고 사람은 무엇으로 사는 지what men live by 배우거라. 세 가지를 다 배우면 하늘로 돌아와도 좋다.'

GRAMMAR POINT

be + p.p. (수동태)

⇨ 주어가 동사의 행위를 '받거나 당하는' 걸 말한다. 행위자는 by로 나타내는데, 문맥상 누구인지 알 수 있거나 일반적인 사람일 때는 생략하는 경우가 많다.

- **I was punished** (by God), but now God has forgiven me.
  나는 (하느님에 의해) 벌을 받았지만, 이제 하느님께서 나를 용서하셨다.

- Learn what **is** not **given** to man. 사람에게 주어지지 않은 게 무엇인지 배워라.

[p. 118-119]

"So I flew back to Earth / and took the mother's soul. The babies fell from her breast. Her body rolled over on the bed / and crushed one of the baby's legs. I tried to fly up to Heaven / with the mother's soul, / but my wings suddenly dropped off. Then, / I fell to Earth. That is / how you found me, Simon."

Simon and Matryna now understood / who had been living with them, / so they began to cry for joy.

The angel Michael said, "I was alone in the field / and naked. I had never known / cold or hunger / until I became a man. I crawled to a church. Then, / I saw a man / coming down the road.

"He frowned / as he passed me, / but he came back / a few minutes later. He gave me some clothes / and brought me to his house. When I entered the house, / his wife seemed very angry. She wanted to send me back into the cold, / but her husband mentioned God to her. The woman changed / at once. When she brought me some food, / I looked at her. I noticed / she had changed. She had become alive, / and God was in her.

"Then, / I remembered the first lesson / God had sent me. God told me, 'Learn / what dwells in man.' I understood. It was love. Love lives in men. God had shown me the first truth, / so I smiled.

"After a year, / a rich gentleman came / to order some boots. I looked at him / and saw the Angel of Death / standing behind him. Only I could see the Angel of Death, / so I knew / that he would die soon. The man was about to die, / yet he wanted boots / that would last for years.

"Then, / I remembered God's second order: 'Learn / what is not given to man.' I learned / that men are not given the knowledge / to know / what they need. So I smiled / for a second time.

- **fly back** 다시 날아가다[날아오다]   • **drop off** 떨어지다, 떨어져 나가다   • **joy** 기쁨 ≠ sadness   • **crawl** 기다
- **frown** 찌푸린, 찡그린   • **alive** 살아 있는, 생기 넘치는   • **stand** 서다

CLOSE UP

1. **That is how you found me** 그렇게 해서 당신이 저를 발견한 겁니다
   〈that is how ~〉는 '그래서 ~하게 되다'라는 뜻으로, 사건의 경위를 나타냄.
2. **The man was about to die** 그 사람은 곧 죽게 될 터였다
   〈be about to ~〉는 '막 ~하려는 참이다'라는 의미.
3. **the knowledge to know what they need** 그들에게 필요한 것이 뭔지 알 수 있는 지식
   knowledge(지식, 분별력)는 know(알다)의 명사형이다.

그래서 저는 다시 지상으로 날아와fly back to Earth 그 어머니의 영혼을 거뒀습니다take the mother's soul. 아기들이 엄마 품에서 떨어졌지요fall from her breast. 여인의 몸이 침대에서 구르면서 roll over on the bed 그 아기의 다리 하나를 뭉갰습니다crush one of the baby's legs. 저는 그 어머니의 영혼을 데리고with the mother's soul 하늘로 날아 올라가려fly up to Heaven 했는데, 갑자기 제 날개 my wings가 떨어져 나갔습니다drop off. 그리고 저는 지상으로 떨어졌지요fall to Earth. 그래서 당신이 저를 발견했던find me 겁니다, 세몬."

세몬과 마트료나는 그제서야 누가 그들과 함께 살고 있었는지 알고는 기뻐서 울기cry for joy 시작했다.

천사 미하일the angel Michael이 말했다. "저는 들판에in the field 홀로alone 벌거벗은 채naked 있었 습니다. 사람이 되고become a man 나서야 비로소 추위나 배고픔cold or hunger을 알게 됐습니다. 기어 서 교회까지 갔지요crawl to a church. 그때 한 남자가 길을 내려오는 게 보였습니다.

그 남자는 저를 지나치면서pass me 눈살을 찌푸렸지만frown 몇 분 뒤에a few minutes later 되돌아오 더군요come back. 그는 제게 옷가지를 주고give me some clothes 저를 자기 집으로 데려갔습니다bring me to his house. 제가 그 집에 들어가자enter the house 그의 부인은 매우 화가 난 듯했습니다seem angry. 부인은 저를 다시 추위 속으로 내쫓고send me back into the cold 싶어 했지만, 남편이 부인에게 하느님 얘기를 했어요mention God. 부인은 즉각at once 태도가 바뀌었습니다change. 부인이 제게 음식 을 갖다 줄bring me some food 때 저는 부인을 살펴봤습니다look at her. 저는 부인의 마음이 바뀌었다는 걸 알아챘지요. 부인은 생기가 넘쳐 있었고become alive, 하느님께서 그 안에 계셨습니다be in her.

그때 하느님께서 제게 보내신 첫 번째 교훈이 떠올랐습니다remember the first lesson. 하느님께서 는 제게 '사람의 내면에 무엇이 깃들어 있는지 배워라.' 하고 말씀하셨죠. 저는 깨달았습니다. 그것은 사랑 love이었습니다. 사람의 내면에는 사랑이 깃들어 있습니다. 하느님께서 제게 첫 번째 진리를 보여 주셨기 에 저는 미소 지었습니다.

1년 뒤after a year 한 부유한 신사a rich gentleman가 장화를 주문하러order some boots 왔습니다. 그를 살펴보니 죽음의 천사the Angel of Death가 그 사람 뒤에 서 있는stand behind him 게 보이더군요. 죽음의 천사는 오로지 저한테만 보였죠. 그래서 저는 그 신사가 곧 죽게 되리란 걸 알았습니다. 그 사람은 곧 죽게 될 터be about to die인데도 몇 년이고 오래갈 장화를 원하더군요.

그때 하느님의 두 번째 명령God's second order, 즉 '사람에게 주어지지 않은 게 무엇인지 깨달아라.' 하는 말씀이 떠올랐습니다. 저는 사람에게는 자신에게 정작 필요한 게 무엇인지what they need 알 수 있 는 능력the knowledge to know이 주어지지 않은 걸 깨달았습니다. 그래서 두 번째로 미소 지었지요.

GRAMMAR POINT

not/never ~ until... : …할 때까지는 ~하지 않다, …하고 나서야 (비로소) ~하다

- I had **never** known cold or hunger **until** I became a man.
  나는 사람이 될 때까지는 추위나 배고픔을 결코 몰랐다. (나는 사람이 되고 나서야 비로소 추위나 배고픔을 알게 되었다.)

- I did **not** realize how much I loved him **until** he died.
  나는 그가 죽을 때까지는 내가 그를 얼마나 사랑하는지 깨닫지 못했다. (나는 그가 죽고 나서야 내가 그를 얼마나 사랑했는지 깨달았다.)

[p. 120-121]

"I still did not know the third truth, / so I have waited / for God to reveal it.

"In my sixth year here, / the woman and the two girls / came. I recognized the girls / and listened to / how the woman had kept them alive. After she told the story, / I realized / that the woman had loved two children / who were not her own. I saw the living God in her, / and then I learned the last lesson: I learned / what men live by. I knew / God had revealed it to me / and had forgiven me, / so I smiled / for a third time."

Just then, / Michael's body / was surrounded by a bright light. He said, "I have learned / that all men live / not by care for themselves / but by love. I did not die / because a man and his wife / took pity on me / and loved me. The orphans stayed alive / because of the love of a woman / who was not their mother. And all men live / because love is in them. A person / who has love / is in God, / and God is in that person / because God is love."

Then, / the roof opened, / and a ray of light / fell down from Heaven. Michael spread his wings / and flew up in the light. Simon stood there, / gazing after him. After a while, / the roof was closed. No one / but Simon and his family / remained.

- **reveal** 드러내다, 보이다, 계시하다 • **recognize** 알아보다, 인식하다 • **be surrounded by** ~에 둘러싸이다
- **orphan** 고아 • **ray of light** 광선 • **spread** 펼치다 • **fly up** 날아 올라가다 • **remain** 남다, 남아있다

CLOSE UP

1. **I have waited for God to reveal it** 저는 하느님께서 그것을 계시해 주기를 기다렸습니다
   〈wait ~ to...〉는 '~가 …하기를 기다리다'라는 의미.
2. **how the woman had kept them alive** 그 여인이 어떻게 그들을 살게 해 왔는지
   〈keep+목적어+보어〉는 '~을 …하게 유지시키다'라는 의미.
3. **not by care for themselves but by love** 자신을 돌보는 마음이 아니라 사랑으로
   〈not ~ but...〉은 '~가 아니라 …'라는 의미. 여기서 care for themselves는 '자기 자신을 돌보는 마음', 즉 '자신에 대한 애착'을 뜻하고, love는 다른 사람을 보살피고 아끼는 마음인 '사랑'을 뜻한다.

Step 4

그래도 여전히 세 번째 진리를 알지 못한 상태라 저는 하느님께서 그것을 계시해 주기를**reveal it** 기다렸습니다.

이곳에서 6년째가 되자**in my sixth year** 그 여인과 두 여자아이가 왔습니다. 저는 그 여자아이들을 알아보았고**recognize the girls**, 그 여인이 어떻게 그 아이들을 살게 해 왔는지**keep them alive** 들었습니다. 여인이 사연을 말한**tell the story** 뒤, 저는 그 여인이 자기 자식도 아닌 그 두 아이들을 사랑해 주었다는 **love two children** 걸 깨달았습니다. 저는 그 여인에게서**in her** 살아 계신 하느님**the living God**을 보았고, 마지막 교훈을 배웠습니다**learn the last lesson**. 사람이 무엇으로 사는지 깨달은 겁니다. 하느님께서 제게 그걸 계시해 주시고 저를 용서하셨다는 걸 알았기 때문에 저는 세 번째로 미소 지었습니다."

바로 그때 미하일의 몸**Michael's body**이 밝은 빛에 둘러싸였다**be surrounded by a bright light**. 미하일이 말했다. "저는 모든 사람들**all men**이 자신을 돌보는 마음(자신에 대한 애착)**care for themselves**이 아니라 사랑으로 살아간다**live by love**는 걸 배웠습니다. 저는 한 남자와 그의 아내**a man and his wife**가 저를 불쌍히 여기고**take pity on me** 저를 사랑해 주었기**love me** 때문에 죽지 않았습니다. 그 고아들**the orphans**은 엄마도 아닌 한 여인의 사랑**the love of a woman**이 있었기에 살아남았습니다**stay alive**. 그리고 모든 사람은 그들 안에 사랑이 있기 때문에 살아갑니다. 사랑을 지닌**have love** 사람은 하느님 안에 있고**be in God**, 하느님께서도 그 사람 안에 계십니다**be in that person**. 하느님은 사랑이시기 **God is love** 때문입니다."

그러자 지붕**the roof**이 열리고**open** 한 줄기 빛**a ray of light**이 하늘에서 내려왔다**fall down from Heaven**. 미하일은 날개를 펼치고**spread his wings** 그 빛 속으로 날아 올라갔다**fly up in the light**. 세몬은 그 자리에 서서**stand there** 미하일의 뒷모습을 가만히 응시했다**gaze after him**. 잠시 후**after a while** 지붕이 닫혔다**be closed**. 세몬과 그의 식구들을 제외하곤**but Simon and his family** 아무도**no one** 남아 있지**remain** 않았다.

Grammar Point

because + 주어 + 동사 : ~하기 때문에   **because of + 명사** : ~ 때문에

⇨ because 다음에는 절이 나오고, because of 다음에는 명사가 나온다.

- I did not die **because** a man and his wife took pity on me and loved me.
  나는 한 남자와 그의 아내가 나를 불쌍히 여기고 나를 사랑해 주었기 때문에 죽지 않았다.
- The orphans stayed alive **because of** the love of a woman.
  그 고아들은 한 여자의 사랑 때문에 살아남았다.
- All men live **because** love is in them. 모든 사람은 그들 안에 사랑이 있기 때문에 살아간다.

[p. 122-123]

How Much Land Does a Man Need?

An elder sister / went to visit her younger sister / in the country. The elder sister was married / to a tradesman in town / and the younger sister / to a peasant in the village. As the sisters sat over their tea talking, / the elder began to boast about / the advantages of town life. She talked about / how comfortably they lived there, / how well they dressed, / what good things they ate and drank, / and how she went to the theater and other types of entertainment.

The younger sister was annoyed / and in turn / mocked the life of a tradesman. She stood up for / the life of a peasant.

"I would not change my way of life / for yours," she said. "We may live roughly, / but at least / **we are free from anxiety**. You live in a better style / than we do, / but though you often earn more / than you need, / **you are very likely to lose / all you have**."

She continued, "We know the proverb / 'Loss and gain are brothers twain.' ==It often happens / that people / who are wealthy one day / are begging for their bread the next.== Our way is safer. Though a peasant's life is not a fat one, / it is long."

Pahom, / the master of the house, / was lying on the top of the stove, / and he listened to the women's chatter.

"It is perfectly true," he said. "**Busy as we are from childhood** / farming Mother Earth, / we peasants have no time / to let any nonsense settle in our heads. ==Our only trouble is / that we haven't got enough land.== If I had plenty of land, / I wouldn't fear the Devil himself!"

The women finished their tea, / chatted a while about dresses, / and then cleared away the tea things / and lay down to sleep. But the Devil had been sitting behind the stove / and had heard all / that was said.

- **married to** ~와 결혼한 • **tradesman** 소매상인, 장사꾼 • **peasant** 소작농 • **boast** 자랑하다, 뻐기다
- **advantage** 이점, 장점 • **entertainment** 오락(물), 여흥 • **annoyed** 짜증이 난, 약이 오른 • **in turn** 차례차례, 번갈아; (~에 대한) 반응으로, (~해서) 결국 • **mock** 놀리다, 조롱하다 • **stand up for** ~을 옹호하다, ~을 변호하다 • **one's way of life** ~의 생활방식 • **anxiety** 근심, 걱정 • **proverb** 속담, 격언 • **twain** 둘 (고어)
- **beg for** ~을 구걸하다 • **the master of the house** 집의 가장 • **lie** 누워 있다 • **chatter** 수다
- **Mother Earth** (어머니인) 대지 • **settle** 자리를 잡다, 정착하다 • **the Devil** 악마 • **clear away** 치우다

CLOSE UP

1. **we are free from anxiety** 우린 근심이 없어
   〈be free from ~〉은 '~이 없는'이라는 의미. 이때의 free는 해롭거나 불쾌한 것이 '없는'이라는 뜻이다.

2. **you are very likely to lose all you have** 너는 전 재산을 잃을 가능성이 높아
   〈be likely to ~〉는 '~한 일이 일어날 것 같다', '~할 가능성이 있다'라는 의미. likely 앞에 very를 붙이면 그럴 가능성이 높다는 뜻이 된다. 〈all you have〉는 '가진 것 전부', 즉 '전 재산'이라는 의미.

3. **Busy as we are from childhood** 우린 어릴 때부터 바쁘긴 하지만
   〈형용사+as+주어+동사〉는 '~이긴 하지만'이라는 의미.

사람에게 필요한 땅은 얼마만큼인가?

언니**an elder sister**가 시골에 있는 동생을 방문하러**visit her younger sister** 갔다. 언니는 도시에 사는 장사꾼과 결혼했고**be married to a tradesman**, 동생은 촌에 사는 농부와**to a peasant** 결혼해서 살고 있었다. 자매가 앉아서 차를 마시며 담소를 나누다가**sit over their tea talking**, 언니가 도시 생활의 장점 **the advantages of town life**을 자랑하기**boast** 시작했다. 언니는 자기들이 거기서 얼마나 안락하게**how comfortably** 사는지**live**, 옷을 얼마나 잘**how well** 차려입는지**dress**, 어떤 좋은 것들**what good things**을 먹고 마시는지**eat and drink**, 그리고 자신은 어떻게 극장**the theater**이나 다른 유형의 오락거리들 **other types of entertainment**을 찾아다니는지 등에 대해 얘기했다.

동생은 약이 오른**be annoyed** 나머지 (이번에는)**in return** 장사꾼의 생활**the life of a tradesman**을 비웃었다**mock**. 동생은 농부의 생활**the life of a peasant**을 두둔했다**stand up for**.

"내 생활방식**my way of life**을 언니의 생활방식과 바꾸지는 않을 거야." 동생이 말했다. "우리가 투박하게 살지는**live roughly** 모르지만, 적어도**at least** 근심은 없거든**be free from anxiety**. 언니네는 우리보다 더 멋지게 살겠지**live in a better style**. 하지만 필요 이상으로 돈을 벌**earn more than you need** 때가 많아도 전 재산**all you have**을 잃을 가능성도 높잖아**be very likely to lose**."

동생은 계속 말을 이었다. "'손실과 이익**loss and gain**은 두 형제**brothers twain**와 같다(벌 때가 있으면 잃을 때도 있다는 의미)'는 속담을 알고 있잖아**know the proverb**. 하루는**one day** 부자였던**be wealthy** 사람들이 다음 날에는**the next** 빵을 구걸하고**beg for their bread** 있는 경우가 비일비재하단 말이야. 우리 (생활)방식이 더 안전해. 농부의 생활이 풍족한 건 아니어도**be not fat one** 오래 가니까**be long**."

그 집의 가장**the master of the house**인 파홈**Pahom**이 난로 위에 누워**lie on the top of the stove**(여기서 stove는 러시아식 벽난로 pechka를 의미함) 있다가 두 여자의 수다를 들었다.

"그렇고 말고." 파홈이 말했다. "우리는 어릴 때부터**from childhood** 대지를 경작하느라**farm Mother Earth** 바쁘긴 하지만, 우리 농부들은 어떤 허튼 생각**any nonsense**도 우리들 머릿속에 자리 잡게**settle in our heads** 내버려 둘 겨를도 없지**have no time to let** (농사 이외의 다른 생각은 하지 않는다는 의미). 우리의 유일한 어려움**our only trouble**은 땅을 충분히 갖고 있지 않다 **haven't got enough land**는 거야. 내게 땅이 많이 있다면**have plenty of land** 악마라도 **the Devil himself** 두렵지 않을 텐데**wouldn't fear**!"

두 여자는 차를 다 마시고**finish their tea** 잠시 옷 얘기를 하더니**chat about dresses**, 다기들**the tea things**을 치우고**clear away** 자리에 누웠다**lie down to sleep**. 그러나 악마**the Devil**가 난로 뒤에 앉아**sit behind the stove** 있으면서 그들이 얘기한 모든 말**all that is said**을 들었다**hear**.

GRAMMAR POINT

주어·보어·목적어로 쓰이는 that절

- **It** often happens **that** people who are wealthy one day are begging for their bread the next.
  하루는 부자였던 사람들이 다음 날에는 빵을 구걸하고 있는 일이 흔하게 일어나.
  (주어: 보통 가주어 it이 문장 앞에 오고, that절은 문장 뒤에 온다.)

- Our only trouble is **that** we haven't got enough land.
  우리의 유일한 어려움은 땅을 충분히 갖고 있지 않다는 거야. (보어: be동사 뒤에 온다.)

- Pahom heard **(that)** a neighbor was going to buy fifty acres of land.
  파홈은 이웃이 땅 50에이커를 살 거라는 말을 들었다. (목적어: 이때의 that은 생략할 수 있다.)

[p. 124-125]

He was pleased to hear / that the man had boasted / that **if he had plenty of land, / he would not fear the Devil himself**.

"All right," thought the Devil. "We will have a contest. I'll give you enough land, / and **by means of that land,** / I will get you into my power."

One day, / Pahom heard / that a neighbor was going to buy fifty acres of land, / so he felt envious. Pahom and his wife / sold some of their property / and borrowed some money. Then, / they bought a farm of forty acres.

So now / Pahom had land of his own. He borrowed seed / and sowed it on the land / he had bought. The harvest was a good one, / and within a year, / **he had managed to pay off his debts**. So he became a landowner. When he went out to plow his fields / or to look at his growing corn, / his heart would fill with joy.

However, / over time, / some of the peasants in the neighborhood / began to trespass across Pahom's land / with their cows and horses. For a long time, / Pahom forgave the owners. But at last / he lost patience / and complained to the district court. He thought, "**I cannot go on overlooking it**, / or they will destroy / all I have. They must be taught a lesson."

Pahom began to fine his neighbors / for trespassing on his land. This made them very upset with him, / so they started to trespass on his land / on purpose. Sometimes, / they even sneaked onto his land at night / and chopped down his trees. Pahom was furious.

He tried to figure out / who was doing it, / and he decided / that it was probably Simon. He took Simon to court, / but Pahom had no evidence / against Simon. The judges let Simon go, / so Pahom got angry at them / and quarreled with the judges / and with his neighbors. Threats to burn his building / began to be uttered.

- **have a contest** 경연을 벌이다, 겨루다 • **by means of** ~을 이용하여 • **feel envious** 부러움을 느끼다
- **property** 재산 • **sow** (씨를) 뿌리다 • **manage to** 그럭저럭 ~하다 • **pay off one's debts** 빚을 갚다
- **landowner** 땅 주인, 지주 • **neighborhood** 이웃 • **trespass** 무단 침입하다 • **lose patience** 인내심을 잃다
- **district court** 지방 법원 • **overlook** 간과하다, 눈감아 주다 • **be taught a lesson** 교훈을 얻다, (잘못에 대해) 따끔한 맛을 보다 • **fine** 벌금을 부과하다; 벌금 • **upset with** ~에 화가 난 • **on purpose** 일부러, 고의로 • **sneak onto** ~로 몰래 들어가다 • **chop down** 베어 넘어뜨리다 • **furious** 분노한 • **figure out** 알아내다 • **take ~ to court** ~를 법정에 세우다 • **evidence** 증거 • **judge** 판사 • **threat** 위협
- **utter** 입 밖에 내다, 말하다

CLOSE UP

1. **by means of that land** 그 땅을 이용하여
   〈by means of ~〉는 '~을 이용하여', '~의 도움으로'라는 의미. 여기서 means는 '수단', '방법'이라는 뜻이다.

2. **he had managed to pay off his debts** 그는 그럭저럭 빚을 다 갚았다
   〈manage to ~〉는 '그럭저럭 ~하다', '간신히 ~하다', '어떻게든 ~하다' 등의 의미. 〈pay off〉는 빚 등을 '다 갚다', '청산하다'라는 의미.

3. **I cannot go on overlooking it** 계속 눈감아 줄 수는 없어
   〈go on+V-ing〉는 '계속 ~하다'라는 의미.

악마는 파홈이 땅만 많으면 악마라도 두렵지 않을 거라고 으스댄 말을 듣고 쾌재를 불렀다.

"좋아all right." 악마는 생각했다. "우리 한번 겨뤄 보는have a contest 거야. 내가 네게 땅을 충분히 주고give you enough land, 그 땅을 이용해서 널 내 손아귀에 넣고get you into my power 말겠다."

어느 날one day 파홈은 이웃a neighbor이 땅 50에이커fifty acres of land를 살 거라는 말을 듣고 부러웠다feel envious. 파홈과 그의 아내는 재산을 약간 팔고sell some of their property 돈을 조금 빌렸다borrow some money. 그런 다음 농지 40에이커a farm of forty acres를 구입했다.

그래서 이제 파홈에게는 자신의 땅land of his own이 생겼다. 파홈은 씨앗(종자)을 빌려다가borrow seed 그가 산 땅에 뿌렸다sow it. 수확이 좋아서 1년 안에within a year 그럭저럭 빚을 다 갚았다pay off his debts. 그래서 파홈은 지주가 되었다become a landowner. 밖에 나가서 밭을 갈거나plow his fields 자라나는 옥수수his growing corn를 보면 마음이 기쁨으로 부풀었다fill with joy.

하지만 시간이 지나면서over time 이웃의 농부 몇 명some of the peasants이 그들의 소와 말을 끌고with their cows and horses 파홈의 땅을 무단 침입하기trespass across Pahom's land 시작했다. 파홈은 오랫동안for a long time 그 마소 주인들을 너그럽게 봐주었다forgive the owners. 그러나 결국에는 at last 인내심을 잃고lose patience 지방 법원에 불만을 호소했다complain to the district court. 파홈은 이렇게 생각했다. "계속 눈감아 줄overlook it 수는 없어. 안 그러면 그자들이 내가 가진 걸 전부 망가뜨리고destroy all I have 말 거야. 그자들은 따끔한 맛을 봐야be taught a lesson 해."

파홈은 자기 땅에 무단 침입한trespass on his land 일로 이웃들에게 벌금을 물리기fine his neighbors 시작했다. 이 때문에 이웃들은 파홈에게 몹시 화가 나서 일부러on purpose 파홈의 땅을 무단 침입하기 시작했다. 때로는 밤에 그의 땅으로 몰래 숨어들어서sneak onto his land 나무들을 찍어 넘어뜨리기까지 했다chop down his trees. 파홈은 노발대발했다be furious.

그는 누가 그런 짓을 하는지 알아내려figure out 애썼고, 십중팔구 세몬probably Simon일 거라고 판단했다. 파홈은 세몬을 법정에 세웠으나take Simon to court 세몬에게 불리한 증거를 하나도 갖고 있지 않았다have no evidence. 판사들the judges이 세몬을 방면하자let Simon go, 파홈은 그들에게 화가 나서get angry at them 판사들 및 이웃들과 언쟁을 벌였다quarrel. 파홈이 사는 건물을 불태워 버리겠다는 협박threat이 나오기 시작했다.

GRAMMAR POINT

if ~ (가정법) ⇨ '가정법 과거' 동사가 쓰이면 현재 사실과 반대되는 가정을 나타냄.

- **If** he **had** plenty of land, he **would** not **fear** the Devil himself.
  그에게 땅만 많으면 악마라도 두려워하지 않을 텐데.

- **If** I **had** plenty of land, I **wouldn't** fear the Devil himself! 내게 땅이 많이 있다면 악마라도 두렵지 않을 텐데.
- **If** it **were** my own land, I **would be** independent. 그게 내 소유의 땅이라면 자립할 수 있게 될 텐데.
  (가정법 과거일 때 if절의 be동사는 항상 were로 씀.)

How Much Land Does a Man Need?

[p. 126-127]

About this time, / there was a rumor / that many people were moving to a new place. "There's no need / for me / to leave my land," thought Pahom. "But some of the others / might leave our village, / and then there would be more room for us. I would take over their land myself / and make my estate a bit bigger."

One day, / Pahom was sitting at home / when a peasant / passing through the village / happened to call on him. The peasant was allowed to stay the night, / and supper was given to him. Pahom had a talk with this peasant / and asked him / where he had come from. The stranger answered / that he had come from beyond the Volga River, / where he had been working. He said / that many people were moving there. Anyone / who moved to the village / was given twenty-five acres of land / for free.

"The land there / is very good," said the peasant. "One peasant moved to the village / with nothing at all, / but now he is very wealthy."

Pahom's heart / was filled with desire. He thought, "Why should I suffer / in this narrow hole / if one can live so well elsewhere? I will sell my land here, / and with the money I get, / I will start all over again / with more land. But I must first go / and find out all about it myself."

So Pahom went down / to the land beyond the Volga. It was / just as the stranger had said. The peasants owned plenty of land. The village gave each person / twenty-five acres of land, / and people could also buy / as much land as they could afford. Pahom moved with his family / to the new settlement.

Pahom had much more land / than before. In fact, / he was ten times better off / than he had been. This made Pahom very happy. But after he got used to it, / he began to think / that even here he did not have enough land. He grew tired of / having to rent other people's land / every year. Wherever there was good land to be had, / the peasants would rush for it / and argue about the land.

- **rumor** 소문, 풍문 • **room** 공간, 여유 • **take over** 이어받다, 인수하다 • **estate** 사유지, 토지 • **pass through** ~을 지나가다 • **call on** ~을 방문하다 • **beyond** ~ 너머 • **for free** 공짜로 • **suffer** 고통받다 • **all over again** (처음부터) 다시 • **find out** 알게 되다, 알아내다 • **can afford** ~할 여유가 있다 • **settlement** 정착지 • **better off** 더 부유한, 더 잘 사는 • **get used to** ~에 익숙해지다 • **grow tired of** ~에 싫증이 나다 • **rush for** ~에 달려들다

CLOSE UP

1. **There's no need for me to leave my land.** 나는 내 땅에서 떠날 필요가 없어.
   〈there's no need to ~〉는 '~할 필요 없다'라는 의미. to부정사의 행위자를 나타내려면 to 앞에 〈for+목적격〉으로 쓴다.

2. **could also buy as much land as they could afford** 자기들 형편이 닿는 대로 많은 땅을 살 수도 있었다
   〈as much/many ~ as...〉는 '…만큼 많은 ~'라는 의미.

3. **he was ten times better off than he had been** 그는 전보다 열 배나 더 부유해졌다
   time은 three times(세 배), four times(네 배)와 같이 배수를 나타낼 수 있다. '두 배'는 two times보다 twice를 더 많이 쓴다.

Step 4

이 무렵about this time 많은 사람들many people이 새로운 곳으로 이주하고move to a new place 있다는 소문이 돌았다. "나는 내 땅에서 떠날leave my land 필요가 없어there's no need." 하고 파홈은 생각했다. "하지만 다른 사람들 몇 명some of the others이 우리 마을을 떠날지도leave our village 모르니까, 그러면 우리가 차지할 수 있는 공간(땅)more room for us이 더 생길 거야. 내가 직접 그들의 땅을 인수해서take over their land 내 사유지를 좀 더 크게 늘려make my estate a bit bigger 봐야지."

어느 날 파홈이 집에 앉아sit at home 있는데, 마을을 지나던pass through the village 한 농부가 우연히 파홈을 방문했다call on him. 농부는 그날 밤을 (파홈의 집에서) 묵도록stay the night 허락받았고 저녁도 대접받았다. 파홈은 이 농부와 얘기를 나누며have a talk 그에게 어디서 왔는지 물었다. 이 낯선 이the stranger는 자신이 볼가 강 너머에서 왔으며come from beyond the Volga River 그곳에서 쭉 일을 했었다고 대답했다. 그는 많은 사람이 그곳으로 이주하고move there 있다고 말했다. 그 마을로 이사 가는move to the village 사람은 누구든지 25에이커의 땅twenty-five acres of land을 무상으로for free 받는다고 했다.

"그곳의 땅the land there은 아주 비옥합니다be very good." 농부가 말했다. "어떤 농부는 그 마을에 전혀 아무것도 안 가지고with nothing 이사 갔지만, 지금은 큰 부자가 됐어요be very wealthy."

파홈의 마음Pahom's heart에 탐욕이 가득 찼다be filled with desire. 그는 이렇게 생각했다. "다른 데서 그렇게 잘 살 수 있다면, 내가 왜 이 좁아터진 데서in this narrow hole 고생을 해야 한단should suffer 말인가? 여기 있는 내 땅을 팔아서sell my land 생긴 돈을 가지고with the money 더 많은 땅을 사서 with more land 처음부터 다시 시작하는start all over again 거야. 하지만 내가 먼저 가서 직접 그에 대한 모든 것을 알아봐야find out all about it 해."

그리하여 파홈은 볼가 강 너머에 있는 땅으로 내려갔다go down. 그곳은 낯선 이가 말했던 그대로였다. 농부들이 많은 땅을 소유하고 있었다own plenty of land. 마을에서 각 개인에게 25에이커의 땅을 주었고, 사람들은 자기들 형편이 닿는 대로 많은 땅을as much land as they can afford 살 수도 있었다. 파홈은 가족을 데리고with his family 그 새로운 정착지로to the new settlement 이주했다.

파홈은 전보다 훨씬 더 많은 땅을 가졌다have much more land. 사실 그전보다 10배나 더 부유해졌다be ten times better off. 이 때문에 파홈은 몹시 행복했다. 그러나 그 생활에 익숙해진get used to it 다음에는 심지어 여기서도 땅을 충분히 갖고 있지 못하다do not have enough land는 생각이 들기 시작했다. 해마다 다른 사람들의 땅을 빌려야rent other people's land 하는 것도 진절머리가 났다grow tired of. 소유하기 좋은 땅good land to be had이 있는 곳은 어디든지 농부들이 그곳으로 몰려들어rush for it 그 땅을 놓고 다투기argue about the land 일쑤였기 때문이다.

GRAMMAR POINT

where (관계부사) : ~하는 (곳), 그곳에서   **wherever (관계부사)** : ~하는 곳은 어디든지

⇨ 관계부사 where는 장소를 나타내는 명사 뒤에 오며, where가 이끄는 관계절은 앞에 나온 장소 명사를 수식하거나 (한정 용법), 그와 관련된 설명을 부가적으로 덧붙인다(서술 용법).

- He went to *a place* **where** they had pitched their tents. 그는 그들이 텐트를 쳐 놓은 곳으로 갔다. (한정 용법)

- He had come from *beyond the Volga River*, **where** he had been working.
  그는 볼가 강 너머에서 왔으며, 그곳에서 쭉 일을 했었다. (서술 용법: where 앞에 쉼표가 있음.)

- **Wherever** there was good land to be had, the peasants would rush for it.
  소유하기 좋은 땅이 있는 곳은 어디든지 농부들이 그곳으로 몰려들곤 했다.

[p. 128-129]

"If it were my own land," thought Pahom, "I would be independent, / and there would not be all this unpleasantness."

So Pahom began looking out for land / which he could buy. One day, / a peddler went by his house. He said / that he was just returning / from the land of the Bashkirs, / which was far away. There, / he had bought / thirteen thousand acres of land / for 1,000 rubles.

"That area has so much land / that you could walk for a year / and still be in the land of the Bashkirs. They sell their land / for very cheap prices. All one has to do / is / make friends with the chief. The land lies near a river, / and the whole prairie is virgin soil."

Pahom was curious, / so he made up his mind / to visit the land of the Bashkirs. Before he went there, / he bought some gifts. The peddler had told him / that it was their custom / to give gifts.

On the seventh day of his travels, / he came to a place / where the Bashkirs had pitched their tents. It was all / just as the peddler had said. The people lived by a river / on the steppes / in felt-covered tents.

They were a simple people. They did not farm at all. The men merely sat around, / drank tea, / ate lamb, / and played their pipes to make music. Still, / despite being uneducated and knowing no Russian, / they were good-natured enough.

As soon as they saw Pahom, / they came out of their tents / and gathered around their visitor. An interpreter was found, / and Pahom told them / he had come about some land. They took Pahom / and led him into one of the best tents. Pahom took some presents out of his cart / and distributed them among the Bashkirs. The Bashkirs were delighted.

- **independent** 독립적인, 자립할 수 있는 • **unpleasantness** 불쾌한 일, 불쾌감; 악감정, 불화 • **look out for** ~을 찾으려고 애쓰다 • **peddler** 행상인 • **virgin soil** 미개간지, 미개척지 • **make up one's mind** 마음을 정하다 • **custom** 관습 • **pitch** (텐트를) 치다 • **steppe** 초원 • **felt-covered tent** 펠트 텐트 • **farm** 농사짓다 • **merely** 단지, 그저 • **despite** ~에도 불구하고 • **uneducated** 교육받지 못한 • **good-natured** 심성이 고운, 선량한 • **interpreter** 통역사 • **take ~ out of...** ~을 …에서 꺼내다 • **distribute** 나눠 주다, 분배하다 • **delighted** 기쁜, 좋아하는

CLOSE UP

1 **All one has to do is (to) make friends with the chief.**
해야 할 일은 족장과 친분을 트는 것뿐이다. (족장과 친분을 트기만 하면 된다.)
〈all ~ have to do is (to)...〉는 '~가 해야 할 일은 …뿐이다', '~는 …하기만 하면 된다'라는 의미.

2 **he made up his mind to visit the land of the Bashkirs** 그는 바시키르인들의 땅을 찾아가기로 마음먹었다
〈make up one's mind to ~〉는 '~하기로 결심하다/마음먹다'라는 의미. 〈decide to ~〉로 바꿔 쓸 수 있다.

3 **As soon as they saw Pahom** 그들은 파홈을 보자마자
〈as soon as ~〉는 '~하자마자'라는 의미.

"그게 내 소유의 땅my own land이라면 자립할 수 있게be independent 될 텐데. 그리고 이 모든 불화all this unpleasantness도 없게 될 텐데." 하고 파홈은 생각했다.

그래서 파홈은 자신이 살 수 있는 땅을 찾아보려고 애쓰기look out for land 시작했다. 어느 날one day 행상 한 명a peddler이 파홈의 집을 지나갔다go by his house. 행상은 자신이 바시키르인들의 땅the land of the Bashkirs에서 막 돌아오는just return 길인데, 그 땅은 멀리 떨어진 곳에 있다be far away고 말했다. 거기에서 그는 13,000에이커의 땅thirteen thousand acres of land을 1,000루블에for 1,000 rubles 샀다고 했다.

"그 지역that area에는 아주 많은 땅이 있어서have so much land 일 년 동안 걸어도walk for a year 여전히 바시키르인들의 땅 안에 있을be in the land of the Bashkirs지도 모릅니다. 그들은 아주 싼 값에 for very cheap prices 자기들 땅을 팔지요sell their land. 해야 할 일all one has to do은 족장과 친분을 트는make friends with the chief 것뿐입니다. 그 땅은 강 근처에 있는데lie near a river, 평원 전체the whole prairie가 미개간지virgin soil입니다."

파홈은 호기심이 생겨서be curious 바시키르인들의 땅에 찾아가visit the land 보기로 마음먹었다 make up his mind. 그는 거기 가기 전에 선물을 몇 개 샀다buy some gifs. 선물을 주는give gifts 것이 그들의 관습their custom이라고 행상이 일러 줬기 때문이다.

여행 7일째 되는 날on the seventh day 파홈은 바시키르인들이 천막을 쳐 놓은pitch their tents 곳에 도착했다. 그곳은 모두 행상이 말했던 그대로였다. 사람들은 어느 강가의by a river 대초원에서on the steppes 펠트로 덮인 천막 안에in felt-covered tents 살고 있었다.

그들은 단순한 민족a simple people이었다. 그들은 전혀 농사를 짓지 않았다do not farm. 남자들은 그냥 빈둥거리며sit around 차나 마시고drink tea, 양고기를 먹고eat lamb, 피리를 불어play their pipes 음악을 연주했다make music. 그러나 교육을 못 받고be uneducated 러시아어도 몰랐지만know no Russian 천성은 그런대로 착한good-natured enough 사람들이었다.

그들은 파홈을 보자see Pahom마자 천막 밖으로 나와come out of their tents 그들의 방문객 주위에 모여들었다gather around their visitor. 통역사an interpreter가 구해지자be found 파홈은 그들에게 자신이 땅 때문에 왔다come about some land고 말했다. 그들은 파홈을 데리고take Pahom 가장 좋은 천막 중 한 군데로into one of the best tents 안내했다. 파홈은 짐수레에서out of his cart 선물 몇 개를 꺼내어take some presents 바시키르인들에게 둘러싸인 가운데 그것들을 나눠 주었다distribute them. 바시키르인들은 몹시 기뻐했다be delighted.

GRAMMAR POINT

which (관계대명사)

⇨ 앞에 나온 사물 명사(선행사)를 대신 받음. which가 이끄는 관계절은 그 명사를 수식하거나(한정 용법), 그와 관련된 설명을 부가적으로 덧붙인다(서술 용법).

- So Pahom began looking out for *land* **which** he could buy.

  그래서 파홈은 자신이 살 수 있는 땅을 찾아보려고 애쓰기 시작했다. (한정 용법)

- He was just returning from *the land of the Bashkirs*, **which** was far away.

  그는 바시키르인들의 땅에서 막 돌아오는 길인데, 그 땅은 멀리 떨어진 곳에 있었다. (서술 용법: which 앞에 쉼표가 있음.)

[p. 130-131]

   The Bashkirs talked for a while / and then told the interpreter to translate. "They wish to tell you," said the interpreter, "that they like you, / and that it is our custom / to do all we can / to please a guest / and to repay him for his gifts. You have given us presents. Now tell us / which of the things we possess / please you best / so that we may present them to you."
   "What pleases me best here," answered Pahom, "is your land. Our land is crowded, / and the soil is exhausted; / but you have plenty of land, / and it is good land." The interpreter translated.
   The Bashkirs talked among themselves / for a while. Then, / they were silent / and looked at Pahom / while the interpreter said, "They wish me to tell you / that in return for your presents, / they will gladly give you / as much land as you want. You have only to point it out / with your hand, / and it is yours."
   The Bashkirs talked again for a while / and began to have a dispute. Pahom asked / what they were arguing about. The interpreter told him / that some of them thought / they ought to ask their chief about the land / and ought not to act in his absence.
   While the Bashkirs were arguing, / a man in a large fox-fur cap / appeared on the scene. They all became silent / and rose to their feet. The interpreter said, "This is our chief himself."
   Pahom immediately took out / the best dressing gown and five pounds of tea, / and he offered these to the chief. The chief accepted them / and seated himself in the place of honor. The Bashkirs at once / began telling him something. The chief listened for a while / and addressed himself to Pahom. Speaking in Russian, / he said, "Well, let it be so. Choose / whatever piece of land / you like. We have plenty of it."

• **translate** 통역하다   • **wish to** ~하기를 원하다   • **repay** 갚다, 보답하다   • **possess** 소유하다, 지니다   • **present** 선물하다; 선물   • **crowded** (사람들이) 붐비는, 북적대는   • **exhausted** 진이 다 빠진, 고갈된   • **in return for** ~에 대한 보답으로   • **point out** 가리키다   • **have a dispute** 논쟁을 벌이다   • **ought to** ~해야 한다   • **chief** 족장   • **in one's absence** ~가 없는 동안에   • **fox-fur cap** 여우 털가죽 모자   • **on the scene** 그 자리에, 현장에   • **rise to one's feet** (자리에서) 일어나다, 일어서다   • **in the place of honor** 상석에   • **at once** 즉시   • **address** 말하다, 연설하다

CLOSE UP

1. **so that we may present them to you** 우리가 그것을 당신에게 선사할 수 있도록
   〈so that ~〉은 '~하기 위해서', '~할 수 있도록'이라는 의미.

2. **in return for your presents** 당신 선물에 대한 보답으로
   〈in return for ~〉는 '~에 대한 보답으로', '~에 대한 대가로'라는 의미.

3. **You have only to point it out** 당신은 그것을 가리키기만 하면 된다
   〈have only to ~〉는 '~하기만 하면 된다'라는 의미.

4. **addressed himself to Pahom** 파홈에게 말을 걸었다
   〈address oneself to ~〉는 '~에게 말을 걸다'라는 의미.

바시키르인들은 잠시 얘기를 나누더니talk for a while 통역사에게 통역하라고translate 말했다. "그들은 당신에게 이렇게 말하고 싶어 합니다wish to tell you." 통역사가 말했다. "그들은 당신이 마음에 든다like you고 하네요. 그리고 손님을 즐겁게 해 주고please a guest 그의 선물에 보답하기repay him for his gifts 위해 우리가 할 수 있는 모든 걸 하는do all we can 게 우리네 풍습our custom이라고 합니다. 당신은 우리한테 선물을 주었습니다give us presents. 이제 우리가 가진 것들the things we possess 중 어떤 것이 가장 마음에 드는지please you best 말해 주면, 우리가 그것을 당신께 선사하겠습니다present them to you."

"이곳에서 가장 마음에 드는 건what pleases me best 당신네 땅your land입니다." 파홈이 대답했다. "우리가 사는 땅our land은 사람들이 붐비고be crowded 토양the soil에 양분이 고갈됐습니다be exhausted. 하지만 당신들은 땅이 많고have plenty of land, 비옥한 땅good land이기도 합니다." 통역사가 통역했다.

바시키르인들은 잠시 자기들끼리 이야기를 나눴다talk among themselves. 그리고는 그들이 조용히 하고be silent 파홈을 바라보는look at Pahom 가운데 통역사가 이렇게 말했다. "저들이 당신께 이렇게 전해 달랍니다. 당신의 선물에 대한 보답으로in return for your presents 기꺼이 당신이 원하는 만큼의 땅as much land as you want을 드리겠습니다. 손으로with your hand 가리키기만point it out 하면 당신 땅이 될 겁니다."

바시키르인들은 다시 잠시 얘기를 나누더니 논쟁을 벌이기have a dispute 시작했다. 파홈은 그들이 무엇 때문에 다투는지 물었다. 통역사는 그들 중 몇 명이 땅에 대해서는 족장에게 물어봐야 하며ought to ask their chief 그가 없을 때in his absence 일을 처리하면 안 된다ought not to act고 생각한다는 말을 파홈에게 해 주었다.

바시키르인들이 논쟁을 벌이고 있는데, 커다란 여우털 모자를 쓴in a large fox-fur cap 남자가 그 자리에 나타났다appear on the scene. 사람들이 모두 조용해지더니become silent 자리에서 일어섰다rise to their feet. 통역사가 말했다. "이분이 우리 족장our chief 본인입니다."

파홈은 즉시 가장 좋은 실내복the best dressing gown과 차 5파운드five pounds of tea를 꺼내어take out 그것들을 족장에게 내밀었다offer these to the chief. 족장은 그것들을 받고accept them 상석에in the place of honor 자리 잡았다seat himself. 바시키르인들이 즉시at once 그에게 무슨 말을 하기tell him something 시작했다. 족장은 잠시 귀 기울여 듣더니listen for a while 파홈에게 말을 건넸다address himself to Pahom. 족장은 러시아어를 써서speak in Russian 이렇게 말했다. "음, 그렇게 합시다let it be so. 어떤 필지의 땅이든whatever piece of land 마음에 드는 걸로 골라 보시오choose. 우리한테는 땅이 많소."

GRAMMAR POINT

ought to : ~해야 한다   **ought not to** : ~하면 안 된다

⇒ 조동사 should와 매우 비슷한 뜻으로, 마땅히 해야 하는 의무나 조언을 나타냄.

- They **ought to** ask their chief about the land and **ought not to** act in his absence.
  그들은 땅에 대해서는 족장에게 물어봐야 하며 그가 없을 때 일을 처리하면 안 된다. (not은 to 앞에 온다.)

- You don't look well. You **ought to** see a doctor. 안색이 안 좋구나. 의사의 진찰을 받아 보는 게 좋겠다.
- We **ought not to** break the rules. 우리는 규칙을 어겨서는 안 돼.

[p. 132-133]

"How can I take / as much as I like?" thought Pahom. "I must get a deed / to make it secure, / or else they may say, 'It is yours,' / and afterward / they may take it away again."

To the chief, / he said, "I must get a deed / as a guarantee, / or else / you may take the land away from me / in the future."

The chief said, "We will go to the town with you / and make a deed for the land."

"And what will be the price?" asked Pahom.

The chief answered, "Our price is always the same: one thousand rubles a day."

Pahom did not understand. "A day? What measure is that? How many acres would that be?"

The chief said, "We don't know / how to figure out the acres, / so we sell land / by the day. As much as you can go round / on your feet / in a day / is yours, / and the price is / one thousand rubles a day."

Pahom said, "But you can walk around / a large tract of land / in a single day."

The chief laughed / and then answered, "It will all be yours. But there is one condition: If you don't return to the spot / where you started / on the same day, / your money is lost. You must make a circle. You may make as large a circle / as you wish, / but you must return to your starting point / before the sun sets. Then, / all of the land / that you walked around / will be yours."

Pahom agreed to the chief's conditions, / and they decided to start / the next morning.

That night, / Pahom lay in bed / thinking about the land. He thought, "I can cover / an enormous amount of land. I can easily walk / thirty-five miles / in one day. Imagine / how much land / that will be."

- **deed** (소유권을 증명하는) 증서 • **secure** 안전한, 확실한 • **or else** 그렇지 않으면 • **afterward** 나중에 • **take away** 빼앗아 가다 • **guarantee** 보증, 보장; 보장하다 • **measure** 측정법, 측정 기준 • **figure out** 계산하다, 알아내다 • **a large tract of land** 넓은 토지 • **condition** 조건 • **spot** 지점, 장소 • **set** (해가) 지다 • **enormous** 거대한, 엄청나게 큰 • **imagine** 상상하다

CLOSE UP

1. **you may take the land away from me** 당신들이 나한테서 그 땅을 빼앗아 갈 수도 있다
   〈take ~ away from...〉은 '~을 …로부터 빼앗다'라는 의미.

2. **how to figure out the acres** 에이커를 계산하는 방법
   여기서 figure out은 양이나 비용 등을 '계산하다, 산출하다'라는 의미. 한편 figure out은 잘 생각한 끝에 '~을 이해하다/알아내다'라는 의미로도 많이 쓰인다. ex) I can't figure out the answer.(나는 그 답을 모르겠어.)

3. **we sell land by the day** 우리는 하루 단위로 땅을 팝니다
   by는 단위를 나타내기도 한다. ex) by the hour(시간 단위로) / by the kilo(킬로 단위로)

"어떻게 내가 원하는 만큼 많이as much as I like 가질 수 있다는 걸까?" 파홈은 생각했다. "확실히 하는make it secure 차원에서 증서를 받아야get a deed 겠어. 그렇지 않으면or else 이 사람들이 '당신 땅입니다.'라고 했다가 나중에afterward 다시 빼앗아 갈지도take it away 몰라."

파홈은 족장에게 말했다. "보증으로as a guarantee 증서를 한 장 받아야겠습니다. 안 그러면 당신들이 나중에in the future 나한테서 그 땅을 빼앗아 갈지도take the land away from me 모르니까요."

족장이 말했다. "우리가 당신과 함께 도시로 가서go to the town 토지 증서a deed for the land를 만들도록 하지요."

"그럼 (땅)값the price이 얼마나 들까요?" 파홈이 물었다.

족장이 대답했다. "우리가 제시하는 값은 항상 똑같소be always the same. 하루에 1,000루블one thousand rubles a day이오."

파홈은 이해하지 못했다. "하루라뇨? 무슨 측량 기준what measure이 그렇지요? 그게 몇 에이커how many acres가 됩니까?"

족장이 대답했다. "우리는 에이커를 따질figure out the acres 줄 모르기 때문에 하루 단위로 해서by the day 땅을 팝니다. 당신이 하루 안에in a day 걸어서on your feet 돌아다닐 수 있는 만큼as much as you can go round이 당신 소유가 되며, 그 값은 하루에 1,000루블이오."

파홈이 말했다. "하지만 하루에in a single day 엄청 넓은 땅a large tract of land을 걸어 다닐walk around 수 있는데요."

족장이 껄껄 웃더니 대답했다. "그게 전부 당신 땅이 되는 거요. 하지만 한 가지 조건one condition이 있소. 만약 당신이 출발했던 지점the spot where you start으로 같은 날에on the same day 돌아오지 못하면don't return, 당신 돈your money을 잃게 되는 거요be lost. 그러니까 당신은 원을 그려야make a circle 해요. 원하는 만큼 큰 원as large a circle as you wish을 그려도 좋소. 하지만 해가 지기the sun sets 전에 출발 지점으로 돌아와야return to your starting point 합니다. 그러면 당신이 걸어 다닌 땅이 전부 당신 것이 될 거요."

파홈은 족장의 조건에 동의했고agree to the chief's conditions, 그들은 다음 날 아침the next morning 작업을 시작하기로 결정했다decide to start.

그날 밤that night 파홈은 잠자리에 누워lie in bed 땅에 대해 생각했다think about the land. "난 엄청나게 넓은 땅an enormous amount of land을 갈cover 수 있어. 하루에in one day 35마일(56km) 은 쉽게 걸을walk thirty-five miles 수 있다고. 그게 얼마나 많은 땅how much land이 될지 상상해 봐imagine."

GRAMMAR POINT

as ~ as... : …만큼 ~한

- How can I take **as much as** I like? 어떻게 내가 원하는 만큼 많이 가질 수 있는 걸까?
- **As much as** you can go round on your feet in a day is yours.
  당신이 하루에 걸어서 돌아다닐 수 있는 만큼이 당신 것이오.
- You may make **as large** a circle **as** you wish. 원하는 만큼 큰 원을 그려도 좋소.
- The people on the hill were **as small as** ants. 언덕 위의 사람들은 개미만큼 작게 보였다.

[p. 134-135]

　　Pahom lay awake all night / and dozed off / only just before dawn. Hardly were his eyes closed / when he had a dream. In his dream, / the chief of the Bashkirs / was sitting in front of a tent / and laughing. "What are you laughing at?" he asked the chief. But the chief was no longer there. Instead, / it was the peddler / who had stopped at his house / and told him about the Bashkirs. Then, the peddler disappeared, / and the peasant / who had told him about the land beyond the Volga River / suddenly appeared. Then, / he saw / that it was not the peasant either, / but the Devil himself / with hoofs and horns, / sitting there and chuckling. There was a man / lying dead in front of the Devil, / and it was Pahom himself. He awoke horror-struck.

　　Looking round, / he saw through the open door / that the dawn was breaking. "It's time / to wake them up," he thought. "We ought to be starting."

　　Pahom, the chief, and the other Bashkirs / met on the land / early in the morning. The chief stretched his arms out / and said, "All of this land—as far as you can see— / belongs to us. You may have / any part of it / you like."

　　The chief took off his fox-fur cap, / placed it on the ground, / and said, "This will be the mark. Start from here / and return here again. All the land / you go around / shall be yours." Pahom took out his money / and put it on the cap.

　　Pahom stood / ready to start / with a spade in his hand. He considered / for some moments / which way he had better go. Then, he concluded, "I will go toward the rising sun."

- **lie awake** (밤새) 깨어 있다, 뜬눈으로 지새다 　• **doze off** 잠깐 잠이 들다, 깜빡 졸다 　• **dawn** 새벽녘, 동틀녘
- **hardly** 거의 ~하지 않다 　• **appear** 나타나다 　• **hoof** (말 등의) 발굽 　• **chuckle** 키득거리다 　• **lying dead** 죽어 누워 있는 　• **horror-struck** 공포에 질린 　• **stretch out** (손, 발을) 쭉 뻗다, 펼치다 　• **spade** 삽

CLOSE UP

1. **the peddler disappeared** 행상이 사라졌다 / **suddenly appeared** 갑자기 나타났다
   appear(나타나다)와 disappear(사라지다)는 서로 반대말이다.

2. **It's time to wake them up.** 이제 그들을 깨워야 할 때야.
   〈it's time to ~〉는 '~해야 할 때이다'라는 의미.

3. **All of this land—as far as you can see** 당신 시야가 미치는 이 땅이 전부
   〈as far as ~〉는 거리 · 범위 · 정도 등이 '~까지'라는 의미.

파홈은 밤새all night 뜬눈으로 누워 있다가lie awake 동트기 직전just before dawn에야 깜박 잠이 들었다doze off. 그는 눈을 감자마자 꿈을 꾸었다have a dream. 꿈속에서in his dream 바시키르인들의 족장the chief of the Bashkirs이 천막 앞에 앉아서sit in front of a tent 웃고laugh 있었다. "뭘 보고 웃는 겁니까?" 파홈이 족장에게 물었다. 그러나 족장은 이제 거기 없었다be no longer there. 대신instead 파홈의 집에 들러stop at his house 바시키르인들에 관해 얘기해tell him about the Bashkirs 준 행상the peddler이 있었다. 그러더니 행상도 사라지고disappear, 파홈에게 볼가 강 너머에 있는 땅the land beyond the Volga River에 대해 얘기해 준 농부the peasant가 난데없이 나타났다suddenly appear. 그 다음에는 그게 농부도 아니고 바로 악마 그 자체the Devil himself라는 걸 파홈은 알았다. 악마는 발굽과 뿔이 달린with hoofs and horns 모습으로 그 자리에 앉아서sit there 낄낄거리고chuckle 있었다. 악마 앞에는in front of the Devil 웬 남자가 죽은 채 누워lie dead 있었는데, 바로 파홈 자신Pahom himself이었다. 파홈은 소스라치게 놀라 잠에서 깼다awake horror-struck.

파홈이 두리번거리며look around 열린 문틈으로through the open door 보니 동the dawn이 트고break 있었다. "그들을 깨울wake them up 때가 됐군it's time." 파홈은 생각했다. "작업을 시작해야 해."

파홈과 족장과 다른 바시키르인들이 해당 토지에서 아침 일찍 만났다. 족장이 팔을 쭉 뻗으며stretch his arms out 말했다. "당신 시야가 미치는as far as you can see 이 땅이 전부all of this land 우리 것이오belong to us. 당신이 원하는 부분이 어떤 것이든 가져도have any part of it 좋소."

족장은 여우털 모자를 벗어서take off his fox-fur cap 땅바닥에 내려놓고place it on the ground 이렇게 말했다. "이게 표지the mark가 될 거요. 여기서 출발해서start from here 다시 여기로 돌아오시오return here. 당신이 돌아다니는 땅이 전부 당신 것이 될 거요." 파홈은 돈을 꺼내어take out his money 모자 위에 놓았다put it on the cap.

파홈은 손에 삽 한 자루를 들고with a spade in his hand 출발할 채비를 갖춘 채 ready to start 서 있었다. 그는 어느 쪽으로 which way 가는 게 나을지 잠시for some moments 숙고했다consider. 그런 다음 결론을 내렸다conclude. "해가 뜨는 방향으로 toward the rising sun 가야겠어."

GRAMMAR POINT

hardly ~ when... : ~하자마자 …했다

⇨ hardly가 있는 주절에는 흔히 과거완료 시제가 쓰이며, hardly 대신 scarcely를 써도 된다.

- **Hardly** were his eyes closed **when** he had a dream. 그는 눈을 감자마자 꿈을 꾸었다.
  (= His eyes were **hardly** closed **when** he had a dream.
  = His eyes had **hardly** been closed **when** he had a dream.)

- **Hardly** had they seen me **when** they ran away. 그들은 나를 보자마자 도망쳤다.
  (= They had **hardly** seen me **when** they ran away.)

[p. 136–137]

Pahom started walking / neither slowly / nor quickly. After having gone a thousand yards, / he stopped, / dug a hole, / and placed pieces of turf one on another / to make it more visible. Then he went on. Now that he had walked off his stiffness, / he quickened his pace. After a while, / he dug another hole.

The weather was getting warmer. He looked at the sun. It was time / to think of breakfast. "It is too soon yet / to turn. I will just take off my boots," he said to himself. He sat down, / took off his boots, / stuck them into his girdle, / and went on. It was easy / to walk now.

"I will go on / for another three miles," he thought, "and then turn to the left. This land here is so nice / that it would be a pity / to lose it."

He went straight on / for a while, / and then he looked back. The people on the hill / where he had started / were as small as ants. "Ah, I have gone far enough / in this direction," he thought. "It's time / to turn and go another direction. Besides, / I'm getting tired / and need something to drink."

He looked at the sun / and saw / that it was noon. He sat down, / ate some bread, / and drank some water. But he did not lie down / as he thought / that if he did, / he might fall asleep. After sitting for a little while, / he went on again. It had become terribly hot, / and he felt sleepy. Still, he went on, / thinking, "An hour to suffer, / a lifetime to live."

He went a long way / in this direction also / and was about to turn to the left again / when he perceived a damp hollow. "It would be a pity / to leave that out," he thought. So he went on past the hollow / and dug a hole / on the other side of it.

"Ah!" thought Pahom, "I have made the sides too long; I must make this one shorter." And he went along the third side / as he moved faster. He looked at the sun. It was nearly halfway to the horizon, / and he had not yet done / two miles of the third side of the square. He was still ten miles from his goal.

- **dig a hole** 구멍을 파다 • **turf** 잔디, 뗏장 • **walk off** 걸어서 ~을 없애다 • **stiffness** 딱딱함, 뻣뻣함
- **quicken** ~을 빠르게 하다 • **take off** 벗다 • **girdle** 허리띠, 벨트 • **stick** (아무렇게나 급히) 집어넣다, 찔러 넣다
- **a pity** 유감, 애석한 일 • **go straight** 똑바로 나아가다 • **look back** 뒤돌아보다 • **lie down** 눕다
- **fall asleep** 잠들다 • **suffer** 고통받다 • **lifetime** 평생, 일생 • **perceive** 감지하다, 인지하다 • **damp** 젖은, 축축한 • **hollow** (골짜기처럼) 움푹 꺼진 곳 • **horizon** 지평선 • **square** 정사각형

CLOSE UP

1. **neither slowly nor quickly** 느리지도 않고 빠르지도 않게
   〈neither ~ nor...〉는 '~도 아니고 …도 아니다'라는 의미.

2. **Now that he had walked off his stiffness** 걷다 보니 뻣뻣하던 몸이 풀려서
   〈now that ~〉은 '~이므로', '~이기 때문에'라는 의미.

3. **It is too soon yet to turn.** 방향을 틀기에는 아직 너무 이르지.
   〈too ~ to...〉는 '…하기에는 너무 ~하다', '너무 ~해서 …할 수 없다'라는 의미.

4. **was about to turn to the left** 왼쪽으로 방향을 틀려는 참이었다
   〈be about to ~〉는 '막 ~하려는 참이다'라는 의미.

파홈은 느리지도 않고neither slowly 빠르지도 않게nor quickly 걷기 시작했다start walking. 1,000야드(900m)를 가고go a thousand yards 나서 걸음을 멈추고stop 구덩이를 하나 판dig a hole 뒤, 뗏장을pieces of turf 차곡차곡one on another 쌓아서 구덩이가 더 잘 보이도록 했다make it more visible. 그리고는 계속 갔다go on. 걷다 보니 뻣뻣하던 몸이 풀려서walk off his stiffness 걸음을 더 빨리 했다quicken his pace. 얼마 있다가 파홈은 구덩이를 또 하나 팠다dig another hole.

날씨가 점점 더 더워지고get warmer 있었다. 파홈은 해를 보았다look at the sun. 아침식사 생각이 나는think of breakfast 때였다. "방향을 틀기에는 아직 너무 이르지. 그냥 장화만이라도 벗어야겠다." 파홈은 혼잣말을 했다. 그는 앉아서sit down 장화를 벗고take off his boots 그것을 허리띠에 찔러 넣은stick them into his girdle 뒤 계속 갔다go on. 이제 걷기가 수월했다.

"3마일(5km)을 더another three miles 계속 가서 왼쪽으로 돌아야지turn to the left." 하고 파홈은 생각했다. "여기 이 땅this land here은 너무 좋아서be so nice 이걸 잃는다면lose it 아쉬울a pity 거야."

파홈은 얼마 동안for a while 계속 똑바로 가고go straight on 나서 뒤를 돌아다봤다look back. 자신이 출발했던 언덕 위의 사람들the people on the hill이 개미처럼 작게as small as ants 보였다. "아, 이 방향으로는in this direction 충분히 멀리 왔군go far enough." 그는 생각했다. "몸을 돌려 다른 방향으로 갈go another direction 때가 됐어. 게다가besides 지쳐서get tired 마실 것도 필요하고."

파홈은 해를 보고 정오noon가 됐다는 걸 알았다. 그는 앉아서 빵을 조금 먹고eat some bread 물도 조금 마셨다drink some water. 하지만 눕지는 않았다do not lie down. 그랬다가는 잠이 들지도fall asleep 모른다는 생각이 들었기 때문이다. 파홈은 잠시 앉아 있다가sit for a little while 다시 계속 갔다go on again. 날씨가 너무 더워져서become terribly hot 졸음이 쏟아졌다feel sleepy. 그렇지만 그는 '잠깐 고생하면an hour to suffer 평생 잘 살 수 있어a lifetime to live.'라고 생각하며 계속 갔다.

파홈은 그 방향으로도 한참을 가서go a long way 다시 왼쪽으로 몸을 돌리려는 참이었는데, 그때 축축한 골짜기를 보게perceive a damp hollow 되었다. "저곳을 빼놓으면leave that out 아쉬울a pity 거야."라는 생각이 들었다. 그래서 그는 골짜기를 지나past the hollow 계속 가서 그 건너편에다on the other side of it 구덩이를 팠다dig a hole.

"이런ah! 내가 두 변을 너무 길게 만들었네make the sides too long." 하고 파홈은 생각했다. "이쪽 변은 더 짧게 해야겠군make this one shorter." 그는 더 빨리 걸음을 옮기며move faster 세 번째 변을 따라 갔다go along the third side. 파홈은 해를 쳐다보았다. 해는 지평선에 거의 반쯤nearly halfway to the horizon 내려와 있었지만, 그는 정사각형 땅의 세 번째 변the third side of the square을 아직 2마일(3km)도 채 가지 못한have not yet done two miles 상태였다. 목표 지점에서 아직 10마일(16km)이나 떨어져ten miles from his goal 있었다.

GRAMMAR POINT

it would be a pity to ~ : ~하는 것은 아쉬운/유감스러운 일일 것이다

⇨ 여기서는 아쉬울 거라고 가정하는 것이므로 조동사 would가 쓰였다.

- This land here is so nice that **it would be a pity to** lose it.
  여기 이 땅은 너무 좋아서 이걸 잃는다면 아쉬울 거야.
- **It would be a pity to** leave that out. 저곳을 빼놓으면 아쉬울 거야.

[p. 138-139]

"I've got to hurry back / in a straight line / now. I shouldn't go too far," he thought. "Besides, / I already have a huge amount of land." So Pahom turned / and hurried toward the hill / that he had started from.

But he now walked with difficulty. He was done in by the heat, / his bare feet were cut and bruised, / and his legs began to fail. He longed to rest, / but it was impossible / if he meant to get back / before sunset. The sun waits for no man, / and it was sinking lower and lower.

"Oh dear," he thought, "if only I had not blundered / by trying for too much. What if I am too late?"

He looked toward the hill / and at the sun. He was still far from his goal, / and the sun was already near the rim.

Pahom walked on and on. It was very hard to walk, / but he went quicker and quicker. He began running. He threw away / his coat, his boots, his flask, and his cap / and kept only the spade / which he used as a support.

"What shall I do?" he thought again. "I have grasped too much / and ruined the whole affair. I can't get there / before the sun sets." This fear / made him still more breathless.

Pahom went on running. His soaking shirt and trousers / stuck to him, / and his mouth was parched. His chest was working / like a blacksmith's bellows, / his heart was beating / like a hammer, / and his legs were giving way / as if they did not belong to him. Though afraid of death, / he could not stop. He gathered the rest of his strength / and ran on.

- **hurry back** 서둘러 돌아가다 • **be done in by** ~에 의해 녹초가 되다, ~에게 당하다 • **bare feet** 맨발
- **bruised** 멍이 든, 타박상을 입은 • **fail** 정지하다, 작동이 안 되다, (다리에서) 힘이 빠지다 • **long to** ~하기를 간절히 원하다
- **sunset** 일몰, 해질 녘 • **sink** (해가) 지다, 가라앉다 • **blunder** (어리석게) 실수하다; (어리석은) 실수 • **try for** ~을 얻으려고 하다 • **rim** 가장자리 • **throw away** 던져 버리다 • **support** 버팀대, 지주 • **grasp** 움켜쥐다 • **ruin** 망치다 • **affair** 일, 사건, 문제 • **fear** 두려움, 공포 • **breathless** 숨이 가쁜, 숨이 찬
- **soaking** 흠뻑 젖은 • **stick** 달라붙다, 들러붙다 • **parched** 몹시 메마른, 바싹 말라 버린 • **blacksmith** 대장장이 • **bellows** 풀무 • **give way** 무너지다, 무너져 내리다

CLOSE UP

1. **I've got to hurry back** 서둘러 돌아가야 해
   〈have got to ~〉는 〈have to ~〉와 같음. '~해야 한다'라는 뜻으로, 필요나 의무를 나타냄.

2. **He longed to rest** 그는 쉬고 싶은 마음이 간절했다
   long에는 동사로 '간절히 바라다'의 뜻이 있다. 이때는 〈long to+동사원형〉 또는 〈long for+명사〉의 형식으로 쓰인다.
   ex) He longed for peace.(그는 평화를 갈구했다.)

3. **If only I had not blundered** 어리석은 실수를 저지른 게 아니라면 좋으련만
   〈if only ~〉는 '~라면 좋을 텐데'라는 의미로, 사실과 반대되는 소망을 나타냄.

4. **What if I am too late?** 너무 늦으면 어쩌지?
   〈What if ~?〉는 '~하면 어쩌지?', '~하면 어떻게 될까?'라는 의미.

5. **as if they did not belong to him** 그들이 마치 그의 것이 아닌 것처럼
   〈as if ~〉는 '마치 ~인 것처럼'이라는 의미.

"이제 직선으로in a straight line 서둘러 돌아가야hurry back 해. 너무 멀리 가면 안 돼shouldn't go too far." 하고 파홈은 생각했다. "게다가 이미 엄청난 양의 땅a huge amount of land을 가졌잖아." 그래서 파홈은 방향을 틀어 출발했던 언덕을 향해 서둘러 갔다hurry toward the hill.

그러나 이제 파홈은 간신히 걷고 있었다walk with difficulty. 더위에by the heat 녹초가 되어 있었고be done in, 맨발his bare feet은 찢어지고 멍들었으며be cut and bruised, 다리his legs는 풀리기fail 시작했다. 그는 쉬고 싶은 마음이 간절했지만long to rest, 해 지기 전에before sunset 돌아갈 생각이라면mean to get back 그건 할 수 없는be impossible 일이었다. 해는 사람을 기다려 주지 않기wait for no man 때문에 점점 더 낮게 가라앉sink lower and lower 있었다.

"아, 이런oh, dear, 너무 많은 걸 얻으려 하다가try for too much 어리석은 실수를 저지른(일을 망쳐버린)blunder 게 아니라면 좋으련만. 너무 늦으면be too late 어떻게 하지?" 하고 파홈은 생각했다.

그는 언덕 쪽을 살펴보고look toward the hill 해도 쳐다봤다. 그는 목표 지점에서 여전히 멀리still far from his goal 있었고, 해는 벌써 지평선 언저리 근처에near the rim 있었다.

파홈은 계속해서 걸었다walk on and on. 걷기가 너무 힘들었지만 점점 더 빨리 갔다go quicker and quicker. 그는 달리기 시작했다begin running. 외투, 장화, 물병, 모자his coat, his boots, his flask, and his cap를 내버리고throw away 버팀대로as a support 쓰는 삽만 가지고 있었다keep only the spade.

"어떻게 하지?" 파홈은 다시 생각했다. "너무 많이 움켜쥐려다가grasp too much 일을 전부 망쳐 버렸어ruin the whole affair. 해 지기 전에 저기 도착할 수 없겠어can't get there." 이런 두려움this fear 때문에 파홈은 더욱 더 숨이 찼다more breathless.

파홈은 계속해서 달렸다go on running. 흠뻑 젖은 셔츠와 바지his soaking shirt and trousers는 몸에 달라붙었고stick to him, 입his mouth은 바싹 말랐다be parched. 가슴his chest은 대장장이의 풀무처럼like a blacksmith's bellows 들썩거렸고work, 심장his heart은 망치질하듯like a hammer 쿵쾅거렸으며beat, 다리his legs는 마치 자기 것이 아닌do not belong to him 것처럼 휘청거렸다give way. 그는 죽음이 두려웠지만afraid of death 멈춰 설 수가 없었다cannot stop. 그는 남은 힘the rest of his strength을 끌어모아gather 계속 달렸다run on.

GRAMMAR POINT

비교급 and 비교급 : 점점 더 ~하게

- The sun waits for no man, and it was sinking **lower and lower**.
  해는 사람을 기다려 주지 않기 때문에 점점 더 낮게 가라앉고 있었다.

- It was very hard to walk, but he went **quicker and quicker**.
  걷기가 너무 힘들었지만, 그는 점점 더 빨리 갔다.

[p. 140-141]

The sun was close to the rim. Now, yes now, / it was about to set. The sun was quite low, / but he was also near his aim. Pahom could already see / the people on the hill / waving their arms / to hurry him up. He could see / the fox-fur cap on the ground / and the money on it, / and the chief / sitting on the ground / holding his sides. And Pahom remembered his dream.

"There is plenty of land," he thought, "but will God let me live on it? I have lost my life. I shall never reach that spot."

Pahom looked at the sun, / which **had reached the earth**. With all his remaining strength, / he rushed on. Just as he **reached the hill**, / it suddenly grew dark. He looked up / —the sun had already set. He gave a cry. "**All my labor has been in vain**," he thought.

He was about to stop, / but he heard the Bashkirs / still shouting. He realized / that the sun seemed to have set, / but the Bashkirs on the hill / could still see it. He took a long breath / and ran up the hill. It was still light there. He **reached the top** / and saw the cap. He fell forward / and **reached the cap** / with his hands.

"Ah, that's a fine fellow!" exclaimed the chief. "He has gained much land."

Pahom's servant / came running up / and tried to raise him, / but he saw / that blood was flowing / from his mouth. Pahom was dead.

The Bashkirs clicked their tongues / to show their pity.

His servant picked up the spade / and ==dug a grave long enough / for Pahom to lie in== / and buried him in it. Six feet / from his head to his heels / was all he needed.

- **aim** 목표 • **hold one's sides** 배를 쥐고 웃다, 포복절도하다 • **lose one's life** 목숨을 잃다 • **labor** 노동, 수고 • **in vain** 허사가 되어, 헛되이 • **be about to** 막 ~하려고 하다 • **seem to** ~하는 것처럼 보이다 • **take a long breath** 숨을 길게 들이마시다 • **fellow** 친구, 녀석, 놈 • **servant** 하인 • **raise** 일으키다, 일으켜 세우다 • **flow** 흘러나오다 • **click one's tongue** 혀를 끌끌 차다 • **grave** 무덤 • **lie in** ~ 안에 눕다 • **bury** 묻다 • **six feet** 6피트, 관을 묻기 위해 땅을 파내는 길이

CLOSE UP

1. **had reached the earth** 이미 땅에 닿아 있었다 / **reached the hill** 언덕에 도달했다 / **reached the top** 꼭대기에 이르렀다 / **reached the cap** 모자를 잡았다
   〈reach ~〉는 '~에 닿다/도달하다/이르다'라는 뜻도 되고, '(손을 뻗어서) ~을 잡다/~에 닿다'라는 뜻도 된다. reach 다음에 to를 붙이지 않도록 주의하자.

2. **All my labor has been in vain.** 내 모든 고생이 헛수고가 되었구나.
   〈be in vain〉은 '허사가 되다', '수포로 돌아가다'라는 의미.

해가 지평선 언저리 가까이close to the rim 걸려 있었다. 이제는, 정말로 이제는, 당장이라도 해가 떨어지려는 참이었다be about to set. 해가 아주 낮게 quite low 떠 있었지만, 파홈 역시 목표에 가까이 near his aim 와 있었다. 파홈은 이미 언덕에서on the hill 팔을 흔들며wave their arms 그를 재촉하는hurry him up 사람들의 모습을 볼 수 있었다. 땅바닥에 놓인 여우털 모자the fox-fur cap와 그 위에 놓인 돈the money on it도 볼 수 있었고, 땅바닥에 앉아sit on the ground 배를 잡고 웃고hold his sides 있는 족장의 모습도 보였다. 그러자 파홈은 자신의 꿈이 생각났다remember his dream.

그는 생각했다. "땅은 많이plenty of land 있어. 그런데 하느님께서 내가 거기에 살도록 허락하실까let me live on it? 내 목숨은 다했어lose my life. 난 결코 저곳에 도달하지 못할never reach that spot 거야."

파홈이 태양을 쳐다보니 이미 땅에 닿아reach the earth 있었다. 파홈은 남은 힘을 모두 쥐어짜서with all his remaining strength 계속 쏜살같이 달렸다rush on. 그가 언덕에 도달하는reach the hill 바로 그 때 날이 갑자기 어두워졌다grow dark. 파홈은 위를 쳐다보았다look up. 해가 이미 진already set 상태였다. 그는 울부짖었다give a cry. "내 모든 고생all my labor이 헛수고가 되었구나be in vain." 하고 그는 생각했다.

파홈이 막 멈춰 서려고 하는데be about to stop, 바시키르인들이 여전히 외치는 소리가 들렸다. (언덕 아래에서는) 해가 진 것처럼 보였지만seem to have set, 언덕 위에 있는 바시키르인들the Bashkirs on the hill에게는 아직 해가 보인다can still see it는 사실을 파홈은 깨달았다. 파홈은 길게 숨을 들이쉬고 take a long breath 언덕을 달려 올라갔다run up the hill. 그곳은 아직 밝은 빛이 남아 있었다. 파홈이 꼭대기에 이르자reach the top 모자가 보였다see the cap. 그는 앞으로 고꾸라지며fall forward 두 손을 뻗어with his hands 모자를 잡았다reach the cap.

"이런ah, 대단한 친구a fine fellow로군!" 족장이 소리쳤다. "엄청난 땅을 얻었어gain much land."

파홈의 하인Pahom's servant이 달려 올라와서come running up 그를 일으켜 세우려raise him 했지만, 그의 입에서from his mouth 피blood가 흐르는flow 게 보였다. 파홈은 숨이 끊어졌던 것이다be dead.

바시키르인들은 혀를 끌끌 차며click their tongues 동정심을 나타냈다show their pity.

파홈의 하인이 삽을 들고pick up the spade 파홈이 충분히 누울 만한 정도로 무덤을 파서dig a grave 시신을 그 안에 묻었다bury him in it. 파홈의 머리부터 발꿈치까지from his head to his heels 6피트(약 180cm)six feet가 그에게 필요한 땅의 전부all he needs였다.

GRAMMAR POINT

enough ~ to... : …할 정도로 충분한 ~ ⇨ enough의 위치에 주의할 것. 명사 앞, 형용사 뒤에 온다.

- His servant dug a grave long **enough** for Pahom **to** lie in.
  그의 하인은 파홈이 누울 만한 길이로 무덤을 팠다.

- That area has **enough** land for all of them **to** farm.
  그 지역은 그들 모두가 경작할 수 있을 만큼의 땅이 있다.

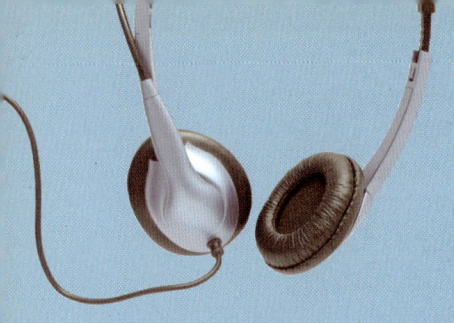

Super Reading Story Training Book

Step

5

A Christmas Carol
– Charles Dickens

A Christmas Carol

One Christmas Eve, / Scrooge sat busy / in his office. It was cold and foggy weather. The city clocks / had just rung three times, / but it was already quite dark.

Scrooge was an old man. **He was known / by everyone / to be mean, miserly, and cold.** He was a greedy sinner. **No warmth could warm him, / and no cold could chill him.** Nobody ever stopped Scrooge / on the street / to say, "My dear Scrooge, how are you?" **No beggars implored him / to give them some money.** Even the dogs seemed to know him, / and they avoided him, / too. But Scrooge did not care / at all. He liked it / that way. People avoided him, / and he avoided people.

He had worked / in the same dark office / for many years. Once / it had been the office / of *Scrooge and Marley*. Scrooge and Marley / had been partners / for many years. And even now, / seven years after Marley had died, / those names were still on the door.

It was a very small room / with a very small fire. The only other person / in the office / was Bob Cratchit, / Scrooge's clerk. Bob was very cold. Scrooge did not give Bob / much wood for his fire / because he did not like to spend money. So the clerk put on his coat / and tried to warm himself / by the light of a candle.

Scrooge did not like anything. He especially hated Christmas.

"Merry Christmas, Uncle," cried a cheerful voice. It was the voice / of Scrooge's nephew Fred.

"Bah, humbug," said Scrooge.

"Oh, come on, Uncle," said Fred. "I'm sure / you don't mean it."

"I do," said Scrooge. "Why are you merry? You're a poor man."

"Well, why aren't you merry? You're a very rich man. And it's Christmas!"

"Bah, humbug," said Scrooge again. "**You keep Christmas / in your own way, / and let me keep it / in mine.**"

- **foggy** 안개가 낀 • **mean** 심술궂은, 잔인한, 비열한 • **miserly** 구두쇠인, 수전노인 • **greedy** 탐욕스러운, 욕심 많은 • **sinner** 죄인 • **chill** 차갑게 하다 • **beggar** 거지 • **implore** 간청하다 • **avoid** 피하다 • **do not care** 개의치 않다 • **clerk** 사무원, 직원, 서기 • **cheerful** 밝고 명랑한 • **bah, humbug** 흥, 허튼소리/같잖은 소리 • **merry** 즐거운

CLOSE UP

1 **He was known by everyone to be mean, miserly, and cold.**
그는 모두에게 비열하고 인색하고 차가운 사람으로 알려져 있었다.
⟨be known to ~⟩는 '~하는 것으로 알려져 있다'라는 의미. by everyone은 모두가 그렇게 생각한다는 것을 강조하기 위해 삽입되었다.

2 **You keep Christmas in your own way, and let me keep it in mine.**
넌 네 방식대로 크리스마스를 축하해라. 난 내 방식대로 할 테니.
⟨in one's own way⟩는 '~ 나름의 방식으로'라는 의미. 여기서 in mine은 in my own way를 줄인 표현이다.

크리스마스 캐럴

어느 크리스마스 전날 밤one Christmas Eve, 스크루지Scrooge가 사무실에in his office 앉아 바쁘게 일하고 있었다sit busy. 춥고 안개가 자욱하게 낀cold and foggy 날씨였다. 도시의 시계들the city clocks이 이제 막 3시를 알렸지만ring three times, 날이 벌써 꽤 어둑어둑했다be quite dark.

스크루지는 늙은 사내an old man였다. 그는 모두에게 비열하고 인색하고 차가운mean, miserly, and cold 사람으로 알려져 있었다. 그는 욕심 많은 죄인a greedy sinner이었다. 어떤 온기도no warmth 그의 마음을 훈훈하게 할warm him 수 없었고, 어떤 냉기도no cold 그의 마음을 차갑게 할chill him 수 없었다(온정이라곤 눈곱만치도 없고 냉정하기 짝이 없었다는 의미). 아무도nobody 한번이라도 길에서 스크루지를 멈춰 세워stop Scrooge "스크루지 영감님, 안녕하세요how are you?"라고 인사한 적이 없었다. 어떤 거지도no beggars 그에게는 돈을 달라고give them some money 간청하지implore 않았다. 심지어 개들도even the dogs 그를 알고 있는 듯했으며, 역시 그를 피해 다녔다avoid him. 그러나 스크루지는 조금도 개의치 않았다do not care. 그는 그런 식으로 지내는 게 좋았다like it that way. 사람들은 그를 피했고, 그도 사람들을 피했다.

스크루지는 여러 해 동안for many years 똑같은 어두운 사무실에서in the same dark office 일해 왔다. 그곳은 한때 '스크루지와 말리Scrooge and Marley'의 사무실이었다. 스크루지와 말리는 여러 해 동안 동업자partners였다. 그리고 말리가 죽고 7년이 지난 지금도 그 문에는 여전히 그 두 이름이 붙어 있었다.

사무실은 아주 작은 난로가 있는with a very small fire 매우 작은 방a very small room이었다. 사무실에 있는 다른 유일한 사람the only other person은 스크루지의 서기Scrooge's clerk 봅 크래칫Bob Cratchit이었다. 봅은 몹시 추웠다be cold. 스크루지는 돈 쓰는spend money 게 싫어서 봅에게 난로에 넣을 장작을 많이much wood for his fire 주지 않았다. 그래서 서기는 외투를 걸치고put on his coat 촛불로by the light of a candle 몸을 따뜻하게warm himself 해 보려고 애썼다.

스크루지는 아무것도 좋아하지 않았다do not like anything. 특히 크리스마스를 싫어했다hate Christmas.

"삼촌, 메리 크리스마스Merry Christmas." 명랑한 목소리가 외쳤다. 스크루지의 조카 프레드Scrooge's nephew, Fred의 목소리였다.

"흥bah, 허튼소리humbug." 스크루지가 말했다.

"에이, 왜 그러세요, 삼촌." 프레드가 말했다. "분명 진심은 아니시겠죠don't mean it."

"진심이다." 스크루지가 말했다. "넌 왜 즐거운be merry 거냐? 가난뱅이a poor man 주제에."

"그럼 삼촌은 왜 즐거워하지 않으세요? 아주 부자a rich man시잖아요. 게다가 크리스마스인걸요!"

"흥, 허튼소리." 스크루지가 다시 말했다. "넌 네 방식대로in your own way 크리스마스를 축하해라keep Christmas. 난 내 방식대로 할 테니."

GRAMMAR POINT

no + 명사 : 어떤 ~도 …아니다 ⇨ 부정의 의미를 강조하고 싶을 때 사용함.

- **No warmth** could warm him, and **no cold** could chill him.
  어떤 온기도 그의 마음을 훈훈하게 할 수 없었고, 어떤 냉기도 그의 마음을 차갑게 할 수 없었다.
- **No beggars** implored him to give them some money. 어떤 거지도 그에게는 돈을 달라고 간청하지 않았다.

[p. 146-147]

"Don't be so angry, Uncle. Come / and have dinner with us / tomorrow."
Scrooge merely answered, "Goodbye."

"I don't want / to be angry with you, / Uncle," said Fred. "So / a Merry Christmas, / Uncle."

"Goodbye," Scrooge only said.

After Scrooge's nephew left, / the clerk **let two other people in**. They were portly gentlemen. They had books and papers / in their hands / and bowed to Scrooge.

"Excuse us. May I ask, / are you Mr. Scrooge / or Mr. Marley?" said one of the gentlemen.

"**Mr. Marley has been dead / these seven years.** He died / seven years ago / this very night," answered Scrooge.

"Mr. Scrooge then," said the man. "At this festive season of the year, / it is nice / for everyone / to give something to people / who have nothing / —no homes, no food."

"Are there no prisons? Any orphanages?" said Scrooge.

"There are. But they always need / a little more. So / a few of us / are raising funds / to buy the poor / some meat, drink, and means of warmth. What shall I put you down for?"

"Nothing!" answered Scrooge.

"You wish / to give an anonymous gift?"

"No. I wish / to be left alone. I don't make merry / at Christmas, / and I can't afford / to make lazy fools merry. I have my work / to worry about."

After the men left, / Scrooge turned to his clerk. "**You'll want / all day off /** tomorrow, / I suppose?" he asked.

"If that's convenient, / sir," the clerk responded.

"It's not convenient, / and it's not fair. Yet you'll still **expect me / to pay you a day's wages** / for no work, / won't you?"

"It's only once a year, / sir."

"That's a poor excuse / for picking a man's pocket / every twenty-fifth of December. But I suppose / you must have the whole day. Be here early / the next morning."

The clerk promised / that he would arrive early. Scrooge walked out of the office / and went back to his empty home.

- **merely** 단지, 그저 • **portly** 다소 뚱뚱한 • **books** (회계) 장부 • **bow** 고개 숙여 인사하다 • **festive** 축제의
- **prison** 감옥 • **orphanage** 고아원 • **raise funds** 기금을 모금하다 • **means of** ~의 방법/수단/도구
- **put down** 적다, 기록하다 • **anonymous** 익명의 • **can't afford to** ~할 여유가 없다 • **lazy** 게으른
- **all day off** 하루 종일 일을 쉼 • **convenient** 편리한, 적합한 • **fair** 공평한 • **wages** 임금 • **poor** 궁색한
- **excuse** 변명 • **pick a man's pocket** 남의 주머니를 털다 • **empty** 텅 빈

CLOSE UP

1. **let two other people in** 다른 사람 두 명을 안으로 들였다
   〈let ~ in〉은 '~을 들어오게 하다', '~을 안으로 들이다'라는 의미.

2. **You'll want all day off** 자네는 하루 종일 쉬고 싶겠지
   off는 '(일을) 쉬는'이라는 의미. ex) I have two days off this week.(나 이번 주에 이틀 휴가야.)

3. **expect me to pay you a day's wages** 내가 자네에게 하루치 임금을 지불하길 기대한다
   〈expect ~ to...〉는 '~가 …하기를 (당연히) 기대하다'라는 의미. 〈pay+사람+돈〉은 '~에게 …을 지불하다'라는 의미.

"삼촌, 그렇게 역정 내지 마세요. 내일 오셔서come 저희와 함께 저녁 드세요have dinner with us."
스크루지는 그저 이렇게 대답했다. "잘 가거라goodbye."
"삼촌한테 화내고 싶지 않아요." 프레드가 말했다. "그러니 크리스마스 즐겁게 보내세요, 삼촌."
"잘 가거라." 스크루지는 그렇게만 말했다.

스크루지의 조카가 떠난 후 서기가 다른 사람 두 명을 안으로 들였다let two other people in. 풍채가 좋은 신사들portly gentlemen이었다. 그들은 손에in their hands 장부와 서류를 들고 있었고have books and papers 스크루지에게 고개 숙여 인사했다bow to him.

"실례합니다excuse us. 여쭤 봐도 되겠는지may I ask, 스크루지 선생이신가요, 말리 선생이신가요?" 두 신사 중 한 명이 말했다.

"말리 씨Mr. Marley는 7년 전에 세상을 떴소be dead. 7년 전seven years ago 바로 오늘 밤에this very night 죽었지die." 스크루지가 대답했다.

"그렇다면 스크루지 선생이시로군요." 신사가 말했다. "이런 연말연시에at this festive season of the year(festive season은 크리스마스와 새해를 포함하는 기간을 의미함) 모든 사람이 집도 없고no homes 음식도 없고no food, 그야말로 아무것도 가진 게 없는have nothing 사람들에게 뭔가를 베푼다면give something 고마운 일일 겁니다be nice."

"감옥이 없단no prisons 말이오? 고아원도any orphanages 없소?" (감옥이나 고아원은 뒀다 뭐하냐는 의미) 스크루지가 말했다.

"있기는 하지요. 하지만 항상 뭔가 좀 더 필요합니다need a little more. 그래서 저희 몇 명a few of us이 가난한 사람들the poor에게 고기meat와 음료drink, 방한용품means of warmth을 사 주려고 기금을 모금하고raise funds 있습니다. 무엇에다 선생의 이름을 올릴까요put you down?"

"아무 데도 올리지 마시오nothing!" 스크루지가 대답했다.

"익명으로 선물하기를give an anonymous gift 바라시는군요?"

"아니오. 나를 그냥 내버려 두면be left alone 좋겠소. 난 크리스마스에 즐겁게 놀지도make merry 않고, 게으른 멍청이들을 즐겁게 해 줄make lazy fools merry 여유도 없소. 내 일로도 골치가 아프단 말이오."

신사들이 떠난 뒤 스크루지는 서기에게 고개를 돌렸다turn to his clerk. "자네 내일 하루 종일 쉬고 싶겠지want all day off, 그렇지?" 스크루지가 물었다.

"그래도 괜찮다면요if that's convenient, 사장님sir." 서기가 대답했다.

"괜찮지도 않고 공평하지도 않아it's not fair. 그렇지만 자넨 아무 일도 안 해도for no work 여전히 내가 자네에게 하루치 임금을 지불하길pay you a day's wages 기대하겠지expect, 안 그런가?"

"일 년에 한 번once a year뿐인걸요, 사장님."

"매년 12월 25일마다every twenty-fifth of December 남의 주머니를 털어 가는pick a man's pocket 데 대한 변명치고는 궁색a poor excuse하군. 하지만 자넨 하루를 꼬박 쉬어야겠지have the whole day. 그다음 날 아침은the next morning 일찍 출근하게be here early."

서기는 일찍 오겠다고arrive early 약속했다promise. 스크루지는 사무실에서 나와walk out of the office 자신의 텅 빈 집으로to his empty home 돌아갔다go back.

GRAMMAR POINT

dead (형용사) : 죽은   **die (동사)** : 죽다

- Mr. Marley has **been dead** these seven years. 말리 씨는 7년 전에 세상을 떴소.
- He **died** seven years ago this very night. 그는 7년 전 바로 오늘 밤에 죽었소.

A Christmas Carol **141**

[p. 148-149]

When Scrooge got to his building, / he put the key / into the lock of the door. But when he looked at the knocker, / he did not see a knocker / but Marley's face. Scrooge stared for a moment, / and then / it was a knocker again. He said, "Pooh, pooh!" / and closed the door / with a bang.

Scrooge went up to his room, / and carefully locked the door. He checked twice / **to see if the door was locked** / and then made a little fire / in the fireplace. He put on his dressing gown, slippers, and nightcap, / and sat down / before the very low fire. As he threw his head back in his chair, / he heard something in the house. It was far away, / but it was coming closer. It sounded / as if some person were dragging a heavy chain / over the casks / in the wine merchant's cellar. Then, / he heard the noise much louder / on the floors below. Then, / it came up the stairs, / and then / it came straight toward his door. It came / right through the heavy door, / and a ghost passed into the room / before his eyes. The face! **He recognized it** / **right away** / **as Marley's.** It was Marley's ghost.

"How now," said Scrooge, / caustic and cold / as ever. "What do you want / with me?"

"Much." Marley's voice, / no doubt about it.

"Who are you?"

"Ask me / who I was."

"Who were you then?" said Scrooge, / raising his voice.

"In life, / I was your partner, / Jacob Marley."

"Mercy! Dreadful apparition, / why do you trouble me? What do you want?" Scrooge's voice trembled / as he spoke.

"I have been traveling / since I died. Though I am dead, / I must walk through / the world of the living. I cannot rest. I cannot stay. I cannot linger anywhere."

"Why?" asked Scrooge.

"Because I'm unhappy. I was very bad to people / when I was alive. If a man stays away from other people / while he is alive, / that man becomes like me," said Marley's ghost.

- **knocker** (문 두드리는) 고리쇠, 문고리 • **stare** 쳐다보다, 응시하다 • **with a bang** 쾅 소리를 내며 • **make a fire** 불을 피우다 • **fireplace** 벽난로 • **dressing gown** (잠옷 위에 입는) 가운, 실내복 • **nightcap** 취침용 모자 • **low fire** (화력이) 낮은 불 • **throw one's head back** 머리를 뒤로 젖히다 • **far away** 멀리서 • **drag** 질질 끌다 • **cask** (술을 담아 두는 나무로 된) 통 • **wine cellar** 와인 보관하는 창고 • **noise** 소리, 잡음 • **pass into** ~로 통과해 들어오다 • **recognize** 알아보다, 인식하다 • **ghost** 유령 • **caustic** 비꼬는, 빈정대는 • **as ever** 언제나처럼 • **dreadful** 무시무시한 • **apparition** 유령 • **linger** (예상보다) 오래 머물다 • **stay away from** ~을 멀리하다 • **alive** 살아 있는

CLOSE UP

1 **to see if the door was locked** 문이 잠겼는지 보려고
〈see if ~〉는 '~인지 확인하다', '~인지의 여부를 알다'라는 의미.

2 **He recognized it right away as Marley's.** 그는 즉시 그것이 말리의 얼굴인 것을 알아봤다.
〈recognize ~ as...〉는 '~이 ...인 것을 알아보다'라는 의미. 여기서 Marley's는 Marley's face를 뜻함.

스크루지는 자기가 사는 건물에 도착하자get to his building 문에 달린 자물쇠에 열쇠를 집어넣었다put the key into the lock. 하지만 문고리를 보니look at the knocker, 문고리로 보이지 않고 말리의 얼굴로 보였다see Marley's face. 스크루지가 잠시for a moment 빤히 바라보니stare, 그것은 다시 문고리로 보였다. 스크루지는 "쳇, 쳇pooh, pooh!" 하며 쾅 하고with a bang 문을 닫았다close the door.

스크루지는 자기 방으로 올라가go up to his room 조심스럽게 문을 잠갔다lock the door. 문이 제대로 잠겼는지 보려고 재차 확인한check twice 다음 벽난로에in the fireplace 작은 불을 피웠다make a little fire. 스크루지는 실내복dressing gown을 입고, 슬리퍼slippers를 신고, 취침용 모자nightcap를 쓴 다음 아주 낮게 타는 불 앞에before the very low fire 앉았다sit down. 그가 의자에 앉아 머리를 뒤로 젖히자throw his head back 집 안에서 무슨 소리가 들렸다hear something. 멀리서 나는 소리였지만 점점 더 가까이 들려왔다come closer. 마치 어떤 사람some person이 포도주 상인의 저장고에 있는 포도주통 위에서over the casks 무거운 쇠사슬을 질질 끄는drag a heavy chain 듯한 소리였다. 그러더니 훨씬 더 큰 소리the noise much louder가 아래층들에서on the floors below 들렸다. 그러더니 소리는 계단을 올라와come up the stairs 곧장 그의 방문을 향해 다가왔다come toward his door. 소리는 바로 육중한 문을 뚫고through the heavy door 들려오더니, 유령 하나a ghost가 방으로 들어와서pass into the room 그의 눈 앞에before his eyes 나타났다. 저 얼굴은the face! 스크루지는 즉시right away 그것이 말리의 얼굴인 것을 알아봤다recognize it as Marley's. 그것은 말리의 유령Marley's ghost이었던 것이다.

"허, 이런how now." 스크루지는 여느 때와 마찬가지로as ever 비꼬듯 차갑게caustic and cold 말했다. "내게 무슨 볼일이 있나?"

"볼일이야 많지." 의심할 바 없이no doubt about it 말리의 목소리Marley's voice였다.

"넌 누구냐who are you?"

"누구였는지를who I was 물어보게."

"그럼 넌 누구였느냐who were you?" 스크루지가 목소리를 높이며 물었다.

"살아 있을 때는in life 자네의 동업자your partner 제이콥 말리Jacob Marley였지."

"맙소사mercy! 끔찍한 유령아dreadful apparition, 왜 나를 괴롭히느냐trouble me? 바라는 게 뭐냐?" 말하는 스크루지의 목소리Scrooge's voice가 가늘게 떨렸다tremble.

"난 죽은 다음부터 내내 떠돌고travel 있다네. 죽었지만 산 자들의 세계the world of the living를 떠돌아야 하지. 난 안식을 누릴 수가 없네cannot rest. 한곳에 머물 수가 없어cannot stay. 어디든 오래 머물 수가 없네cannot linger."

"어째서why?" 스크루지가 물었다.

"불행하기be unhappy 때문이라네. 난 살아 있을be alive 때 사람들에게 아주 못되게 굴었네be bad to people. 살아 있을 때 다른 사람들과 가까이 지내지 않으면stay away from other people, 그 사람은 나처럼 된다네become like me." 말리의 유령이 대답했다.

GRAMMAR POINT

as if ~ (가정법) : 마치 ~인 것처럼 ⇨ 실은 그렇지 않지만 마치 그런 것 같다는 의미.

- It sounded **as if** some person **were dragging** a heavy chain over the casks.
  그것은 마치 어떤 사람이 포도주통 위에서 무거운 쇠사슬을 질질 끄는 듯한 소리였다. **(가정법 과거)**

- They were as happy **as if** they **had eaten** a king's meal.
  그들은 마치 왕의 식사를 먹은 것처럼 행복해했다. **(가정법 과거완료)**

[p. 150-151]

"I am here tonight / to warn you / that you have yet a chance / and hope of escaping my fate," said Marley's ghost.

"This is the chain / I made during my lifetime. **Every time / I refused to help / those in need**, / the chain became longer and heavier. When I died, / our chains were about the same, Scrooge, / but now, / after seven years, / yours is much longer than mine. I want to help you / not to be unhappy / like me / when you die."

"How?" asked Scrooge.

"You will be visited / by three more ghosts," answered Marley's ghost. "Expect the first / tonight / when the bell tolls one. Expect the second / tomorrow night / at the same hour. The third will come / the next night, / when the last stroke of twelve / has rung."

The ghost began floating out the window.

"But wait. Will I see you again? Can't you tell me more?"

"No, Scrooge, / you won't see me again. Remember / what I told you, / for your own sake, / or you will soon / see your own heavy chain."

The ghost disappeared out the window, / which was wide open.

As Scrooge went to the window / to see / where Marley had gone, / he suddenly heard some crying / down below. Again, / Scrooge's heart froze. The voices **came / not from people, / but from ghosts**. He quickly closed the window. He tried to say, "Humbug," / but he stopped / at the first syllable.

"**This couldn't have happened.** I will go to sleep, / and tomorrow / everything will be fine," he thought. Then, he went to bed / and fell into a troubled sleep.

When Scrooge awoke, / it was still so dark. "Was it all a dream?" he wondered. Just then, / the clock tolled / a deep, dull, hollow one.

Light flashed up / in the room / in an instant, / and the curtains of his bed / were drawn aside / by a strange figure. The ghost was an old man / with long white hair. He held / a branch of fresh green holly / in his hand. From the top of his head, / a bright clear jet of light / sprang.

"I am / the Ghost of Christmas Past," he said.

"Whose past?"

"Your past," answered the ghost.

- **warn** 경고하다, 강력히 충고하다 • **escape** 벗어나다, 피하다 • **fate** 운명 • **toll** (종 소리가) 울리다 • **stroke** 치기, 때리기, (시계, 종 등의) 치는 소리 • **ring** 울리다 • **float** 떠다니다 • **for one's own sake** ~을 위하여
- **disappear** 사라지다 • **freeze** 얼어붙다 • **syllable** 음절 • **troubled sleep** 편치 않은 잠 • **awake** (잠에서) 깨다 • **hollow** 속이 빈, 공허한, 허로우른 • **flash up** 번쩍 빛나다 • **in an instant** 즉시, 이내 • **draw ~ aside** ~을 옆으로 젖히다 • **figure** 형상, (사람) 형체 • **holly** 호랑가시나무 • **a jet of light** 광선, 빛줄기 • **spring** (갑자기) 튀어오르다, 확 나타나다

CLOSE UP

1. **Every time I refused to help those in need** 내가 궁핍한 사람들을 도와주는 걸 거절할 때마다
   ⟨every time ~⟩은 '~할 때마다', ⟨refuse to ~⟩는 '~하기를 거절하다'라는 의미. ⟨in need⟩는 '어려움에 처한, 궁핍한'이라는 뜻.

2. **came not from people, but from ghosts** 사람들이 아니라 유령들한테서 나왔다
   ⟨not ~ but...⟩은 '~가 아니라 …'라는 의미.

3. **This couldn't have happened.** 설마 이런 일이 일어났을 리가 없어.
   ⟨could have p.p.⟩는 '~했을 수도 있다'라는 뜻이고, ⟨couldn't have p.p.⟩는 '~했을 리가 없다'라는 의미.

"내가 오늘 밤 여기 온 이유는 자네한테 아직 나처럼 되는 운명을 피할escape my fate 수 있는 기회와 희망a chance and hope이 있다는 걸 경고하기warn you 위해서일세." 말리의 유령이 말했다.

"이건 내가 살아 있을 때during my lifetime 만든 쇠사슬the chain일세. 내가 궁핍한 사람들those in need을 도와주는 걸 거절할refuse to help 때마다 쇠사슬은 더 길고 무거워졌지become longer and heavier. 내가 죽었을 때 우리의 쇠사슬은 (길이가) 거의 같았다네be about the same, 스크루지. 하지만 7년이 지난after seven years 지금은 자네의 것이 내 것보다 훨씬 더 길지be much longer. 자네가 죽어서 나처럼 불행해지지 않도록 자네를 돕고help you 싶네."

"어떻게 말인가how?" 스크루지가 물었다.

"자네한테 유령 셋이 더three more ghosts 찾아올 걸세." 말리의 유령이 대답했다. "첫 번째the first 유령은 오늘 밤tonight 종소리가 1시를 알릴toll one 때 찾아올 걸세. 두 번째the second 유령은 내일 밤tomorrow night 같은 시각에at the same hour 찾아올 거라네. 세 번째the third 유령은 그다음 날 밤the next night 12시를 치는 마지막 종소리the last stroke of twelve가 울렸을 때 찾아올 거야."

유령이 창밖으로 유유히 떠돌며 나가기float out the window 시작했다.

"하지만 기다리게wait. 자네를 다시 만나게 되겠나? 내게 더 얘기해 줄tell me more 수 없겠나?"

"아니, 스크루지. 자네는 날 다시는 보지 못할 걸세. 내가 자네를 위해for your own sake 한 말을 기억하게. 그렇지 않으면 자네는 자네 자신의 무거운 쇠사슬your own heavy chain을 곧 보게 될 걸세."

유령은 창밖으로 사라졌고disappear out the window, 창문은 활짝 열려 있었다be wide open.

말리가 어디로 갔는지 보려고 스크루지가 창가로 가자go to the window, 갑자기 아래쪽에서down below 울부짖는 소리가 들렸다hear some crying. 다시 한번 스크루지의 심장이 얼어붙었다freeze. 그 목소리들은 사람이 아니라 유령들한테서 나오는come from ghosts 소리였다. 스크루지는 재빨리 창문을 닫았다close the window. 그는 "속임수야humbug."라고 말하려 했으나 첫 음절에서 멈추고 말았다.

"설마 이런 일이 일어났을 리가 없어couldn't have happened. 잠을 자야지go to sleep. 그럼 내일은 모든 게 괜찮아질 거야." 하고 스크루지는 생각했다. 그리고는 잠자리에 들어go to bed 뒤숭숭한 잠이 들었다fall into a troubled sleep.

스크루지가 잠에서 깼을awake 때는 여전히 아주 캄캄했다. "그 모든 게 꿈a dream이었나?" 스크루지는 의아해했다. 바로 그때just then 시계가 깊고 둔탁하고 허허롭게deep, dull, hollow 1시를 울렸다.

순식간에in an instant 방 안에 빛light이 번쩍 비치더니flash up, 그의 침대 커튼the curtains of his bed이 이상한 형체a strange figure에 의해 옆으로 젖혀졌다be drawn aside. 그 유령은 흰 수염을 길게 기른with long white hair 노인an old man이었다. 유령은 싱싱한 초록색 호랑가시나무fresh green holly 가지를 손에 들고hold a branch 있었다. 유령의 머리 꼭대기에서는from the top of his head 밝고 선명한 빛줄기a bright clear jet of light가 뿜어져 나왔다spring.

"나는 과거의 크리스마스 유령the Ghost of Christmas Past이다." 유령이 말했다.

"누구의 과거whose past란 말이오?"

"너의 과거your past다." 유령이 대답했다.

> **GRAMMAR POINT**
>
> **be + p.p. (수동태)** ⇨ 주어가 동사의 행위를 '받거나 당하는' 걸 말한다. 행위자는 by로 나타냄.
>
> - You will **be visited by** three more ghosts. 자네는 유령 셋의 방문을 더 받을 걸세.
> - The curtains of his bed **were drawn** aside **by** a strange figure.
>   그의 침대 커튼이 이상한 형체에 의해 옆으로 젖혀졌다.

[p. 152-153]

"What do you want?"

"Rise / and walk with me."

Scrooge got up from his bed. He held the ghost's hand, / and they passed through the wall together. Suddenly, / they were standing in the country / where he had lived / as a boy. It was clear enough / by the decorations in the shops / that there, too, / it was Christmastime.

They saw / many boys and girls / going home across the fields, / happily shouting "Merry Christmas" / to each other. Scrooge remembered / the happiness and joy / when he was a child. He could feel tears / on his cheek.

"Are you sad?" asked the ghost.

"No, no, I am ... happy," said Scrooge.

"They are not real. They are only spirits / from Christmas past. They cannot see us."

But Scrooge knew the spirits, / just as he knew / the streets, the houses, and the townspeople. Then, / they saw Scrooge as a boy, / reading on his own / in an empty classroom. Seeing himself / as he had once been, / Scrooge sat down at a desk / next to him / and began to cry.

"It's me. Once / when I was a boy, / I was left alone here / on Christmas. My father and mother / weren't at home. Now, suddenly, / I wish I would ..." Scrooge's voice grew quiet.

"What do you wish?" the ghost asked.

"Last night, / a young boy / came to my office window / and sang me a Christmas carol. I just got angry / and told him to leave. I wish / I'd given some money to that poor boy," said Scrooge / with heavy sadness.

The ghost smiled. "Let's see / another Christmas," he said.

This time, / Scrooge saw the office / where he had first worked. He saw Mr. Fezziwig, / the man whom he had worked for. Young Scrooge was helping them / prepare the office / for a Christmas party. Soon, / there were / many young people / there. They were his fellow apprentices. They were enjoying themselves / and dancing. Even he, / Scrooge himself, / was dancing and enjoying himself.

- **rise** (자리에서) 일어나다 • **get up from** ~에서 일어나다 • **hold one's hand** ~의 손을 잡다 • **pass through** ~을 통과하다 • **decoration** 장식 • **tear** 눈물 • **spirit** 영혼, 유령 • **on one's own** 혼자서 • **sit down** 앉다 • **be left alone** 혼자 남겨지다 • **grow quiet** 조용해지다 • **get angry** 화를 내다 • **prepare** 준비하다 • **fellow** 동료 • **apprentice** 견습생, 도제

CLOSE UP

1. **Seeing himself as he had once been** 옛날의 자기 모습을 보고
   〈as he is〉 하면 '현재의 그의 모습'을 뜻한다. 따라서 〈as he had once been〉은 '예전의 그의 모습'이 되겠다.

2. **They were enjoying themselves** 그들은 즐거운 시간을 보내고 있었다
   〈enjoy oneself〉는 '즐기다', '흥겨워하다', '즐거운 시간을 보내다'라는 의미.

"원하는 게 뭐요?"

"일어나서rise 나와 함께 가자walk with me."

스크루지는 침대에서 일어났다get up from his bed. 그는 유령의 손을 잡았고hold the ghost's hand, 그들은 함께 벽을 통과했다pass through the wall. 갑자기 둘은 스크루지가 소년이었을 때as a boy 살던 시골에 서 있었다stand in the country. 여러 상점 안의in the shops 장식으로 보아by the decorations 거기서도 크리스마스 때Christmastime인 게 매우 분명했다be clear enough.

많은 소년 소녀들many boys and girls이 들판을 가로질러across the fields 집으로 가면서go home 서로에게to each other "메리 크리스마스"라고 즐겁게 외치는happily shout 모습이 보였다. 스크루지는 어린 시절의 행복과 기쁨the happiness and joy을 떠올렸다. 그는 뺨에 눈물이 흐르는 게 느껴졌다feel tears.

"슬픈가?" 유령이 물었다.

"아니, 그게 아니라, 난…… 행복하오." 스크루지가 대답했다.

"저들은 실제로 존재하는 사람이 아니다be not real. 과거의 크리스마스에 속한 영혼들spirits from Christmas past일 뿐이지. 그들에게는 우리가 보이지 않는다cannot see us."

그러나 스크루지는 그 거리와 집들, 도시 주민들을 알고 있듯이 그 영혼들도 알고 있었다. 그러고 나서 그들은 어린 스크루지Scrooge as a boy가 빈 교실에서in an empty classroom 홀로on his own 책을 읽고 있는 모습을 보았다. 옛날의 자기 모습을 본see himself 스크루지는 어린 스크루지 옆에 있는 책상에 앉아sit down at a desk 울기 시작했다begin to cry.

"내 모습이야it's me. 어렸을 때 한번은 크리스마스 날on Christmas 이곳에 홀로 남겨진be left alone here 적이 있었지. 아버지와 어머니가 집에 계시지 않았어be not at home. 이제 새삼스레 내가 바라는 건……." 스크루지의 목소리가 잦아들었다grow quiet.

"바라는 게 뭔가?" 유령이 물었다.

"어젯밤last night 한 어린 소년a young boy이 내 사무실 창가에 와서 come to my office window 내게 크리스마스 캐럴을 한 곡 불러 줬소sing me a Christmas carol. 난 그냥 화를 내며get angry 그 애한테 가라고 했지tell him to leave. 그 불쌍한 아이that poor boy한테 돈이라도 조금 줬다면give some money 좋았을 텐데." 스크루지는 깊은 슬픔에 잠겨with heavy sadness 말했다.

유령이 미소를 지었다. "다른 크리스마스를 살펴보자see another Christmas." 유령이 말했다.

이번에this time 스크루지는 자신이 처음 일했던 사무실을 보았다see the office. 스크루지의 고용주였던 페지위그 씨도 보였다see Mr. Fezziwig. 젊은 스크루지는 크리스마스 파티를 위해for a Christmas party 그들이 사무실을 준비하는prepare the office 걸 돕고 있었다. 얼마 안 있어 많은 젊은이들many young people이 그곳에 모였다. 그들은 스크루지의 동료 견습생들his fellow apprentices이었다. 그들은 흥겨워하며enjoy themselves 춤을 추고dance 있었다. 심지어 스크루지 자신도 춤을 추며 즐거운 시간을 보내고 있었다.

GRAMMAR POINT

where (관계부사) ⇨ 장소를 나타내는 명사 뒤에 오며, where가 이끄는 관계절은 그 명사를 수식함.

- Suddenly, they were standing in *the country* **where** he had lived as a boy.

  갑자기 그들은 스크루지가 소년이었을 때 살던 시골에 서 있었다.

- This time, Scrooge saw *the office* **where** he had first worked.

  이번에 스크루지는 자신이 처음 일했던 사무실을 보았다.

A Christmas Carol

[p. 154-155]

At the end of the party, / Mr. and Mrs. Fezziwig said / "Merry Christmas" / to everybody.

"It's old Mr. Fezziwig's office. He was such a happy, kind boss."

The ghost looked at Scrooge / and asked, "What's the matter?"

"I was thinking of my clerk, / Bob Cratchit. I wish / I'd said something to him / yesterday," said Scrooge.

The ghost smiled again. "Come, / my time grows short," said the ghost. "Another Christmas," he said.

The scene changed. Scrooge again / saw himself. He was older now / —a man in the prime of life. He was sitting / with a young woman. She had once been his girlfriend. She was crying.

"No, it's too late. You have another love now," she said.

"What? What other love?" Scrooge asked.

"Money. / You love only money now, / not me. Goodbye."

"No more! Ghost! Please remove me / from this place," Scrooge cried / in pain.

"No, Scrooge. I told you / that these were shadows / of the things / that have been," said the ghost. "There is / one more scene."

Years had passed / since the last scene. Scrooge saw a beautiful woman / smiling with her children / in a warm house. The door opened, / and the father came in. His arms / were full of Christmas presents. He gave one / to each of his children. The children laughed and shouted / as they opened the presents.

Scrooge looked at the mother. She was the woman / from Scrooge's past. She had left him / because he had been more interested in money / than in her. Looking at the happy family, / Scrooge realized / what he had lost.

"No more! Leave me, ghost," shouted Scrooge.

"This was your life. These things happened / and cannot be changed. Only the future / can be changed," the ghost said.

"Please, ghost, / I cannot bear it. Haunt me / no longer!" Scrooge shouted sadly.

As Scrooge struggled with the spirit, / he suddenly became exhausted. He was overcome by drowsiness / and sank into a heavy sleep.

- **boss** 상사, 사장   - **scene** 장면   - **the prime of life** 인생의 전성기, 장년기   - **remove** 내보내다, 제거하다
- **in pain** 고통스럽게   - **shadow** 그림자   - **be interested in** ~에 관심 있다   - **bear** 참다, 견디다
- **haunt** (유령이) ~에 나타나다, (계속) 따라다니다   - **struggle with** ~와 싸우다, ~와 씨름하다   - **exhausted** 녹초가 된, 기운이 빠진   - **overcome by** ~에 압도된, ~에 꼼짝 못하는   - **drowsiness** 졸음   - **sink into** ~에 빠지다

CLOSE UP

1. **grows short** 줄어들고 있다 / **became exhausted** 진이 빠지게 되었다
   〈grow/become + 형용사〉는 '~하게 되다'라는 뜻으로 상태의 변화를 나타냄. grow는 느리면서 점진적인 변화를 나타낸다.
2. **remove me from this place** 나를 이곳에서 벗어나게 해 주시오
   〈remove ~ from...〉은 '~을 ...에서 내보내다/제거하다'라는 의미.
3. **had been more interested in money than in her** 그녀보다 돈에 더 관심이 있었다
   〈be interested in ~〉은 '~에 관심을 가지다'라는 의미. 여기서 money와 her는 관심의 대상으로 서로 비교되고 있음.
4. **was overcome by drowsiness** 졸음을 이기지 못했다
   〈be overcome by ~〉는 '~을 이겨 내지 못하다', '~에 꼼짝 못하다'라는 의미.

파티가 끝날 무렵 페지위그 부부가 모두에게 "메리 크리스마스"라고 인사했다.

"옛날 페지위그 씨의 사무실이군. 참 행복하고 친절한 사장님such a happy, kind boss이셨지."

유령이 스크루지를 보며 물었다. "뭐가 문제인가what's the matter?"

"내 서기인 봅 크래칫 생각을 하고think of my clerk, Bob Cratchit 있었소. 어제 그에게 무슨 말이라도 했더라면say something to him 좋았을 텐데." 스크루지가 말했다.

유령이 다시 미소를 지었다. "가자come, 내 시간my time이 줄어들고 있다grow shorter." 유령이 말했다. "다른 크리스마스another Christmas로 가자." 하고 유령이 말했다.

장면the scene이 바뀌었다change. 스크루지는 다시 자신의 모습을 보았다see himself. 이제 그는 나이가 좀 더 들어서be older 한참 인생의 전성기에 있는in the prime of life 사나이였다. 그는 젊은 여자와 함께with a young woman 앉아 있었다. 여자는 한때 그의 여자친구his girlfriend였다. 그녀는 울고cry 있었다.

"안 돼요. 너무 늦었어요. 당신한테는 이제 다른 사랑이 있잖아요have another love." 여자가 말했다.

"뭐라고what? 다른 사랑이라니what other love?" 스크루지가 물었다.

"돈 말이에요. 당신은 이제 내가 아니라 오직 돈만 사랑하잖아요love only money. 잘 있어요."

"이제 그만no more! 유령이여! 나를 이곳에서 벗어나게 해 주시오remove me from this place." 스크루지가 고통에 차서in pain 소리쳤다.

"아니, 스크루지. 이것들은 과거에 있던 일들the things that have been의 그림자shadows라고 내가 얘기했지 않나." 유령이 말했다. "한 장면이 더one more scene 있다."

마지막 장면 이후 세월이 흘렀다. 스크루지는 어떤 아름다운 여인a beautiful woman이 따뜻한 집에서in a warm house 아이들과 함께with her children 미소 짓고 있는 모습을 보았다. 문이 열리고 아버지the father가 안으로 들어왔다come in. 그의 팔his arms에는 크리스마스 선물이 한가득 들려 있었다be full of Christmas presents. 아버지는 아이들 각각에게to each of his children 선물을 하나씩 주었다give one. 아이들은 선물을 열어 보며open the presents 웃고 소리쳤다laugh and shout.

스크루지는 그 어머니를 바라보았다look at the mother. 스크루지의 그 과거의 여인the woman from Scrooge's past이었다. 스크루지가 그 여자보다 돈에 더 관심을 보여서be more interested in money 그를 떠났던leave him 여인이었다. 그 행복한 가정을 보고 스크루지는 자신이 무엇을 잃었는지 깨달았다.

"이제 그만! 유령이여, 내게서 떠나 주시오leave me." 스크루지가 소리쳤다.

"이게 그대의 인생your life이었다. 이런 일들these thins은 이미 일어났고happen 바뀔 수도 없다cannot be changed. 오직 미래만이only the future 바뀔 수 있지can be changed." 유령이 말했다.

"제발, 유령이여. 난 견딜 수가 없소cannot bear it. 더는 내게 나타나지haunt me 마시오no longer!" 스크루지가 애처롭게 소리쳤다.

스크루지는 유령과 씨름하느라struggle with the spirit 갑자기 진이 빠져 버렸다become exhausted. 그는 졸음을 이기지 못하고be overcome by drowsiness 깊은 잠에 빠져들었다sink into a heavy sleep.

GRAMMAR POINT

I wish ~ (가정법)

⇨ I wish 뒤에 나오는 종속절에 '가정법 과거완료' 동사가 쓰이면 과거 사실과 반대되는 소망을 나타냄.

- **I wish I'd said** something to him yesterday. 어제 그에게 무슨 말이라도 했더라면 좋았을 텐데.

- **I wish I'd given** some money to that poor boy. 그 불쌍한 아이에게 돈을 좀 주었더라면 좋았을걸.

A Christmas Carol 149

[p. 156–157]

Scrooge awoke / in his bedroom. It was one in the morning again / —time for the second ghost. He looked around his bedroom. There was nobody / there. He went to the door of his living room.

"Come in, / Ebenezer Scrooge," said a voice.

He opened the door / and saw something very surprising. The room looked so different. The walls were covered with Christmas trees. Heaped upon the floor / were / turkeys, geese, pigs, sausages, plum puddings, chestnuts, apples, and great bowls of punch. Upon the couch / in the center of the room / sat a happy giant, / holding a glowing torch / which lit the room.

"Come in. Come in. I am / the Ghost of Christmas Present," said the giant.

"Ghost, / I learned a lot / from the ghost / last night. Tonight, / if you have / something to teach me, / take me / anywhere you want," said Scrooge.

"Touch my robe," said the giant.

Scrooge did / as he was told. Scrooge found / they were walking / in a London street / on Christmas morning. The ghost took him / to the Cratchits' house. At the door, / the ghost smiled and stopped / to bless Bob Cratchit's dwelling.

Mrs. Cratchit, Bob's wife, / was preparing their Christmas dinner. Just then / Bob Cratchit was coming back from church / with the youngest son, Tiny Tim. Tiny Tim was ill / and used a crutch / to walk.

The family sat down / to eat their meal. They had only / one goose, some potatoes, and a small Christmas pudding. It seemed very small / for such a large family, / but nobody complained. Though it was a very simple Christmas meal, / they were still as happy / as if they had eaten a king's meal. After dinner, / all the Cratchit family / gathered around the fire. Bob proposed, "A Merry Christmas / to us all, my dears. God bless us!"

- **surprising** 놀라운 • **be covered with** ~로 덮여 있다 • **be heaped upon** ~에 수북이 쌓이다
- **bowl of punch** 펀치가 담긴 그릇 • **couch** (긴) 소파 • **glowing torch** 타오르는 횃불, 눈부시게 빛나는 횃불
- **light** ~에 불을 밝히다, ~에 빛을 비추다 • **find** 발견하다, 깨닫다 • **the Cratchits** 크래칫 일가, 크래칫네 (= the Cratchit) • **bless** 축복하다 • **crutch** 목발 • **complain** 불평하다 • **as if** 마치 ~인 것처럼 • **gather** 모이다 • **propose** 제안하다

CLOSE UP

1 were covered with Christmas trees 크리스마스트리로 덮여 있었다
〈be covered with ~〉는 '~으로 덮여 있다'라는 의미.

2 Heaped upon the floor were turkeys, geese, pigs, ...
바닥에는 칠면조 고기, 거위 고기, 돼지고기,…… 등이 잔뜩 쌓여 있었다
정상적인 어순은 〈Turkeys, geese, pigs,... were heaped upon the floor.〉인데, heaped upon the floor가 문장 앞으로 나가면서 주어(turkeys, geese, pigs,...)와 동사(were)가 도치되었다. 주어가 너무 길거나 새로운 주어를 소개할 때 이와 같은 도치 구조가 쓰이는데, 문학이나 설명문 등에서는 흔히 볼 수 있는 구조이다.

3 Upon the couch in the center of the room sat a happy giant
거실 한복판의 소파 위에는 행복한 거인이 앉아 있었다
역시 도치된 문장. 정상적인 어순은 〈A happy giant sat upon the couch in the center of the room.〉이다.

스크루지는 자신의 침실에서in his bedroom 잠을 깼다awake. 다시 새벽 1시one in the morning였다. 두 번째 유령이 나타나기로 한 시각time for the second ghost이었다. 스크루지는 침실을 두리번거렸다look around his bedroom. 거기엔 아무도 없었다nobody. 그는 거실 문으로 갔다go to the door of his living room.

"들어와라come in, 에브니저 스크루지Ebenezer Scrooge." 웬 목소리가 말했다.

스크루지가 문을 열었더니open the door 아주 놀라운 광경something very surprising이 보였다. 거실이 너무 달라 보였다look so different. 벽the walls은 크리마스트리로 덮여 있었다be covered with Christmas trees. 바닥에는upon the floor 칠면조 고기turkeys, 거위 고기geese, 돼지고기pigs, 소시지sausages, 자두 푸딩plum puddings, 밤chestnuts, 사과apples, 펀치가 담긴 큰 그릇들great bowls of punch이 잔뜩 쌓여 있었다be heaped. 거실 한복판의in the center of the room 소파 위에는upon the couch 행복한 거인a happy giant이 앉아 있었는데, 거실을 밝히는light the room 타오르는 횃불a glowing torch을 들고hold 있었다.

"들어와라. 들어와. 나는 현재의 크리스마스 유령the Ghost of Christmas Present이다." 거인이 말했다.

"유령이여, 난 어젯밤에 온 유령으로부터 많은 걸 배웠소learn a lot. 오늘 밤 당신이 내게 가르칠 게 something to teach me 있다면 당신이 원하는 곳 어디든지anywhere you want 나를 데려가시오take me." 스크루지가 말했다.

"내 옷을 만져라touch my robe." 거인이 말했다.

스크루지는 시키는 대로as he is told 했다. 그러자 스크루지는 자신들이 크리스마스 아침에on Christmas morning 어느 런던 거리를 걷고walk in a London street 있다는 걸 깨달았다. 유령은 그를 크래칫네 집으로 데려갔다take him to the Cratchits' house. 문 앞에서at the door 유령은 미소를 지으며 멈춰 서서smile and stop 봅 크래칫의 집에 축복을 빌었다bless Bob Cratchit's dwelling.

봅의 아내Bob's wife인 크래칫 부인Mrs. Cratchit이 크리스마스 만찬을 준비하고prepare their Christmas dinner 있었다. 바로 그때 봅 크래칫은 막내 아들the youngest son 타이니 팀Tiny Tim과 함께 교회에서 돌아오고come back from church 있었다. 타이니 팀은 아파서be ill 목발을 짚고use a crutch 걸었다.

식구들이 식사를 하기eat their meal 위해 자리에 앉았다. 그들에게는 거위 한 마리one goose, 감자 몇 알some potatoes, 그리고 조그만 크리스마스 푸딩 하나a small Christmas pudding밖에는 없었다. 그런 대가족이 먹기에는for such a large family 아주 적은 양 같았지만seem very small 아무도 불평하지 않았다. 아주 소박한 크리스마스 식사a very simple Christmas meal였지만, 그래도 그들은 흡사 왕의 식사를 한eat a king's meal 것처럼 행복해했다. 저녁식사 후after dinner 크래칫 식구들은 모두all the Cratchit family 난로 주위에 모였다gather around the fire. 봅이 이렇게 말했다. "사랑하는 우리 가족 모두에게to us all 메리 크리스마스. 하느님, 우리 가족을 축복하소서bless us!"

GRAMMAR POINT

such a/an + 형용사 + 명사 : 그렇게 ~한 … ⇨ 그 정도가 높다는 것을 나타냄.

- It seemed very small for **such a large family**. 그런 대가족이 먹기에는 아주 적어 보였다.
- Mr. Fezziwig was **such a happy, kind boss**. 페지위그 씨는 참으로 행복하고 친절한 사장님이었지.

[p. 158–159]

"God bless us every one!" said Tiny Tim. Tiny Tim sat / very close to his father's side / upon his little stool. He was very sick. Bob held his withered little hand / in his / as if he loved the child / and wished to keep him by his side, / but he dreaded / that Tiny Tim might be taken from him.

"Will he be here / next Christmas?" Scrooge asked.

"With help," replied the ghost.

Scrooge raised his head / when he heard his name spoken.

"Let's drink / to Mr. Scrooge," said Bob.

"To Scrooge?" Mrs. Cratchit's face reddened, / and she said, "Why should we drink / to that old, stingy, unfeeling man?"

"My dear," was Bob's mild answer, "it's Christmas Day."

"Well, you are right. I'll drink to him. But nothing we do / could make that mean old man / feel happy or merry," said Mrs. Cratchit.

The mention of his name / cast a dark shadow / on the party, / which lasted / for a full five minutes. After some time, / the Cratchits became cheerful again. They were not a handsome family. They were not well dressed. But they were happy, grateful, and pleased with one another.

The ghost took Scrooge away / from the Cratchits' house. The two of them / walked through the streets of London. People were going to parties / with their friends and families. Suddenly, / they were in a cold, dark, empty place. They looked through the window / of a small house. Inside, / there was / a big family / in a very small room. Yet they were happy / and were singing Christmas carols together.

Scrooge asked, "Who are they?"

"They are poor miners," answered the ghost. "They have hard lives / working inside the Earth / to dig up coal."

Slowly, / the scene vanished, / and Scrooge suddenly heard / a hearty laugh. It was his nephew Fred's house. Fred was telling everyone / about his visit to his uncle.

- **stool** 스툴, 등받이가 없는 의자 • **withered** 메마른, 여위고 약한 • **dread** 몹시 두려워하다 • **be taken from** ~에게서 빼앗기다 • **redden** 빨개지다 • **stingy** 구두쇠의, 인색한 • **unfeeling** 무정한, 냉정한 • **mention** 언급, 거론 • **cast a shadow** 그림자를 드리우다 • **last** 지속되다 • **cheerful** 밝은, 명랑한 • **well dressed** 잘 차려 입은 • **grateful** 감사하는 • **pleased with** ~에 만족하는, ~에 기뻐하는 • **take ~ away from...** ~을 …에서 데려가다 • **look through** ~을 통해 들여다보다 • **Christmas carol** 크리스마스 캐럴 • **miner** 광부 • **dig up** ~을 (땅에서) 파내다 • **vanish** 사라지다

CLOSE UP

1 **Let's drink to Mr. Scrooge.** 스크루지 씨를 위해 건배하자.
〈drink to ~〉는 '~을 위해 건배하다'라는 의미.

2 **nothing we do could make that mean old man feel happy or merry**
우리가 하는 어떤 것도 그 못된 영감을 행복하거나 즐겁게 만들 수 없을 거예요
주어는 nothing we do이고, 동사는 could make이다. that mean old man은 목적어, feel happy or merry는 목적보어. 즉, 〈make + 목적어 + 목적보어〉의 구조를 가진 문장으로 '~을 …하게 만들다'라고 해석하면 된다.

"하느님, 우리 식구 한 사람 한 사람을 축복해 주세요bless us every one!" 타이니 팀이 말했다. 타이니 팀은 아버지 곁에 바짝 붙어서close to his father's side 그의 작은 의자에upon his little stool 앉아 있었다. 그 아이는 매우 아팠다. 밥은 그 아이를 사랑해서love the child 자신의 곁에 계속 두고keep him by his side 싶은 듯, 자신의 손으로 아들의 작고 여윈 손his withered little hand을 잡고hold 있었지만, 타이니 팀이 자신의 곁에서 떠나게 될까be taken from him 봐 두려웠다dread.

"저 아이가 내년 크리스마스에도next Christmas 이곳에 (살아) 있겠소be here?" 스크루지가 물었다.

"도움을 받는다면with help." 유령이 대답했다.

스크루지는 자신의 이름이 거론되는 걸 듣고hear his name spoken 고개를 들었다raise his head.

"스크루지 씨를 위해 건배하자drink to Mr. Scrooge." 밥이 말했다.

"스크루지를 위해서라고요?" 크래칫 부인의 얼굴이 붉어졌다. "우리가 왜 그 늙고 인색하고 인정머리 없는old, stingy, unfeeling 사람을 위해 건배해야 해요?" 하고 부인이 말했다.

"여보, 크리스마스 날이잖소." 밥의 부드러운 대답이었다.

"뭐, 당신 말이 맞네요. 그를 위해 건배하죠. 하지만 우리가 하는 어떤 것도 그 못된 영감that mean old man을 행복하거나 즐겁게feel happy or merry 해 줄 수 없을 거예요." 크래칫 부인이 말했다.

스크루지의 이름이 거론되자the mention of his name 파티에는on the party 어두운 그림자가 드리워졌고cast a dark shadow, 그런 분위기가 5분이나 계속for a full five minutes 지속됐다last. 얼마 후 after some time 크래칫 가족the Cratchits은 다시 쾌활해졌다become cheerful. 그들은 잘난 가족a handsome family은 아니었다. 좋은 옷을 입고 있지도be well dressed 않았다. 하지만 행복하고 감사해하며be grateful 서로에게 만족했다be pleased with one another.

유령이 크래칫네 집에서from the Cratchits' house 스크루지를 데리고 떠났다take Scrooge away. 그 둘the two of them은 런던 거리를 거닐었다walk through the streets of London. 사람들이 친구들이나 식구들과 함께with their friends and families 파티에 가고go to parties 있었다. 갑자기 둘은 춥고 어두운 공터a cold, dark, empty place에 있었다. 둘은 어떤 작은 집a small house의 창문을 들여다보았다look through the window. 안에는 아주 작은 방에in a very small room 대식구a big family가 모여 있었다. 그래도 그들은 행복했고 함께 크리스마스 캐럴을 부르고sing Christmas carols 있었다.

스크루지가 물었다. "이들은 누구요?"

"가난한 광부들poor miners이다." 유령이 대답했다. "그들은 석탄을 캐느라dig up coal 땅속에서 일하며work inside the Earth 어렵게 살고 있다have hard lives."

서서히 그 장면the scene이 사라지고vanish, 스크루지에게 갑자기 호탕한 웃음소리가 들렸다hear a hearty laugh. 그의 조카 프레드의 집Fred's house이었다. 프레드는 모든 사람에게 자기 삼촌을 방문했던his visit to his uncle 얘기를 하고 있었다.

GRAMMAR POINT

which (관계대명사) ⇨ 앞에 나온 절의 전체 내용을 대신 받기도 함.

- The mention of his name cast a dark shadow on the party, **which** lasted for a full five minutes.
  그의 이름이 거론되자 파티에는 어두운 그림자가 드리워졌고, 그런 분위기가 5분이나 계속 지속됐다.

- He visited Fred's house, **which** pleased everyone there.
  그는 프레드의 집을 방문했는데, 그것이 그곳에 있던 모든 이를 기쁘게 했다.

A Christmas Carol

[p. 160–161]

"So when I said 'Merry Christmas' to him, / he replied 'Bah, humbug!'" said Fred. Everyone laughed.

"He's a strange old man," said Fred. "He is rich, / but he doesn't do anything good / with his money. He even lives / like he's poor. I invite him / to have Christmas dinner with us / every year, / but he never comes. Someday, / perhaps / he will change his mind. And someday / perhaps / he will pay poor Bob Cratchit more money / as well."

For the rest of the evening, / Scrooge and the ghost / watched his nephew and friends / enjoy their Christmas party. Then, / the clock struck twelve. Scrooge looked around for the ghost, / but he saw the ghost / no more. Then, / he remembered Marley's prediction, / and he lifted his eyes.

Scrooge saw a solemn phantom coming / like a mist along the ground / toward him. Unlike the others, / he could not see / this one's face or body. It was covered / from head to toe / in a long black garment. The only visible part / of the phantom / was one outstretched hand.

The phantom moved / slowly and silently. As it came near him, / Scrooge bent down upon his knee, / for the ghost seemed to scatter / gloom and mystery / as it moved. The ghost did not speak at all.

"I am in the presence of / the Ghost of Christmas Yet to Come," said Scrooge. "You are about to show me the things / which have not happened yet, / but will happen / in the time before us," Scrooge said, / looking at the strange ghost. "Is that so, / Spirit?"

The ghost silently moved its head a little / and pointed with its hand. Scrooge suddenly found himself / in the middle of the city. The ghost stopped / beside a group of businessmen. Scrooge could hear / some of them talking.

"I don't know much about it. I only know / he's dead," said one great fat man.

"When did he die?" inquired another.

"Last night, / I believe."

"What has he done / with his money?" asked a red-faced gentleman.

"I haven't heard," responded the first man. "He didn't leave it to me / though. That's / all I know."

"At least / his funeral will be very cheap," said one man.

- **change one's mind** 마음을 바꾸다 • **strike** (종 등이) 치다 • **prediction** 예측, 예견 • **solemn** 근엄한, 엄숙한 • **phantom** 유령 • **mist** 엷은 안개 • **unlike** ~와 달리 • **from head to toe** 머리부터 발끝까지 • **garment** 의복, 옷 • **visible** 볼 수 있는, 보이는 • **outstretched** 밖으로 뻗어 나온 • **bend down upon one's knee** 무릎을 꿇다 • **scatter** 흩뿌리다, 흩어지게 하다 • **gloom** 음울, 암울 • **mystery** 신비로움 • **point** 가리키다 • **funeral** 장례식

CLOSE UP

1 Unlike the others 다른 유령들과 달리
unlike는 like(~처럼, ~와 비슷하게)의 반대말이다. '~와 달리', '~와 다르게'라는 의미.

2 I am in the presence of the Ghost of Christmas Yet to Come.
내가 미래의 크리스마스 유령 앞에 있는 거로군.
〈be in the presence of ~〉는 '~의 면전에/앞에 있다'라는 의미.
〈yet to come〉은 '아직 오지 않은', '앞으로 다가올'이라는 의미로, 여기서는 '미래(future)'를 뜻한다.

"그래서 내가 삼촌한테 '메리 크리스마스'라고 했더니, '흥, 허튼소리!'라고 대답하시지 뭐야." 하고 프레드가 말했다. 모든 사람이 웃었다.

"이상한 노인 양반a strange old man이지 뭐야." 프레드가 말했다. "부자인데도 그 돈으로with his money 좋은 일을 하나도 하지 않는단don't do anything good 말이야. 심지어 가난한 사람인 것처럼 산다니까. 내가 해마다every year 우리와 함께with us 크리스마스 만찬을 드시자고have Christmas dinner 청하는데도invite him 절대로 안 오셔never come. 언젠가는someday 아마 마음을 바꾸시겠지change his mind. 그리고 언젠가는 어쩌면 가엾은 밥 크래칫한테도 봉급을 더 주시겠지pay more money."

남은 저녁 내내 스크루지와 유령은 그의 조카와 친구들his nephew and friends이 크리스마스 파티를 즐기는enjoy their Christmas party 모습을 지켜보았다. 그러고 나서 시계가 12시를 쳤다strike twelve. 스크루지가 두리번거리며 유령을 찾아보았지만, 유령은 이제 보이지 않았다. 그때 스크루지는 말리의 예언이 떠올라서remember Marley's prediction 눈을 치켜떴다lift his eyes.

스크루지는 근엄한 유령a solemn phantom이 지면에 낀 엷은 안개a mist along the ground처럼 자기 쪽으로 오는 걸 보았다. 다른 유령들과 달리unlike the others, 이 유령의 얼굴이나 몸통은 알아볼 수 없었다. 이 유령은 머리부터 발끝까지from head to toe 기다란 검은 옷에in a long black garment 덮여 있었다be covered. 그 유령에게서 유일하게 보이는 부분the only visible part이라곤 뻗어 나온 한 손one outstretched hand이 전부였다.

유령은 천천히 말 없이slowly and silently 움직였다. 유령이 자기에게 가까이 다가오자come near him 스크루지는 무릎을 꿇었다bend down upon his knee. 유령이 움직이면서 우울함과 신비로움gloom and mystery을 흩뿌리는scatter 것 같았기 때문이다. 유령은 전혀 말을 하지 않았다do not speak.

"내가 미래의 크리스마스 유령the Ghost of Christmas Yet to Come 앞에 있는 거로군." 스크루지가 말했다. "아직 일어나지는 않았지만 앞으로in the time before us 일어날 일들을 이제 내게 보여 주려는 show me 거겠지." 스크루지는 그 이상한 유령을 바라보며 말했다. "그런 거요, 유령이여?"

유령이 잠자코 머리를 살짝 움직이더니move its head a little 손으로 가리켰다point with its hand. 스크루지는 별안간 자신이 도시 한복판에in the middle of the city 있는 걸 깨달았다. 유령이 한 무리의 사업가들a group of businessmen 옆에 멈춰 섰다. 스크루지는 그들 중 몇 명이 하는 말을 들을 수 있었다.

"나도 그 일에 대해 자세히는 모릅니다don't know much about it. 그가 죽었다는 것만 알죠." 덩치 크고 뚱뚱한 사내가 말했다.

"언제 죽었는데요?" 다른 사내가 물었다.

"어젯밤인 것 같아요."

"그는 자기 돈을 어떻게 했답니까?" 얼굴이 붉은 신사가 물었다.

"들은 바 없어요haven't heard." 맨 처음 사내가 대답했다. "그러나 나한테는 남기지 않았죠don't leave it to me. 그게 내가 아는 전부all I know예요."

"적어도at least 그의 장례식his funeral은 매우 싸게 치르겠군요be very cheap." 한 사내가 말했다.

GRAMMAR POINT

for + 주어 + 동사 : 왜냐하면 ~이므로

⇨ 나중에 부가적으로 덧붙이는 이유를 나타냄. 이때 for가 이끄는 절은 항상 문장 뒤에 오며, 그 앞에는 쉼표를 넣는다.

- Scrooge bent down upon his knee, **for** the ghost seemed to scatter gloom and mystery.
  스크루지는 무릎을 꿇었다. 유령이 우울함과 신비로움을 흩뿌리는 것 같았기 때문이다.

- I didn't follow them, **for** something dangerous was likely to happen.
  나는 그들을 따라가지 않았다. 뭔가 위험한 일이 생길 것 같아서였다.

[p. 162-163]

"That's true. He had no friends. No one liked him, / so nobody will go to his funeral."

Scrooge did not understand / why the ghost wanted him / to listen to this conversation, / but he knew / the ghost would not answer him, / so he did not ask.

They left the busy scene / and went to an obscure part of the town. The streets were dark and small. They visited a dirty shop / full of horrible old things / you can imagine / —iron, old rags, bottles, clothes, and bones. It was a place / where people came to sell their things / when they needed money.

Scrooge watched / as three people brought things / to sell to the shopkeeper. They were from the same dead man's house.

"What have you got / to sell?" asked the shopkeeper.

One woman took out / some towels, silver teaspoons, and other small things, / and said, "He doesn't need these now."

"No indeed, ma'am," answered the shopkeeper.

"Take a look at these," said the other woman. "Bed curtains and blankets. He isn't likely to catch a cold / without them / now."

Scrooge listened to this dialogue / in horror. "Ghost, I see. The case of this unhappy man / might be my own."

The scene had suddenly changed, / and Scrooge found himself / in another terrible room. There was a bare bed / with no blankets / or curtains around it. A pale light from outside / fell straight upon the bed. On it, / unwatched, unwept, and uncared for, / was the dead body / of the unknown man. He was covered by a thin sheet.

The ghost, / as silent as ever, / merely pointed at the body. Scrooge realized / that the ghost wanted him / to look at the face of the dead man, / but he could not do it.

"I cannot look at his face," cried Scrooge. "Let me see some tenderness / connected with this death, / or this dark chamber / will be forever in my memory."

The scene changed to another home. A woman stood up / as her husband entered the room. "Have you gotten any news?" she asked.

- **obscure** 잘 알려지지 않은, 무명의 • **horrible** 끔찍한, 지독한 • **bone** 뼈 • **shopkeeper** 가게 주인 • **take out** 꺼내다 • **indeed** 실로, 정말로 • **catch a cold** 감기에 걸리다 • **in horror** 무서워서, 오싹하여 • **case** 경우, 상황, 처지 • **terrible** 지독한, 소름끼치는 • **bare** 아무것도 안 덮인, 맨~ • **pale light** 희미한 불빛 • **unwatched** 지켜보는 이 없는 • **unwept** 슬퍼할 이 없는 • **uncared for** 돌보는 이 없는 • **dead body** 사체 • **be covered by** ~으로 덮이다 • **sheet** 천 • **point at** ~을 가리키다 • **tenderness** 부드러움, 친절, 다정함 • **connected with** ~와 연결된 • **chamber** ~실, 방 • **stand up** 일어서다

CLOSE UP

1 **On it, ..., was the dead body of the unknown man.** 그 위에는 … 그 모르는 사내의 시신이 놓여 있었다.
부사구 on it이 문장 앞으로 나오고, 주어(the dead body of the unknown man)와 동사(was)가 도치된 문장.

2 **as silent as ever** 여전히 침묵을 지키며
⟨as ~ as ever⟩는 '여전히/변함없이 ~한'이라는 의미. ex) He is as greedy as ever.(그는 여전히 탐욕스럽다.)

156 Step 5

"맞아요. 그에게는 친구가 없었어요have no friends. 아무도no one 그를 좋아하지like him 않았으니 아무도nobody 그의 장례식에 가지go to his funeral 않겠죠."

스크루지는 유령이 왜 자신이 이 대화를 듣길listen to this conversation 바라는지 이해하지 못했지만, 유령이 대답하지 않으리라는 걸 알았기 때문에 물어보지 않았다.

둘은 그 분주한 장면을 떠나leave the busy scene 도시의 잘 알려지지 않은 어느 지역an obscure part of the town으로 갔다. 거리는 어둡고 좁았다be dark and small. 둘은 다리미iron, 낡은 넝마old rags, 병bottles, 옷clothes, 뼈다귀bones 등 상상할 수 있는 온갖 끔찍하고 낡은 물건들horrible old things이 가득 찬 어떤 지저분한 가게를 찾아갔다visit a dirty shop. 그곳은 사람들이 돈이 필요할need money 때 자신들의 물건을 팔러sell their things 오는 곳이었다.

스크루지는 세 사람three people이 가게 주인에게to the shopkeeper 팔 물건들을 가져오는bring things 걸 지켜보았다. 그들은 아까와 똑같은 그 죽은 사람의 집에서 온 것이었다.

"뭘 파시겠소?" 가게 주인이 물었다.

한 여자가 수건 몇 장some towels과 은 찻숟가락silver teaspoons, 그리고 다른 잡동사니들other small things을 꺼내며take out 말했다. "그 사람한테는 이제 이것들이 필요 없어요."

"그렇고 말고요, 부인." 가게 주인이 대답했다.

"이것들 좀 보세요take a look at these." 다른 여자가 말했다. "침대 커튼bed curtains과 담요blankets 예요. 그 사람은 이제 이것들이 없어도without them 감기에 걸릴catch a cold 것 같지 않네요."

스크루지는 공포에 질린 채in horror 이 대화를 들었다listen to this dialogue. "유령이여, 알겠소. 이 불행한 사내의 처지the case of this unhappy man가 내 처지가 될 수도 있다는 거잖소."

장면이 갑자기 바뀌었고, 스크루지는 자신이 소름 끼치는 다른 방에in another terrible room 와 있는 걸 알았다. 담요도 없고 주위에 커튼도 없이 덩그러니 놓인 맨 침대a bare bed가 하나 있었다. 밖에서 들어오는 희미한 빛a pale light이 곧장 침대에 비쳤다fall upon the bed. 침대 위에는 지켜보는 사람도 없고unwatched, 슬퍼해 주는 사람도 없고unwept, 돌보는 사람도 없는uncared for, 그 모르는 사내the unknown man의 시신the dead body이 놓여 있었다. 시신은 얇은 천으로by a thin sheet 덮여 있었다be covered.

유령은 여전히 침묵을 지키며as silent as ever 그저 시신을 가리킬point at the body 뿐이었다. 스크루지는 유령이 자신에게 원하는 게 죽은 사내the dead man의 얼굴을 보는look at the face 거라는 걸 깨달았지만 그렇게 할 수가 없었다.

"그의 얼굴을 보지 못하겠소." 스크루지가 소리쳤다. "이 죽음과 관련하여connected with this death 어떤 따뜻한 구석이 있다면some tenderness 좀 보여 주시오let me see. 안 그러면or 이 어두운 방this dark chamber이 내 뇌리에in my memory 영원히forever 남을 것 같소."

장면이 또 다른 집으로 바뀌었다change to another home. 어떤 여인이 남편이 방으로 들어오자enter the room 자리에서 일어섰다stand up. "무슨 소식any news이라도 있나요?" 여인이 물었다.

GRAMMAR POINT

be likely to ~ : ~할 것 같다   **it is likely that ~** : ~할 것 같다

⇨ ⟨be likely to ~⟩는 ⟨it is likely that ~⟩으로 바꿔 쓸 수 있다.
　⟨be not likely to ~⟩ 하면 '~할 것 같지 않다'라는 의미.

- He **isn't likely to** catch a cold without them now.
  = **It isn't likely that** he will catch a cold without them now.
  그는 이제 이것들이 없어도 감기에 걸릴 것 같지 않군요.

A Christmas Carol

[p. 164–165]

"When I visited him / to find out / if we could pay the money / one week later," he answered, "an old woman told me / he was dead."

"That's great news," she said. "I'm sorry for saying that. I mean / that now we have time to get the money / that we have to pay."

"No, ghost! Show me someone / who's sorry about a death, / not someone / who's happy because of a death," shouted Scrooge.

The ghost took him / to poor Bob Cratchit's house. Scrooge saw the family / sitting quietly around the fire. They were talking about Tiny Tim.

"I met Fred, / Mr. Scrooge's nephew," said Bob. "And he said / that he was very sorry / to hear about Tiny Tim."

Bob turned to his family / and said, "We must never forget / what a good boy Tiny Tim was."

"No, never father," shouted all the children.

Then, / Bob Cratchit broke down / all at once. He couldn't help it / as the tears flowed down his face.

"Ghost," said Scrooge, "something informs me / that our parting moment / is at hand. Tell me. Who was the dead man / we saw?"

The Ghost of Christmas Yet to Come / took Scrooge to a churchyard. The ghost stood among the graves / and pointed down to one. Scrooge crept toward it, / trembling as he went, / and followed the finger / to read the name on the neglected grave: EBENEZER SCROOGE.

"Am I that man / who lay upon the bed? No, ghost! Oh no, no. I am not / the man I was. I will not be / the man I must have been / but for this evening. Why show me this / if I am past all hope? Assure me / that I may yet change these shadows."

- **be sorry about** ~을 유감스럽게 생각하다 • **break down** (감정을 주체하지 못하고) 허물어지다, 울음을 주체하지 못하다 • **all at once** 갑자기 • **cannot help it** 어쩔 수 없다 • **inform** 알리다 • **parting moment** 헤어질 시간 • **at hand** 가까이에 있는 • **churchyard** 교회 경내 (흔히 묘지로 쓰임) • **grave** 무덤 • **creep** 살금살금 움직이다, 살살 기다 • **neglected** 방치된 • **lie** 누워 있다 • **be past all hope** 전혀 가망이 없다 • **assure** 확언하다, 장담하다

CLOSE UP

1. **to find out if we could pay the money one week later** 한 주 늦게 돈을 지불해도 되겠는지 알아보려고
   여기서 if는 '~인지 아닌지'의 의미. 문맥에 따라 적절한 의미를 파악하도록 하자.

2. **he was very sorry to hear about Tiny Tim** 그는 타이니 팀에 대한 소식을 듣고 매우 안타까워했다
   sorry는 '미안하다'는 뜻 외에 '가엾어하는', '안타까워하는', '유감스러워하는'의 의미로도 많이 쓰인다.

3. **our parting moment is at hand** 우리가 헤어질 순간이 다가왔다
   〈~ be at hand〉는 '~이 가까이 다가왔다'라는 의미.

4. **the man I was** 과거의 그 사내 / **the man I must have been** 보나마나 그렇게 되었을 법한 그런 사내
   was는 be동사의 과거형이므로, 전자는 과거에 어떤 사람이었는가를 뜻한다. been은 be동사의 p.p.형이다. 〈must have p.p.〉는 '~였음에 틀림없다(강한 추측)'라는 뜻이므로, 후자는 그런 사람이 되었을 거라는 추측을 나타낸다.

5. **but for this evening** 오늘 밤이 없었더라면 (오늘 밤이 아니었더라면)
   〈but for ~〉는 '~이 없다면/없었더라면' 또는 '~이 아니라면/아니었더라면'이라는 의미.
   ex) I would have failed but for your help. (네 도움이 없었더라면 나는 실패했을 거야.)

"우리가 한 주 늦게one week later 돈을 지불해도pay the money 되겠는지 알아보려고find out 그를 찾아갔는데visit him, 어떤 노부인이 그가 죽었다be dead고 하지 뭐요." 남편이 대답했다.

"잘됐네요great news." 여인이 말했다. "이렇게 말해서 미안해요. 내 말은mean, 이제 우리가 갚아야 할 돈을 구할get the money 시간이 생겼다have time는 뜻이에요."

"그만, 유령이여! 죽음 때문에because of a death 기뻐하는be happy 사람 말고, 죽음을 애석해하는be sorry about a death 사람을 보여 주시오show me." 스크루지가 소리쳤다.

유령이 스크루지를 불쌍한 봅 크래칫의 집으로to poor Bob Cratchit's house 데려갔다take him. 스크루지는 식구들이 조용히 난롯가에 둘러앉아sit around the fire 있는 모습을 보았다. 그들은 타이니 팀에 관해 얘기하고talk about Tiny Tim 있었다.

"내가 스크루지 씨의 조카Mr. Scrooge's nephew 프레드를 만났단다meet Fred." 봅이 말했다. "그 사람이 타이니 팀의 소식을 듣고hear about Tiny Tim 매우 안됐다고be very sorry 하더구나."

봅이 식구들을 돌아보며turn to his family 말했다. "우리는 타이니 팀이 얼마나 착한 아이what a good boy였는지 절대로 잊으면 안 된다never forget."

"결코 잊지 않을게요, 아버지." 자녀들이 모두 큰 소리로 말했다.

그러자 봅 크래칫은 갑자기all at once 무너져 내렸다(울음을 주체하지 못했다)break down. 눈물the tears이 얼굴에 흘러내리는데도flow down his face 어찌할 수 없었다cannot help it.

"유령이여." 스크루지가 말했다. "우리가 헤어질 순간our parting moment이 가까워졌음be at hand을 뭔가가 알려 주는구려inform me. 말해 주시오tell me. 우리가 봤던 그 죽은 사내는 누구였소?"

미래의 크리스마스 유령은 스크루지를 교회 묘지로to a churchyard 데려갔다. 유령은 무덤들 사이에 서서stand among the graves 한 무덤을 가리켰다point down to one. 스크루지는 덜덜 떨며tremble 그곳을 향해 살금살금 다가갔다creep toward it. 그리고 유령의 손가락을 따라follow the finger 방치되어 있는 그 무덤the neglected grave에 새겨진 이름을 읽었다read the name. 에브니저 스크루지.

"내가 그 침대 위에 누워 있던lie upon the bed 그 사내란 말이오? 아니오, 유령이여! 아니오, 안 돼. 난 과거의 그 사내the man I was가 아니오. 오늘 저녁이 없었다면but for this evening 보나마나 그렇게 되었을 법한 그런 사내the man I must have been는 되지 않겠소. 내게 전혀 가망이 없다면be past all hope 왜 이런 걸 보여 주는show me this 거요? 내가 아직은 이런 그늘을 바꿀change these shadows 수도 있다고 확실히 말해 주시오assure me."

GRAMMAR POINT

관계대명사 ⇨ 앞에 나온 명사(선행사)를 대신 받으며, 관계대명사가 이끄는 절은 그 명사를 수식한다.

- Now we have time to get *the money* **that** we have to pay.
  이제 우리가 갚아야 할 돈을 구할 시간이 생겼군요.
- Show me *someone* **who**'s sorry about a death, not *someone* **who**'s happy because of a death.
  죽음 때문에 기뻐하는 사람 말고, 죽음을 애석해하는 사람을 보여 주시오.
- Who was *the dead man* **(whom)** we saw? 우리가 본 그 죽은 사내는 누구였소?
- Am I *that man* **who** lay upon the bed? 내가 그 침대 위에 누워 있던 그 사내란 말이오?

[p. 166-167]

Scrooge continued, "I will honor Christmas / in my heart / and try to keep it / all the year. I will live / in the past, present, and future. I will never forget the lessons / that I have been taught."

Then, / the phantom began to disappear, / and Scrooge realized / that he was back in his own bedroom. Best and happiest of all, / time was before him. He had time / to make amends.

Scrooge heard the church bells / ringing loudly. Running to the window, / he opened it / and put out his head. It was a clear, bright, stirring, golden day.

"What day is it today?" cried Scrooge / to a boy down on the street.

"Today? It's Christmas Day, sir," answered the boy.

"Christmas!" Scrooge was surprised. All of the visits from the ghosts / had taken place / in one night.

"Do you know / the butcher's shop down the street?" Scrooge asked. "Please go / and tell the butcher / I'll buy a big goose. Come back with the man, / and I'll give you a nice tip." The boy ran off quickly.

"I'll send it to Bob Cratchit's. He won't know / who is sending it. **It's twice the size of Tiny Tim**," Scrooge thought to himself.

Scrooge then dressed himself / in his Sunday best / and went out onto the streets. Many people were on the streets, / and Scrooge gave each of them / a delighted smile. He said, "Good morning, sir," or "A Merry Christmas to you," to everyone he passed.

Later in the afternoon, / he walked toward his nephew's house. He passed the door / a dozen times / before he had the courage / to go up and knock. But he finally did.

Fred was very surprised / to see his uncle. "Uncle, why are you here?" he asked.

"I have come to dinner. Will you let me in, Fred?" Scrooge asked.

"Of course you may!" cried out Fred.

Fred was very happy, / and so were his wife and all their friends. They had a wonderful party together.

- **honor** 기리다, 지키다 • **lesson** 교훈 • **make amends** 보상하다, 만회하다 • **stirring** 마음을 뒤흔드는, 신나는 • **take place** 일어나다, 발생하다 • **butcher's shop** 정육점 • **butcher** 정육점 주인 • **tip** 팁 • **think to oneself** 혼자 마음속으로 생각하다 • **dress oneself** 옷을 입다 • **one's Sunday best** 가장 좋은 옷 • **delighted** 아주 기뻐하는, 즐거워하는 • **a dozen times** 열두 번 • **courage** 용기 • **uncle** 삼촌

CLOSE UP

1 **It's twice the size of Tiny Tim.** 그것은 크기가 타이니 팀의 두 배는 되겠군.
〈배수+명사〉는 '~의 … 배'라는 의미. '두 배'는 twice이고, 세 배부터는 three times(세 배), four times(네 배)와 같이 〈기수+times〉로 표현한다. *ex*) five times the length of the road(그 도로 길이의 다섯 배)

2 **Scrooge then dressed himself in his Sunday best** 그런 다음 스크루지는 가장 좋은 옷으로 차려입었다
〈dress oneself in ~〉은 '~(옷)을 차려입다'라는 의미.

Step 5

스크루지는 계속 말을 이었다. "크리스마스를 마음에in my heart 기리고honor Christmas 일 년 내내 all the year 그렇게 하도록keep it 노력하겠소. 과거와 현재와 미래에도in the past, present, and future 그렇게 살겠소. 내가 배운 교훈을 결코 잊지 않겠소never forget the lessons."

그때 유령이 사라지기disappear 시작했고, 스크루지는 자신이 다시 자기 침실에in his own bedroom 돌아와 있다는be back 걸 깨달았다. 무엇보다 좋고 행복한 것은best and happiest of all 자신 앞에 시간이 남아 있다는 사실이었다. 그에게는 (잘못을) 보상할make amends 시간이 있었다have time.

스크루지는 교회의 종들the church bells이 크게 울리는ring loudly 소리를 들었다. 그는 창가로 달려가서run to the window 창문을 열고open it 고개를 내밀었다put out his head. 맑고clear 밝고bright 설레이고stirring 황금처럼 빛나는golden 날이었다.

"오늘이 무슨 요일what day이냐?" 스크루지가 아래 거리에 있는 소년에게 소리쳐 물었다.

"오늘이요? 크리스마스 날Christmas Day이에요, 어르신." 소년이 대답했다.

"크리스마스라고!" 스크루지는 깜짝 놀랐다be surprised. 유령들의 방문the visits from the ghosts이 모두 하룻밤 사이에in one night 일어난take place 일이었던 것이다.

"거리 아래쪽에 있는down the street 푸줏간the butcher's shop을 아느냐?" 스크루지가 물었다. "가서 푸줏간 주인한테 내가 커다란 거위를 살buy a big goose 거라고 전해 주렴. 그 사람을 데리고with the man 돌아오면come back 내가 심부름 값을 두둑이a nice tip 주마." 소년은 냉큼 달려갔다run off.

"거위는 봅 크래칫 가족에게 보낼 거야. 누가 보내는 건지 모를 테지. 거위 크기가 타이니 팀의 두 배twice the size of Tiny Tim는 되겠군." 스크루지는 마음 속으로 생각했다.

그런 다음 스크루지는 가장 좋은 옷으로in his Sunday best 차려입고dress himself 거리로 나섰다go out onto the streets. 거리에는 사람들이 많이many people 있었고, 스크루지는 그들에게 일일이each of them 아주 즐거운 미소를 보냈다give a delighted smile. 그는 지나는 사람 모두에게 "안녕하시오good morning, 선생."이라거나 "메리 크리스마스a Merry Christmas to you."라고 인사했다.

오후 늦게later in the afternoon 스크루지는 조카의 집을 향해toward his nephew's house 걸어갔다. 그는 열두 번a dozen times이나 그 대문을 지나친pass the door 뒤에야 올라가서go up 문을 두드릴knock 용기가 났다have the courage. 마침내 스크루지는 그렇게 했다.

프레드는 삼촌을 보고see his uncle 몹시 놀랐다. "삼촌, 여긴 어쩐 일이세요why are you here?" 프레드가 물었다.

"저녁 먹으러 왔다come to dinner. 들어가게 해 주겠니let me in, 프레드?" 스크루지가 물었다.

"물론이죠!" 프레드가 소리쳤다.

프레드는 몹시 기뻐했고, 그의 아내와 친구들도 모두 아주 기뻐했다. 그들은 함께 근사한 파티를 열었다have a wonderful party.

GRAMMAR POINT

So am I. : 나도 그래.

- You are happy. **So am I.** (= I **am also** happy.) 너 행복하구나. 나도 그래.
- Fred was very happy, and **so were** his wife and all their friends.
  = Fred was very happy, and his wife and all their friends **were also very happy**.
  프레드는 몹시 기뻐했고, 그의 아내와 친구들도 모두 아주 기뻐했다.

A Christmas Carol

[p. 168-169]

The next day, / Scrooge went to the office / early in the morning. He wanted to be there / before Bob got there. Bob was eighteen minutes late. As Bob walked in, / Scrooge said, "Hello. **What do you mean / by coming here at this time of day?**"

"I'm very sorry, sir. I'm late," replied Bob.

"Yes, I think you are," said Scrooge.

"Now, I'll tell you what, / my friend," said Scrooge. "**I'm not going to stand this sort of thing** / any longer. And therefore ... therefore, / **I am going to pay you more money**!"

Scrooge continued, "I'll raise your salary / and assist your struggling family. We will discuss your affairs / this very afternoon," Scrooge said / with a nice smile.

That afternoon, / Scrooge took Bob out for a drink / and **explained** / **how he was going to help him**.

Scrooge was better than his word. He did everything / **he said he was going to do** / and more. He became a friend of the Cratchit family, / and to Tiny Tim, / who did not die, / he was like a second father. He became as good a friend, / as good a master, / and as good a man / as the city ever knew.

Some people laughed at him / because he had changed. Scrooge did not mind. Scrooge's own heart laughed, / and that was quite enough for him. He had no further dealings with ghosts, / but he lived happily ever afterward.

- **stand** 참다 • **this sort of thing** 이런 (종류의) 일 • **raise salary** 월급을 올리다 • **assist** 돕다, 도와주다
- **struggling** 고군분투하는, 버둥거리는, 기를 쓰는 • **affairs** 일, 사건 • **this very afternoon** 바로 오늘 오후
- **second father** 제2의 아버지, 아버지와 다름없는 사람 • **laugh at** ~을 비웃다 • **do not mind** 신경 쓰지 않다, 개의치 않다 • **dealings with** ~와의 거래 관계, ~와의 교제 • **ever afterward** 그 후로 계속

CLOSE UP

1. **What do you mean by coming here at this time of day?** 이 시간에 오면 어쩌자는 건가?
   〈What do you mean by + V-ing ~?〉는 '도대체 어쩔 셈으로 ~하느냐?'라는 의미.

2. **I'm not going to stand this sort of thing** 이런 일을 참지 않겠네 /
   I am going to pay you more money 자네에게 봉급을 더 주겠네 /
   explained how he was going to help him 자기가 어떻게 그를 도울지 설명했다 /
   he said he was going to do 자기가 해 주겠다고 말한
   〈be going to ~〉는 '~할 것이다'라는 의미. 이미 계획하거나 결정해서 앞으로 하게 될 일, 또는 현재의 상황으로 보아 앞으로 곧 일어나게 될 일 등을 말할 때 쓰인다. 여기서 쓰인 was going to는 주절의 동사 explained 및 said와 시제를 일치시키기 위해 쓰인 과거형이다.

Step 5

그다음 날the next day 스크루지는 아침 일찍early in the morning 사무실로 출근했다go to the office. 밥이 도착하기get there 전에 사무실에 가 있고be there 싶었던 것이다. 밥은 18분 늦었다eighteen minutes late. 밥이 걸어 들어오자walk in 스크루지는 이렇게 말했다. "어서 오게hello. 이 시간에at this time of day 출근하면come here 어쩌자는 건가?"

"정말 죄송합니다, 사장님. 제가 지각을 하고 말았네요be late." 밥이 대답했다.

"그래, 그런 것 같군." 스크루지가 말했다.

"자, 여보게, 자네한테 할 얘기가 있네tell you what." 스크루지가 말했다. "난 이런 일this sort of thing을 더는 참지 않겠네. 그래서 말인데therefore…… 그래서 자네에게 봉급을 더 주기로pay you more money 했네!"

스크루지의 말이 이어졌다. "자네의 봉급을 올려 주고raise your salary 고군분투하는 자네 가족your struggling family도 도와주겠네assist. 당장 오늘 오후에this very afternoon 자네 문제를 상의해 discuss your affairs 보세." 스크루지는 친절한 미소를 지으며with a nice smile 말했다.

그날 오후that afternoon 스크루지는 밥을 데리고 나가서take Bob out 술 한잔 사 주며for a drink 자신이 어떻게 그를 도울지help him 설명했다explain.

스크루지는 자신이 약속한 것보다 더 잘해 주었다be better than his word. 자신이 해 주겠다고 말한 모든 것과 그 이상everything and more을 베풀었던 것이다. 스크루지는 크래칫 가족의 친구가 되었고become a friend, 목숨을 건진 타이니 팀에게는 아버지와 다름없는 사람like a second father이 되었다. 스크루지는 그 도시에서 여태 알고 있는 사람 중에 가장 좋은 친구이자, 가장 훌륭한 주인이자, 가장 착한 사람이 되었다.

어떤 사람들은 그가 바뀌었기 때문에 그를 비웃었다laugh at him. 스크루지는 개의치 않았다do not mind. 스크루지 자신의 마음Scrooge's own heart이 웃고 있었기laugh 때문에, 그에게는 그걸로도 아주 충분했다be quite enough. 스크루지는 더 이상 유령들과 만나는 일dealings with ghosts이 없었다. 하지만 그 후로도 계속ever afterward 행복하게 살았다live happily.

GRAMMAR POINT

as ~ as ~ ever... : 여태껏 …한 중에 가장 ~한 ⇨ 〈as+형용사+a/an+명사〉의 어순에 주의하자.

- He became **as good** a friend, **as good** a master, and **as good** a man **as** the city **ever** knew.
  그는 그 도시에서 여태 알고 있는 사람 중에 가장 좋은 친구이자, 가장 훌륭한 주인이자, 가장 착한 사람이 되었다.

- He is **as greedy** a man **as** we've **ever** known.
  그는 우리가 여태껏 알았던 사람 중에 가장 탐욕스러운 사람이다.

Super Reading Story Training Book

Step 6

The Last Leaf

– O. Henry

The Last Leaf

[p. 172-173]

In a little district / west of Washington Square, / the streets have run crazy / and broken themselves into small strips / called "places." These "places" / make strange angles and curves. One street crosses itself / a time or two. An artist once discovered / a valuable possibility / on this street. Suppose / a collector with a bill / for paints, paper, and canvas / should, / **in taking this route**, / suddenly meet himself coming back, / **without a cent having been paid** on account.

So, / to quaint old Greenwich Village, / the art people soon came prowling, / hunting for north windows and eighteenth-century gables and Dutch attics and low rents. Then, / they imported pewter mugs and a dish or two / from Sixth Avenue / and became a "colony."

At the top of / an ugly, three-story brick house, / Sue and Johnsy had their studio. "Johnsy" was a nickname for Joanna. One was from Maine; / the other from California. They had met at the restaurant Delmonico's / on Eighth Street / and **had found** / **that their tastes in art, food, and clothes** / **were so similar** / **that the joint studio resulted**.

That was in May. In November, / a cold, unseen stranger, / whom the doctors called Pneumonia, / visited the colony, / touching one here and there / with his icy fingers. Over on the east side, / this ravager strode boldly, / claiming scores of victims, / but his feet trod slowly / through the maze of the narrow and moss-grown "places."

Mr. Pneumonia was not / what you would call a gentleman. A small woman / with blood thinned by the warm California zephyrs / was no match for the tough

---

- **district** 지역, 지구, 구역
- **run crazy** (도로 등이) 제멋대로 뻗다
- **strip** 가늘고 긴 조각, 좁고 긴 땅
- **valuable** 값비싼, 소중한
- **possibility** 가능성
- **suppose** 가정하다, 생각하다
- **collector** 징수원, 수집가
- **take a route** 길을 따르다, 경로를 취하다
- **on account** 외상으로, 신용으로
- **quaint** 진기한, 예스러운, 색다른
- **prowl** 살금살금 돌아다니다
- **gable** 박공, 합각(지붕)
- **attic** 다락방
- **rent** 집세, 임차료
- **import** (외국에서) 들여오다, 수입하다
- **colony** (같은 취향이나 동종업자들끼리의) 부락, 집단
- **three-story** 3층의
- **studio** (예술가들의) 작업실, 원룸 아파트
- **nickname** 별명, 애칭
- **result** (~의 결과로) 발생하다
- **pneumonia** 폐렴
- **ravager** 파괴자, 약탈자
- **stride** 성큼성큼 걷다, 활보하다
- **boldly** 대담하게
- **scores of** 수십의
- **victim** 희생자
- **tread** 발을 디디다
- **maze** 미로
- **moss-grown** 이끼 낀
- **zephyr** 산들바람, 미풍
- **be no match for** ~의 적수가 되지 못하다, ~을 당할 수 없다

CLOSE UP

1. **in taking this route** 이 길로 들어섰다가 / **without a cent having been paid** 한 푼도 받지 못하고
   〈in+V-ing〉는 '~하다가/~하는 중에'라는 의미. 〈without+V-ing〉는 '~하지 않고'라는 의미.
   여기서 a cent는 동명사구 having been paid의 의미상 주어이다.

2. **had found that their tastes in art, food, and clothes were so similar that the joint studio resulted** 예술과 음식과 옷에 대한 서로의 취향이 아주 비슷하다는 걸 알게 되어 공동 화실이 꾸려지게 되었다
   〈that their tastes in art, food, and clothes were so similar〉 부분은 had found의 목적어.
   문장 전체적으로는 '아주 ~해서 …하다'라는 의미의 〈so ~ that...〉 구문이다.

마지막 잎새

워싱턴 광장Washington Square 서쪽에 있는 한 작은 구역에서는in a little district 길들the streets이 이리저리 제멋대로 뻗어 나가서run crazy '플레이스'라 불리는called "places" 좁은 골목들로 나뉘어져 있다break themselves into small strips. 이들 '플레이스'는 기묘한 각도와 곡선을 이루고 있다make strange angles and curves(기묘하게 꺾이고 구부러져 있다는 의미). 하나의 길one street이 한두 번씩은a time or two 제 자신과 교차하는cross itself 것이다(길 하나를 따라가다 보면 어느새 왔던 길을 다시 지나가게 된다는 의미). 일찍이once 한 화가an artist는 이 거리에서 있을 법한 값진 가능성a valuable possibility(이로운 점)을 발견하기도 했다. 그림물감과 종이, 캔버스 대금 청구서를 들고 온 수금원a collector with a bill이 이 길로 들어섰다가take this route, 외상값은 한 푼도 받지 못한 채, 느닷없이suddenly 다시 그 자리로 되돌아온 자신을 발견하게 된다면meet himself coming back 어떻겠는가.

그리하여 이 색다르고 고풍스러운quaint old 그리니치 빌리지Greenwich Village에는, 북향으로 난 창문north windows과 18세기풍의 박공 지붕eighteenth-century gables과 네덜란드풍의 다락방Dutch attics과 값싼 셋방How rents을 찾아, 이내 예술가들the art people이 살금살금 찾아들었다come prowling. 그리고는 모두들 6번가에서from Sixth Avenue 백랍으로 만든 컵 몇 개pewter mugs와 접시 한두 개씩a dish or two을 사들여 와서는import '예술인 동네'를 이루었다become a "colony".

한 볼품없는 3층짜리 벽돌집an ugly, three-story brick house 꼭대기 층에는at the top 수와 존시Sue and Johnsy의 화실이 있었다have their studio. '존시'는 조애너의 애칭a nickname for Joanna이었다. 한 사람one(수를 가리킴)은 메인 주 출신from Maine이었고, 다른 한 사람the other(존시를 가리킴)은 캘리포니아 주 출신from California이었다. 두 사람은 8번가에 있는 델모니코 식당에서 만났는데, 예술과 음식과 옷에 대한in art, food, and clothes 서로의 취향their tastes이 아주 비슷하다는be so similar 걸 알고는 공동 화실the joint studio이 꾸려지게 된 것이었다result.

그게 5월의in May 일이었다. 11월이 되자in November 의사들이 폐렴Pneumonia이라고 부르는 냉혹하고 눈에 보이지 않는 불청객a cold, unseen stranger이 이 예술인 동네에 찾아와visit the colony 그 얼음장처럼 차가운 손가락으로with his icy fingers 여기저기서 사람들을 건드리고touch one here and there 다녔다. 이 파괴자this ravager는 저편 동쪽에서는over on the east side 대담하게 활보하며stride boldly 수십 명의 희생자를 냈지만claim scores of victims, 이 비좁고 이끼 낀 '플레이스'의 미로를 통과하면서는through the maze 발걸음이 느려졌다tread slowly.

폐렴 선생Mr. Pneumonia은 신사라고 부를 만한 녀석이 아니었다. 따뜻한 캘리포니아의 미풍the warm California zephyrs을 받고 자란 핏기 없는(연약한)with blood thinned 자그마한 여자a small woman는 이 거칠고 치명적인 질병the tough and deadly illness의 상대가 되지 못했다no match.

GRAMMAR POINT

one / the other ⇒ 두 개 중에서 '하나'는 one, '나머지 하나'는 the other로 표현한다.

- **One** was from Maine; **the other** from California.
  한 사람은 메인 주 출신이고, 다른 한 사람은 캘리포니아 주 출신이었다.

- Two artists lived in the building. **One** lived on the first floor; **the other** lived at the top.
  그 건물에는 두 명의 화가가 살았다. 한 사람은 1층에 살고, 다른 한 사람은 꼭대기 층에 살았다.

[p. 174-175]

and deadly illness. But he attacked Johnsy, / and she lay, / scarcely moving, / on her painted iron bedstead, / looking through the small Dutch windowpanes / at the blank side of the next brick house.

One morning, / the busy doctor invited Sue into the hallway.

"She has one chance in— / let us say, ten," he said, / as he shook down the mercury / in his clinical thermometer.

"And that chance is / for her to want to live. Sometimes / when people give up trying to live, / it doesn't matter / what medicines I give. Your friend has made up her mind / that she's not going to get well. Has she anything on her mind?"

"She ... she wanted to paint the Bay of Naples / some day," said Sue.

"Paint? Bosh! Does she have anything on her mind / worth thinking about twice, / like a man, for instance?"

"A man?" said Sue, / with a hard sound in her voice. "Is a man worth— / but, no, Doctor. There is nothing of the kind."

"Well, it is the weakness then," said the doctor. "I will do all / that science, / so far as it may be employed by me, / can accomplish. But whenever my patient / begins to count the carriages / in her funeral procession, / I subtract fifty percent / from the power of medicine to cure. If you can get her to ask one question / about the new winter styles in cloak sleeves, / I will promise you / a one-in-five chance for her / instead of one in ten."

After the doctor left, / Sue went into the workroom / and cried a napkin to a pulp. Then, / she swaggered into Johnsy's room / with her drawing board, / whistling a popular tune.

Johnsy lay, / scarcely making a move under the bedclothes, / with her face toward the window. Sue stopped whistling, / thinking she was asleep.

- **deadly** 치명적인 • **scarcely** 거의 ~ 않다 • **bedstead** 침대틀 • **windowpane** 창유리, 유리창
- **blank** 비어 있는 • **shake down** 흔들어 내리다 • **mercury** 수은 • **clinical thermometer** 체온계
- **give up** 포기하다 • **it doesn't matter** 중요하지 않다, 상관없다 • **make up one's mind** 마음을 정하다
- **get well** 회복되다 • **weakness** 나약함, 힘이 없음; 약점 • **accomplish** 이루다 • **funeral procession** 장례 행렬 • **subtract** 빼다, 삭감하다 • **cure** 낫게 하다, 치유하다 • **get ~ to...** ~을 설득해서 …하게 하다 • **cloak** 망토, 코트 • **cry a napkin to a pulp** 종이 냅킨이 흐늘흐늘해질 때까지 • **pulp** 걸쭉한 것, 곤죽; (종이 재료) 펄프 • **swagger** 으스대며 걷다, 활보하다 • **whistle** 휘파람을 불다 • **popular tune** 유행하는 곡조

CLOSE UP

1. **Has she anything on her mind? / Does she have anything on her mind?**
   그녀가 뭔가 마음을 쓰고 있는 일이 없을까?
   〈have ~ on one's mind〉는 '~을 염두에 두다', '~에 마음을 쓰다, 걱정하다'라는 의미.

2. **so far as it may be employed by me** 그것(의술)이 나에게 이용될 수 있는 한까지
   so far as I may employ it의 수동태이고, it은 science를 가리킴. 여기서 employ는 '쓰다, 이용하다'라는 뜻이고, science는 '의술'을 뜻함. 〈so far as ~〉는 '~하는 한'이라는 의미.

그러나 폐렴은 존시를 공격했고attack Johnsy, 그래서 그녀는 거의 움직이지도 않고scarcely move 페인트를 칠한 철제 침대에 누워서lie, 조그만 네덜란드풍 유리창을 통해 벽돌로 지은 옆집the next brick house의 텅 빈 벽을 바라보고look at the blank side 있었다.

어느 날 아침, 분주한 의사the busy doctor가 수를 복도로 불러냈다invite Sue into the hallway.

"저 아가씨가 회복될 가능성은…… 그러니까let us say 열에 하나one chance in ten 정도요." 의사가 체온계의in his clinical thermometer 수은주를 흔들어 낮추면서 shake down the mercury 말했다.

"그나마 그 가능성that chance도 저 아가씨가 살고 싶어 할want to live 때의 얘기지. 간혹 사람들이 살려는 노력을 포기할give up trying to live 때는, 내가 무슨 약을 처방하느냐what medicines I give가 중요하지 않거든it doesn't matter. 아가씨의 친구는 낫지get well 않겠다고 마음먹은make up her mind 상태요. 혹시 환자가 뭔가 마음을 쓰고 있는 일anything on her mind이 없을까?"

"쟤는…… 언젠가는some day 나폴리 만을 그리고paint the Bay of Naples 싶어 했어요." 수가 말했다.

"그림이라고? 바보같은 소리bosh! 뭔가 더 골똘히 생각할 만한worth thinking about 것을 마음속으로 품고 있는 게 없느냐 말이오. 예를 들면for instance 남자친구라든가like a man?"

"남자라고요?" 수가 딱딱한 목소리로 말했다. "그럴 만한 남자가…… 아뇨, 선생님. 그런 건 없어요 nothing of the kind."

"흠, 그렇다면 문제the weakness로군." 의사가 말했다. "나는 의술이 이룰 수 있는science can accomplish 모든 것을 할 거요will do all. 내가 그것(의술)을 이용할 수 있는 한까지so far as it may be employed by me 말이요(자기가 할 수 있는 범위의 의술은 다 동원해 보겠다는 의미). 하지만 내 환자my patient(존시를 가리킴)가 자기 장례식 행렬의in her funeral procession 마차 수를 세기count the carriages 시작할 때마다 난 약효the power of medicine to cure에서 50퍼센트를 제합니다subtract fifty percent(약효가 절반으로 줄어든다는 의미). 만약 아가씨가 그녀를 잘 설득해서 겨울에 새로 유행할 외투 소매 스타일styles in cloak sleeves에 관해 한 가지 질문이라도 하게ask one question 만들 수 있다면, 회복 가능성이 열에 하나one in ten가 아니라 다섯에 하나one in five라고 약속하지요."

의사가 떠난 뒤 수는 작업실로 가서go into the workroom 종이 냅킨이 흠뻑 젖어 흐늘흐늘해질 때까지 울었다cry a napkin to a pulp. 그런 다음 화판을 들고with her drawing board 휘파람으로 유행하는 곡조를 부르며whistle a popular tune 존시의 방으로 씩씩하게 걸어 들어갔다swagger into Johnsy's room.

존시는 이불 속에서under the bedclothes 거의 꼼짝도 않고scarcely make a move, 얼굴을 창문 쪽으로 돌리고 누워 있었다. 수는 존시가 잠들었다be asleep고 생각하고 휘파람을 멈췄다stop whistling.

GRAMMAR POINT

분사구문 ⇨ 접속사와 주어는 생략되고 분사가 이끄는 절을 '분사구문'이라 한다.

- she lay, scarcely **moving**, ... **looking** through the small Dutch windowpanes ...
  그녀는 거의 움직이지 않고 누워서 … 조그만 네덜란드풍 유리창을 통해 바라보고 있었다
- Johnsy lay, scarcely **making** a move under the bedclothes,...
  존시는 이불 속에서 거의 꼼짝 않고 누워 있었다
- Sue stopped whistling, **thinking** she was asleep. 수는 그녀가 잠들었다고 생각하고 휘파람을 멈췄다.

The Last Leaf

[p. 176-177]

She arranged her board / and began a pen-and-ink drawing / to illustrate a magazine story. Young artists must **pave their way to Art** / by drawing pictures / for the magazine stories / that young authors must write / to **pave their way to literature**.

As Sue was sketching / a pair of elegant horseshow riding trousers and a monocle / on the figure of the hero, / an Idaho cowboy, / she heard a low sound, / several times repeated. She quickly went to the bedside.

Johnsy's eyes were open wide. She was looking out the window / and counting backward. "Twelve," she said, / and a little later, "eleven"; / and then "ten," and "nine"; / and then "eight" and "seven" almost together.

Sue looked out the window. What was there / to count? There was only a bare, dreary yard / to be seen, / and the blank side of the brick house / twenty feet away. An old, old ivy vine, / twisted and decayed at the roots, / climbed halfway up the brick wall. The cold breath of autumn / had taken most of its leaves from the vine / until its skeleton branches clung, / almost bare, / to the bricks.

"What is it, / dear?" asked Sue.

"Six," said Johnsy, / in almost a whisper. "They're falling faster now. Three days ago, / there were almost a hundred. **It made my head ache** / **to count them.** But now it's easy. **There goes another one.** There are only five left now."

"Five what, / dear? Tell your Sudie."

"Leaves. On the ivy vine. When the last one falls, / I must go, too. I've known that / for three days. Didn't the doctor tell you?"

"Oh, I have never heard of such nonsense," complained Sue, / with magnificent scorn. "What have old ivy leaves to do with your getting well? And you used to love that vine so, / you naughty girl. Don't be like that. Why, / the doctor told me this morning / that your chances for getting well real soon / were / —let's see exactly what he said— / he said / the chances were ten to one. Why, / that's almost as good a chance as we have in New York / when we ride on the streetcars / or walk past a new building."

- **arrange** 준비하다, 배치하다 • **pen-and-ink drawing** 펜화 • **illustrate** 삽화를 넣다 • **literature** 문학 • **horseshow** 마술 쇼, 마술 대회 • **riding trousers** 승마용 바지 • **monocle** 외알 안경 • **count backward** 거꾸로 세다 • **bare** 아무것도 없는, 황량한 • **dreary** 음울한, 따분한, 황량한 • **yard** 마당 • **ivy vine** 담쟁이덩굴 • **twisted** 뒤틀린, 일그러진 • **decayed** 썩은 • **skeleton branches** 앙상한 나뭇가지들 • **cling to** ~에 매달리다, ~에 들러붙다 • **nonsense** 헛소리, 말도 안 되는 생각 • **with magnificent scorn** 아주 무시하는 태도로 • **have to do with** ~와 관계가 있다 • **ten to one** 90퍼센트(의 가능성) • **as good a chance as** ~만큼 좋은/높은 가능성

CLOSE UP

1. **pave their way to Art** 미술의 길을 닦다 / **pave their way to literature** 문학의 길을 닦다
   〈pave one's way to ~〉는 '~의 길을 닦다', '~에 대한 기틀을 마련하다'라는 의미.

2. **It made my head ache to count them.** 그걸 세려면 머리가 아팠지.
   〈make+목적어+동사원형〉은 '~을 …하게 만들다'라는 의미. 한편, 여기서 It은 가주어이고, to count them이 진주어이다.

3. **There goes another one.** 또 하나 떨어진다.
   〈there goes ~〉는 '~이 가다', '~이 사라져 버리다', '(기회 등)이 날아가다'라는 의미.

Step 6

수는 화판을 배치하고arrange her board 어느 잡지 소설에 삽화로 들어갈illustrate a magazine story 펜화a pen-and-ink drawing를 그리기 시작했다. 젊은 화가들young artists은, 젊은 작가들young authors이 문학의 길을 닦아 나가기pave their way to literature 위해 써야 하는 잡지 소설에 들어갈 삽화를 그림으로써 미술의 길을 닦아 나가야pave their way to Art 하는 것이다.

　　수가 소설의 주인공the hero인 아이다호 카우보이an Idaho cowboy의 모습 위에 미술 쇼에서 입는 우아한 승마 바지와 외알 안경을 스케치하고sketch 있는데, 나지막한 소리a low sound가 여러 차례 반복해서several times repeated 들렸다. 수는 급히 침대 옆으로 갔다go to the bedside.

　　존시가 눈을 말똥말똥 뜨고 있었다be open wide. 그녀는 창밖을 내다보며look out the window 수를 거꾸로 세고count backward 있었다. 존시는 "열둘twelve"이라고 말하더니, 조금 있다가a little later "열하나eleven", 이어and then "열ten", "아홉nine", 그리고는 거의 한꺼번에almost together "여덟eight"과 "일곱seven"이라고 했다.

　　수는 창밖을 내다봤다. 셀 게 뭐가 있지? 보이는to be seen 거라곤 살풍경하고 황량한 마당a bare, dreary yard과 20피트 떨어져 있는twenty feet away 벽돌집의 텅 빈 벽the blank side뿐이었다. 뿌리가 뒤틀리고 썩어 버린twisted and decayed 늙디 늙은 담쟁이덩굴an old, old ivy vine이 벽돌 벽을 반쯤 타고 올라가 있었다climb halfway up the brick wall. 가을의 차가운 입김the cold breath of autumn이 담쟁이덩굴에서from the vine 잎사귀 대부분을 휩쓸어 가는take most of its leaves 바람에 앙상한 가지들its skeleton branches만 거의 헐벗은 채로almost bare 벽돌에 달라붙어 있었다cling to the bricks.

　　"얘, 뭐가 말이니?" 수가 물었다.

　　"여섯six." 존시가 거의 속삭이듯 말했다. "이제 더 빨리 떨어지고fall faster 있어. 사흘 전에는three days ago 거의 백 개almost a hundred가 있었는데. 그걸 세려면count them 머리가 아팠지make my head ache. 하지만 지금은 수월하네. 또 하나another one 떨어진다. 이제 다섯 개만 남았구나only five left."

　　"얘, 뭐가 다섯 개라는 거야five what? 너의 수디(수의 애칭)한테 말해 보렴."

　　"잎사귀들leaves 말이야. 담쟁이덩굴에 붙어 있는on the ivy vine. 마지막 하나the last one가 떨어지면fall 나도 가야겠지must go. 사흘 전부터 알고 있었어. 의사가 너한테 말하지 않던?"

　　"아, 그런 어처구니없는 소리such nonsense는 들어 본 적이 없다." 수가 몹시 무시하는 투로with magnificent scorn 투덜거렸다complain. "늙은 담쟁이 잎사귀들old ivy leaves이 네가 회복되는 것your getting well과 무슨 상관이 있니? 게다가 넌 저 담쟁이덩굴을 아주 좋아했잖아love that vine so, 이 심술꾸러기 아가씨야you naughty girl. 그러지 마라don't be like that. 참, 의사 선생님이 오늘 아침에 나한테 말씀하셨어. 네가 진짜 빨리 나을 가능성your chances for getting well이…… 그러니까 선생님 말씀what he said을 그대로 보자면…… 가능성이 90퍼센트ten to one(10대 1, 열에 아홉은 회복될 수 있다는 의미)이라고 하셨어. 뭐, 그건 우리가 뉴욕에서in New York 전차를 타거나ride on the streetcars 새 건물을 지나쳐 걸어가게walk past a new building 될 확률과 거의 비슷하게 좋은 거야."

GRAMMAR POINT

동명사의 의미상 주어 ⇨ 소유격 또는 목적격으로 나타냄.

- What have old ivy leaves to do with **your/you** getting well?
  늙은 담쟁이 잎사귀들이 네가 회복되는 것과 무슨 상관이 있니?

- She was upset about **Johnsy's/Johnsy** giving up trying to live.
  그녀는 존시가 살려는 노력을 포기해서 속상했다.

[p. 178-179]

"Try to have some broth now, / and let Sudie go back to her drawing, / so she can sell it to the editor. Then, / I'll buy port wine for her sick child / and pork chops for her greedy self."

"You don't need to get / any more wine," said Johnsy, / keeping her eyes fixed out the window.

"There goes another. No, I don't want any broth. That leaves just four. I want to see the last one fall / before it gets dark. Then, I'll go, too."

"Johnsy, dear," said Sue, / bending over her, "will you promise / to keep your eyes closed / and not to look out the window / until I am done working? I must hand my drawings in / by tomorrow. I need the light, / or I would pull the shade down."

"Couldn't you draw / in the other room?" Johnsy asked coldly.

"I'd rather be here / beside you," said Sue. "Besides, / I don't want you / to keep looking at those silly ivy leaves."

"Tell me / as soon as you have finished," said Johnsy, / closing her eyes, / and lying white and still / as a fallen statue, "because I want to see the last one fall. I'm tired of waiting. I'm tired of thinking. I want to turn loose my hold on everything / and go sailing down, down, / just like one of those poor, tired leaves."

"Try to sleep," said Sue. "I must call Behrman up / to be my model for the old hermit-miner. I'll just be gone / for a minute. Don't try to move / until I come back."

Old Behrman was a painter / who lived on the ground floor / beneath them. He was past sixty / and had a long beard / like Michelangelo's Moses / curling down from his wide head. Behrman was a failure in art. He had been painting / for forty years, / but he had never produced anything noteworthy. He had always been about to paint a masterpiece, / but he had never yet begun it. For several years, / he had painted nothing / except for minor advertisements here and there.

- **broth** 걸쭉한 수프, 고기 국물 • **port wine** 포트 와인 • **fixed** 고정된 • **bend over** ~ 위로 몸을 굽히다 • **hand in** ~을 제출하다 • **shade** 차양, 빛 가리개 • **I'd rather** (차라리) ~하겠다 • **fallen** 쓰러진 • **statue** 조각상 • **turn loose** 놓아주다 • **call up** 부르다, 연락하다 • **hermit-miner** 은둔 광부(hermit 은둔자 + miner 광부) • **beard** 턱수염 • **Moses** 모세 • **failure** 실패, 실패자 • **noteworthy** 주목할 만한 • **masterpiece** 걸작 • **minor** 작은, 중요하지 않은 • **advertisement** 광고

CLOSE UP

1. **here beside you** 여기 네 옆에 / **Besides, I don't want you to** ~ 게다가 네가 ~하는 게 싫어
   〈beside ~〉는 전치사로 '~ 옆에'라는 의미. 〈besides〉는 부사일 때는 '게다가', 전치사일 때는 '~ 외에도'라는 의미.

2. **I'm tired of waiting. I'm tired of thinking.** 나는 기다리는 데 지쳤어. 생각하기도 지쳤고.
   〈be tired of ~〉는 '~하는 데 지치다/싫증 나다'라는 의미.

3. **except for minor advertisements** 자잘한 광고 말고는
   〈except for ~〉는 〈except ~〉와 같은 의미. '~을 제외하고는'이라는 뜻이다.

"이제 수프를 좀 먹어have some broth 봐. 그리고 수디가 다시 그림을 그리게go back to her drawing 해 줘. 그래야 (잡지) 편집자한테 팔sell it to the editor 수 있지. 그러면 앓고 있는 우리 아기her sick child(존시를 말함)를 위해서는 포트와인port wine을 사 오고 먹성 좋은 나her greedy self를 위해서는 돼지갈비pork chops를 사 올 거야."

"포도주는 더 살 필요 없어." 존시가 시선을 창밖에 고정한 채keeping her eyes fixed 말했다.

"한 개가 또another 떨어지네. 아니, 수프는 먹고 싶지 않아. 이제 네 개만just four 남았구나. 어두워지기 전에 마지막 잎이 떨어지는 걸 보고see the last one fall 싶어. 그러면 나도 가게 될 거야will go."

"얘, 존시." 수가 존시 위로 몸을 숙이며bend over her 말했다. "내가 일을 마칠 때까지 눈을 감고keep your eyes closed 창밖을 내다보지 않겠다고 약속해 줄래? 나 내일까지by tomorrow 내 그림들을 넘겨줘야hand my drawings in 해. 나한테는 빛이 필요해need the light. 그렇지만 않으면or 가리개를 내리겠는데pull the shade down 말이야."

"다른 방에서 그릴draw in the other room 수는 없겠니?" 존시가 쌀쌀맞게 물었다.

"차라리 여기here 네 옆에beside you 있을래." 수가 말했다. "게다가besides 네가 저 바보 같은 담쟁이 잎들those silly ivy leaves을 계속 보고 있는keep looking at 것도 싫고."

"다 끝나면finish 바로 내게 알려 줘tell me." 존시는 눈을 감고close her eyes 쓰러진 조각상처럼as a fallen statue 창백한 얼굴로 가만히 누운lie white and still 채 말했다. "마지막 잎이 떨어지는 걸 보고 싶으니까 말이야. 이제 기다리는 거 지친다be tired of waiting. 생각하는 것도 지치고be tired of thinking. 모든 것에 대한 내 미련my hold on everything을 놓아 버리고turn loose 아래로 아래로 떨어져 내려가고go sailing down, down 싶어. 저 가엾고 지친 잎사귀들 중 하나처럼 말이야."

"잠을 좀 자도록 해 봐try to sleep." 수가 말했다. "나는 베어먼 영감님을 불러다가call Behrman up 은둔한 늙은 광부 그림의 모델이 되어be my model 달라고 해야 하니까. 잠깐만for a minute 갔다 올게will be gone. 내가 돌아올come back 때까지 꼼짝하지 마."

베어먼 영감Old Behrman은 그들 아래쪽beneath them 1층에on the ground floor 살고 있는 화가a painter였다. 나이는 예순이 넘었고be past sixty, 미켈란젤로의 모세상처럼 이마가 넓은 머리에서부터from his wide head 구불구불 늘어진curl down 긴 수염을 기르고 있었다have a long beard. 베어먼은 화가로서 실패한 사람a failure in art이었다. 40년 동안 그림을 그려paint for forty years 왔지만, 주목할 만한 작품anything noteworthy을 내놓은 적이 한 번도 없었다never produce. 언제나 당장이라도 걸작을 그릴paint a masterpiece 태세였지만, 아직 시작해 본 적이 한 번도 없었다never begin it. 몇 년 동안for several years 여기저기서here and there 의뢰받은 자잘한 광고 그림minor advertisements 말고는 아무것도 그린 게 없었다paint nothing.

GRAMMAR POINT

not + to부정사 ⇒ to부정사를 부정할 때는 to부정사 앞에 not을 붙인다.

- Will you promise **to keep** your eyes closed and **not to look** out the window?
  눈을 감고 창밖을 내다보지 않겠다고 약속해 줄래?

- I tried **to sleep**. 나는 자려고 노력했다.
- I tried **not to sleep**. 나는 자지 않으려고 노력했다.

[p. 180-181]

He earned a little / by serving as a model / for those young artists in the colony / who could not pay for a professional. He drank gin to excess / and still talked about his coming masterpiece. For the rest, / he was a fierce little old man, / who made fun of anyone who was soft / and who regarded himself as a bulldog / ready to protect the two young artists / living in the studio above him.

Sue found Behrman / smelling strongly of juniper berries / in his dimly lit den below. In one corner / was a blank canvas on an easel / that had been waiting there / for twenty-five years / to receive the first line of the masterpiece. She told him about Johnsy's fancy / and how she feared / she would, / indeed, light and fragile as a leaf herself, / float away / when her slight hold upon the world / grew weaker.

Old Behrman, / with his red eyes plainly streaming, / shouted about / how silly Johnsy's idea was.

"What!" he cried. "Are there people in this world / so foolish to believe / that they will die / when a leaf falls off a vine? I have never heard of such a thing. No, I will not pose as a model / for you. Why did you allow such a silly thought / to enter her head? Oh, that poor little Miss Johnsy."

"She is very ill and weak," said Sue, "and the fever has left her mind / filled with thoughts of death and other horrible things. Very well, Mr. Behrman, / if you do not care to pose for me, / you don't have to. But I think / you are a horrid old man."

"You are just like a woman!" yelled Behrman. "Who said / I will not pose? Go on. I will go with you. For half an hour, / I have been trying to say / that I am ready to pose. God, this is not a place / in which someone / as pretty as Miss Johnsy / should lie sick. Someday, / I will paint a masterpiece, / and we shall all go away. God, yes."

- **pay for** ~에 대한 대금을 지불하다
- **professional** 전문적인, 직업적인
- **to excess** 과도하게, 지나치게
- **for the rest** 그 외에는, 그 밖의 것에 관하여는
- **fierce** 사나운, 험악한, 과격한
- **make fun of** ~을 조롱하다, ~을 놀리다
- **dimly lit** 희미하게 빛나는, (불빛이) 흐릿한
- **den** 작업실, 골방, 굴
- **fancy** 환상
- **fear** 두려워하다, 우려하다
- **fragile** 깨지기 쉬운, 허약한
- **float away** 떠가다, 날아가 버리다
- **slight hold upon the world** 세상에 대한 작은 미련
- **plainly** 분명히, 숨김없이
- **stream** 줄줄 흐르다
- **pose (as a model)** (모델로서) 포즈를 취하다
- **horrid** 지독한, 고약한
- **lie sick** 아파서 누워 있다, 몸져눕다

CLOSE UP

1. **regarded himself as a bulldog** 자신을 불독(경비견)으로 자처했다
   〈regard ~ as...〉는 '~을 …로 여기다/간주하다'라는 의미. 여기서 bulldog은 '경비견'의 의미로 보면 되겠다.

2. **with his red eyes plainly streaming** 그의 충혈된 눈에 눈물을 주르륵 흘리며
   〈with + 목적어 + 보어〉 형식의 동시상황 구문. 목적어는 his red eyes이고, 보어는 plainly streaming이다.

3. **allow such a silly thought to enter her head** 그런 멍청한 생각이 그녀의 머릿속에 들어가게 내버려 두다
   〈allow ~ to...〉는 '~이 …하도록 용납하다/허락하다'라는 의미.

4. **has left her mind filled with thoughts** 그녀의 마음을 생각들로 가득 차게 했다
   〈leave + 목적어 + 보어〉는 '~을 …한 상태가 되게 하다', '~을 …한 상태로 내버려 두다'라는 의미.

베어먼은 예술인 동네에서in the colony 전문 모델료를 지불할 수 없는cannot pay for a professional 젊은 화가들에게 모델 노릇을 해 주고serve as a model 푼돈을 벌었다earn a little. 그는 진을 과도하게 마셨고drink gin to excess, 머지않아 그리게 될 걸작his coming masterpiece에 대해 여전히 떠벌렸다. 그 밖에도(또한)for the rest, 과격한 성미에 체구가 작은 늙은이a fierce little old man였으며, 나약한 사람은 누구든지anyone who is soft 놀려 댔고make fun of, 자신을 위층 화실에 살고 있는 두 젊은 화가(수와 존시)를 기꺼이 보호할 각오가 된ready to protect 경비견으로 자처하고regard himself as a bulldog 있기도 했다.

수는 베어먼이 아래층에 있는 그의 침침한 골방에서in his dimly lit den 노간주나무 열매(진에 들어가는 열매) 냄새를 물씬 풍기고smell strongly 있는 모습을 보았다. 한쪽 구석에는in one corner (아무것도 그려지지 않은) 텅 빈 캔버스a blank canvas가 이젤 위에on an easel 놓여 있었는데, 그것은 거기서 걸작의 첫 획이 그어지기를receive the first line 25년간이나for twenty-five years 기다리며 있는 것이었다. 수는 베어먼에게 존시의 망상Johnsy's fancy에 대해 얘기하고, 그야말로 그녀 자신이 나뭇잎처럼as a leaf 가볍고 허약한light and fragile 존시가 세상에 대한 자신의 약한 미련her slight hold upon the world마저 더 약해지면grow weaker 둥둥 떠서 날아가 버리게float away 될까 봐 얼마나 걱정되는지 얘기했다.

베어먼 영감은 충혈된 눈his red eyes에 눈물을 주르륵 흘리며plainly stream 존시의 생각Johnsy's idea이 얼마나 어리석은지how silly에 대해 고함을 질러댔다.

"뭐라고what!" 베어먼이 소리쳤다. "잎사귀 하나a leaf가 담쟁이에서 떨어진다고fall off a vine 자기도 죽을 거라will die 믿는 그런 멍청한so foolish 사람들이 이 세상에 있단 말이야? 그런 말은 들어 본 적도 없다. 아니, 자네의 모델 노릇은 못해 주겠네will not pose as a model. 자네는 왜 그런 멍청한 생각such a silly thought이 그녀의 머릿속에 들어가도록enter her head 내버려 둔 건가? 아, 가엾은 존시 양."

"그 애는 몹시 아프고 약해요be ill and weak." 수가 말했다. "그래서 열the fever이 나더니 마음이 온통 죽음과 다른 끔찍한 것들death and other horrible things에 대한 생각으로 꽉 차게 됐다고요. 좋아요very well, 베어먼 영감님. 저의 모델이 되고 싶지 않다면do not care to pose 그러시지 않아도 돼요don't have to. 하지만 영감님이 정말 고약한 노인a horrid old man이라는 생각이 드네요."

"자네도 어쩔 수 없는 여자just like a woman로군!" 베어먼이 소리쳤.  "누가 모델을 안 하겠다고 했나? 가세. 나도 따라갈go with you 테니. 난 30분 전부터 언제라도 모델이 되겠다고be ready to pose 말하려고 했었어. 맙소사god, 이곳은 존시 양 같이 예쁜as pretty as Miss Johnsy 사람이 병들어 누워 있을lie sick 만한 데가 아니란 말이야. 언젠가 나는 걸작을 그릴 거야. 그럼 우리 모두 멀리 떠나자고go away. 암, 그렇고 말고."

GRAMMAR POINT

관계대명사 ⇨ 보통 관계대명사는 선행사 바로 뒤에 오지만, 때로 그 사이에 수식어구 등이 놓일 수도 있다.

- ... for *those young artists* in the colony **who** could not pay for a professional
  예술인 동네에서 전문 모델료를 지불할 수 없는 젊은 화가들에게

- ... *a blank canvas* on an easel **that** had been waiting there for twenty-five years ...
  거기서 25년간 기다려 온 텅 빈 캔버스가 이젤 위에

[p. 182-183]

Johnsy was sleeping / when they went upstairs. Sue pulled the shade down to the windowsill / and **motioned Behrman to go into the other room**. In there, / they fearfully peered out the window / at the ivy vine. Then, / they looked at each other / for a moment / without speaking. **A persistent, cold rain / was falling / along with some snow.** Behrman, / in his old blue shirt, / took his seat / as the hermit-miner / on an upturned kettle for a rock.

When Sue awoke from an hour's sleep / the next morning, / she found Johnsy / with dull, wide-open eyes / staring at the drawn green shade.

"Pull it up. I want to see," she ordered in a whisper.

Wearily, Sue obeyed.

But, incredibly, / despite the beating rain and fierce gusts of wind / that had lasted throughout the entire night, / there still remained one ivy leaf / against the wall. It was the last one / on the vine. Still dark green near its stem, / but, **with its serrated edges tinted yellow** / as it was beginning to decay, / it hung bravely from a branch / some twenty feet above the ground.

"It is the last one," said Johnsy. "I thought / it would surely fall during the night. I heard the wind. It will fall today, / and I shall die / at the same time."

"Dear, dear!" said Sue, / leaning her worn face down to the pillow. "Think of me, / if you won't think of yourself. What would I do?"

- **windowsill** 창틀, 창문턱 • **motion** 동작을 해 보이다, 손짓하다 • **fearfully** 무서워하며, 걱정스럽게 • **peer out** ~ 밖을 응시하다 • **persistent** 끈질긴, 끊임없이 지속되는 • **take one's seat** 자리를 잡다, 자리에 앉다 • **upturned** 뒤집힌, 거꾸로인 • **wearily** 맥없이, 힘없이, 녹초가 되어 • **incredibly** 놀랍게도 • **despite** ~에도 불구하고 • **gusts of wind** 강한 바람, 돌풍 • **remain** 남다, 남아 있다 • **serrated** 톱니 모양의 • **tinted** (~한 색으로) 물든 • **decay** 썩다, 쇠약해지다 • **worn face** 지친 얼굴, 수척해진 얼굴

CLOSE UP

1. **motioned Behrman to go into the other room** 베어먼에게 다른 방으로 들어가라고 손짓했다
   〈motion ~ to...〉는 '~에게 …하라고 손짓/몸짓하다'라는 의미.

2. **A persistent, cold rain was falling along with some snow.**
   그칠 줄 모르는 차가운 비가 약간의 눈과 함께 내리고 있었다.
   〈along with ~〉는 '~와 함께'라는 의미.

3. **with its serrated edges tinted yellow** 톱니 모양의 가장자리는 노란빛으로 물든 채
   〈with + 목적어 + 보어〉 형식의 동시상황 구문. 목적어는 its serrated edges이고, 보어는 tinted yellow이다.

두 사람이 위층으로 올라갔을go upstairs 때 존시는 잠을 자고 있었다. 수는 가리개를 창턱까지 내리고pull the shade down to the windowsill 베어먼에게 다른 방으로 들어가라고go into the other room 손짓했다. 그 방에서in there 두 사람은 창밖의 담쟁이덩굴을 걱정스레 쳐다봤다fearfully peer. 그리고는 잠시for a moment 서로를 말 없이without speaking 바라보았다. 그칠 줄 모르는 차가운 비a persistent, cold rain가 약간의 눈과 함께along with some snow 내리고 있었다. 베어먼은 낡아빠진 파란 셔츠를 입고in his old blue shirt 바위 대용으로for a rock 뒤집어 놓은 주전자 위에on an upturned kettle 은둔한 광부의 모습으로as the hermit-miner 자리 잡았다take his seat.

수가 한 시간쯤 자고an hour's sleep 다음 날 아침the next morning 깨어나 보니awake 존시가 흐릿한 눈을 크게 뜨고with dull, wide-open eyes (창문에) 쳐져 있는 초록색 가리개를 응시하고stare at the drawn green shade 있었다.

"저것 좀 올려 봐pull it up. 보고 싶으니까." 존시가 속삭이는 소리로 명령했다.

녹초가 된wearily 수는 시키는 대로 했다obey.

그런데, 믿을 수 없게도incredibly, 밤새도록throughout the entire night 계속된 세찬 비the beating rain와 사나운 돌풍fierce gusts of wind에도 불구하고, 담쟁이 잎 하나one ivy leaf가 여전히 벽에 붙어against the wall 있었다. 그것은 담쟁이의 마지막 잎새the last one on the vine였다. 줄기 가까이는 near its stem 아직도 짙은 초록색dark green이었지만, 톱니 모양의 가장자리its serrated edges는 시들어 가기 시작하는begin to decay 것처럼 노란빛으로 물든 채tinted yellow, 땅에서 20피트쯤 올라간 some twenty feet above the ground 가지에 대견하게 매달려 있었다hang bravely from a branch.

"마지막 잎새구나." 존시가 말했다. "밤사이during the night 틀림없이 떨어질surely fall 거라 생각했는데. 바람 소리를 들었거든hear the wind. 저 잎새는 오늘 떨어질fall today 거야. 그러면 나도 동시에 죽게die at the same time 될 거야."

"얘, 얘dear, dear!" 수가 지친 얼굴을 베개에 내려 놓으며 말했다. "내 생각 좀 해 줘think of me. 네 자신을 생각하지 않을 거라면 말이야. 난 어떡하란 말이니what would I do?"

GRAMMAR POINT

despite : ~에도 불구하고 (= in spite of) ⇨ 잘못해서 despite of로 쓰지 않도록 주의하자.

- **Despite** the beating rain and fierce gusts of wind, ... there still remained one ivy leaf against the wall. 세찬 비와 사나운 돌풍에도 불구하고 … 담쟁이 잎 하나가 여전히 벽에 붙어 있었다.

- **Despite** my effort to keep her alive, she died. 그녀를 살리려는 내 노력에도 불구하고 그녀는 죽고 말았다.

[p. 184-185]

But Johnsy did not answer. The most lonesome thing / in the entire world / is a soul / when it is making ready / to go on its mysterious, far journey. The fancy seemed to possess her / more strongly / as, / one by one, / **the ties that bound her to friendship and to Earth** / were loosed.

The day passed, / and even in the twilight, / they could see the lone ivy leaf / clinging to its stem against the wall. And then, / with the coming of the night, / the north wind again began to blow / while the rain still beat against the windows / and ran down the eaves.

When it was light enough, / Johnsy, the merciless, / commanded that the shade be raised.

The ivy leaf was still there.

Johnsy lay for a long time / looking at it. And then she called to Sue, / who was stirring her chicken broth / over the gas stove.

"I've been a bad girl, Sudie," said Johnsy. "Something has made / that last leaf stay there / to show me / how wicked I was. It is a sin / to want to die. You may bring me a little broth now / and some milk with a little port in it, / and … No, bring me a hand-mirror first, / and then pack some pillows about me, / and I will sit up / and watch you cook."

An hour later, / she said, "Sudie, / someday I hope to paint the Bay of Naples."

The doctor came in the afternoon, / and Sue had an excuse / to go into the hallway / as he left.

"**Even chances**," said the doctor, / taking Sue's thin, shaking hand / in his. "With good nursing, / you'll win. And now **I must see another case** / I have downstairs. Behrman, his name is / —some kind of an artist, / I believe. Pneumonia, too. He is an old, weak man, / and the attack is acute. There is no hope for him, / but he goes to the hospital today / to be made more comfortable."

- **make ready to** ~할 준비를 하다 • **possess** 사로잡다, 소유하다 • **ties** 끈, 연대 • **be loosed** 풀리다, 헐거워지다 • **twilight** 황혼, 땅거미 • **beat** 때리다, 두들기다 • **eave** 처마, 차양 • **merciless** 잔인한, 인정사정없는 • **command** 명령하다 • **stir** 휘젓다 • **wicked** 사악한, 나쁜 • **sin** 죄 • **pack** 싸다, 가득 채우다 • **sit up** 일어나 앉다 • **have an excuse to** ~할 구실을 만들다 • **even chances** 절반의 가능성 • **acute** (질병이) 급성의, 극심한

CLOSE UP

1. **the ties that bound her to friendship and to Earth** 그녀를 우정과 세상에 묶어 주던 끈들
   〈bind ~ to...〉는 '~을 …에 묶다'라는 의미. 〈that ~ Earth〉 부분은 the ties를 수식하는 관계절.

2. **Even chances** 반반의 가망 (50:50의 동일한 가망)
   even을 '~조차'라는 뜻의 부사로만 알고 있는 경우가 많은데, 형용사로 '동일한', '고른', '대등한', '평평한', '짝수의' 등의 뜻도 있다는 걸 알아두자. ex) They are even in length.(그것들은 길이가 같다.) / an even number(짝수)

3. **I must see another case** 다른 환자를 봐야겠군
   case의 기본 의미는 '(특정한) 경우, 사례'인데, '환자'라는 뜻으로도 쓰인다. '질병에 걸리거나 부상당한 사례'라고 이해하면 되겠다.

178 Step 6

그러나 존시는 대답하지 않았다. 이 세상에서in the entire world 가장 외로운 것the most lonesome thing은 신비에 싸인 머나먼 여행을 떠날go on its mysterious, far journey 채비를 하고make ready 있는 사람a soul이다. 존시를 우정과 세상에 묶어 주던bind her to friendship and to Earth 끈들the ties이 하나씩one by one 풀리면서be loosed, 그 망상the fancy은 더욱 강하게more strongly 그녀를 사로잡고possess her 있는 듯했다.

하루가 지나고 땅거미가 질 무렵in the twilight에도, 그들은 그 홀로 남은 담쟁이 잎the lone ivy leaf이 벽에 붙은 줄기에 매달려 있는cling to its stem 모습을 볼 수 있었다. 그러다가 밤이 되자with the coming of the night 또 다시 북풍the north wind이 몰아치기blow 시작하는 한편, 빗줄기the rain는 여전히 창문을 때리고beat against the windows 처마 밑으로 떨어졌다run down the eaves.

날이 충분히 밝아지자be light enough 인정사정없는 존시Johnsy, the merciless는 가리개를 올리라고the shade be raised 명령했다command.

담쟁이 잎은 여전히 그 자리에still there 있었다.

존시는 한참 동안for a long time 누워서 그것을 바라보았다look at it. 그러더니 수를 불렀다call to Sue. 그녀는 가스 난로 위에 올려놓은 닭고기 수프를 젓고stir her chicken broth 있는 중이었다.

"난 나쁜 계집애a bad girl였어, 수디." 존시가 말했다. "내가 얼마나 못됐는지how wicked 보여 주려고show me 무언가가 저 마지막 잎새that last leaf를 저기에 그대로 있게stay there 했나 봐. 죽고 싶어 하다니want to die 죄받을 일a sin이지. 이제 내게 수프를 조금 갖다 줘bring me a little broth. 포트와인을 약간 탄 우유도 좀some milk 갖다 주고, 그리고……, 아니다, 손거울부터 먼저a hand-mirror first 갖다 주고, 내게 베개를 몇 개 받쳐 줘pack some pillows about me. 일어나 앉아서sit up 네가 요리하는 모습을 봐야겠다watch you cook."

한 시간 뒤an hour later 존시가 말했다. "수디, 나는 언젠가someday 나폴리 만을 그리고paint the Bay of Naples 싶어."

오후에in the afternoon 의사가 왔고, 의사가 돌아갈 때 수는 핑계를 대고have an excuse 복도로 나갔다go into the hallway.

"가망이 반반even chances이오." 의사가 수의 떨고 있는 여윈 손을 자신의 손으로 잡으며 말했다. "잘 간호하면with good nursing 아가씨가 이길win 거요. 그럼 이제 나는 아래층에 있는 다른 환자를 봐야겠군see another case. 베어먼이라던가 그 사람 이름이, …… 무슨 화가some kind of an artist라던데. 역시 폐렴pneumonia, too이야. 나이가 많고 몸도 약한 사람an old, weak man인데, 급성으로 걸렸지the attack is acute 뭔가. 그에게는 가망이 없지만no hope, 오늘 입원하면go to the hospital 좀 더 편해지겠지be made more comfortable."

GRAMMAR POINT

command that + 주어 (+ should) + 동사원형

⇨ 제안, 요구, 주장, 명령 등과 관련된 일부 동사(suggest/demand/insist/command/…) 뒤에 목적어로 나오는 that절에서, 동사 형태는 〈should+동사원형〉을 쓰거나 should 없이 그냥 〈동사원형〉만 쓴다.

- Johnsy, the merciless, **commanded** that the shade **(should) be raised**.
  인정사정없는 존시는 가리개를 올리라고 명령했다.

- The doctor **insisted** that he **(should) go** to the hospital. 의사는 그가 입원해야 한다고 주장했다.

[p. 186-187]

The next day, / the doctor said to Sue, "She's out of danger. You've won. Nutrition and care now / —that's all she needs."

That afternoon, / Sue went to the bed / where Johnsy lay, / contentedly knitting / a very blue and very useless woolen shoulder scarf, / and she put one arm around her, pillows and all.

"I have something to tell you, / my dear," she said. "Mr. Behrman died of pneumonia / in the hospital today. He was ill / for only two days. The janitor found him / on the morning of the first day / in his room downstairs / helpless with pain. His shoes and clothing / were soaked and icy cold. They couldn't imagine / where he had been / on such a dreadful night. And then they found / a lantern, still lit, / a ladder that had been dragged from its place, / some scattered brushes, / and a palette with green and yellow colors mixed on it, / and—look out the window, dear, / at the last ivy leaf on the wall. Didn't you wonder / why it never fluttered or moved / when the wind blew? Ah, darling, / it's Behrman's masterpiece. He painted it there / the night that the last leaf fell."

- **out of danger** 위험에서 벗어난 • **nutrition** 영양(섭취) • **contentedly** 만족스럽게, 흐뭇한 표정으로
- **die of** ~으로 죽다 • **janitor** 수위, 관리인, 잡역부 • **helpless** 속수무책인, 무기력한 • **be soaked** 흠뻑 젖다
- **dreadful** 끔찍한 • **drag** (질질) 끌다, 끌고 가다 • **scattered** 흐트러진 • **flutter** 흔들리다, 펄럭이다

CLOSE UP

1 **on such a dreadful night** 그렇게 끔찍했던 밤에
〈such a/an+형용사+명사〉의 구조일 때 such는 '아주 ~한'의 뜻으로 정도를 강조함.

2 **a palette with green and yellow colors mixed on it** 초록색과 노란색이 그 위에 섞여 있는 팔레트
〈with+목적어+보어〉 형식의 동시상황 구문. 목적어는 green and yellow colors이고, 보어는 mixed on it이다.
여기서 it은 a palette를 가리킴.

그다음 날the next day 의사가 수에게 말했다. "환자가 위험한 고비는 넘겼소be out of danger. 아가씨가 이겼네. 이제부터는 영양과 보살핌nutrition and care, 그게 환자에게 필요한 전부all she needs요."

그날 오후that afternoon 수는 존시가 아주 파란색very blue의 도무지 쓸모없는very useless 모직 어깨걸이a woolen shoulder scarf를 만족스럽게 짜며knit 누워 있는 침대로 가서, 한 팔로 그녀와 베개와 모든 것을 끌어안았다.

"얘, 네게 할 말이 있어have something to tell you." 수가 말했다. "베어먼 영감님Mr. Behrman이 오늘 병원에서in the hospital 폐렴으로 돌아가셨단다die of pneumonia. 딱 이틀간for only two days 앓으셨어be ill. 첫날 아침on the morning of the first day 건물관리인the janitor이 아래층에 있는 그분 방에서in his room 영감님이 아파서 꼼짝도 못하고helpless with pain 있는 걸 발견했대. 영감님의 신발과 옷his shoes and clothing은 흠뻑 젖어서 얼음처럼 차가웠고be soaked and icy cold. 사람들은 그렇게 끔찍했던 밤에on such a dreadful night 영감님이 어디에 있었는지where he has been 상상도 못했어can't imagine. 그러다가 아직도 불이 켜져 있는still lit 랜턴a lantern과, 원래 있던 자리에서 끌고 온be dragged from its place 사다리a ladder와, 흩어져 있는 붓 몇 자루some scattered brushes와, 초록색과 노란색이 섞여 있는with green and yellow colors mixed on it 팔레트a palette를 발견한 거야. 그리고 얘, 창밖을 좀 내다봐look out the window. 벽에 붙어 있는 저 마지막 담쟁이 잎새the last ivy leaf 좀 봐. 바람이 부는데도 왜 전혀 팔랑대거나 움직이지 않는지never flutter or move 궁금하지 않던? 아아, 얘, 저건 베어먼 영감님의 걸작Behrman's masterpiece이란다. 영감님이 마지막 잎새the last leaf가 떨어지던 날 밤에 저 자리에 저걸 그리셨던paint it there 거야."

GRAMMAR POINT

die of / die from : ~으로 죽다

⇨ 보통 질병으로 죽었을 때는 of를 쓰고, 부상이나 부주의 등으로 죽었을 때는 from을 쓴다.

- Mr. Behrman **died of** pneumonia in the hospital today. 베어먼 영감님이 오늘 병원에서 폐렴으로 돌아가셨어.
- She **died from** injuries after the car accident. 그녀는 자동차 사고 후 부상으로 죽었다.

Super
Reading
Story
Training
Book

Answers
and
Translations

Step 1

The Magic Cooking Pot

p. 12-13

Stop & Think

- Why did the little girl begin to cry? 어린 소녀는 왜 울기 시작했는가?
  ⇨ She could not find anything to eat. 먹을 것을 찾을 수 없어서. /
  She was hungry but had no food. 배가 고픈데 먹을 게 없어서.
- What did the old woman have? 할머니는 무엇을 가지고 있었나?
  ⇨ She had a magic cooking pot. 마법의 솥단지를 가지고 있었다.

Check Up

1 The little girl lived — b. with her mother.
2 The little girl searched for food — c. in the forest.
3 The old woman had — a. a magic cooking pot.
4 The pot started — d. cooking porridge.

1 어린 소녀는 엄마와 함께 살았다.
2 어린 소녀는 숲에서 먹을 게 있나 살펴보았다.
3 할머니는 마법의 솥을 가지고 있었다.
4 솥은 죽을 만들기 시작했다.

p. 14-15

Stop & Think

- What should the little girl do to stop the pot from cooking? 어린 소녀가 어떻게 해야 솥이 요리를 멈추는가?
  ⇨ She should say, "Stop, little pot, stop." "멈춰라, 작은 솥단지야, 멈춰라."라고 말해야 한다.
- Why did the mother decide to eat without her daughter? 엄마는 왜 딸 없이 식사하기로 마음먹었나?
  ⇨ Her daughter went out for a long time, and she became hungry.
  딸이 오랫동안 밖에 나가 있었고, 엄마는 배가 고파졌기 때문에.

Check Up

1 The little girl took the pot and <u>ran back</u> to her home.
2 Soon, the pot was <u>full</u> of porridge.
3 The pot <u>immediately</u> stopped cooking.
4 The little girl and her mother ate <u>porridge</u> every day.

1 어린 소녀는 솥을 가지고 집으로 뛰어 돌아왔다.
2 얼마 안 있어 솥은 죽으로 가득 찼다.
3 솥은 즉시 요리를 멈췄다.
4 어린 소녀와 엄마는 날마다 죽을 먹었다.

p. 16-17

Stop & Think

- Why did the pot keep making porridge? 솥단지는 왜 계속해서 죽을 만들었는가?
  ⇨ The little girl's mother forgot the magic words. 어린 소녀의 엄마가 주문을 잊어버려서.

CHECK UP

1. The mother did not remember how to make it stop.
2. The porridge spilled onto the floor.
3. Every house in the village had porridge in it.

1. 엄마는 그것을 멈추게 하는 법이 생각나지 않았다.
2. 죽이 바닥으로 흘러내렸다.
3. 마을의 집집마다 죽 범벅이 되었다.

The Shoemaker and the Elves

p. 18-19

Stop & Think

- Were there many customers in the shop? 가게에는 손님이 많았는가?
  ⇨ No, few people visited the shop. 아니다. 가게를 찾는 사람들이 거의 없었다.

- Who made the beautiful shoes? 누가 그 아름다운 구두를 만들었는가?
  ⇨ We don't know. 알 수 없다. /
  Somebody made the shoes for the shoemaker. 누군가 구두장이를 대신하여 그 구두를 만들었다.

CHECK UP

1. The shoemaker was very poor. T
2. The shoemaker finished his last pair of shoes. F
3. The lady gave the shoemaker three gold coins for the shoes. T
4. The next morning, the shoemaker made two more pairs of shoes. F

1. 구두장이는 아주 가난했다.
2. 구두장이는 그의 마지막 구두를 완성했다.
3. 귀부인은 구두장이에게 구둣값으로 금화 세 닢을 주었다.
4. 다음 날 아침 구두장이는 구두를 두 켤레 더 만들었다.

p. 20-21

Stop & Think

- Why did the shoemaker and his wife hide downstairs? 구두장이 부부는 왜 아래층에 숨어 있었는가?
  ⇨ To find out who was making the shoes. 누가 구두를 만드는지 알아보려고.

CHECK UP

1. The next morning, the shoemaker and his wife came down.
2. They saw two beautiful pairs of shoes on the table.
3. The two customers paid twelve gold coins for the four pairs of shoes.
4. The shoemaker and his wife hid downstairs.

1 다음 날 아침 구두장이 부부가 아래로 내려왔다.
2 그들은 아름다운 구두 두 켤레가 작업대 위에 놓여 있는 걸 보았다.
3 두 손님들은 구두 네 켤레에 금화 열두 닢을 지불했다.
4 구두장이 부부는 아래층에 숨어 있었다.

p. 22-23

Stop & Think

- Who made the beautiful shoes? 누가 그 아름다운 구두들을 만들었는가?
  ⇨ **Two elves made the shoes.** 꼬마요정 둘이 구두를 만들었다.

- Why did the elves leave? 꼬마요정들은 왜 떠났는가?
  ⇨ **The shoemaker and his wife knew about them.** 구두장이 부부가 그들에 대해 알고 있어서.

CHECK UP

1 Two <u>elves</u> made the shoes at night.
2 The shoemaker and his wife made tiny <u>clothes</u>.
3 The <u>elves</u> left and never came back.
4 The shoemaker and his wife became <u>rich</u>.

1 꼬마요정 둘이 밤에 구두를 만들었다.
2 구두장이 부부는 조그만 옷을 만들었다.
3 꼬마요정들은 떠나서 다시 돌아오지 않았다.
4 구두장이 부부는 부자가 되었다.

Jack and the Beanstalk

p. 24-25

Stop & Think

- What did the strange old man offer Jack? 낯선 노인은 잭에게 무엇을 내놓았는가?
  ⇨ **He offered Jack some magic beans.** 노인은 잭에게 마법의 콩 몇 알을 내놓았다.

CHECK UP

1 What did Jack sell the strange old man? (c)
   a. magic beans   b. some food   c. a cow
2 What did Jack's mother do with the beans? (b)
   a. She ate them.   b. She threw them out the window.   c. She planted them.

1 잭은 낯선 노인에게 무엇을 팔았는가?
   a. 마법의 콩   b. 약간의 식량   c. 암소
2 잭의 어머니는 콩알을 어떻게 했는가?
   a. 먹었다.   b. 창밖으로 던졌다.   c. 심었다.

p. 26-27

Stop & Think

- Who lived in the castle? 성에 누가 살았는가?
  ⇨ **The giant and his wife lived in the castle.** 성에는 거인과 그의 아내가 살았다.

- Why did Jack climb the beanstalk again? 잭은 왜 다시 콩나무에 올라갔는가?
  ⇨ He ran out of gold. 황금이 다 떨어져서.

CHECK UP

1 The giant's wife — b. was kindhearted.
2 The giant's huge bag — c. was filled with gold.
3 Jack stole — a. the giant's gold.

1 거인의 아내는 마음씨가 고왔다.
2 거인의 거대한 자루에는 황금이 가득 들어 있었다.
3 잭은 거인의 황금을 훔쳤다.

p. 28–29

Stop & Think

- Why did Jack cut down the beanstalk? 잭은 왜 콩나무를 찍어 넘어뜨렸나?
  ⇨ The giant was chasing him. 거인이 그를 쫓아오고 있어서. /
  To stop the giant from coming down. 거인이 내려오지 못하게 하려고.

CHECK UP

1 The hen <u>laid</u> golden eggs.
2 The <u>harp</u> played beautiful music.
3 Jack <u>stole</u> the harp and ran out of the castle.
4 Jack <u>cut down</u> the beanstalk with an axe.

1 암탉은 황금 알을 낳았다.
2 하프는 아름다운 음악을 연주했다.
3 잭은 하프를 훔쳐서 성 밖으로 달아났다.
4 잭은 도끼로 콩나무를 찍어 넘어뜨렸다.

The Ugly Duckling

p. 30–31

Stop & Think

- How did the seventh egg look? 일곱 번째 알은 어떻게 생겼는가?
  ⇨ It was bigger than the other ones. 다른 알들보다 더 컸다.
- How did the ugly duckling look? 미운 오리 새끼는 어떻게 생겼는가?
  ⇨ He was big, gray, ugly, and strange looking. 몸집이 크고 회색인데다 못생기고 이상해 보였다.

CHECK UP

1 Mother Duck did not remember the seventh egg.   T
2 The last baby duckling looked strange.   T
3 The ugly duckling looked like the old duck.   F

1 어미 오리는 일곱 번째 알을 기억하지 못했다.
2 그 마지막 새끼 오리는 이상하게 생겼다.
3 미운 오리 새끼는 늙은 오리를 닮았다.

p. 32-33

Stop & Think

- Why was the ugly duckling sad? 미운 오리 새끼는 왜 슬펐나?
  ⇨ Nobody loved him. 아무도 그를 사랑하지 않아서.
- Who killed the two geese? 누가 두 기러기를 죽였는가?
  ⇨ Hunters killed the geese. 사냥꾼들이 기러기를 죽였다.

CHECK UP

1. The ugly duckling was a <u>good</u> swimmer.
2. The farm girl <u>disliked</u> the ugly duckling.
3. The ugly duckling <u>ran away from</u> the farm.
4. Hunters with <u>rifles</u> killed the two geese.

1. 미운 오리 새끼는 헤엄을 잘 쳤다.
2. 농장 주인의 딸은 미운 오리 새끼를 싫어했다.
3. 미운 오리 새끼는 농장에서 뛰쳐나갔다.
4. 총을 든 사냥꾼들이 두 기러기를 죽였다.

p. 34-35

Stop & Think

- What did the ugly duckling see in the sky? 미운 오리 새끼는 하늘에서 무엇을 보았는가?
  ⇨ He saw three swans. 백조 세 마리를 보았다.
- How did the ugly duckling survive the winter? 미운 오리 새끼는 어떻게 겨울을 견뎌 냈는가?
  ⇨ A farmer took the ugly duckling to his home. 한 농부가 미운 오리 새끼를 자기 집으로 데려갔다.

CHECK UP

1. Why couldn't the ugly duckling swim in the lake? (c)
   a. There was no water.   b. He was a bad swimmer.   c. The water froze.
2. When did the farmer set the ugly duckling free? (b)
   a. in the winter   b. in the spring   c. in the summer

1. 미운 오리 새끼는 왜 호수에서 헤엄을 칠 수 없었나?
   a. 물이 없어서.   b. 헤엄을 잘 못 쳐서.   c. 물이 얼어붙어서.
2. 농부는 언제 미운 오리 새끼를 놓아주었는가?
   a. 겨울에   b. 봄에   c. 여름에

p. 36-37

Stop & Think

- What was the ugly duckling? 미운 오리 새끼의 정체는 무엇이었나?
  ⇨ He was a swan. 백조였다.

CHECK UP

1. The ugly duckling <u>flew</u> into the sky.
2. The ugly duckling saw his <u>reflection</u> in the water.
3. He was not an <u>ugly</u> duckling anymore.
4. The ugly duckling was <u>the most</u> beautiful of all the swans.

1 미운 오리 새끼는 하늘로 날아올랐다.
2 미운 오리 새끼는 물에 비친 자기 모습을 보았다.
3 그는 이제 미운 오리 새끼가 아니었다.
4 미운 오리 새끼는 모든 백조들 중에서 가장 아름다웠다.

The Ant and the Grasshopper

p. 38-39

Stop & Think

- Why does the ant work hard every day? 개미는 왜 날마다 열심히 일하는가?
  ⇨ To save food for the winter. 겨울을 대비해 식량을 비축하려고.
- What does the grasshopper do every day? 베짱이는 날마다 무엇을 하는가?
  ⇨ He plays and sings every day. 날마다 놀면서 노래를 부른다.

Check Up

1 The ant <u>gathers</u> a lot of food for the winter.
2 In winter, the <u>grasshopper</u> has no food to eat.
3 The grasshopper realizes how <u>foolish</u> he was.
4 Is the grasshopper in the field in the next spring? (No)

1 개미는 겨울에 먹을 식량을 많이 모은다.
2 겨울에 베짱이는 먹을 식량이 하나도 없다.
3 베짱이는 자기가 얼마나 어리석었는지 깨닫는다.
4 베짱이는 이듬해 봄에 들판에 있는가? (아니다)

The Hare and the Tortoise

p. 40-41

Stop & Think

- Why did the tortoise and the hare race? 거북이와 토끼는 왜 경주를 했는가?
  ⇨ To find out who the faster animal was. 누가 더 빠른 동물인지 알아보려고.

Check Up

1 The hare bragged — b. about how fast he could run.
2 The tortoise bet — d. he could beat the hare.
3 The tortoise — a. kept walking to the finish line.
4 The hare woke up — c. too late.

1 토끼는 자신이 얼마나 빨리 달릴 수 있는지 자랑했다.
2 거북이는 자신이 토끼를 이길 수 있다고 장담했다.
3 거북이는 결승선까지 꾸준히 걸었다.
4 토끼는 잠에서 너무 늦게 깨어났다.

The Sick Lion

p. 42-43

Stop & Think

- What did the lion do? 사자는 무슨 짓을 했는가?
  ⇨ He ate the animals that entered his cave. 자신의 굴에 들어오는 동물들을 잡아먹었다.
- Why did the fox refuse to enter the cave? 여우는 왜 굴에 들어가기를 거부했는가?
  ⇨ He only saw footprints entering the cave. 굴에 들어간 발자국만 보였기 때문에.

CHECK UP

1. The lion could not <u>hunt</u> animals anymore.
2. The animals felt <u>sorry</u> for the lion.
3. The lion <u>pretended</u> to be sick.
4. The fox looked at the <u>footprints</u> outside the cave.

1. 사자는 더는 동물 사냥을 할 수 없었다.
2. 동물들은 사자를 가엾게 여겼다.
3. 사자는 아픈 척했다.
4. 여우는 굴 밖에서 발자국들을 살펴보았다.

The Boy Who Cried Wolf

p. 44-45

Stop & Think

- Why did the shepherd boy yell, "Wolf!" the first time? 양치기 소년이 처음에 "늑대다!"라고 소리친 이유는?
  ⇨ He was bored watching the sheep by himself. 혼자서 양들을 지키는 게 따분했기 때문에.
- Why did the villagers not go to help the shepherd boy? 마을 사람들은 왜 양치기 소년을 도우러 가지 않았는가?
  ⇨ They thought he was tricking them again. 소년이 또 자기들을 속이고 있다고 생각했기 때문에.

CHECK UP

1. The shepherd boy tricked the villagers by crying out, "Wolf!"   T
2. A wolf attacked the shepherd boy's sheep.   T
3. The shepherd boy killed the wolf.   F

1. 양치기 소년은 "늑대다!"라고 소리쳐서 마을 사람들을 속였다.
2. 늑대 한 마리가 양치기 소년의 양들을 공격했다.
3. 양치기 소년은 늑대를 죽였다.

Step 2

The Little Mermaid

p. 48-49

CHECK UP

1. The Little Mermaid had a <u>beautiful</u> singing voice.
2. All mermaids have a <u>tail</u> instead of legs.
3. The Little Mermaid dreamed of the <u>land</u> above the water.

1. 인어공주는 고운 노래하는 목소리를 가졌다.
2. 인어들은 모두 다리 대신 꼬리를 가지고 있다.
3. 인어공주는 물 밖의 육지에 관한 꿈을 꾸었다.

p. 50-51

Stop & Think

- Who did the Little Mermaid see inside the ship? 인어공주는 배 안에서 누구를 보았는가?
  ⇨ She saw many handsome gentlemen and a prince. 잘생긴 신사 여럿과 왕자를 보았다.

CHECK UP

1. The Little Mermaid thought the prince was handsome.   T
2. The prince could breathe underwater.   F
3. The Little Mermaid saved the prince's life.   T

1. 인어공주는 왕자가 잘생겼다고 생각했다.
2. 왕자는 물속에서 숨을 쉴 수 있었다.
3. 인어공주는 왕자의 생명을 구했다.

p. 52-53

Stop & Think

- Who found the prince on the beach? 누가 해변에서 왕자를 발견했는가?
  ⇨ A pretty girl found the prince. 예쁜 소녀가 왕자를 발견했다.
- What did the Little Mermaid wish? 인어공주의 소원은 무엇이었나?
  ⇨ She wished to become a human. 인간이 되고 싶어 했다.

CHECK UP

1. The Little Mermaid hid behind some <u>rocks</u>.
2. The Little Mermaid only thought about the <u>prince</u>.
3. <u>Mermaids</u> live for 300 years.
4. Humans have <u>souls</u>, but mermaids do not.

1. 인어공주는 바위들 뒤로 숨었다.
2. 인어공주는 왕자에 대한 생각만 했다.
3. 인어들은 300년을 산다.
4. 인간에게는 영혼이 있지만 인어에게는 없다.

p. 54-55

Stop & Think

- How can a mermaid get a soul? 인어는 어떻게 영혼을 얻을 수 있는가?
  ⇨ A man must love her and marry her. 인간 남자가 인어를 사랑해서 결혼해야 한다.
- How can the Little Mermaid become a human? 인어공주는 어떻게 인간이 될 수 있는가?
  ⇨ She has to drink the magic drink before sunrise. 해 뜨기 전에 마법의 물약을 마셔야 한다.

CHECK UP

1. Humans think — d. tails are ugly.
2. The sea witch's house — b. was made from bones.
3. The Little Mermaid — a. wanted a pair of human legs.
4. The Little Mermaid's tail — c. will split in two.

1. 인간들은 꼬리가 추하다고 생각한다.
2. 바다마녀의 집은 해골로 만들어져 있었다.
3. 인어공주는 인간의 다리를 갖고 싶어 했다.
4. 인어공주의 꼬리는 둘로 갈라질 것이다.

p. 56-57

Stop & Think

- What did the sea witch take from the Little Mermaid? 바다마녀는 인어공주에게서 무엇을 가져갔는가?
  ⇨ She took the Little Mermaid's voice. 인어공주의 목소리를 가져갔다.

CHECK UP

1. What will happen to the Little Mermaid if the prince marries someone else? (b)
   a. She will lose her voice.   b. She will turn into foam.   c. She will get a soul.
2. What happened right after the Little Mermaid drank the magic drink? (c)
   a. She became a human.   b. She found the prince.   c. She passed out.

1. 왕자가 다른 사람과 결혼하면 인어공주는 어떻게 되는가?
   a. 목소리를 잃게 된다.   b. 물거품으로 변한다.   c. 영혼을 얻는다.
2. 인어공주는 마법의 물약을 마신 후 바로 어떻게 되었는가?
   a. 인간이 되었다.   b. 왕자를 찾았다.   c. 정신을 잃었다.

p. 58-59

Stop & Think

- Where did the prince take the Little Mermaid? 왕자는 인어공주를 어디로 데려갔는가?
  ⇨ He took her inside his castle. 자신의 성 안으로 데려갔다.
- What did the Little Mermaid do at the prince's party? 인어공주는 왕자가 연 파티에서 무엇을 했는가?
  ⇨ She danced beautifully. 아름답게 춤을 추었다.

CHECK UP

1. Some girls sang for the prince at the party.
2. The Little Mermaid and the prince did everything together.
3. The Little Mermaid missed her family.

1 몇몇 소녀가 파티에서 왕자를 위해 노래했다.
2 인어공주와 왕자는 모든 것을 함께 했다.
3 인어공주는 식구들을 그리워했다.

p. 60-61

Stop & Think

- How did the prince feel about the Little Mermaid? 인어공주에 대한 왕자의 감정은 어떠했는가?
  ⇨ He loved her like a sister. 여동생처럼 사랑했다.

Check Up

1 The prince did not think of marrying the Little Mermaid.   T
2 The king ordered the prince to marry the Little Mermaid.   F
3 The prince met the girl he had been looking for.   T
4 The princess of the next kingdom saved the prince's life.   F

1 왕자는 인어공주와 결혼할 생각이 없었다.
2 왕은 왕자에게 인어공주와 혼인하라고 명했다.
3 왕자는 그가 찾고 있던 소녀를 만났다.
4 이웃 나라 공주가 왕자의 목숨을 구했다.

p. 62-63

Stop & Think

- What did the Little Mermaid do at the wedding? 인어공주는 결혼식에서 무엇을 했는가?
  ⇨ She danced more beautifully than ever. 그 어느 때보다 더 아름답게 춤췄다.

Check Up

1 The prince and the princess — a. got married on the ship.
2 The Little Mermaid's sisters — b. couldn't kill the prince.
3 The Little Mermaid had to kill — c. gave their hair to the sea witch.
4 The Little Mermaid — d. the prince before the sun rose.

1 왕자와 공주는 배 위에서 결혼했다.
2 인어공주의 언니들은 자신들의 머리카락을 바다마녀에게 주었다.
3 인어공주는 해가 뜨기 전에 왕자를 죽여야 했다.
4 인어공주는 왕자를 죽일 수 없었다.

p. 64-65

Stop & Think

- What did the Little Mermaid become? 인어공주는 무엇이 되었는가?
  ⇨ She became a fairy of the air. 공기의 요정이 되었다.

- Why did the prince look sad? 왕자는 왜 슬퍼 보였나?
  ⇨ The Little Mermaid was gone. 인어공주가 없어졌기 때문에.

Check Up

1 The Little Mermaid became a <u>fairy</u> of the air.
2 The Little Mermaid can get a <u>soul</u>.

3 The prince guessed what had happened to the Little Mermaid.
4 The Little Mermaid kissed the prince and princess.

1 인어공주는 공기의 요정이 되었다.
2 인어공주는 영혼을 얻을 수 있다.
3 왕자는 인어공주에게 무슨 일이 생겼는지 짐작했다.
4 인어공주는 왕자와 공주에게 입을 맞췄다.

Step 3

Beauty and the Beast

p. 68-69

Stop & Think

- What kind of a person was Beauty? 뷰티는 어떤 사람이었는가?
  ⇨ She was pretty, kind, and smart. 예쁘고 마음씨 곱고 영리했다.
- What happened to the merchant's ships? 상인의 배에 무슨 일이 생겼는가?
  ⇨ They sank in a storm at sea. 바다에서 폭풍을 만나 침몰했다.

Check Up

1 Beauty's sisters were selfish and greedy.
2 Beauty was beautiful and enjoyed reading.
3 The merchant sold his house and moved to the countryside.
4 Their new house was very tiny.

1 뷰티의 언니들은 이기적이고 욕심이 많았다.
2 뷰티는 아름다웠고 독서를 즐겼다.
3 상인은 집을 팔고 시골로 이사했다.
4 그들의 새 집은 매우 작았다.

p. 70-71

Stop & Think

- How did Beauty's sisters like their new house? 뷰티의 언니들은 새 집을 얼마나 마음에 들어 했는가?
  ⇨ They disliked it and complained a lot. 집이 마음에 들지 않아서 몹시 투덜댔다.
- What happened to Beauty's father's ship? 뷰티 아버지의 배에는 무슨 일이 일어났나?
  ⇨ Pirates stole all the ship's gold and silver, and the ship had many holes in it.
  해적들이 배의 모든 금과 은을 훔쳐가고 배에는 많은 구멍이 났다.

CHECK UP

1. Beauty worked hard and — a. cleaned every day.
2. One of Beauty's father's ships — c. did not sink.
3. Some pirates stole — d. the gold and silver.
4. Beauty's father could not — b. afford to fix the ship.

1 뷰티는 매일 열심히 일하고 청소했다.
2 뷰티 아버지의 배들 중 한 척이 침몰하지 않았다.
3 해적들이 금과 은을 훔쳐 갔다.
4 뷰티의 아버지는 배를 수선할 형편이 안 되었다.

p. 72-73

Stop & Think

- What did Beauty's father see in the dining room? 뷰티의 아버지는 식당에서 무엇을 보았는가?
  ⇒ There were a table full of food and a plate with a knife and fork beside it.
  음식이 가득 차려진 식탁이 있었고, 접시와 그 옆에 나이프와 포크가 있었다.

CHECK UP

1. The weather suddenly became very <u>cold</u>.
2. Beauty's father saw a <u>light</u> in the forest.
3. There was <u>no one</u> in the castle.
4. Beauty's father sat down at the table and <u>ate</u> the food.

1 날씨가 갑자기 몹시 추워졌다.
2 뷰티의 아버지는 숲 속에서 불빛을 하나 보았다.
3 성 안에는 아무도 없었다.
4 뷰티의 아버지는 식탁에 앉아 음식을 먹었다.

p. 74-75

Stop & Think

- Why did Beauty's father go to the garden? 뷰티의 아버지는 왜 정원에 갔는가?
  ⇒ To pick a rose for Beauty. 뷰티에게 줄 장미 한 송이를 꺾으려고.
- What did the Beast want Beauty's father to do in return for sending him home?
  야수는 뷰티의 아버지를 집에 보내 주는 대신 그가 어떻게 하기를 원했는가?
  ⇒ The Beast wanted Beauty's father to send his daughter to live in his castle with him.
  그의 딸을 보내어 자신의 성에서 자신과 함께 살게 하기를 원했다.

CHECK UP

1. The garden had many yellow roses.   F
2. The Beast wanted to eat Beauty's father.   F
3. The Beast gave Beauty's father a box of gold.   T

1 정원에는 노란 장미가 많이 있었다.
2 야수는 뷰티의 아버지를 잡아먹고 싶어 했다.
3 야수는 뷰티의 아버지에게 금 한 상자를 주었다.

p. 76-77

Stop & Think

- What did Beauty ask her father about the Beast? 뷰티는 아버지에게 야수에 관해 무엇을 물었는가?
  ⇨ She asked if the Beast was ugly. 야수가 흉하게 생겼는지 물었다.
- Who met Beauty at the castle? 성에서 누가 뷰티를 맞아 주었는가?
  ⇨ No one met her. 아무도 맞아 주지 않았다.

CHECK UP

1. What did Beauty's father show her? (a)
   a. a box of gold   b. a picture of the Beast   c. a red rose
2. What was on the dining table? (b)
   a. nothing   b. Beauty's favorite foods   c. some cakes and pies

1 뷰티의 아버지는 뷰티에게 무엇을 보여 주었는가?
   a. 금 한 상자   b. 야수의 초상화   c. 빨간 장미
2 식탁 위에 무엇이 있었는가?
   a. 아무것도 없었다   b. 뷰티가 제일 좋아하는 음식들   c. 케이크와 파이

p. 78-79

Stop & Think

- What did Beauty find in the book? 뷰티는 책에서 무엇을 발견했는가?
  ⇨ She found a note from the Beast. 야수가 쓴 쪽지를 발견했다.

CHECK UP

1. The <u>sign</u> on the door read "Beauty's Room."
2. The Beast had hair like a <u>lion</u>.
3. Beauty told the Beast that he was <u>ugly</u>.
4. Beauty thought the Beast was not so <u>frightening</u>.

1 문 위에 붙어 있는 표지판에는 '뷰티의 방'이라고 적혀 있었다.
2 야수는 사자처럼 털이 나 있었다.
3 뷰티는 야수에게 보기 싫게 생겼다고 말했다.
4 뷰티는 야수가 그다지 무섭지 않다고 생각했다.

p. 80-81

Stop & Think

- What did the Beast ask Beauty to do? 야수는 뷰티에게 무엇을 요청했는가?
  ⇨ He asked Beauty to marry him. 자기와 결혼해 달라고 청했다.
- Why did Beauty want to go home? 뷰티는 왜 집에 가고 싶어 했는가?
  ⇨ Her father was sick in bed and all by himself. 아버지가 아파서 몸져누워 홀로 있었기 때문에.

CHECK UP

1. The Beast gave Beauty — c. a magic mirror.
2. Beauty and the Beast — a. had dinner together every night.
3. Beauty saw her father — b. sick in bed.

196 Answers and Translations

1 야수는 뷰티에게 마법 거울을 주었다.
2 뷰티와 야수는 매일 밤 함께 만찬을 먹었다.
3 뷰티는 아버지가 몸져누워 있는 것을 보았다.

p. 82-83

Stop & Think

- Why did the Beast give Beauty a ring? 야수는 뷰티에게 왜 반지를 주었는가?
  ⇨ So Beauty could go to see her father and come back to the castle.
  뷰티가 아버지를 보러 갔다가 성으로 돌아올 수 있게 하려고.

- How did Beauty feel about the Beast? 뷰티는 야수에 대해 어떤 감정을 느꼈는가?
  ⇨ She liked him and almost loved him. 야수를 좋아했고 사랑하기 직전이었다.

Check Up

1 Beauty put on the ring and went to bed.
2 In the morning, Beauty was in her father's house.
3 Beauty's sisters were very unhappy.

1 뷰티는 반지를 끼고 잠자리에 들었다.
2 아침에 뷰티는 아버지의 집에 있었다.
3 뷰티의 언니들은 매우 불행했다.

p. 84-85

Stop & Think

- Where did Beauty see the Beast? 뷰티는 어디에서 야수를 보았는가?
  ⇨ She saw the Beast in her dream. 꿈에서 보았다.

- What did Beauty tell the Beast? 뷰티는 야수에게 무슨 말을 했는가?
  ⇨ She loved him and wanted to marry him. 그를 사랑하며 그와 결혼하고 싶다고 했다.

Check Up

1 The Beast was dying in Beauty's dream.   T
2 Beauty woke up from the dream and removed the ring.   T
3 Beauty found the Beast in the dining room.   F

1 뷰티의 꿈에서 야수는 죽어 가고 있었다.
2 뷰티는 잠에서 깨어 반지를 뺐다.
3 뷰티는 식당에서 야수를 발견했다.

p. 86-87

Stop & Think

- What did the fairy do to the prince? 요정은 왕자에게 무슨 일을 했는가?
  ⇨ The fairy cursed the prince and turned him into the Beast. 왕자에게 저주를 내려서 야수가 되게 했다.

Check Up

1 How did Beauty break the spell? (c)
   a. She kissed the Beast.   b. She married the Beast.   c. She loved the Beast.

2 What did the fairy promise Beauty and the prince? (a)
   a. many children   b. long lives   c. lots of money

Answers and Translations 197

1 뷰티는 어떻게 주문을 풀었나?
   a. 야수에게 입을 맞췄다.   b. 야수와 결혼했다.   c. 야수를 사랑했다.
2 요정은 뷰티와 왕자에게 무엇을 약속했나?
   a. 많은 자녀   b. 장수   c. 많은 돈

The Stars

p. 88-89

Stop & Think

- Who did the shepherd sometimes see? 양치기는 가끔씩 누구를 보았는가?
  ⇨ A loner and some coal miners 은둔자와 광부들
- What news interested the shepherd the most? 양치기에게 가장 흥미로운 소식은 무엇이었나?
  ⇨ News about Stephanette 스테파네트에 관한 소식

Check Up

1 The shepherd spent most of his time alone.   T
2 A person delivered supplies to the shepherd every week.   F
3 The shepherd often spoke with Stephanette.   F
4 One Sunday, the delivery boy arrived at ten o'clock.   F

1 양치기는 대부분의 시간을 혼자서 보냈다.
2 매주 한 사람이 양치기에게 물품을 배달했다.
3 양치기는 종종 스테파네트와 얘기를 나눴다.
4 어느 일요일에 배달 소년이 10시에 도착했다.

p. 90-91

Stop & Think

- Why did Stephanette come to the field? 스테파네트는 왜 들판에 왔는가?
  ⇨ The farmhand was sick, and the old woman was visiting her children.
    농장 머슴은 아프고, 나이 든 아주머니는 자녀들을 방문하러 가서.

Check Up

1 The heavy rain delayed the delivery person.
2 The person on the mule was Stephanette.
3 Stephanette got lost on her way to the field.
4 Had the shepherd ever spoken to Stephanette before? (No)

1 심한 비가 배달부를 지체시켰다.
2 노새를 타고 온 사람은 스테파네트였다.
3 스테파네트는 들판으로 오는 동안 길을 잃었다.
4 양치기는 전에 스테파네트와 얘기한 적이 있는가? (없다)

p. 92-93

Stop & Think

- What did the shepherd say to Stephanette? 양치기는 스테파네트에게 무슨 말을 했는가?
  ⇨ He said nothing to her. 아무 말도 하지 않았다.

198   Answers and Translations

- Why did Stephanette return to the shepherd? 스테파네트는 왜 양치기에게 돌아왔는가?
  ⇨ She could not cross the river. 강을 건널 수 없었기 때문에.

CHECK UP

1. The shepherd's bed was — c. made of straw and sheepskin.
2. The shepherd was — a. embarrassed in front of Stephanette.
3. Stephanette left to go — d. back to the farm.
4. The water in the river — b. had risen too high.

1. 양치기의 침대는 지푸라기와 양가죽으로 만들어졌다.
2. 양치기는 스테파네트 앞에서 쑥스러워했다.
3. 스테파네트는 농장으로 돌아가려고 떠났다.
4. 강물의 수위가 너무 높아졌다.

p. 94-95

Stop & Think

- How did the shepherd feel about taking care of Stephanette?
  양치기는 스테파네트를 돌보는 일에 대해 어떤 기분을 느꼈는가?
  ⇨ He felt proud of his responsibility. 자신의 임무를 뿌듯해했다.
- What did Stephanette suddenly do? 스테파네트는 갑자기 무엇을 했는가?
  ⇨ She came out of the barn and sat by the fire. 헛간에서 나와 모닥불 옆에 앉았다.

CHECK UP

1. Where did the shepherd make a bed for Stephanette? (b)
   a. by the fire   b. in the barn   c. in the pasture
2. How did the noises make Stephanette feel? (b)
   a. warm   b. frightened   c. angry

1. 양치기는 스테파네트의 잠자리를 어디에 만들어 주었는가?
   a. 불 옆에   b. 헛간 안에   c. 초원에
2. 소리들은 스테파네트에게 어떤 기분이 들게 했는가?
   a. 따스한   b. 깜짝 놀란   c. 화가 난

p. 96-97

Stop & Think

- What did the shepherd show Stephanette in the sky? 양치기는 스테파네트에게 하늘에 있는 무엇을 알려 주었는가?
  ⇨ He showed her the Milky Way and the constellations. 은하수와 별자리를 알려 주었다.

CHECK UP

1. Stephanette pointed to a shooting star in the sky.
2. The Milky Way stretches across all of France.
3. Shepherds can tell time by looking at stars.

1. 스테파네트는 하늘에 있는 별똥별을 가리켰다.
2. 은하수는 프랑스 전역을 가로질러 뻗어 있다.
3. 양치기들은 별을 보고 시간을 알 수 있다.

p. 98-99

Stop & Think

- How did Stephanette fall asleep? 스테파네트는 어떻게 잠이 들었는가?
  ⇨ With her head on the shepherd's shoulder. 양치기의 어깨에 머리를 기대고.

Check Up

1. The Evening Star is the most beautiful star of all.
2. Stephanette fell asleep in front of the fire.
3. Stephanette laid her head on the shepherd's shoulder.

1. 개밥바라기는 가장 아름다운 별이다.
2. 스테파네트는 모닥불 앞에서 잠들었다.
3. 스테파네트는 양치기의 어깨에 머리를 기댔다.

Step 4

What Men Live By

p. 102-103

Stop & Think

- Why couldn't Simon pay for the sheepskins? 세몬은 왜 양가죽 값을 치를 수 없었나?
  ⇨ His customers did not give him any money. 그의 고객들이 그에게 돈을 주지 않아서.
- What did Simon see behind the church? 세몬은 교회 뒤에서 무엇을 보았는가?
  ⇨ He saw a naked man. 벌거벗은 남자를 보았다.

Check Up

1. Simon had five rubles.   F
2. Simon wanted to buy some sheepskins.   T
3. There was a robber next to the church.   F
4. Simon was afraid of the naked man.   T

1. 세몬에게는 5루블이 있었다.
2. 세몬은 양가죽을 사고 싶었다.
3. 교회 옆에 강도가 한 명 있었다.
4. 세몬은 벌거숭이 사내가 두려웠다.

p. 104-105

Stop & Think

- What did Simon give the man? 세몬은 사내에게 무엇을 주었는가?
  ⇨ He gave the man his coat, boots, and a stick. 그의 외투와 장화, 지팡이를 주었다.
- What did Simon's wife think about her husband? 세몬의 아내는 남편에 대해 무슨 생각을 했는가?
  ⇨ She thought he had been out drinking. 밖에서 술을 마셨다고 생각했다.

Check Up

1. The man said that — d. God had punished him.
2. Simon felt glad — b. to help another person.
3. Matryna was — a. very disappointed with Simon.
4. Matryna thought that Simon — c. was a drunkard.

1 사내는 하느님께서 그에게 벌을 내리셨다고 말했다.
2 세몬은 다른 사람을 도와줘서 기뻤다.
3 마트료나는 세몬에게 매우 실망했다.
4 마트료나는 세몬이 술주정뱅이라고 생각했다.

p. 106–107

Stop & Think

- What did Simon say to make Matryna calm down? 세몬은 마트료나를 진정시키려고 무슨 말을 했는가?
  ⇨ He said that anger is a sin. 분노는 죄악이라고 말했다.

Check Up

1. What did Matryna feel for the stranger? (c)
   a. concern   b. love   c. pity
2. What happened after the man smiled? (a)
   a. A light came from his face.   b. Simon felt pity for him.   c. Matryna's heart softened.

1 마트료나가 낯선 이에게 느낀 감정은?
   a. 염려   b. 애정   c. 연민
2 남자가 미소를 짓자 무슨 일이 일어났는가?
   a. 그의 얼굴에서 광채가 났다.   b. 세몬이 그에게 연민을 느꼈다.   c. 마트료나의 마음이 누그러졌다.

p. 108–109

Stop & Think

- What work did Michael know? 미하일은 무슨 일을 할 줄 알았는가?
  ⇨ He did not know anything. 아무것도 몰랐다.

- Who was in the carriage? 마차에는 누가 타고 있었나?
  ⇨ A gentleman in a fur coat was in the carriage. 모피 외투를 입은 신사가 타고 있었다.

Check Up

1. Simon and Matryna had no more of bread.
2. The stranger's name was Michael.
3. Simon offered Michael food and shelter in return for work.
4. Michael became a very skilled bootmaker.

1 세몬과 마트료나에게는 더 이상 빵이 없었다.
2 낯선 이의 이름은 미하일이었다.
3 세몬은 미하일에게 일을 하는 대가로 음식과 거처를 제공했다.
4 미하일은 매우 솜씨 좋은 제화공이 되었다.

p. 110–111

Stop & Think

- What did Michael do when he looked behind the gentleman? 미하일은 신사의 뒤쪽을 바라보며 무엇을 했는가?
  ⇨ He smiled. 미소를 지었다.

Check Up

1. The gentleman showed Simon some <u>expensive</u> leather.
2. The gentleman <u>terrified</u> Simon.
3. The gentleman wanted his boots in <u>two days</u>.
4. Michael made <u>slippers</u> for the gentleman.

1. 신사는 세몬에게 비싼 가죽을 보여 주었다.
2. 신사는 세몬을 몹시 겁나게 했다.
3. 신사는 장화를 이틀 후에 찾고 싶어 했다.
4. 미하일은 신사가 신을 슬리퍼를 만들었다.

p. 112–113

Stop & Think

- What happened to the gentleman? 그 신사는 어떻게 되었는가?
  ⇨ He died in the carriage. 마차에서 죽었다.

Check Up

1. Michael smiled two times in six years. — T
2. A woman with two girls came to Simon's hut. — T
3. The two girls were cousins. — F
4. The woman was the girls' mother. — F

1. 미하일은 6년 동안 두 번 미소 지었다.
2. 한 여인이 두 여자아이를 데리고 세몬의 오두막에 왔다.
3. 두 여자아이는 사촌지간이었다.
4. 여인은 여자아이들의 엄마였다.

p. 114–115

Stop & Think

- How did the girl's leg get injured? 여자아이의 다리는 어떻게 다치게 되었는가?
  ⇨ Her mother rolled on it and crushed it when she died.
  아이 어머니가 죽을 때 그 다리 위로 굴러서 다리를 짓눌렀다.

- What happened as everyone was talking? 모두가 말을 하고 있을 때 무슨 일이 생겼는가?
  ⇨ A bright light filled the room. 밝은 빛이 방을 가득 채웠다.

Check Up

1. The woman said the girls — b. were precious to her.
2. Michael asked Simon and Matryna — c. to forgive him.
3. Simon realized that Michael — a. was not an ordinary man.

1. 여인은 소녀들이 자신에게 소중하다고 말했다.
2. 미하일은 세몬과 마트로나에게 자신을 용서해 달라고 했다.
3. 세몬은 미하일이 평범한 사람이 아님을 깨달았다.

p. 116–117

Stop & Think

- Why did God punish Michael? 하느님은 왜 미하일에게 벌을 내렸는가?
  ⇨ He disobeyed God. 하느님을 거역했기 때문에.

- What did God order Michael to learn about? 하느님은 미하일에게 무엇을 배워 오라고 명했는가?
  ⇨ To learn three truths: Learn what dwells in man. Learn what is not given to man. And learn what men live by. 세 가지 진리–사람의 내면에는 무엇이 깃들어 있는지, 사람에게 주어지지 않은 게 무엇인지, 그리고 사람은 무엇으로 사는지–를 배워 오라고 했다.

CHECK UP

1. Why did Michael smile three times? (a)
   a. He learned three truths.   b. He saw God.   c. He knew the little girls.

2. Whose soul was Michael supposed to take? (b)
   a. Simon's soul   b. the mother's soul   c. the girls' souls

1. 미하일은 왜 세 번 미소 지었는가?
   a. 세 가지 진실을 깨달아서.   b. 하느님을 보아서.   c. 그 어린 여자아이들을 알고 있어서.

2. 미하일은 누구의 영혼을 거두기로 되어 있었나?
   a. 세몬의 영혼   b. 그 (아기) 어머니의 영혼   c. 그 여자아이들의 영혼

p. 118–119

Stop & Think

- What did Michael do when he returned to Earth? 미하일은 지상으로 돌아와서 무엇을 했는가?
  ⇨ He took the mother's soul. 그 어머니의 영혼을 거두었다.

- What was the second truth? 두 번째 진리는 무엇이었나?
  ⇨ Men are not given the knowledge to know what they need. 사람에게는 자신에게 정작 필요한 게 무엇인지 알 수 있는 능력이 주어지지 않았다.

CHECK UP

1. Michael could return to <u>Heaven</u> after he learned all three truths.
2. Michael learned the <u>first</u> truth from Matryna.
3. Michael learned another truth from the <u>rich man</u>.

1. 미하일은 세 가지 진리를 모두 배운 후에 하늘로 돌아갈 수 있었다.
2. 미하일은 마트료나에게서 첫 번째 진리를 배웠다.
3. 미하일은 부자 신사에게서 또 다른 진리를 배웠다.

p. 120–121

Stop & Think

- What was the third truth? 세 번째 진리는 무엇이었나?
  ⇨ All men live because love is in them. 모든 사람은 내면에 사랑이 있기 때문에 살아간다.
    All men live by love. 모든 사람은 사랑으로 살아간다.

CHECK UP

1. Michael learned the <u>third</u> truth from the woman.
2. A <u>bright</u> light surrounded Michael's body.
3. Did Michael fly away from Simon's house? (Yes)

1 미하일은 그 여인에게서 세 번째 진리를 배웠다.
2 밝은 빛이 미하일의 몸을 감쌌다.
3 미하일은 세몬의 집에서 멀리 날아갔는가? (그렇다)

How Much Land Does a Man Need?

p. 122–123

Stop & Think

- Why was the younger sister annoyed? 동생은 왜 약이 올랐는가?
  ⇨ The elder sister was boasting about the advantages of town life. 언니가 도시 생활의 장점을 자랑했기 때문에.
- How would Pahom feel if he had plenty of land? 파홈은 땅이 많으면 어떤 기분이겠는가?
  ⇨ He would not fear the Devil himself. 악마라도 두렵지 않을 것이다.

Check Up

1 How did the younger sister feel about her way of life? (b)
   a. She felt anxious.   b. She liked it.   c. She wanted to change it.
2 Where was the Devil sitting? (b)
   a. on the stove   b. behind the stove   c. under the stove

1 동생은 자신의 생활방식에 대해 어떤 기분을 느끼고 있었는가?
   a. 근심했다.   b. 마음에 들어 했다.   c. 바꾸고 싶어 했다.
2 악마는 어디에 앉아 있었는가?
   a. 난로 위   b. 난로 뒤   c. 난로 밑

p. 124–125

Stop & Think

- Why did Pahom fine his neighbors? 파홈은 왜 이웃들에게 벌금을 물렸는가?
  ⇨ They were trespassing on his land. 그들이 파홈의 땅에 무단 침입했기 때문에.

Check Up

1 The Devil decided to — c. have a contest with Pahom.
2 Pahom bought a farm — a. and became a landowner.
3 Pahom's neighbors began to — b. trespass on his land on purpose.
4 Pahom took Simon — d. to court for trespassing.

1 악마는 파홈과 겨뤄 보기로 결심했다.
2 파홈은 농지를 사서 지주가 되었다.
3 파홈의 이웃들은 일부러 파홈의 땅을 무단 침범하기 시작했다.
4 파홈은 세몬을 무단침입죄로 법정에 세웠다.

p. 126–127

Stop & Think

- What did the stranger tell Pahom about the village? 낯선 이는 파홈에게 그 마을에 대해 무슨 말을 했는가?
  ⇨ Anyone who moved there was given twenty-five acres of land for free.
     그곳으로 이주한 사람은 누구나 25에이커의 땅을 무상으로 받았다.

- Why was Pahom not happy in the village? 파홈은 왜 마을에서 행복하지 않았는가?
  ⇨ He had to rent other people's land every year. 해마다 다른 사람들의 땅을 빌려야 했기 때문에.

CHECK UP

1. The peasant came from a land beyond the Volga River.   T
2. The village beyond the Volga gave everyone 250 acres of land for free.   F
3. Pahom visited the village to find out about the land.   T
4. Pahom was ten times better off than before.   T

1. 농부는 볼가 강 너머에 있는 땅에서 왔다.
2. 볼가강 너머에 있는 그 마을은 모든 사람에게 250에이커의 땅을 무상으로 주었다.
3. 파홈은 그 땅에 대해 알아보려고 그 마을을 찾아갔다.
4. 파홈은 전보다 10배 부유해졌다.

p. 128-129

Stop & Think

- How much land did the peddler buy? 행상은 얼마나 많은 땅을 샀는가?
  ⇨ He bought thirteen thousand acres of land. 13,000에이커의 땅을 샀다.

CHECK UP

1. The peddler said that the Bashkirs sold their land for cheap prices.
2. Pahom decided to visit the land of the Bashkirs.
3. The Bashkirs pitched their tents beside a river.
4. Pahom told the interpreter that he had come about some land.

1. 행상은 바시키르인들이 싼값에 땅을 판다고 말했다.
2. 파홈은 바시키르인들의 땅에 찾아가 보기로 마음먹었다.
3. 바시키르인들은 강가에 천막을 쳤다.
4. 파홈은 통역사에게 자신이 땅 때문에 왔다고 말했다.

p. 130-131

Stop & Think

- What did Pahom say about the Bashkirs' land? 바시키르인들의 땅에 대해 파홈은 무슨 말을 했는가?
  ⇨ They had plenty of it, and it was good land. 땅이 많은데다 비옥한 땅이다.

- What did Pahom give to the chief? 파홈은 족장에게 무엇을 주었는가?
  ⇨ He gave the chief the best dressing gown and five pounds of tea. 가장 좋은 실내복과 차 5파운드를 주었다.

CHECK UP

1. The Bashkirs wanted to repay Pahom for his gifts.
2. The Bashkirs told Pahom to point out the land he wanted.
3. The chief arrived while the Bashkirs were arguing.
4. Did the chief speak to Pahom in Russian? (Yes)

1. 바시키르인들은 파홈에게 그가 준 선물에 대해 보답하고 싶어 했다.
2. 바시키르인들은 파홈에게 그가 원하는 땅을 가리키라고 했다.
3. 바시키르인들이 논쟁을 벌이는 동안 족장이 도착했다.
4. 족장은 파홈에게 러시아어로 말했는가? (그렇다)

p. 132-133

Stop & Think

- How much was the land Pahom wanted to buy? 파홈이 사고 싶어 한 땅은 얼마였는가?
  ⇒ It was one thousand rubles a day. 하루에 1,000루블이었다.

- What was the condition the chief gave Pahom? 족장이 파홈에게 제시한 조건은 무엇이었나?
  ⇒ He had to return to the spot where he started on the same day, or he would lose his money. 출발했던 지점으로 같은 날 돌아와야 한다. 그렇지 않으면 돈을 잃게 된다.

Check Up

1. What did Pahom want the chief to give him with the land? (a)
   a. a deed   b. some money   c. some servants
2. How far did Pahom think he could walk in one day? (b)
   a. 20 miles   b. 35 miles   c. 50 miles

1. 파홈은 족장이 땅과 함께 무엇을 주기를 원했는가?
   a. 증서   b. 돈   c. 하인 몇 명
2. 파홈은 자신이 하루에 얼마나 멀리 걸을 수 있다고 생각했는가?
   a. 20마일   b. 35마일   c. 50마일

p. 134-135

Stop & Think

- What happened to Pahom in his dream? 꿈속에서 파홈에게 무슨 일이 생겼는가?
  ⇒ He was lying dead in front of the Devil. 악마 앞에서 죽은 채 누워 있었다.

- What did the chief put down to mark the starting spot? 족장은 출발 지점을 표시하려고 무엇을 내려놓았는가?
  ⇒ He put down his fox-fur cap on the ground. 여우털 모자를 땅바닥에 내려놓았다.

Check Up

1. Pahom had a dream — b. the night before the contest.
2. The Devil was — c. laughing in Pahom's dream.
3. Pahom put his money — a. on the fox-fur cap.

1. 파홈은 겨루기 전날 밤 꿈을 꾸었다.
2. 악마는 파홈의 꿈속에서 웃고 있었다.
3. 파홈은 돈을 여우털 모자 위에 놓았다.

p. 136-137

Stop & Think

- Why did Pahom not lie down at lunch? 점심 때 파홈은 왜 눕지 않았는가?
  ⇒ He did not want to fall asleep. 잠들고 싶지 않아서.

Check Up

1. Pahom walked for 100 yards on the first side of the square.   F
2. Pahom did not stop to have lunch.   F
3. Pahom made the first side and the second side of the square too long.   T

1 파홈은 정사각형 땅의 첫 번째 변에서 100야드를 걸었다.
2 파홈은 점심을 먹으려고 멈춰 서지 않았다.
3 파홈은 정사각형 땅의 첫 번째 변과 두 번째 변을 너무 길게 만들었다.

p. 138-139

Stop & Think

- What did Pahom throw away while he was returning to the hill? 파홈은 언덕으로 돌아가는 동안 무엇을 버렸는가?
  ⇨ He threw away his coat, boots, flask, and cap. 외투, 장화, 물병, 모자를 버렸다.
- What was Pahom afraid of as he returned to the hill? 파홈은 언덕으로 돌아갈 때 무엇이 두려웠나?
  ⇨ He was afraid of death. 죽음이 두려웠다.

CHECK UP

1 Pahom thought he had tried for too much land.
2 Pahom kept his spade and used it as a support.
3 Pahom's heart was beating like a hammer.

1 파홈은 자신이 너무 많은 땅을 얻으려 했다고 생각했다.
2 파홈은 삽을 계속 가지고 있으면서 버팀대로 사용했다.
3 파홈의 심장은 망치질하듯 쿵쾅거렸다.

p. 140-141

Stop & Think

- How much land did Pahom need? 파홈에게 필요한 땅은 얼마만큼이었나?
  ⇨ He needed six feet from his head to his heels. 머리부터 발꿈치까지 6피트가 필요했다.

CHECK UP

1 The sun set at the bottom of the hill faster than at the top.
2 The chief said that Pahom had gained much land.
3 Pahom's servant saw that he was dead.
4 Did the Devil win his contest with Pahom? (Yes)

1 태양은 언덕 꼭대기보다 기슭에서 더 빨리 졌다.
2 족장은 파홈이 많은 땅을 얻었다고 말했다.
3 파홈의 하인은 파홈이 죽었다는 걸 알았다.
4 악마가 파홈과 겨루어 이겼는가? (그렇다)

Step 5

A Christmas Carol

p. 144-145

Stop & Think

- How did people feel about Scrooge? 사람들은 스크루지를 어떻게 생각했는가?
  ⇨ They avoided him. 그를 피했다. / They didn't like him. 그를 좋아하지 않았다.

CHECK UP

1. Scrooge was a greedy man.　　　　　　　T
2. Scrooge and Marley still worked together.　F
3. Bob Cratchit was Scrooge's boss.　　　　F

1. 스크루지는 욕심 많은 사내였다.
2. 스크루지와 말리는 여전히 함께 일했다.
3. 밥 크래칫은 스크루지의 상사였다.

p. 146-147

Stop & Think

- What did Scrooge's nephew ask him to do? 스크루지의 조카는 그에게 무엇을 하라고 청했는가?
  ⇨ To go to Christmas dinner. 크리스마스 만찬에 오라고. /
  To have dinner with his family. 자신의 가족과 함께 저녁을 먹자고.

- What did Scrooge give Bob Cratchit for Christmas? 스크루지는 크리스마스를 맞아 밥 크래칫에게 무엇을 주었는가?
  ⇨ He gave Bob Cratchit the day off. 하루 쉬게 해 주었다.

CHECK UP

1. Scrooge said that Marley _died_ seven years ago.
2. The men asked Scrooge to give them some _money_.
3. Scrooge paid Bob Cratchit his day's _wages_ for Christmas.
4. Bob Cratchit promised to arrive _early_ the day after Christmas.

1. 스크루지는 말리가 7년 전에 죽었다고 말했다.
2. 신사들은 스크루지에게 돈을 좀 달라고 요청했다.
3. 스크루지는 밥 크래칫에게 크리스마스 날에 대한 임금을 지불했다.
4. 밥 크래칫은 크리스마스 다음 날 일찍 출근하겠다고 약속했다.

p. 148-149

Stop & Think

- What went into Scrooge's room? 무엇이 스크루지의 방으로 들어왔는가?
  ⇨ Marley's ghost went into Scrooge's room. 말리의 유령이 스크루지의 방으로 들어왔다.

CHECK UP

1. What kind of noise did Scrooge hear? (b)
   a. a screaming man   b. a dragging chain   c. a laughing woman
2. What could Marley not do? (a)
   a. rest   b. speak   c. move

1 스크루지는 어떤 소리를 들었는가?
   a. 남자의 비명   b. 쇠사슬 끄는 소리   c. 여자의 웃음소리
2 말리가 할 수 없었던 것은?
   a. 안식하기   b. 말하기   c. 움직이기

p. 150-151

Stop & Think

- How many ghosts will visit Scrooge? 얼마나 많은 유령이 스크루지를 방문할 예정인가?
  ⇨ Three ghosts will visit him. 유령 셋이 그를 방문할 것이다.
- What was the first ghost to visit Scrooge? 스크루지를 방문한 첫 번째 유령은 무엇이었는가?
  ⇨ The first ghost was the Ghost of Christmas Past. 첫 번째 유령은 과거의 크리스마스 유령이었다.

CHECK UP

1. Marley said that Scrooge's <u>chain</u> was longer than his own.
2. The first ghost was going to come at <u>one</u> in the morning.
3. The first ghost looked like <u>an old man</u>.

1 말리는 스크루지의 쇠사슬이 자신의 것보다 더 길다고 말했다.
2 첫 번째 유령은 새벽 1시에 찾아올 예정이었다.
3 첫 번째 유령은 노인 같아 보였다.

p. 152-153

Stop & Think

- What time of year did the ghost take Scrooge to? 유령은 스크루지를 1년 중 어느 때로 데려갔는가?
  ⇨ The ghost took Scrooge to Christmastime. 크리스마스 때로 데려갔다.

CHECK UP

1. Scrooge and the ghost — c. passed through the wall together.
2. The images Scrooge saw — a. were not real.
3. Scrooge once worked — b. in an office for Mr. Fezziwig.

1 스크루지와 유령은 함께 벽을 통과했다.
2 스크루지가 본 형상들은 실제로 존재하는 것이 아니었다.
3 스크루지는 한때 페지위그 씨의 사무실에서 일했다.

p. 154-155

Stop & Think

- Who did Scrooge see with himself? 스크루지는 누가 자신과 함께 있는 모습을 보았나?
  ⇨ He saw his old girlfriend. 옛 여자친구를 보았다.
- What did Scrooge tell the ghost? 스크루지는 유령에게 무슨 말을 했는가?
  ⇨ Scrooge told the ghost to leave him. 자신을 떠나 달라고 말했다.

CHECK UP

1. Scrooge never had a girlfriend in his entire life. **F**
2. Scrooge loved money more than people. **T**
3. The beautiful woman Scrooge saw was his mother. **F**
4. Scrooge asked the ghost to show him some more scenes. **F**

1. 스크루지는 평생 한 번도 여자친구가 없었다.
2. 스크루지는 사람보다 돈을 더 사랑했다.
3. 스크루지가 본 아름다운 여인은 그의 어머니였다.
4. 스크루지는 유령에게 더 많은 장면을 보여 달라고 부탁했다.

p. 156-157

Stop & Think

- Who was the second ghost? 두 번째 유령은 누구였는가?
  ⇨ It was the Ghost of Christmas Present. 현재의 크리스마스 유령이었다.

- What did Bob Cratchit's family have to eat? 밥 크랫칫의 가족은 먹을 게 어떤 게 있었는가?
  ⇨ They had a goose, some potatoes, and a small Christmas pudding.
     거위 한 마리, 감자 몇 알, 조그만 크리스마스 푸딩 하나가 있었다.

CHECK UP

1. There was a <u>giant</u> sitting in the middle of Scrooge's living room.
2. The ghost told Scrooge to <u>touch</u> his robe.
3. <u>Tiny Tim</u> needed to use a crutch to walk.
4. The Cratchits had a simple meal, but they <u>enjoyed</u> it.

1. 스크루지의 거실 한복판에 한 거인이 앉아 있었다.
2. 유령은 스크루지에게 자신의 옷을 만지라고 말했다.
3. 타이니 팀은 걸을 때 목발을 써야 했다.
4. 크래칫 가족은 소박한 식사라도 즐겁게 먹었다.

p. 158-159

Stop & Think

- Who did Bob Cratchit propose a toast to? 밥 크랫칫은 누구를 위해 건배를 제안했나?
  ⇨ He proposed a toast to Scrooge. 스크루지를 위해 건배를 제안했다.

CHECK UP

1. How did Mrs. Cratchit feel about drinking to Scrooge? **(c)**
   a. pleased   b. nervous   c. unhappy

1. 크래칫 부인은 스크루지를 위해 건배하는 것에 대해 기분이 어떠했는가?
   a. 기뻤다   b. 신경질이 났다   c. 기쁘지 않았다

p. 160-161

Stop & Think

- Who was the third ghost? 세 번째 유령은 누구였는가?
  ⇨ It was the Ghost of Christmas Yet to Come. 미래의 크리스마스 유령이었다.

CHECK UP

1. Fred wanted Scrooge to give Bob Cratchit more <u>money</u>.
2. The third ghost wore <u>black</u> clothes.
3. The third ghost said <u>nothing</u>.
4. Were the people the ghost showed Scrooge talking about a marriage? <u>(No)</u>

1 프레드는 스크루지가 봅 크래칫에게 돈을 더 많이 주기를 바랐다.
2 세 번째 유령은 검은 옷을 입고 있었다.
3 세 번째 유령은 아무 말도 하지 않았다.
4 유령이 스크루지에게 보여 준 사람들은 결혼식 얘기를 하고 있었는가? (아니다)

p. 162-163

Stop & Think

- Where did the three people get the items they were selling? 세 사람이 팔리는 물건들은 어디서 난 것인가?
  ⇨ They got them from the dead man's house. 죽은 사내의 집에서 가져온 것이다.

CHECK UP

1. The shopkeeper asked the women — a. what they had to sell.
2. One woman was selling — b. bed curtains and blankets.
3. The ghost pointed at — c. a dead body covered by a sheet.

1 가게 주인은 여자들에게 무엇을 팔 건지 물었다.
2 한 여자는 침대 커튼과 담요를 팔고 있었다.
3 유령은 천에 덮여 있는 시신을 가리켰다.

p. 164-165

Stop & Think

- Why was the Cratchit family sad? 크래칫 가족은 왜 슬퍼했는가?
  ⇨ Tiny Tim died. 타이니 팀에 죽어서.

CHECK UP

1. The Ghost of Christmas Yet to Come took Scrooge to a churchyard.   <u>T</u>
2. Scrooge wanted to know who the dead man was.   <u>T</u>
3. The name on the grave was Scrooge's.   <u>T</u>

1 미래의 크리스마스 유령은 스크루지를 교회 묘지로 데려갔다.
2 스크루지는 죽은 사내가 누구인지 알고 싶어 했다.
3 무덤에 새겨진 이름은 스크루지의 이름이었다.

p. 166-167

Stop & Think

- What did Scrooge tell the boy to do? 스크루지는 소년에게 무엇을 해 달라고 말했는가?
  ⇨ Go to the butcher's shop and bring the butcher back. 푸줏간에 가서 푸줏간 주인을 데려오라고 했다.

CHECK UP

1. Scrooge realized that all three ghosts had visited him in <u>one night</u>.
2. Scrooge sent <u>the goose</u> to Bob Cratchit's house.

3 Scrooge went to his nephew's house to have dinner.

1 스크루지는 유령 셋이 모두 하룻밤 사이에 자신을 방문했다는 걸 깨달았다.
2 스크루지는 거위를 봅 크래칫의 집으로 보냈다.
3 스크루지는 저녁식사를 하러 조카의 집으로 갔다.

p. 168–169

Stop & Think

- What did Scrooge tell Bob Cratchit he was going to do? 스크루지는 봅 크래칫에게 자신이 무슨 일을 할 거라고 말했는가?
  ⇨ Scrooge said that he would raise his salary and assist his family.
  봉급을 올려주고 가족을 도와주겠다고 말했다.
- How did Scrooge act toward Tiny Tim? 스크루지는 타이니 팀에게 어떻게 행동했는가?
  ⇨ He became a second father to Tiny Tim. 타이니 팀에게 아버지와 다름없는 사람이 되었다.

CHECK UP

1 What did Scrooge promise Bob Cratchit? (c)
   a. a bigger house   b. a healthy family   c. a higher salary
2 What kind of man did Scrooge become? (b)
   a. a greedy man   b. a good man   c. a silly man

1 스크루지는 봅 크래칫에게 무엇을 약속했는가?
   a. 더 큰 집   b. 건강한 가족   c. 더 많은 봉급
2 스크루지는 어떤 사람이 되었는가?
   a. 욕심 많은 사람   b. 착한 사람   c. 미련한 사람

The Last Leaf

p. 172–173

Stop & Think

- What kind of people went to old Greenwich Village? 어떤 사람들이 고풍스러운 그리니치 빌리지로 갔는가?
  ⇨ Art people went there. 예술가들이 갔다.
- What happened in the colony in November? 11월에 예술인 동네에 무슨 일이 생겼는가?
  ⇨ Many people caught pneumonia. 많은 사람이 폐렴에 걸렸다.

CHECK UP

1 There were "places" in Washington Square.
2 People went to old Greenwich Village looking for low rents.

3 Sue and Johnsy lived together.
4 Did many people get pneumonia in May? (No)

1 워싱턴 광장에는 많은 '플레이스'가 있었다.
2 사람들은 값싼 셋방을 찾아서 고풍스러운 그리니치 빌리지로 갔다.
3 수와 존시는 함께 살았다.
4 많은 사람들이 5월에 폐렴에 걸렸는가? (아니다)

p. 174-175

Stop & Think

- What did the doctor say Johnsy needed to do? 의사는 존시가 무엇을 해야 한다고 말했는가?
  ⇨ She needed to want to live. 살고 싶어 해야 한다.
- What did the doctor want Sue to do? 의사는 수가 무엇을 하기를 바랐는가?
  ⇨ Get Johnsy to think of something valuable to her. 존시가 자신에게 소중한 뭔가를 생각해 보도록 하는 것.

Check Up

1 The doctor said Johnsy had one chance in ten to live.
2 Medicine is less effective when patients think about death.
3 Sue cried very hard after the doctor left.

1 의사는 존시가 살아날 가망성이 열에 하나라고 말했다.
2 약은 환자가 죽음을 생각하면 효과가 줄어든다.
3 의사가 떠난 뒤에 수는 매우 심하게 울었다.

p. 176-177

Stop & Think

- What was Johnsy counting? 존시는 무엇을 세고 있었나?
  ⇨ She was counting the leaves on the ivy vine. 담쟁이덩굴에 달린 잎사귀 수를 세고 있었다.

Check Up

1 Johnsy was counting backward.   T
2 Johnsy said she would die when the last leaf fell.   T
3 Sue said Johnsy's chances of living were ten to one. T

1 존시는 거꾸로 수를 세고 있었다.
2 존시는 마지막 잎새가 떨어지면 자신도 죽게 될 거라고 말했다.
3 수는 존시가 살아날 확률이 10대 1이라고 말했다.

p. 178-179

Stop & Think

- What did Sue ask Johnsy to do? 수는 존시에게 무엇을 하라고 부탁했는가?
  ⇨ Close her eyes and not look out the window. 눈을 감고 창밖을 내다보지 말라고.
- Who was Behrman? 베어먼은 누구였는가?
  ⇨ He was a painter who lived downstairs from Sue and Johnsy. 수와 존시의 화실 아래층에 살고 있는 화가였다.

Check Up

1 What did Johnsy ask Sue to do? (a)
   a. draw in another room   b. give her some broth   c. pull the shade down

Answers and Translations

2 What kind of an artist was Behrman? (c)
   a. a successful one   b. an average one   c. a failed one

1 존시는 수에게 무엇을 하라고 요청했는가?
   a. 다른 방에서 그림을 그리라고   b. 수프를 좀 달라고   c. 가리개를 내리라고
2 베어먼은 어떤 화가였나?
   a. 성공한 화가   b. 보통 화가   c. 실패한 화가

p. 180-181

Stop & Think

- What did Behrman drink too much of? 베어먼은 무엇을 과음했는가?
  ⇨ He drank too much gin. 진을 과음했다.

Check Up

1 Behrman worked as — c. a model for artists in the colony.
2 There was a blank canvas — a. in one corner of Berhman's den.
3 Behrman thought Johnsy's idea — d. was silly.
4 Behrman decided to — b. pose as a model for Sue.

1 베어먼은 예술인 동네에서 화가들의 모델이 되어 주는 일을 했다.
2 베어먼의 방 한 구석에는 빈 캔버스가 있었다.
3 베어먼은 존시의 생각이 어리석다고 생각했다.
4 베어먼은 수의 모델이 되어 주기로 마음먹었다.

p. 182-183

Stop & Think

- What did Johnsy tell Sue to do when she woke up? 존시는 잠에서 깨자 수에게 무엇을 하라고 말했는가?
  ⇨ She told Sue to pull up the shade. 가리개를 올리라고 말했다.
- What did Johnsy and Sue see outside? 존시와 수는 밖에서 무엇을 보았는가?
  ⇨ They saw one ivy leaf against the wall. 담쟁이 잎사귀 한 개가 벽에 붙어 있는 걸 보았다.

Check Up

1 Sue and Behrman looked out the window at the ivy vine.
2 There was still one leaf left on the vine.
3 Johnsy thought the last leaf would fall during the night.
4 Was Johnsy ready to die? (Yes)

1 수와 베어먼은 창밖의 담쟁이덩굴을 내다봤다.
2 덩굴에는 여전히 잎사귀 하나가 남아 있었다.
3 존시는 마지막 잎새가 밤에 떨어질 거라고 생각했다.
4 존시는 죽음을 맞을 준비가 되어 있었나? (그렇다)

p. 184-185

Stop & Think

- What did Sue and Johnsy see the next morning? 다음 날 아침 수와 존시는 무엇을 보았는가?
  ⇨ The ivy leaf was still on the vine. 담쟁이 잎사귀가 여전히 덩굴에 붙어 있는 걸 보았다.